T0310674

Agile Scrum Implementation and Its Long–Term Impact on Organizations

Kenneth R. Walsh
University of New Orleans, USA

Sathiadev Mahesh
University of New Orleans, USA

Cherie C. Trumbach
University of New Orleans, USA

A volume in the Advances in Systems Analysis,
Software Engineering, and High Performance
Computing (ASASEHPC) Book Series

Published in the United States of America by
    IGI Global
    Engineering Science Reference (an imprint of IGI Global)
    701 E. Chocolate Avenue
    Hershey PA, USA 17033
    Tel: 717-533-8845
    Fax: 717-533-8661
    E-mail: cust@igi-global.com
    Web site: http://www.igi-global.com

Copyright © 2021 by IGI Global. All rights reserved. No part of this publication may be reproduced, stored or distributed in any form or by any means, electronic or mechanical, including photocopying, without written permission from the publisher. Product or company names used in this set are for identification purposes only. Inclusion of the names of the products or companies does not indicate a claim of ownership by IGI Global of the trademark or registered trademark.

Library of Congress Cataloging-in-Publication Data

Names: Walsh, Kenneth R., 1966- editor. | Mahesh, Sathiadev, editor. |
  Trumbach, Cherie C., 1974- editor.
Title: Agile scrum implementation and its long-term impact on organizations
  / Kenneth R. Walsh, Sathiadev Mahesh, and Cherie C. Trumbach, editors.
Description: Hershey, PA : Engineering Science Reference, 2020. | Includes
  bibliographical references and index. | Summary: "This book contains
  research and practice topics in the scrum software development
  methodology"-- Provided by publisher.
Identifiers: LCCN 2020010858 (print) | LCCN 2020010859 (ebook) | ISBN
  9781799848851 (h/c) | ISBN 9781799856313 (s/c) | ISBN 9781799848868
  (eISBN)
Subjects: LCSH: Agile software development. | Scrum (Computer software
  development) | Computer software--Management.
Classification: LCC QA76.76.D47 A3838 2020 (print) | LCC QA76.76.D47
  (ebook) | DDC 005.1/112--dc23
LC record available at https://lccn.loc.gov/2020010858
LC ebook record available at https://lccn.loc.gov/2020010859

This book is published in the IGI Global book series Advances in Systems Analysis, Software Engineering, and High Performance Computing (ASASEHPC) (ISSN: 2327-3453; eISSN: 2327-3461)

British Cataloguing in Publication Data
A Cataloguing in Publication record for this book is available from the British Library.

All work contributed to this book is new, previously-unpublished material. The views expressed in this book are those of the authors, but not necessarily of the publisher.

For electronic access to this publication, please contact: eresources@igi-global.com.

Advances in Systems Analysis, Software Engineering, and High Performance Computing (ASASEHPC) Book Series

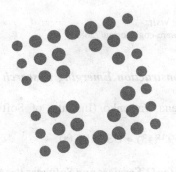

Vijayan Sugumaran
Oakland University, USA

ISSN:2327-3453
EISSN:2327-3461

MISSION

The theory and practice of computing applications and distributed systems has emerged as one of the key areas of research driving innovations in business, engineering, and science. The fields of software engineering, systems analysis, and high performance computing offer a wide range of applications and solutions in solving computational problems for any modern organization.

The **Advances in Systems Analysis, Software Engineering, and High Performance Computing (ASASEHPC) Book Series** brings together research in the areas of distributed computing, systems and software engineering, high performance computing, and service science. This collection of publications is useful for academics, researchers, and practitioners seeking the latest practices and knowledge in this field.

COVERAGE

- Software Engineering
- Human-Computer Interaction
- Distributed Cloud Computing
- Computer Networking
- Computer System Analysis
- Virtual Data Systems
- Enterprise Information Systems
- Performance Modelling
- Parallel Architectures
- Metadata and Semantic Web

IGI Global is currently accepting manuscripts for publication within this series. To submit a proposal for a volume in this series, please contact our Acquisition Editors at Acquisitions@igi-global.com or visit: http://www.igi-global.com/publish/.

The Advances in Systems Analysis, Software Engineering, and High Performance Computing (ASASEHPC) Book Series (ISSN 2327-3453) is published by IGI Global, 701 E. Chocolate Avenue, Hershey, PA 17033-1240, USA, www.igi-global.com. This series is composed of titles available for purchase individually; each title is edited to be contextually exclusive from any other title within the series. For pricing and ordering information please visit http://www.igi-global.com/book-series/advances-systems-analysis-software-engineering/73689. Postmaster: Send all address changes to above address. Copyright © 2021 IGI Global. All rights, including translation in other languages reserved by the publisher. No part of this series may be reproduced or used in any form or by any means – graphics, electronic, or mechanical, including photocopying, recording, taping, or information and retrieval systems – without written permission from the publisher, except for non commercial, educational use, including classroom teaching purposes. The views expressed in this series are those of the authors, but not necessarily of IGI Global.

Titles in this Series

For a list of additional titles in this series, please visit:
http://www.igi-global.com/book-series/advances-systems-analysis-software-engineering/73689

Formal and Adaptive Methods for Automation of Parallel Programs Construction Emerging Research and Opportunities
Anatoliy Doroshenko (Institute of Software Systems, Ukraine) and Olena Yatsenko (Institute of Software Systems,Ukraine)
Engineering Science Reference • © 2021 • 279pp • H/C (ISBN: 9781522593843) • US $195.00

Balancing Agile and Disciplined Engineering and Management Approaches for IT Services and Software Products
Manuel Mora (Universidad Autónoma de Aguascalientes, Mexico) Jorge Marx Gómez (University of Oldenburg, Germany) Rory V. O'Connor (Dublin City University, Ireland) and Alena Buchalcevová (University of Economics, Prague, Czech Republic)
Engineering Science Reference • © 2021 • 354pp • H/C (ISBN: 9781799841654) • US $225.00

Urban Spatial Data Handling and Computing
Mainak Bandyopadhyay (DIT University-Dehradun, India) and Varun Singh (MNNIT-Allahabad, India)
Engineering Science Reference • © 2020 • 300pp • H/C (ISBN: 9781799801221) • US $245.00

FPGA Algorithms and Applications for the Internet of Things
Preeti Sharma (Bansal College of Engineering, Mandideep, India) and Rajit Nair (Jagran Lakecity University, Bhopal, India)
Engineering Science Reference • © 2020 • 257pp • H/C (ISBN: 9781522598060) • US $215.00

Advancements in Instrumentation and Control in Applied System Applications
Srijan Bhattacharya (RCC Institute of Information Technology, India)
Engineering Science Reference • © 2020 • 298pp • H/C (ISBN: 9781799825845) • US $225.00

Cloud Computing Applications and Techniques for E-Commerce
Saikat Gochhait (Symbiosis Institute of Digital and Telecom Management, Symbiosis International University, India) David Tawei Shou (University of Taipei, Taiwan) and Sabiha Fazalbhoy (Symbiosis Centre for Management Studies, Symbiosis International University, India)
Engineering Science Reference • © 2020 • 185pp • H/C (ISBN: 9781799812944) • US $215.00

Soft Computing Methods for System Dependability
Mohamed Arezki Mellal (M'Hamed Bougara University, Algeria)
Engineering Science Reference • © 2020 • 293pp • H/C (ISBN: 9781799817185) • US $225.00

701 East Chocolate Avenue, Hershey, PA 17033, USA
Tel: 717-533-8845 x100 • Fax: 717-533-8661
E-Mail: cust@igi-global.com • www.igi-global.com

Table of Contents

Section 5
Organization Assessment

Detailed Table of Contents

Section 1
Previous Literature

Chapter 1

    Cherie C. Trumbach, University of New Orleans, USA
    Kenneth R. Walsh, University of New Orleans, USA
    Sathiadev Mahesh, University of New Orleans, USA

This chapter starts with a brief history of software development from a summary of traditional approaches and presents the conditions that led to agile approaches such as product complexity, shortened life cycle of the market and eventually to the widespread acceptance of Scrum. The authors then compare the narrative to the bibliometric analysis of abstract records that can be found in the Web of Science database. They parse the terms from the abstract records to identify research trends over time and map the underlying structure of agile research. Finally, they consider the future of Agile-Scrum in light of the current pandemic.

Section 2
Industry Perspectives

Chapter 2

    S. M. Balasubramaniyan, Digital Core Technologies, India

Agile Manifesto refers to Leadership and Team characteristics in three out of the twelve principles of Agile software. Clearly, the 'people' in the organisation play a critical role in the success of Agile software development. Many studies have been done on the various aspects of the Leadership and Team characteristics in respect of the role, the behaviour, the process and the structure. While most of these studies are related to the role and behaviour aspects of the leadership and the teams, this chapter attempts to supplement them with those aspects that are related to structure, internal and external interfaces and interactions, to ensure that the Agile engagements are planned and executed successfully and consistently. The emphasis in this chapter is the Organisation Culture that must be conducive for sure success of Agile projects and Scrum teams.

Chapter 3

The purpose of this chapter to is examine the issues involved in the integration of Agile teams into existing organizations that have not previously incorporated Agile teams, and suggest mechanisms that can make the integration process more efficient and effective. Issues and solutions discussed include conflicting environmental viewpoints, differing project end-point definitions, organizational reporting, budgeting and financial performance reporting challenges, and the special challenge of legacy technologies to Agile teams. Methods discussed for successful integration of Agile teams into existing organizations include leadership selection, use of cross-functional team members, appropriate performance measures, funding for the team, and effective communication within and among the organizational members.

Jeff Sutherland worked on the first Scrum project in 1993, but the framework as we know it now was formally coined by Jeff and Ken Schwaber in 1995. Since then IT divisions have seen the growing adoption of Scrum within their organization. However, this growth has been peppered with poor examples of adoption leading to lackluster results. This chapter explores why there is such a prevalence of "Bad" Scrum and the impact it has on the culture of the organization. This chapter explores the impact of poorly led transformations and will also provide some ways to reconsider how transformations should pivot.

This chapter discusses the steps necessary to incorporate appropriate Scrum procedures into maintenance and enhancement projects on legacy systems, developed and maintained using a systems development life cycle (SDLC). It considers the benefits of introducing a more modular approach to system development, where the characteristics of existing systems have created interdependent modules, functions, and application architecture. Although these systems represent an investment in money, resources, time, and knowledge that make decommissioning them inexpedient, the process can and must be improved and incorporating Scrum procedures and practices will improve the success rate of maintenance and enhancements to these systems.

Section 3
Significant Scrum Organizational Issues

Chapter 6

This chapter discusses how the method selected to manage a project can play a role in the success of that project. Certain projects are better suited to particular models of project management. The traditional, or "waterfall," approach; the agile approach; and a more refined agile approach known as Scrum, which will be evaluated. The Scrum approach to project management is gaining a lot of momentum in recent years but all projects may not be well suited for this method. By analyzing the different styles of project management, a discussion of the benefits and pitfalls of each approach will be completed as well as how those characteristics may contribute to risks. An examination of project types, project roles, and project management experience will be completed to provide insight for when the Scrum approach to project management is most appropriate to contribute to the overall success of a project and when it may be best to apply a different management style.

Chapter 7

The utilization of the Scrum methodology delineates a separation of roles for a product team, with the Product Owner being responsible for identifying and describing product backlog items and making decisions regarding the priority of these items, ensuring business requirements are being met, and providing feedback throughout the project to the team to ensure that there is success in the deployment of the IT solution. Despite the importance of this role, there is scant research to examine the effectiveness of the Product Owner in the outcomes of the Scrum effort. In this chapter, the authors study and empirically evaluate the efficacy of the Product Owner and the practices and procedures that are inherent to the Scrum methodology, as well as the intervening effects of the challenges of the development process and the changing requirements. They conclude by presenting the results of the analysis and the implications of the findings for future work in Scrum, as well as what the research means for Product Owners within organizations that are employing the Scrum methodology.

Chapter 8

The adoption of agility at a large scale often requires the integration of agile and non-agile development practices into hybrid software development and delivery environment. This chapter addresses software testing related issues for Agile software application development. Currently, the umbrella of Agile methodologies (e.g. Scrum, Extreme Programming, Development and Operations – i.e., DevOps) have become the preferred tools for modern software development. These methodologies emphasize iterative and incremental development, where both the requirements and solutions evolve through the collaboration between cross-functional teams. The success of such practices relies on the quality result of each stage of development, obtained through rigorous testing. This chapter introduces the principles of software testing within the context of Scrum/DevOps based software development lifecycle.

Chapter 9

The value agile scrum process can generate is not guaranteed simply by mere adoption. Rather the process creates an opportunity for improvement in the development process. Mismanagement of the approach by an organization can reduce the potential added value or in extreme situations have a negative impact. Therefore, appropriate management procedures are necessary to realize the full potential of the agile scrum approach. This chapter focuses on the human resource challenges the agile scrum approach creates for an organization. The dynamic pace, cross-functional composition, and self-directed team approach requires special consideration in the development of most human resource functions. In particular, the authors will review changes to the employee selection, performance management, and learning and career development processes. These changes will better align these functions with the values and principals of the agile scrum approach and help organizations manage this sometimes chaotic approach to innovation without constraining it.

Chapter 10

As the use of software is present in so many activities today, it is important for business in particular to be aware of challenges that may seem different today than before the prevalence of software in our lives. Agile project management is one example: this more recent and nimble approach to software development presents its own challenges. Fortunately, the guiding legal principles related to traditional contract formation and execution are based in principles of fairness and equity, making the customization of legal principles to Agile contracting a reasonable endeavor. This chapter presents basic contract law and such law as it more specifically relates to contracts dealing with Agile software development.

Section 4
Education

Chapter 11

The LEGO®-Scrum simulation-based training (SBT) described here shows how LEGO® bricks can help professionals learn first-hand about Scrum methodology, an Agile approach to software development projects. The chapter's objectives are 1) to present the modalities of the LEGO®-Scrum SBT, 2) to demonstrate how LEGO® bricks can help professionals learn, first-hand, about Scrum, and 3) to illustrate how this learning can be relevant and impactful for participants. Based on observations, interviews, and a data collection by questionnaire carried out with 198 participants, the proposed SBT appears to provide a significant, relevant, and valuable learning experience. In addition, four experienced Scrum masters and IT project managers, who played key roles in the SBT, argued that the LEGO®-Scrum SBT provides a realistic representation of real-world Scrum projects; that it is dynamic, complex, challenging, and motivating; and that participants' learning is evocative and relevant, since they learn by doing.

Chapter 12

    David Parsons, The Mind Lab, New Zealand
    Kathryn MacCallum, University of Canterbury, New Zealand
    Hayley Sparks, The Mind Lab, New Zealand

Students who are innovating in a project-based context need appropriate frameworks to support applied research that is easily understandable, flexible to different contexts, and appropriate to their needs. Such support is particularly important when the research involves the development of a technology-related artifact, where students need empirical methods for the design and evaluation of that artifact, in addition to guidance in meeting the academic requirements of their courses. This chapter describes a Scrum-based approach for supporting innovations in learning contexts, extending previous proposals in the literature. The context of the research is two academic programs where students undertake innovative technology-based research projects. The new research model is designed to provide a better supporting framework to assist them to effectively manage their projects by integrating the adaptive cycles and ceremonies of the Scrum agile method with complementary concepts and phases from Design Thinking, Design Science, and Design-Based Research.

Chapter 13

An Agile Method to Support Students With Special Educational Needs in Regular Education
    Alfredo Mendoza González, Universidad Autonoma de Zacatecas, Mexico
    Jaime Muñoz-Arteaga, Autonomous University of Aguascalientes, Mexico

In Mexico there are units of consultants that help schools to make students with special needs be included in regular education they provide the necessary help to enhance the learning process. Their work implies adapting the learning methodology, complementing the planned academic activities, adapting learning goals to the students' needs, providing specific technological tools, analyze the knowledge acquisition, etc. Additionally, there are many factors that can affect these goals and complicate the whole intervention process. The COVID-19 pandemic is making attitudinal changes of students, together with the long academic brake, and the forced on-line learning. Together, consultants, teachers, parents, and scientists have analyzed gaps in the intervention process of the supporting units, related with collaboration, teamwork, adaptations in activities and knowledge acquisition, and proposed a solution to it. In this chapter, the authors present Scrum process as a feasible solution, making easy and stronger the collaboration, role definition, and goals prioritization.

Section 5
Organization Assessment

Chapter 14

Sathiadev Mahesh, University of New Orleans, USA
Kenneth R. Walsh, University of New Orleans, USA
Cherie C. Trumbach, University of New Orleans, USA

Scrum technologies have been applied in business software for two decades and are an important part of organizations' innovation processes. This exploratory study examines whether the use of Scrum within an organization can be detected from its financial statements by reviewing references to scrum in corporate financial reports filed with the US Securities and Exchange Commission (SEC). While scrum use is widespread in software development, there are very few references to scrum in corporate financial reports. Fewer than one-half percent of businesses filing reports with the Securities and Exchange Commission include scrum capabilities in their business strategy or business competency sections. It appears that senior management has not yet recognized the value of the technology and evaluated its impact on investor evaluation of business prospects. Investors need to seek other media to evaluate scrum implementation at the business.

Foreword

While neither agile development, in general, nor Scrum, in particular, are new concepts, they remain largely unexploited and often misunderstood in many organizations. Missed opportunities lie not just with client organizations, but, all too frequently, with those who have most to be gained from their use—the systems development group. On the other hand, those organizations that have harnessed agile development tools, like Scrum, have found them to be powerful tools that can be used to efficiently and effectively build and realign systems in response to rapidly evolving business requirements.

The books editors identified organizations that have successfully met the challenge of agile development, and then enlisted as authors experts who have either been at the center of the transition to agile development or who have studied it intensely. The result is a compelling read for systems development managers still struggling with the journey to agile—though those with considerable experience and many successes will still draw useful lessons and see opportunities to fine-tune their own development, implementation, and management processes. The individual chapters also will appeal to scholars of system development and those who teach courses in systems development. However, in what follows I concentrate on the collections' value to practicing system developers and those responsible for the system development organization.

The overarching theme of the book is developing systems to respond rapidly to organizational change—that is, "How can we create systems faster while adapting to concomitant organizational and environmental change?" We live in an ever more dynamic world, even more so in the current pandemic-driven economy. Unfortunately, the information systems that all of our organizations depend upon are in many, perhaps most, cases anything but adaptable. Computer code is like a very fast and very precise network of deeply buried piping, but like a pipe it can also be very rigid and difficult to divert should the need arise. Increasingly information systems managers find themselves being pushed to change the information systems infrastructure to meet some pressing competitive need. Tried and true development methodologies based on the system development lifecycle, long the go-to tool, while still useful in many situations, are an anathema to agile. Moreover, the kinds of systems where the life cycle model does apply, now in many cases enter the organization as purchased packages or Web services. Systems that are left to internal developers are often accompanied by cry-outs for "Can you get me something by next month?", "next week", or even "next day." In these situations the lifecycle model completely fails us, and with it too fails a hidebound systems development organization.

Agile systems development methods offer clear improvements to matching software development to dynamic situations, however challenges still remain in organizations. In this fine book, you will find chapters addressing the most pressing challenges and opportunities that accompany Agile adoption in your organization. For the practitioner audience, chapters two through six look at the challenges of integrating agile methods with legacy systems and the drag of organizational inertia. The challenges addressed in these very applied chapters include organizational culture, team building and team resistance, when to turn to Scrum rather than to a life cycle approach, and how to apply Scrum to the maintenance and enhancement of systems developed with life cycle approaches.

In subsequent chapters other subject matter experts delve deeply into organizational change and implementation issues that accompany an organizations adoption of Agile. Among these are the changing role of the product owner, differences in human resource requirements, different approaches to system testing, and how to draw up a contract for a development activity that has no formal requirements document.

The remaining chapters of the book may be more appealing to professors and graduate students as they focus on teaching and the use of Scrum in student innovation projects, and how Scrum has been leveraged in the education of special needs students. A final chapter looks at Scrum from a considerably higher perspective—reporting on a study examining mentions of Scrum in corporate financial reports. That author's objective is to assess how the market values Scrum.

Some practitioners will read this book from cover to cover, while others will pull it from their shelves as a reference as problems arise, for example, in contracting, or hiring, or in overcoming resistance from traditional developers or project managers. Professors who teach systems development too will find the book useful, as will scholars doing research in this very important arena.

If you are using, or considering using, Scrum in your organization, classroom, or research, I know you will find value in this book.

Blake Ives
University of Houston, USA

Blake Ives *holds the C. T. Bauer Chair in Business Leadership at the C. T. Bauer School of Business in the University of Houston. Blake is a past President of the Association for Information Systems and a Fellow and awardee of The LEO award for life time achievement. He previously served on the Board of Directors for the Society of Information Management International and is a past Director of Research for the Society for Information Management's Advanced Practice Council. Blake received his Ph.D. in Management Information Systems at the University of Minnesota. Blake is past editor-in-chief of MIS Quarterly.*

Foreword

In assembling this collection of expertly crafted chapters, the editors have selected a set of works that paint a rich portrait of agile systems development, the Scrum methodology and the role of Agile development within the organization. There will be numerous take-aways for systems development managers, and I recommend the book to that audience. But, in what follows, I solely consider the value of the book for an academic reader, particularly those doing research in systems development and project management.

The way developers, and most recently "citizen developers," go about implementing and introducing an information system into an organization has always been a complicated and difficult task. After all, organizations are complex entities, and so are information systems. A seamless amalgamation of both seems, at best, challenging to achieve. It is therefore not surprising that scholars often use the word "assemblage" in their descriptions and are sometimes in disagreement about how to best achieve adaptability of information systems to a broad range of contexts.

From a philosophical perspective, information systems can be viewed as artifacts, built by human beings for other human beings and utilizing some arrangement of hardware, software, data, processes and people. From an organizational perspective, information systems can be viewed as supporting business processes, and the set of enterprise systems as representative of the organization itself. From an analytical perspective, information systems can simply be viewed as processors, delivering high-quality information as their output.

Whatever the perspective is, the development of an information systems and its installation within the organization remains an np-, if not, np-complete endeavor.

Approaching it academically will therefore keep scholars busy for many years to come. In the meantime, this book provides a goldmine of practical nuggets. Scholars, and future scholars alike, who seek to gain a quick but deep understanding of the agile development phenomenon are well advised to delve into the book. Questions, such as "When should agile be employed?" "What are the challenges a successful implementation faces?" or "What new opportunities does agile development present?" are just some of many that scholars will learn about. The chapters in the book, all authored by subject matter experts, are full of advice, much of it backed up by hard-earned experience rather than rigorous science. But these descriptions—be it describing success or failure—along with the prescriptions of the experts, provide a rich educational foundation for subsequent scholarship. After all, bodies of expertise lay the necessary groundwork to ensure the research questions eventually identified and addressed are the ones that executives are actually wrestling with. Such compendiums, if done as carefully as this one, fill an essential role!

Iris Junglas

College of Charleston, USA

Iris Junglas *is the Noah T. Leask Distinguished Professor of Information Management and Innovation in the Supply Chain and Information Management Department at the College of Charleston. Over her 20-year career, she has worked inside as well as outside of academia, including a variety of IT consulting firms. Dr. Junglas' research sits at the intersection of technology innovation and business analytics. Her work has been published in the leading journals of the discipline. She is a Fulbright Recipient and a Senior Associate Editor of the European Journal of Information Systems and an Associate Editor for the Communications of Association of Information Systems and Management Information Quarterly Executive.*

Preface

INTRODUCTION

Software development continues to be a dynamic and innovative component of products, services, and organizations and the challenges to create the best software of the highest quality remain. Both development technologies and business needs are evolving at such a fast pace that detailed planning for software projects can be exceedingly difficult, if not impossible, to do in an accurate way. Earlier attempts to create software development life cycles have tended to prove too rigid and can lead to detailed documentation prior to an understanding of what a final system might look like.

Agile development methods have stepped in to create more dynamic development practices that can pivot as more is learned about the requirements and capabilities of the projected system. By focusing on just enough planning, teams can begin work sooner, adapt to changes, and realize value earlier than more traditional approaches. Ken Schwaber and Jeff Sutherland are widely credited for developing Scrum which has been used since the 1990's and has become the most common of the Agile frameworks.

Although no longer new in concept, agile approaches with just enough planning and the ability to pivot can run counter to organizational culture. Other departments of an organization may not use agile approaches and may look at agile as an excuse for less detailed planning. Even IT departments that have been operating for years with more traditional approaches and find the change a cultural shift. Several chapters in this volume discuss those integration issues that still exist.

The audience for this volume is decidedly for both the practitioner and academic communities because in such a practical science of software development an understanding of both perspectives is important. The real world is quite messy indeed as software development occurs within the milieu of product innovation, process innovation, and broader societal changes. The brisk speed of change makes detailed analysis fleeting while conceptual analysis may be difficult to apply. In this volume, many of the chapters describe the rich environment from which their recommendations are derived to help practitioners apply or adapt the findings and to help researchers understand the relevant intervening constructs.

Section 1, Previous Literature, sets the stage by using text analysis techniques to summarize previously published work and trends.

For researchers who want to gain an understanding of the environment faced by real world practitioners, Section 2, Industry Perspectives, was written by authors who are experts in the field. Each offers their perspective on both the challenges and the methods to face those challenges. It is clear from their accounts that in real world settings, many work in environments where traditional project planning is the driving culture of the organization if not the software development department. In such cases, the Agile culture of iterative development may clash with predominant organization thinking. These authors have described such situations and offer hard learned lessons of communicating and operating in such mixed culture environments.

For those interested in a deeper dive into particular issues within the scrum process or implications for the broader organization, see Section 3, Significant Organizational Issues. This section includes chapters on specific Scrum issues such when is Scrum a good fit, product owner practices, and software testing. It also includes the broader organizational issues of human resource management and contracting in organizations that use Scrum.

Section 4, Education, includes chapters on teach Scrum and teach using Scrum. Section 5, Organization Assessment, looks at what can be understood from an organization financial statements about its Scrum and more broadly, innovation posture.

ORGANIZATION OF THE BOOK

In Chapter 1, "A Historical and Bibliometric Analysis of the Development of Agile," Trumbach, Walsh, and Mahesh offer a brief literature review of the evolution of Scrum and a bibliographic analysis showing more recent trends in publication.

In Chapter 2, "Leadership and Team Dynamics for a Successful Agile Organisational Culture," Balasubramaniyan discusses the role of senior leadership and the skill of the people involved. He argues that such leadership and well developed team skills are needed for successful agile projects.

In Chapter 3, "Integrating Agile Teams into the Organization," Goodwin and Logan discuss the conflicts that arise between Agile management practices and general management practices where the iterative approach of Scrum may be at odds with traditional project management. The chapter offers solutions that senior management can use to develop better teams.

In Chapter 4, "A Wrinkle in the Promise of Scrum," Chandrasekharan identifies problems with Scrum adoption within organization. teams and identifies solutions. This chapter explores the impact of poorly led transformations and will also provide some ways to reconsider how transformations should pivot.

In Chapter 5, "Integrating Scrum Processes Into SDLC Maintenance and Enhancement Projects," Jewkes discuss the opportunities and challenges found when Scrum methods are used with the maintenance and enhancement of legacy computing systems.

In Chapter 6, "When Is It a Good Fit to Apply the Scrum Approach to Project Management," Chen argues that Scrum may not always be the best approach. Chen details the risks and benefits of Scrum versus traditional approaches and offers guidelines on choosing between approaches.

In Chapter 7, "An Investigation Into Product Owner Practices in Scrum Implementations," Schwarz, Baham, and Davis investigate the critical link between product owner and software quality. The Scrum role of product owner is a key link between the business customer and the Scrum team and has a major impact on project success and they demonstrate the impact with empirical evidence. Their work is important both in addressing the business issues surrounding the product owner as well as in conducting empirical research in this critical area.

In Chapter 8, "Software Testing Under Agile, Scrum, and DevOps," Pal and Karakostas discuss the importance of software testing as well as the consequences of software deficiencies. They then offer a systematic approach to testing in Scrum settings.

In Chapter 9, "Human Resource Management in Agile Scrum Processes," Zingoni looks at how the human resource needs of an organization change when pursuing Agile Scrum processes. In particular, the changing needs in talent acquisition and management. Zingoni finds that although talent acquisition is not wholly different for Agile professionals, the weighting of certain characteristics may be altered and the use of panel interviews, a focus on group-fit, and supporting assessments are all the more significant. In terms of employee performance, Zingoni points out how to tweak the how, when and where of feedback in Agile settings. In terms of talent development, Zingoni highlights that importance of team assignments in an agile environment that will have a less defined career ladder.

In Chapter 10, "Traditional or Agile Contracting for Software Development: Decisions, Decisions," Payne looks at legal contracts for software projects that are being conducted using Agile Scrum and where a complete requirements document would not be available for such a contract.

In Chapter 11, "Learning SCRUM: A LEGO®-Scrum Simulation," Bourdeau, Romero-Torres, and Petit show how Scrum can be taught using a LEGO simulation. They chose the LEGO approach because it was easy to introduce to learners, but still provided for experiential learning practice. They show their method to be immersive and active in ways that activate participant learning. Their experience, observation, and testing of the method shows it to be quite promising as a way to create an authentic and well received experience for learners, making it a useful way to introduce people to such techniques across a wide variety of backgrounds.

In Chapter 12, "Integrating Scrum With Other Design Approaches to Support Student Innovation Projects," Parsons, MacCallum, and Sparks show how a Scrum based approach can be applied to teaching research methods in an environment where technology artifacts are developed as part of the process. Their method helps to balance the needs of time management and flexibility with the confines of a course schedule. The method also helps keep a balanced focus on the research objective with the development of the technology artifact.

In Chapter 13, "An Agile Method to Support Students With Special Educational Needs in Regular Education After COVID-19 Contingency," González and Muñoz-Arteaga show how the Scrum method can be used in a process to adapt a standard curriculum to one for special needs students.

In Chapter 14, "The Market Value of Scrum: A Note on References to Scrum in U.S. Corporate Financial Reports," Mahesh, Walsh, and Trumbach identify the lack of references to Scrum in US Financial Reports. The industry needs to communicate the value of the approach to top management more effectively.

CONCLUSION

This volume represents an important evolution and integration of practitioner, academic, and broader organizational thinking on the now mainstream process framework of Scrum. When Scrum is practiced by experts on innovative projects in organizations with a high level of trust in the team, remarkable results have been documented. However, as the practice has gone mainstream, a number of challenges emerge and this volume lays those practical challenges on the table and discusses the range of solutions. It also gives insight to what the practitioner faces to help researchers model the problem realistically.

Further, as Scrum becomes more common, contracting and human resource development need to adapt as well. This volume shows how contracting for software development can evolve. It also shows how the human resource department can adapt their methods to hire and develop the best talent for a Scrum work environment.

Finally, the volume addresses methods of teaching Scrum and using Scrum to inform adaptive teaching more broadly. Knowledge of Scrum is needed by a diverse constituency across organizations and methods that can educate the technology and no technology participants alike can aid in the process cultural change organizations face. Further, educational environments are becoming more dynamic and can apply Scrum processes to curriculum change and adaptation.

Acknowledgment

The editors would like to acknowledge the help of all the people involved in this project and, more specifically, to the authors and reviewers that took part in the review process. Without their support, this book would not have become a reality.

In particular, the editors would also like to thank Jillian C. Borukhovich, Anya R. Trumbach, and Kassidy R. Walsh for their critical help in editing submissions.

The editors also are thankful for the support of the Department of Management and Marketing, University of New Orleans.

Kenneth R. Walsh
University of New Orleans, USA

Sathiadev Mahesh
University of New Orleans, USA

Cherie C. Trumbach
University of New Orleans, USA

Section 1
Previous Literature

Chapter 1
A Historical and Bibliometric Analysis of the Development of Agile

Cherie C. Trumbach
University of New Orleans, USA

Kenneth R. Walsh
University of New Orleans, USA

Sathiadev Mahesh
University of New Orleans, USA

ABSTRACT

This chapter starts with a brief history of software development from a summary of traditional approaches and presents the conditions that led to agile approaches such as product complexity, shortened life cycle of the market and eventually to the widespread acceptance of Scrum. The authors then compare the narrative to the bibliometric analysis of abstract records that can be found in the Web of Science database. They parse the terms from the abstract records to identify research trends over time and map the underlying structure of agile research. Finally, they consider the future of Agile-Scrum in light of the current pandemic.

INTRODUCTION

"Project management" can be defined as a series of activities and processes performed as part of a project by a defined set of people, from same or different areas with the aim of generating new or improved organizational products, services, and/or processes (Jrad and Sundaram, 2015). In this chapter, we discuss agile project management. This is a method of project management focused on collaboration and frequent communication. Project management techniques should help the chances of project success. In the early years of software development, project failure was too common, resulting in the development

DOI: 10.4018/978-1-7998-4885-1.ch001

Copyright © 2021, IGI Global. Copying or distributing in print or electronic forms without written permission of IGI Global is prohibited.

of structured approaches that sought to ensure successes. Traditional structured approaches to software project management, sometimes referred to as the systems development life cycle or the waterfall method, became accepted practice. As these structured methods became standard practice, software project failure remained high and experts recognized that such a dynamic environment may require rethinking software development management. Agile methods then took the assumption that all requirements cannot be known at project initiation and that the dynamic business and technology environments will cause change during the project.

Agile software development was formalized as a methodology in 2001 with the creation of the Agile Manifesto. It refers to a set of computer programming methodologies that emphasize flexibility, collaboration, efficiency, simplicity, and most of all, delivering working products to end users within short timeframes (Codington-Lacerte, 2018). However, as time has passed, agile principles have spread into additional industries including general project management. According to Hayat (2019) almost every software company uses agile development, particularly Scrum, and these companies have experienced many positive results from its use.

This chapter starts with a brief history of Software Development from a summary of traditional approaches and presents the arguments made for agile approaches and the eventual widespread acceptance of Scrum. We then compare the narrative to the bibliometric analysis of abstract records that can be found in the Web of Science database. Finally, we consider the future of Agile-Scrum in light of the current pandemic.

BACKGROUND

From Traditional Software Development to Scrum

Early software development was done by developers who had both responsibility for analysis and coding. Such a two-step process was thought to be adequate for small scale development, but led to numerous problems for large software systems (Royce, 1970). A simple solution may have been to introduce a more sophisticated methodology with increased documentation and decomposition to allow more people to work in concert. However, such an approach is risky because errors found will inevitably lead to rework of previous steps (Royce, 1970). As an answer to this, a more sophisticated development timeline including iteration, documentation, and testing was proposed (Royce, 1970). The result of this line of thinking was an iterative and adaptive model of the phases of large-scale software development (Royce, 1970). Boehm (1983) reiterated the importance of a planned and phased approach. Boehm (1983 also emphasized the importance of documenting and completing phases before moving on to subsequent phases, although he also discussed using prototyping, incremental development, and scaffolding as ways to not necessarily defer coding until specifications were complete. This process was formalized into the familiar "analysis-design-implementation-test" steps. As the process became more formalized, particularly in the 1980s, the opportunity to automate parts of the process became more evident. However, with formalization by a wide range of practitioners, the structure of the phases may have been refined and the expense of the concepts of iteration and adaptation.

In the early stages of agile software development, prototypes followed by incremental steps were utilized. These were the first steps toward agile processes. However, these increments and prototypes were limited. They may have been applied in just one cycle where a prototype was refined to produce a finished product. Small iterations only occurred where earlier results needed to be corrected. The mindset was that iterations indicated the existence of a problem with the initial design. At this point in time, the technology to support agile development was non-existent and the development process was considered linear. The linear approach was customer friendly in that the final result of the project was clearer. As software development became more sophisticated, quality, productivity, and scalability became the focus of improving the process. More tools were developed to support the process and the models expanded to cover more aspects of the overall process. (Kneuper, 2017)). The early formal methodologies offered a solid, consistent project structure with clear management procedures and homogenous project teams. (Jovanovic and Beric, 2018). The methodologies were plan-driven with upfront requirements, documentation and detailed plans. Two examples are the waterfall and the spiral model (Li and Armin, 2009). The traditional methods do an excellent job utilizing graphical tools to support communication as well as support reports and review meetings. However, the tools used to support these methodologies such as Work Breakdown Structures, Gantt charts, and cost schedules all assume a linear process (Rodrigues and Bowers, 1996).

A traditional project has well-defined boundaries aligned with corporate goals, clear roles and responsibilities, and clear objectives. The techniques are more aligned with the operational aspects of projects. However, many fields have more complex projects with increasing uncertainty concerning project parameters. In these circumstances, traditional methodologies are insufficient for the web of risks. These projects need a broader more strategic view of project management (Jrad and Sundaram, 2015; Rodrigues and Bowers, 1996). As projects have become more complex, project failure has become more common. There are more cost overruns, schedule delays, and cancelled projects. (Rodrigues and Bowers, 1996) There are both internal and external reasons for project failures. The failures generally fall in one of three categories: political/social environment, legal agreements, and human factors. Traditional project management techniques are not designed to address these areas.

Additionally, since the traditional method is linear and structured in approach, it is difficult to change directions or make changes to the project plan. Additionally, since client and stakeholder input are focused into the earliest stages of the linear process, therefore there is minimal input from clients and stakeholders when changes are needed or to ensure that requirements are actually being met along the way (Jovanovic and Beric, 2018).

Given the limitations of traditional approaches, new approaches were needed to address the rigidity of traditional approaches and lack of methods to address the human elements of projects. As time-to-market became increasingly more important and digital markets enabled by the World Wide Web expanded, iterative approaches began to infiltrate certain aspects of the software development process. The first model to explicitly include iterations in the process beyond coding and testing was Boehm's spiral model in 1988. A few years later, rapid application development was published (J. Martin, Rapid Application Development, MacMillan, 1991). Object-Oriented development also changed the direction of software development (Kneuper, 2017).

The agile concept can be traced back to the manufacturing industry in 1991 through lean manufacturing. M. A. Youssef coined the term "agile manufacturing" in a paper in 1992 (Li and Armin, 2009; Youssef, 1992). The rise of knowledge workers and the knowledge economy along with the move toward lean production also drove the push toward new ways of thinking about project management and the introduction of Scrum as a method (Takeuchi and Nonaka) and "many new development methodologies were introduced, such as Scrum, Extreme Programming, Dynamic Systems Development Method, the Crystal family of methods, and Feature Driven Development". Together these methods added the concepts of intensive communications between the customer and the project team, fast feedback, and self-organizing teams. In comparison to traditional methodologies, agile methodologies allow for a more flexible project structure. Additionally, the process makes provision for working with the customer to change directions or alter requirements. Additionally, each software release is fully functional within a short time between each release allowing for more opportunities to get feedback and make changes. A key component of agile manufacturing is a strong relationship with clients (Jovanovic and Beric, 2018). Customer involvement is a key element in the agile methodology.

According to Ionel (2009), the two main differences between traditional and agile methodologies are based on two assumptions. Traditional methodologies assume that customers need guidance from the developers regarding the requirements. The biggest assumption is that developers actually know and understand not only what customers' need at the start of the project, but also what customers will need in the future. Since the design process is all done in one shot and the result is a completed product, the developers end up overdesigning the system, incorporating functionality that the customer often does not need. There is also a delay as a system that meets not only current requirements, but future requirements anticipated by developers, is built. Agile does not assume that the developer knows more than the customer about their needs. Neither does it assume that the customer knows their future needs. It assumes that neither the customers nor the developers fully know what the requirements should be. A simpler product is completed quickly, and additional functionality is added with each succeeding version. Such an approach accommodates future requirement changes. The flexibility build into agile methodologies can handle changes in cost, scope, and quality of software based on customer needs, even as those needs change or are revealed (Hayat et al, 2019).

In 2001, the Agile Manifesto was developed establishing agile as a formal category for methodologies. As software projects and the nature of information system changes became more complex and more unpredictable, agile methodologies were widely accepted. The mantra "faster, cheaper, quicker" continues to rule software development projects (Jrad and Sundaram, 2015).

Scrum

"Scrum is the framework of Agile Methodology" (Hayat et al, 2019). Scrum has three iterative stages: Product backlog development, main sprint, and daily sprints. The model is iterative throughout the product development process (Sommer et al, 2013). Almost every company uses Agile /Scrum and it has a positive impact on software project management. 95% of users state that Scrum has a positive impact on cost and provides an easy way to manage changes in both time and cost. When using Scrum, work is divided in small chunks and sprints are defined, developers develop their chunks on time and within budget (Hayat et al, 2019).

Over time, agile principles have spread into other areas outside of the software project management. In particular, agile principles have been of interest in the realm of product development for industrial manufacturers. The stage-gate model for product development projects has been criticized as being too simplistic. Spiral models and circular models have proven difficult to implement. However, even though Agile is beneficial, agile methodologies must be modified for these projects for successful implementation. Industrial Manufacturers integrate customer-focused agile process models like Scrum into their existing Product Development models as a hybrid model. The benefits of a hybrid model that integrates the traditional stage-gate approach applied to physical products are a faster and more adaptive response to changing customer needs, better integration of voice-of-the-customer, better team communication, improved development productivity and faster time to market.

Scrum has shown positive results in product development performance. Sommer et al (2013) presents three cases with different levels of incorporating Scrum in a hybrid manner. In all three cases, product development performance was improved. However, what is unclear, is the contribution of specific elements of Agile to improved performance.

BIBLIOMETRIC ANALYSIS

This study uses the Web of Science database. Web of Science is an electronic database which abstracts and indexes publications from 8600 journals across multiple disciplines. Our data is based on the search string "(agile or scrum) and (project or software or methodology)". This search string was selected to capture as many relevant records while excluding noise, or irrelevant records. A total of 2,826 articles fit within our topic. The abstracts were downloaded and imported into VantagePoint text mining software. VantagePoint is a text mining software specifically designed to import, parse the fields and analyze a corpus of technology abstract records, particularly abstracts from technology-focused databases. The full abstract records are parsed by field (title, keywords, author(s), author affiliation, country, year, abstract, publication) and the free text fields are parsed by words and phrases. As a result, the analysis contains information about authors, organizations, publications, countries, and topics over a timeline. These lists created from individual fields were cleaned to identify spelling variations which refer to the same underlying concept. In the next step, various groups were created to conduct further analysis. The results are captured below.

Figure 1 depicts the number of records published using the search string each year. The data for 2020 contains only those articles that were indexed in Web of Science through February 2020. There is also some delay between publication and record indexing. The number of articles per year provides an indication of the level of interest in a topic. Two pieces of data worth noting are the first time that a term appears in the literature and the trends from year to year, more so than the exact number of records. For example, as seen in our earlier discussion of the history of agile methodologies, "Agile Manufacturing" was a term coined in 1992. This indicates when discussion of the topic first appears in the public sphere. For our search term, there was a steady, but small, increase in research interest until 2001. Then, in 2001, the year of the Agile Manifesto, there was an upward turn in Agile interest that continued to increase through 2005. In 2006, there started to be a decline in the occurrence of research publication records related to agile methodologies. However, in 2008 there was a turnaround in interest that steadily continued to rise with the exception of the year 2013. This small dip in 2013 is likely to be a statistical aberration Interestingly, 2008 is also the year that the term "scrum methodology" first appeared in the abstract records, though other variations of the term "scrum" appeared earlier. Scrum added clarification for implementation and gave more specific direction to the body of agile methodologies. Abrahamsson et al (2008) describe a study in which agile methodologies including Scrum were evaluated for the impact on communication practices of software development teams. Agile practices were found to positively impact communication, but other approaches were also needed to achieve the desired overall results. There is a rapid increase in the number of records through 2019. Note that 2020 data was only collected for a couple of months.

Figure 1. Number of Articles Published for Each Year

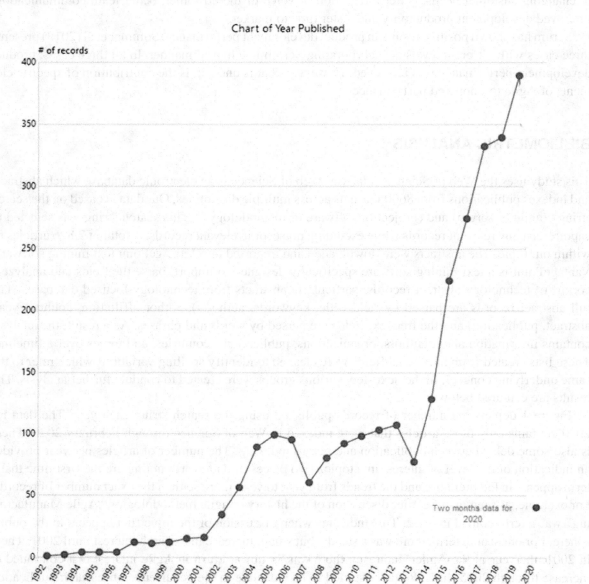

Continuing the analysis required the parsing of the abstract into terms. However, these terms must be cleaned in order to combine terms with slightly different representations but are actually the same concept. For example, the terms "agile project methodology" and "agile methodology" represent the same concept. The terms from the Abstract phrases and keywords were combined and cleaned into topic areas to demonstrate the main topics covered in the research and how those topics developed over time. The decision as to which terms to combine is somewhat subjective but should generally be done at the same level of specificity. For this first analysis, a broad generalization was used to combine terms that represent a wider topic area. The final list used for analysis contained 58 terms/topic areas. Table 1 shows the top 20 topic areas and the number of records where the topic was identified. The most common topic area is "agile teams". Some terms were basic terms that are expected from our search string, such as "project management" and "scrum methodologies" while other terms are more pertinent to research in general, such as "future research". Some notable observations are the prevalence of terms such as "supply chain", "quality requirements", "engineering education" and "risk management".

Table 1. List of Top 20 Topics

	# Records	Topic List
1	1213	Agile Teams
2	247	Supply Chain
3	216	Project Management
4	209	Manufacturing Organizations
5	195	Practical Experience
6	182	Business Environment
7	166	Information Systems
8	159	Research Limitations/Implications
9	138	Requirements Management
10	127	Extreme Programming (XP)
11	125	End-users
12	114	Process Management
13	111	Decision-making Process
14	101	Knowledge Base
15	87	Quality Requirements
16	84	Future Research
17	70	Competitive Environment
18	68	Engineering Education
19	64	Scrum Methodology
20	52	Risk Management

Another level is analysis is to review the terms as they appear by year. When did various terms first start to occur in the public sphere? When did certain terminology become more popular? How did the conversation about the topic change over time? One way to visualize the development in the conversation over time is with a Bubble Chart as shown in Figure 2. Conceptually important terms primarily from Table 2 were used as the input into the Bubble Chart. Each bubble represents the years in which those topics appear in the literature and the size of the bubble indicates the relative number of records containing that topic.

The number of references associated with all of the topics in the topic list show a growth trend of "agile" as a research topic. One very interesting finding is that while the Agile Manifesto did not occur until 2001, the discussion of agile ideas with these topics were occurring long before then. The Manufacturing industry was talking about agile ideas in 1994, the earliest of all of these major topic areas.

Figure 2. Topics by Year

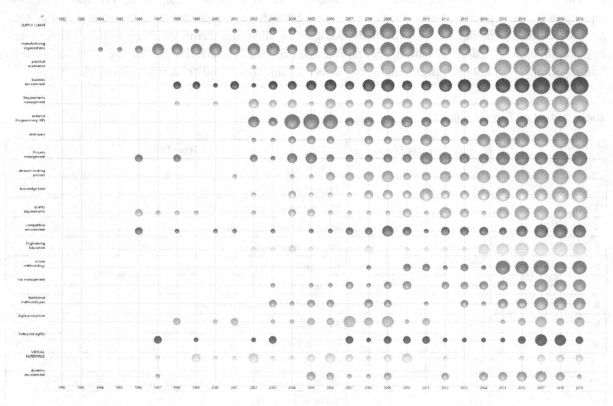

This occurrence makes sense considering that lean manufacturing began discussing agile topics in 1991. Some topics have steadily grown over time. Others have sputtered along. While manufacturing was the first area with an interest in agile ideas, it has seen very little growth over time. Another term, "traditional methodologies" had a small steady stream of overlap in Agile records but in 2019, there has been a resurgence of discussion about traditional methods with Agile. As agile methodologies are applied in areas outside of traditional software project methods and into areas that have been dominated by traditional project management techniques, we should expect that those methods would be studied more frequently in comparison to Agile. In addition, our literature review indicated that there has been a growing interest in combining Scrum with traditional stage-gate methodologies in the realm of new product development in the industrial manufacturing industry. Hence, more references to those traditional methodologies. The most significant increases in interest have been in the areas of the competitive environment, risk management, data analysis, and quality requirements. Also, in 2014, the increase in interest in Agile in engineering education was substantial. Two noteworthy topics that are among the newest additions but have made a quick impact are "success factors" and "systematic review". A scan of titles with these two terms indicates the progression of research in Agile toward a review of research in Agile particularly with the goal of identifying the factors that make agile project management successful. Interestingly, one area that has seen interest wane in the last 8 years is agile in the virtual enterprise. Given the current state of the world, the interest in Agile or Scrum in the context of the virtual enterprise may increase.

Table 3 depicts the top journals in which our search terms were found for each year considered. Again, here we see that interest in agile topics are first found lightly scattered through production related journals, indicating the interest in agile manufacturing. While research continues in these journals, just a few years after the Agile Manifesto is released, agile topics are quickly spread out to a variety of software engineering, computer science and technology journals. Notice that in 2008, IEEE Latin American Transactions began to publish Agile and Scrum related topics, indicating a rising interest in Latin America in these topics.

Now, let's take a look at the underlying topic structure in Agile-Scrum literature. Figure 3 shows a Factor Map created using the cleaned list of Combined Keywords and Abstract Phrases that occur in at least 10 Records. The analysis ends up including 313 terms. A process is used using PCA analysis to create clusters of terms based on the co-occurrence of terms with one another. Though all of the terms are included in the analysis, not all of the terms are included in the final cluster sets. The resulting 13 clusters which indicate the underlying topic-structure and relationships in the literature are described in the following table (Table 4).

SCRUM, THE PANDEMIC, AND THE FUTURE

As with many areas, Covid-19 has forced many changes to organizations and most will never go back to pre-Covid times. Some organizations have had to adapt quickly to handle the variety of challenges that have occurred as a result of the pandemic. The most obvious changes are that the pandemic has forced people to work from home and use new technologies to do so. Digital adoption has increased at a phenomenal rate. A survey conducted by McKinsey and Company found that across a range of industries, there has been a 19% to over 100% increase in digital adoption due to Covid-19. The percentage of individuals working full time from home has seen an even far greater increase. For example, the percent of individuals working at home in the Media and Technology sector grew from 9% to 84%, in Professional and Business Services 5% to 74% and in Financial Activities from 5% to 70%. When asked if they expected to continue working remotely after the pandemic, 75% of those now working remotely expect to continue (Baig, et al, 2020). This is a fundamental shift in the structure of the work environment. Along with this change in the work environment, comes many challenges. The most fundamental challenge is that of physical distance from co-workers. This physical distance is an impediment to the typical ways in which employees interact not just for meetings but in the ability to chat with a co-worker in their office or engage in spontaneous break room conversations. However, the physical distance is compounded by additional challenges related to home responsibilities as parents may also be home with children who are now homeschooling or unable to attend daycare. There may not be sufficient space at home for private workspace or parents may have to assist with homeschooling. Such rapid transformational changes also require an agile approach to change management. Yet, the usual approach to agile methodologies like Scrum are based on colocation.

In addition to the rapid change in the structure of the workday, many businesses have required a short turn around on software applications with new capabilities to support a remotely operating business. Their survival might depend on it. This need has created opportunities for software development, who utilize agile development methods and can quickly respond to unique requests. Companies and/ or countries are asking for an array of applications that will possibly allow them to continue to operate in their physical space such as social distancing apps for retail store reservations and check-ins, and

Table 3. Journals by Year

# Recs	Publication Name	1994	1995	1996	1997	1998	1999	2000	2001	2002	2003	2004	2005	2006	2007	2008	2009	2010	2011	2012	2013	2014	2015	2016	2017	2018	2019	2020
110	INFORMATION AND SOFTWARE TECHNOLOGY											1	1	1	2	3	3	3	9	7	5	11	20	12	8	13	9	2
107	JOURNAL OF SYSTEMS AND SOFTWARE												3	2		6	3	6	2	11	6	7	9	15	17	13	7	
68	EXTREME PROGRAMMING AND AGILE PROCESSES IN SOFTWARE ENGINEERING, PROCEEDINGS											24	27	17														
60	JOURNAL OF SOFTWARE-EVOLUTION AND PROCESS																			5	2	10	2	4	11	12	11	
53	IEEE SOFTWARE					1		1		2	3	2	6	2	3	1	7	7		1	1	1	1	4		3	6	1
43	INTERNATIONAL JOURNAL OF ADVANCED COMPUTER SCIENCE AND APPLICATIONS																						6	5	12	10	10	
35	EMPIRICAL SOFTWARE ENGINEERING											1	1	3		2		4		2		3	7	2	3	4	1	
30	SUPPLY CHAIN MANAGEMENT-AN INTERNATIONAL JOURNAL											1	1	3	1	1	3	2	1	2		4	1	3	1		5	
27	BENCHMARKING-AN INTERNATIONAL JOURNAL																						2	7	5	10	3	
26	INTERNATIONAL JOURNAL OF PRODUCTION RESEARCH				1	1	2	2	1	2	2			1		3		2	3	2			1		1	1	1	
25	INTERNATIONAL JOURNAL OF OPERATIONS & PRODUCTION MANAGEMENT	1				1		1	2			1	2	1	6	1	1		1	2		1	2	1		1		
24	IEEE ACCESS																						1		2	8	12	1
24	INTERNATIONAL JOURNAL OF SOFTWARE ENGINEERING AND KNOWLEDGE ENGINEERING													1	1	1	1	1		2	2	4	1	4	1	1	4	
23	PROJECT MANAGEMENT JOURNAL																	3	1	1		2	2	2	5	6		
21	EXTREME PROGRAMMING AND AGILE METHODS - XP/ AGILE UNIVERSE 2004, PROCEEDINGS											21																
19	IEEE LATIN AMERICA TRANSACTIONS																1	1	1	2			4	7	1	1	1	
17	INTERNATIONAL JOURNAL OF PRODUCTION ECONOMICS					1				1	1					3	3	2	2		1		1	1				
17	JOURNAL OF MANUFACTURING TECHNOLOGY MANAGEMENT																						3	4	2	5	2	1
16	IET SOFTWARE															1		2	1	2		1				2		7

thermal monitoring apps. Government organizations may need applications to help slow the spread of the virus such as location tracking, facial recognition, quarantine management or risk management applications. Hospitals may also need smart routing applications to manage and monitor the flow of patients and supplies around the hospital to ensure the safety of all the patients (Preimesberger, 2020). Organizations that have incorporated the Scrum methodology have the advantage of already operating as

Table 4. Cluster Descriptions

Cluster Defining Terms	Cluster description
Agile teams, software development teams, team members, software teams, team performance	All of the terms in this cluster are related to the team aspect of Agile. Teamwork, team collaboration, and effective team management are critical to the success of agile projects.
Product quality, software quality	A main driver in implementing agile methodologies is to improve the quality of the final product. These articles discuss the impact of Agile on quality.
Extreme programming	Extreme programming is a type of agile software development framework.
Global software development, systematic literature review	As an innovative idea progresses, researchers conduct systematic literature reviews. In this cluster, those reviews are related to the use of Agile in global software development.
Agile transformation, agile adoption	In any organization, Agile implementation must take preparation to adopt the practices. It will also transform the organization. These articles address those considerations.
Software Engineering Education, capstone course, effort estimation	This cluster primarily consists of articles addressing the introduction of Agile/Scrum into university curriculum, particularly in software engineering programs.
Agile capabilities, organizational agility, enterprise agility, agile strategies, agile organizations, critical factors, large organizations	Agile is not just a methodology. It will impact the organization. The organization itself must be agile in order to successfully utilize agile methodologies.
Agility evaluation, mass customization, manufacturing organization, fuzzy logic, agility assessment	When utilizing agile practices in manufacturing, measuring manufacturing agility allows the ability to quantify results.
Research limitations, practical implications, supply chain management, supply chain strategy	This is a cluster addressing practical implications of Agile, particularly as it relates the Supply chain.
Business performance, agile manufacturing, information-technology, virtual enterprise, operational performance, structural equation modeling	This cluster contains a wide variety of topics related to the business operations.
Product development, new products	These records address the specific area of Agile product development
Process planning, changing markets, concurrent engineering	This cluster topics are related to agile manufacturing and the need for Agile in the context of concurrent engineering due to the changing markets.

an agile organization but also must adjust as well because the basis of Scrum and other agile processes rests on physical proximity. Agile methods are based on team collocation. Almost all agile software implementations have collocated teams, often in one (small) room. This arrangement is almost impossible due to the pandemic. However, with some digital adjustments, these organizations have a strong foundation of principles from which to build. The five Scrum values of courage, focus, commitment, respect, and openness can guide companies through a transition to remote operations. The organization has to maintain a focus on scrum principles and goals and adjust the processes accordingly. It will be interesting to see how these forced changes will change the trajectory of the Scrum Methodology. These companies and the methodology must grow from its strength in being accustomed to change and flexibility. However, even beyond strength and flexibility, agile principles are conducive to the change to remote work. Rigid prioritization, small cross-functional autonomous teams, regular meetings, and agile leadership all translate well to remote operations. Organizations need to focus on core elements of iteration and collaboration while finding new ways to connect remotely.

Figure 3. Key Terms Factor Map

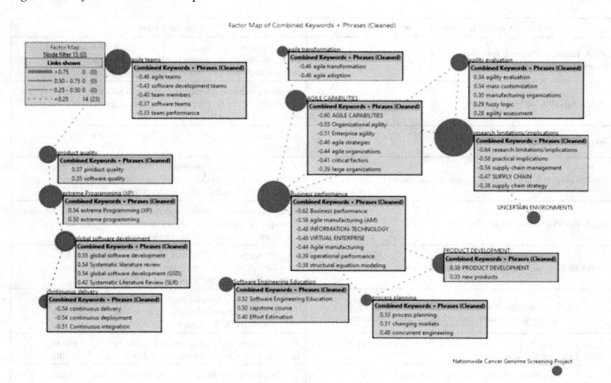

In order to guide a team through these changes, there are some questions to consider. How agile is the project team? What does a project leader need to do to keep a project progressing? Rehburg, et. al. (2020) from Boston Consulting Group maintains that it is imperative for leadership to ensure that teams stay focused on the organization's purpose, strategy, and priorities. It is imperative that leaders also communicate intent to aid team members in efforts to stay focused. The online workday must include elements that maintain the structure for agile development. Rehburg advocates for daily 15-30-minute meetings and a weekly meeting lasting 60-90 minutes. He also stresses the importance of being available on instant messaging and making calendar availability visible. Finally, virtual tools can greatly aid in collaboration. Conferencing tools that allow for always-on connection opportunities can facilitate informal connections. However, constant online visibility may be difficult given the exceptional challenges of working from home. These challenges are not insurmountable but should not be ignored. Another level of flexibility is needed within the Scrum framework. For example, one organization allowed parents to block out periods of time on the team calendar to attend to family matters. Another organization doubled their lunch break. This flexibility allows workers to take care of home matters more easily when needed and focus on work otherwise. Organizations have also focused on ensuring that these additional meetings are working sessions that produce tangible results and not time wasters. Using a different strategy, some organizations have decided to schedule meeting-free time blocks (Agile Actors, 2020). Companies are trying different approaches to overcome these obstacles. Currently, these examples are anecdotes by consultants who have seen positive results. More research is needed to determine the impact on productivity by these various approaches.

The overall goal is to set up virtual spaces that mirror the effectiveness of physical spaces. According to Comella-Dorda, et. al. (2019) from McKinsey and Company, remote work results in inefficiency and reduced cohesion, but the causal problems can be addressed. McKinsey and Company lays out recommendations for continuing to use agile approaches with remote teams that are more detailed than Rehburg's suggestions. Table 5 shows these recommendations along with an example as to how the recommendation can be implemented remotely. The authors also reiterate that teams that were functioning cohesively prior to being thrust into remote operations will function better afterwards. Perhaps the team has ground rules about how individuals would have their turn to speak or how feedback on suggestions are provided. These same ground rules still apply in the virtual environment but altered to take advantage of the capabilities in the technology. Some of these changes may require additional training or revisions to the specific rule. Documentation is more important in remote operations, but how do you encourage the team to document more? Meetings can be recorded with transcriptions, but what meetings should be recorded and how will they be organized for efficient retrieval by others?

Table 5. Remote Agile Recommendations

Recommendations	Example
Revisit the norms and ground rules for interaction	Consider ground rules for virtual tools like whiteboards and video conferencing
Cultivate bonding and morale	Virtual team building and assume best intentions
Adapt coaching and development	Reinvent face-to-face activities but more frequently
Recalibrating remote agile processes	Start with outcomes and work backward, particularly for ceremonies
Establish a single source of truth	Documentation is more important
Adjust to synchronous collaboration	Use it but don't over rely on them
Keep teams engaged during long ceremonies	Short exercise breaks as an example
Adapting leadership approach	Be deliberate with engagement

CONCLUSION

As projects have become more complicated and there is a drive for a faster turnover of product improvements along with higher expectations in quality, agile methodologies like Scrum have become increasingly popular. Interest in agile methods has moved from Manufacturing to software development using Scrum to just about every industry. While the idea of the agile organization has been gaining in popularity, Covid-19 has thrust many organizations into new territories that would highly benefit from agile approaches, like Scrum. However, a team already operating using agile principles is in a better position to make adjustments to operating remotely than teams that are not accustomed to change. The challenge for agile teams is that the current models and tools are built upon collocation. While any change is a challenge, there are many software tools already on the market that support the same objectives in a remote situation.

REFERENCES

Abrahamsson, P., Pikkarainen, M., Salo, O., Haikara, J., & Still, J. (2008). The impact of agile practices on communication in software development. *Empirical Software Engineering*.

Agile Actors. (2020). *Solutions to common remote work issues during COVID.* Downloaded August 24, 2020, from https://www.scruminc.com/solutions-to-common-remote-work-issues-during-covid/

Baig, A., Hall, B., Jenkins, P., Lamarre, E., & McCarthy, B. (2020). *The covid-19 recovery will be digital: A plan for the first 90 days.* Retrieved August 24, 2020, from https://www.mckinsey.com/business-functions/mckinsey-digital/our-insights/the-covid-19-recovery-will-be-digital-a-plan-for-the-first-90-days

Boehm, B. W. (1983). Seven basic principles of software engineering. *Journal of Systems and Software*, *3*(1), 3–24. doi:10.1016/0164-1212(83)90003-1

Codington-Lacerte, C. (2018). *Agile software development.* Salem Press Encyclopedia.

Comella-Dorda, S., Garg, L., Thareja, S., & Vasquez-McCall, B. (2019). *Revisiting agile teams after an abrupt shift to remote.* Retrieved August 23, 2020 from https://wwww.mckinsey.com/business-functions/organization/our-insights/revisiting-agile-teams-after-an-abrupt-shift-to-remote#

Cooper, R. G., & Sommer, A. F. (2016). From experience: The agile-stage-gate hybrid model: A promising new approach and a new research opportunity. *Journal of Product Innovation Management*, *33*(5).

Hayat, F., Rehman, A. U., Arif, K. S., Wahab, K., & Abbas, M. (2019). *The influence of agile methodology (Scrum) on software project management.* IEEE Computer Society.

Ionel, N. (2009). Agile software development methodologies: An overview of the current state of research. *Annals of Faculty of Economics*, *4*(1).

Jiang, L., & Eberlein, A. (2009). An analysis of the history of classical software development and agile development. *IEEE International Conference on Systems, Man, and Cybernetics*. 10.1109/ICSMC.2009.5346888

Jovanovic, P., & Beric, I. (2018). Analysis of the available project management methodologies," management. *Journal of Sustainable Business and Management Solutions in Emerging Economies*, *23*(3), 1. doi:10.7595/management.fon.2018.0027

Jrad, R. B. N., & Sundaram, D. (2015). Challenges of inter-organizational information and middleware system projects: Agility, complexity, success, and failure. *6th International Conference on Information, Intelligence, Systems and Applications (IISA)*. 10.1109/IISA.2015.7387960

Kneuper, R. (2017). *Sixty years of software development life cycle models. IEEE Annals of the History of Computing*.

Lynch, W. (2019). *The brief history of Scrum.* Retrieved August 21, 2020, from https://medium.com/@warren2lynch/the-brief-of-history-of-scrum-15efb73b4701#:~:text=Jeff%20Sutherland%20originated%20the%20first,a%20formal%20process%20in%201995

Preimesberger, C. (2020). *Startup vantiq comes to rescue in covid-19 use cases.* Retrieved August 21, 2020, from https://www.eweek.com/innovation/startup-vantiq-comes-to-rescue-in-covid-19-use-cases

Rehburg, B., Danoesastro, M., Kaul, S., & Stutts, L. (2019). *How to remain remotely agile through covid-19.* Retrieved August 22, 2020, from https://www.bcg.com/en-us/publications/2020/remaining-agile-and-remote-through-covid.aspx

Rising, L., & Janoff, N. (2000). The Scrum software development process for small teams. *IEEE Software*, *17*(4), 26–32. doi:10.1109/52.854065

Rodrigues, A., & Bowers, J. (1996). Systems dynamics in project management: A comparative analysis with traditional methods. *System Dynamics Review*, *12*(2), 121–139. doi:10.1002/(SICI)1099-1727(199622)12:2<121::AID-SDR99>3.0.CO;2-X

Royce, W. W. (1970). Managing the development of large software systems. *Proceedings of IEEE WESCON,* 1-9.

Singh, R., Kumar, D., & Sagar, B. B. (2019). Analytical study of agile methodology in information technology sector. *4th International Conference on Information Systems and Computer Networks (ISCON).* 10.1109/ISCON47742.2019.9036280

Sommer, A. F., Slavensky, A., Nguyen, V. T., Steger-Jenson, K., & Dukovska-Popovska, I. (2013). Scrum integration in stage-gate models for collaborative product development – A case study of three industrial manufacturers. *IEEE International Conference on Industrial Engineering and Engineering Management (IEEM).* 10.1109/IEEM.2013.6962616

Youssef, M. A. (1992). Agile manufacturing: A necessary condition for competing in global markets. *Industrial Engineering, 18*(20).

Section 2
Industry Perspectives

Chapter 2
Leadership and Team Dynamics for a Successful Agile Organisational Culture

S. M. Balasubramaniyan

Digital Core Technologies, India

ABSTRACT

Agile Manifesto refers to Leadership and Team characteristics in three out of the twelve principles of Agile software. Clearly, the 'people' in the organisation play a critical role in the success of Agile software development. Many studies have been done on the various aspects of the Leadership and Team characteristics in respect of the role, the behaviour, the process and the structure. While most of these studies are related to the role and behaviour aspects of the leadership and the teams, this chapter attempts to supplement them with those aspects that are related to structure, internal and external interfaces and interactions, to ensure that the Agile engagements are planned and executed successfully and consistently. The emphasis in this chapter is the Organisation Culture that must be conducive for sure success of Agile projects and Scrum teams.

INTRODUCTION

The importance of Leadership and the Team dynamics in the Agile projects' success has been adequately brought out through three of the twelve principles in Agile Manifesto (Agile Alliance, 2001). These principles state that (i) Business people and the developers must work together daily throughout the project, (ii) Build projects around motivated individuals. Get them the environment and support they need and trust them to get the job done and (iii) At regular intervals, the team reflects on how to become more effective, then tunes and adjusts its behaviour accordingly. In essence, the role and needed behaviour of the Agile teams and the leaders can be derived out of these principles.

Stray et.al. (2020) deal with the leadership considerations from the group dynamics perspective. Many organisations transform to Agile mode through 'Appointed Leaders' rather than identifying and preparing for such a role. The challenges in such a set up are listed as Team maturity, Team design and Culture

DOI: 10.4018/978-1-7998-4885-1.ch002

Copyright © 2021, IGI Global. Copying or distributing in print or electronic forms without written permission of IGI Global is prohibited.

and mindset. How do we address such challenges? Parris and Peachey (2013) recommend that Servant Leadership is the answer. While no consensus exists on the definition of Servant Leadership, according to them, it is a viable Leadership theory. Ethics, virtues and morality are some of the key components of Servant Leadership. However, the research of Parris and Peachey (2013) lacks the concrete direction for Servant Leadership. Lean CX (2019) describes the role, attitude and the activities played by the Project Manager and the Scrum Master in specifically removing the 'blockers' as the Servant Leadership. De Smet, Lurie and St. George (2018), in the McKinsey & Company's report strongly suggests that new capabilities are required to lead Agile transformation in the 21st century organisations. They are categorised under Agile ways of working, Agile mindsets and behaviour and Agile Organisation design and culture. This study suggests ways to get such leadership qualities.

Moe et. al. (2009) recommend Diffused leadership rather than Centralised leadership for successful Agile organisation. The leadership is shared between Product owner, Scrum Master and the members of the team. A case study has been presented to substantiate the theory, however, from this author's experience, it is found that this is an idealistic proposition and may not be practical in many instances.

Anthony Mersino (2018) lists the successful characteristics of Agile leaders as Growth mindset, self-awareness, ownership, Humility, Empathetic listening, Courage, Risk taking, trust, ability to see and optimise and the ability to inspire others. This research also lists Establishing teams, Shaping the environment, coaching and leading organisational change as the key responsibility of the Agile leaders. While these activities and characteristics of leaders are listed as the necessary ingredients of Agile leaders, it is felt that they are equally relevant and applicable for leaders of any organisational culture. It is felt that some more specifics around Agile mode of working should have been considered. Riggins (2019) lists Disconnect with the Executives, Scaling management and Exhaustive nature of work as the three main challenges of new Agile leaders. Hence, it is realised that certain organisational characteristics need to be established to assist the Agile leaders in overcoming the challenges.

Druskat and Wheeler (2001) propose a concept of managing from the boundary, which uses an external team leader as an option. According to them, how to effectively manage and Self-Managed team is largely unanswered. 13 behaviours, largely grouped under 4 types of behavioural groups viz. Relating, Empowering, Persuading and Scouting, are the key characteristics of an external leader. Interestingly, the success of such leaders is their ability to support the team to self-manage and the take care of the external boundary management, read, issues at the external interfaces and interactions.

Srivastava and Jain (2017) bring up the important current reality of Leadership for Distributed Agile teams. It is practically not possible for every sub team at different locations to have a Scrum master. The proposition in this study is that the team members take turns to play the role of Scrum Master in key locations. This study also defines and describes the behavioural aspects to assist playing the Scrum Master role. Along these lines is another study (Pearce & Sims, 2002) that weighs the pros and cons of 'Vertical' and 'Shared' leadership concept. The study considers aversive, directive, transactional, transformational and empowering behaviours of Agile leaders to gather information, statistically analyse the data and the conclusions are that shared leadership is better than vertical leaders in Agile scenario. However, in the experience of the author of this chapter, the Vertical leadership can be as much effective, if not better, than the shared leadership. The ways to accomplish this have been covered in this study.

Kaczor (2019), in the white paper on Agile leadership in and beyond the Scrum team looks at the focus of the Agile leaders inside of the Agile team and beyond the team boundaries. This is seen to be another important aspect of building and sustaining successful Scrum teams. Inside the team, the Agile leader is a Servant Leader and beyond the team, they play the role for organisational level enablement.

This study recommends that an organisational level Executive leader is ideally suited for this purpose. The author of this chapter considers this dimension as one of the non-behaviour related aspects of sustained success of Agile.

Agile leadership checkbook (Agile Cxo, 2017) and Agile leadership tool kit (Roning, 2019) are suggested as the supporting aids by the respective authors to systematically and quantitatively manage the roles of Agile leadership. The author of this chapter sees them as important surrounding considerations for the successful agile culture transformation in an organisation and leverages on these studies.

Leading and enabling are the responsibilities of the leadership; learning and implementing are the vital requirements of the teams. Together they create success stories. Gren et al. (2017) present their research on Group development and group maturity of Agile teams through their study of psychological aspects of Agile teams. Both qualitative measurements using semi structured interviews and quantitative measurement have been researched. This study mainly deals with teams post their formation. While it has its merits, it is felt that a proactive approach before team formation would be more valuable. While bringing out the importance of Retrospectives to improve the productivity and efficiency of Scrum teams, Kortum, Klunder and Schneider (2019) highlight that issues related to Social driven team behaviour, communication, mood and satisfaction of the team members contribute to low performance. The recommendation here is to go for automated feedback to positively impact the performance. Extensive analysis has been done on the impact of feedback on the psychological aspects of the team.

Aghina et. al. (2018, Dec) deal with the important aspects of identifying, selecting and developing individuals for successful Agile teams. This study extensively deals with the traits and behaviour of agile teams. In the order of importance, handling ambiguity, agreeableness, extroversion, conscientiousness, openness, neuroticism are presented as the traits required. Pride in the product / work, openness to change, customer centrism, self-transcendence, self enhancement and conservation are listed as the preferred behaviour. In another McKinsey report (Aghina, 2018, Jan) suggests Strategy, Structure, Process, People and Technology as the Five Trademarks of a successful Agile organisation. Cross functional teams, self-managed teams, flow-to-the-work pools of staff are indicated as the key ingredient of a high trust environment. This chapter builds over these concepts in its Discovery.

At the operating level, communication is a key driver in the Agile project's success (Vilmate, 2019). Poorly organised communication, lack of documentation, lack of commitment, the ever changing environment are seen to contribute to the challenges of agile engagements. 'Make haste slowly' is a strong recommendation in this study.

Parker et. al. (2015) identifies the need for the senior management to let go their control over the teams. This study also suggests the self-organised teams' limited understanding of the benefits and its detrimental effects bring down the organisational productivity.

The foregoing narration amply brings out the importance of the roles played by Leadership as well as the teams in successful Agile organisations. It can be noted that most of the research works cited deal with the behavioural, role and personal attributes of the two entities viz. leaders and the team. It is further noted that some of the observations mentioned in the references like the preference of one leadership style over the other based on the limitations observed at the time of the research, have successfully been overcome over a period of time.

Therefore, the attempt in this chapter is to touch upon those behavioural aspects which have found newer solutions in recent times and more importantly, supplement the findings in these citations with the structural and organisational dynamics dimensions of the organisation. These are seen to be critical as well as supplemental to the personal and behavioural aspects of successful Agile organisations.

APPROACH

A few organisations, almost all of them in the Information and Communication Technology sector, around the world are early adopters of the Agile framework and have learnt and grown with the maturity of the Agile mode of working and Scrum teams. These organisations have experimented, adapted and defined many aspects of Agile working that were seen beneficial in the organisation's context as well as at the Industry level. They have been translated into Standard Operating Procedures of the organisation, white papers in formal and informal communications and shared through professional forums. The theoretical approaches followed, primarily by the Academia through literature study, are through interviews, qualitative and quantitative analysis of the information gathered. They form the hypothesis in most of the instances for further study or experimentation. In the industry, the practical experience of implementation, the successes and failures on the ground helps to substantiate and take views of the various aspects of Agile working and the characteristics of an Agile organisation. During the course of such experimentation in the industry, certain not-so-strongly perceived as Agile related factors are also employed and many of them are seen to be beneficial. Hence, this chapter adopts an Autoethnography approach to study the leadership and team dynamics considerations.

The treatment of the subject topic in this chapter, therefore, includes some references to the behavioural and attitudinal aspects of Leadership and team while most of the discussions are around the Structure and organisational dynamics stand points.

DISCOVERY

The probability of success of Agile projects significantly improves in a unified Agile environment. Organisation wide unified environment translates into Organisational culture. It is, therefore, beneficial that an organisation that intends to follow Agile methods for a significant number of its project engagements, establishes an Agile culture in the organisation to improve on the sustained success of Agile engagements.

The primary factors that determine the culture of an organisation is the attitude and behaviour of its people. From the Roles and Responsibilities stand point, the people in the organisation can be broadly classified into 'Leadership / Management Group' and the 'Team / Operative Group'. In any disciplined organisation, the leadership team and the operative teams follow one of the many styles of working which are time proven. The style of working consisting of the practices, the approaches to situations, the preparedness, the behaviour, the responsiveness and the like, determines the organisational culture. An Agile organisational culture varies, significantly to moderately, from the many conventional cultures that are time tested for their efficacy for traditional businesses.

Leadership Traits for Agile Culture in an Organisation

Leadership adopts multiple styles of functioning depending on the nature of business, the profile of the employees, the geographical region of operations, the customer expectations & needs and their own experiences and beliefs. Bill Joiner and Stephen Josephs (2007) indicate Five levels of Leadership Agility and Four leadership Agility competencies. Their study reveals that only about 10% of the managers reach the required level of Leadership agility. Denning (2019) mentions about Five biggest challenges facing Agile and remarks that getting top management buy-in and professionalising Agile as two of them which directly relates to the leadership consideration. This section would discuss and recommend some of the recent practices and critical considerations to address them.

Considering that the key requirement of an Agile organisation is SPEED, the leadership needs to have speed in decision making, speed in implementing decisions, speed in finding solutions to issues and speed in proactively identifying and nullifying potential problems and managing the execution and delivery needs on the go but with utmost quality and uncompromised actions. The best suited style of management functioning is situational leadership.

Situational Leadership is about Adoptability. Leaders do not practice just one style; they use multiple leadership styles as the situation demands. Daniel Goleman (Goleman, 1995) defines six types of situational leadership traits, from Coaching Leaders to Coercive Leaders, all of which may be required in different instances in managing the work force to be agile. Blanchard and Hersey model the situational leadership around Task Behaviour and Relationship Behaviour as Telling leadership, Selling leadership, Participating leadership and Delegating leadership (Kenton, 2020). How do the various situational leadership traits manifest in the actual activities of the management teams?

This section focuses on the few considerations that are very relevant for the Agile culture.

Executive Presence

The Leadership needs to be physically and virtually present at every critical instance in a project engagement. Early involvement in the planning process and communication process makes a significant difference to the smooth execution and successful completion of the objectives of the projects. When this is extended to all the aspects of running an organisation, the leadership needs to possess agility in its working itself.

Leadership agility can be best achieved by organising the management team itself as a Scrum team. Organisational goals are the product backlog for this team. Sprints of objectives broken down 'minimum viable accomplishment' would help to steer the operations of the organisation to be agile. Daily scrums would help in the decision making. Standish Group report indicates that 'Decision Latency' costs the projects in a big way impacting its success (Johnson & Mulder, 2017). Empirically, the report says, the decision-making time reduction by 80% results in the success rate improvement of the project by nearly four times.

Self Organising Teams

It is the responsibility of the Management team to form Self Organising teams in the organisation for the successful execution of the customer and internal projects. It is a carefully crafted and designed initiative and does not happen by accident. The Leadership team needs to budget, invest and provide for time, energy and financial support to build such teams over a period of time. The earliest it is done in the effort to make the organisation Agile-ready, the better.

It helps to know that there are basically three modes of failure in raising the teams. Firstly, the team not being efficient for the objective of the work for which it is assembled. The requirement for a competent team for the purpose must be clearly understood, translated into action by the proper identification of candidates, communicating the expectations and handholding the team for an initial period of time.

Secondly, while the expectation of the team to be Agile, the management should not be working on a Waterfall model. This has two significant impacts. One, the interactions between the leadership and teams will not be synchronised leading to failure of the purpose. More importantly, the confidence of the team in the leadership is likely to be eroded leading to the failure of the team.

Thirdly, not screening and selecting appropriate practices will lead to the failure of the team. It is a critical supporting and over-arching consideration. The select practices supplement the team competency in making the team efficiency optimal.

Business Process Integration

Cross functional teams accomplish Agility in the organisation and is the key consideration in Scrum. For the seamless working of the cross functional teams to achieve the business goals, it is essential that there is synergy between the teams so that the outcome is maximised towards the objectives of the project.

While a number of tools and systems are available to integrate the business processes of an organisation, the right outcome is achieved by the careful sequencing of flow of the integration. Management team plays a critical role in this process.

While, at a broad level, the business processes of an organisation are standard such as Financial management, Workforce management, Customer engagement and relationship management, Resource management, Marketing and Sales etc., every organisation has its own method and way of working of these functions. Typically, there is history and reasons for following a business process as it is practiced. This is best understood by the management team.

Thus, the leadership team should assist in migrating the various business processes of the organisation into a unified system. What is critical for the working of the function, what are the desirable processes, what needs to be retained and what can change are attributes that are best decided by the management team.

The next step is to critically look at the processes for their adequacy and applicability for the purpose viz. to build organisational agility. Keeping the imperatives as above in mind, the leadership team needs to determine the aids and blocks in the various business processes for their integration towards achieving the needed base for an Agile organisation. These must be clearly articulated and communicated to the people who are responsible for the integration.

Subsequently, the business processes may have to be re-engineered to bridge the gaps identified. While the process constructors will do the job, the management team has the responsibility of oversight and regular reviews to ensure that the intended changes are brought in.

Implementation of the integrated business process is one of the toughest jobs. There is likely to be a natural resistance to any change in every organisation and it is the role of the leadership team in communicating, assisting in understanding, facilitating the implementation of the integrated processes, either in phases or wholesale, depending on the size and nature of business. Once the team accepts and practices the new integrated business process, the cross functional teams can be formed and a new way of working, if applicable, can be rolled out. In this phase, the leadership team needs to carefully watch for the defects and inefficiencies in the process by carefully collecting the data and indications. In a periodical manner, these defects have to be corrected and the processes improved to yield the best results.

Once the integrated business processes are seen to be working towards the objectives of an Agile organisations, the Standard Operating Procedures and the management systems need to be updated and the systems created for sustained working.

Customer Engagement

No Agile engagement is successful without the involvement of the client, internal or external. The customer engagement happens at two levels, one at the executive management level and secondly, at the operating management level.

The connection at the executive management level helps to understand the broad picture of the purpose of the project. Supplementing the stated specifications of the product or service being developed for the client, the unstated and implied needs need to be taken care of at the upstream phases of the customer engagement. The experience and the capabilities of the leadership team helps in realising them. They may translate into augmented specifications and specific processes of development.

While the Agile Manifesto does not promote zero documentation, minimised effort and need for optimal and not elaborate documentation is a winner. The clear understanding of the larger picture by every member of the cross functional team can accomplish this.

At the operational level, the customer engagement greatly assists in taking timely decisions, critical reviews to ensure that the development is in line with the intended outcome and quicker issue resolution. Basically, the customer team can be part of the sprint activities to the extent needed. Moreover, the sprint backlog decision will be significantly helped by the plan of the customer in the phased release of the product or service.

Change Management

Change Management is one of the difficult activities but a critical need for continued success of an Agile organisational culture. While all the members of the organisation need to embrace the change as required, often there is a need for executive intervention in deciding on the change and in what form the change needs to be adopted and implemented.

Change Management process starts with a Change Management strategy. There are multiple options of models available for Change Management strategy like McKinsey's 7 S Model, Lewin's model, the ADKAR model etc. The leadership team needs to consider and choose one of the models that would work best for them.

Emotional Intelligence

While the business world focused on Intelligence Quotient for a long time in their leadership members, the recent developments have brought to focus and in front, the importance of Emotional Quotient in them. This is equally applicable in organisations running on conventional mode of working but most importantly for setting up an Agile culture.

The teams comprised of people with different backgrounds, experiences, states of mind and work cultures. When they are assembled to work on Agile environment, the probability is high that it disrupts some of the members significantly. Leaders should be able to identify the emotional needs of the members such as fear, loss of confidence, apathy, confusion and the like and be prepared for it. Support systems if required must be put in place including professional help. The management team should be prepared to spend adequate time to manage the emotional needs of the team members so that, over a short period of time, all the members of all teams are in a minimal level of comfortable state of mind to work towards the objectives of the project and the initiatives.

The leadership team needs to demonstrate that they are leading from within. That means that there is a perceived belief in the changes and the way of working that are promoted by them. This brings the necessary confidence to the team members for them to adopt the new culture.

Supply Chain

Supply Chain management is a critical business process in any organisation. It gains importance all the more in an organisation with Agile culture. The success or failures of the Sprint cycles are dependent on the availability of all types of resources, man power, material and systems at the appropriate time without fail. This calls for a highly efficient and highly dependable supply chain system.

Setting up an efficient and reliable supply chain system is an art by itself. Agile projects certainly need Just-In-Time input. This is one of the pre-requisites in setting an organisation for Agile culture. Supply chain partners need to be evaluated for their efficiencies and capabilities, their financial stability, their levels of commitments, track record and management before signing them up. Enough but not excess redundancy needs to be built in the system in order to manage exigencies.

Technology Assimilation

The leadership team needs to equip the organisation with a dedicated team of Technology enablers to ensure agility in its operations. Considering that most of the customers who are hard pressed to develop products and services in the Agile way are likely to be operating in the cutting edge technologies where incremental product development which can test the market and provide the much needed revenue with every increment, the organisation which services the customer also needs to be technically abreast.

There are two areas where Technology assimilations are critically required in an Agile organisation. Firstly, it is in the products and services delivered to the customers. If the organisation has to raise up to the expectations of the clients in quickly turning around the requirements, not much time can be spent by the organisation in the introduction of the technology into the team. They may have to be proactive.

Secondly, the support systems that aid the development of the products and services for the customer must also be constantly evaluated and upgraded. The teams need to work at the maximum possible efficiency and the latest tools and techniques need to be inducted into the organisation. This technology assimilation is also an important need that would justify the dedicated team of technology introducers in the company. Management team needs to give special attention in this area.

Governance and Accountability

Running an organisation and running a project are significantly different. Compliance to local and federal regulations, company laws, Human Resource practices, facility management and such aspects are important to the running of an organisation. Stakeholders' management is another critical aspect of Governance of an organisation. While an Agile organisation cuts down the lengthy procedures, care must be taken that no compliance and regulatory requirements are breached at any point for any reason. It is a challenge and it also brings out the calibre of the management team to take care of this.

Similarly, the accountability matrix of every aspect of the governance and operations must be clearly thought through, responsibilities assigned and well communicated. There should never be an instance where for any exception or compliance, an assigned individual is not available to take the decision.

Both in large corporations and in small enterprises, this is one of the negative factors that bring down the efficiency of the operation and thereby the outcome. For many issues, the management team scouts around to find the right person to respond when an issue surfaces and, in the process, valuable time is lost in resolving the issue.

Agility does not mean no documentation; it is about appropriate documentation for the purpose and the clear understanding of the aspects of policies and operations which are not explicitly stated. The leadership team needs to possess the required information about the team members so that the optimisation of the documentation can be carefully and rightfully planned and made. It is highly recommended that the Accountability matrix is made and published so that everyone knows where the bug stops when it comes out.

Continuous Improvement Culture

An Agile organisation is set on a path of continuous improvement. The learning never stops in an organisation that embraces Agility in its entire working. It is highly desirable to have Continuous Improvement facilitators, also known as Black Belts, who could identify the problems and improvement areas, design CI projects, facilitate the stakeholders' involvement, apply the methodology options and produce the desired improvement.

Organisational performance is determined by the Metrics of the Operations and the customer perception is determined by formal feedback from the customers. Collectively these two inputs help the organisation to determine the improvement areas and the quantum of improvement. Targets need to be set and improvement projects undertaken to achieve them.

Peter Drucker famously said, what cannot be measured cannot be managed. It is the responsibility of the management team to state the imperatives of running the organisation. Qualified and trained professionals of Business Excellence translate them into measurable parameters and set the goals in consultation with the management team. These goals are communicated to the appropriate teams for them to plan their strategy and activities to achieve them.

The Metrics plan of an organisation typically consists of the Business Level metrics and Operation level metrics. Both are equally important and the performance of the organisation needs to be periodically and consistently measured. An agile leadership would review the performance at close intervals to take actions to correct any course deviations. As mentioned earlier, decision latency significantly deteriorates the success of the agile working.

Innovation and Experimentation

The culture of innovation and experimentation needs to be inculcated in the organisation if it needs to pursue a path of Agility. The foregoing sections describe in detail the characteristics that the organisation and leadership team need to possess if Agile way of working is to be introduced and sustained.

Aspects like Technology assimilation and Business process integration may have no precedence when one is in the cutting edge of technology or business. What makes the attempts successful is the culture of innovation and experimentation. The foresight and the planning process of the leadership team prepares the execution teams adequately with the outcome of their exploration so that when the customer engagement execution happens the teams are adequately prepared, know the pitfalls and success factors and ensure that the sprints of short durations are highly productive and successful. There may not be enough time and provision to fail and find alternates.

The culture of Innovation and experimentation helps to fail fast. What it means is that there is adequate time to isolate the failure modes and carefully address them in the execution process.

The leadership team plays a significant role in planning, designing and operationalising this enabling process.

Team Dynamics for Agile Culture in an Organisation

Having considered the necessary ingredients for the Leadership traits in an Agile organisation, it must be understood that the team characteristics are also equally, if not more, important for the organisation to be Agile-ready. The realisation of the Scrum framework is largely with the team members in an organisation. Some product and service developments are naturally amenable to Scrum framework but some may need proper articulation to get the best benefit out of the agile mode of development. The team dynamics need to support such an operation.

Besides the skills and the competency factors that are required for forming scrum teams in the organisation for effectively and successfully carrying out the projects, there are a few considerations that demand higher attention than in a conventional mode of working. We will look at a few such characteristics in this section.

Psychological Safety

Any change brings with it a substantial amount of anxiety, fear and resistance. While the leadership team does its best to address this situation as described in an earlier section, it is essential that the team members are also prepared for the same. The probability of success of Agile engagements come down drastically when the teams work in an apprehensive mode. The teams are liable to make mistakes, lack the required attention and be disengaged with the work. This is a highly dysfunctional state of affairs.

To receive the support the leadership team would extend in this regard, the team must be prepared to get the best benefit out of it. Senior members of the team or the team lead should identify the emotional requirement of the various team members and spend time with them to bring them up to a threshold level of preparedness so that the emotional support extended by the leadership team provides the necessary confidence in all the team members. At the end of the day, the members of the team feel and be confident that they can adapt to the changes, perform to the new expectations and be successful in the new normal. This is a critical non-technical base on which successful scrum teams would perform.

Meaning and Impact

Resulting out of psychological safety, the team members start feeling that the work is personally important to them. This frame of mind brings the best out of them which is essential for the success of sprint execution. The team members develop the belief that their work matters and gladly be part of the change process. Once the new agile culture sets in, they are comfortable working in the new environment and voluntarily create the changed culture that is required.

Fractal Organisation

Fractal is a structure, as some people define as "Form of sustainable ordered chaos". Contrary to a hierarchical organisation structure where command and control works, fractal organisation thrives on expanding from within. At any magnification of its parts, the same pattern is exhibited. The fundamental principle of fractal organisation is that "the whole is more than the sum of the parts".

Fractal organisations display some unique characteristics. Firstly, the members interact with each other in a random manner. Interaction patterns emerge from this behaviour to accomplish the goals.

Second, there are greater variety in the organisations. The higher level of ambiguities and contradictions are not seen as dysfunctional but as innovative ways to create new possibilities.

Third characteristics is that the members are in their own environment and also part of a larger system. When the member characteristic changes, the environment also changes. So, the evolution is concurrent.

Fourthly, in fractal organisation, the members share the information freely and iteratively so that decision making is collective and efficient. The responses to the changes are most effective.

All the members of the fractal organisation have the Shared Purpose. Integrity, Continuous improvement, efficacy of decision making is most optimal in such scenarios. The leadership enables the energy of the organisation to be directed outwards rather than inward looking.

Finally, fractal organisations believe they need not be perfect. Sub optimal performance is acceptable as long as it is better than the above average in the marketplace. Time and energy are not spent on making the performance perfect but to make the performance as required for a satisfied customer delivery.

Organisational Mitosis

As the organisation grows, it is inevitable that new teams are formed to address the business requirement. As teams split and form new teams, they exhibit the same characteristics of the original teams. As in cell biology these characteristics of team formation is known as Mitosis. The team formation carefully considers this aspect as the recipe for sustained success in the Agile environment. The leadership plays a vital role in ensuring that the tested and successful team dynamics are retained and replicated in the new teams as well.

Visible Culture of Excellence

The unified view of the team is one of excellence is what they do. The culture of excellence can be described as excellence in people, excellence in technology and excellence in process.

People's excellence come from individual and team behaviour. All the members of the team should have the shared outlook, should own their work and be accountable for the same without having to be monitored and followed up (self-organising team) and possess a high degree of emotional intelligence. They respect each other, show respect to fellow members and support in the growth of every team member. This is critical to avoid wasted time of team and leadership and efforts in resolving inter-personnel issues.

Engineering excellence or excellence in technology is critical for the success of work. The above characteristics of the team also help build the learning and experimentation culture, coaching and assisting, understanding the business and technology needs of the customers.

Process excellence results in a predictable and consistent outcome from the organisation. It also helps in baselining the performance of the organisation for evaluating the adequacy of the teams for the need of the business and customers' expectations and to design and deploy system level improvements.

These three dimensions of excellence culture ensures that the Scrum mode of working of the organisation is highly efficient and productive.

Intrepid Teams

Successful agile teams have members who are fearless and challenging each other. They do not filter communication and at the same time more purpose and result oriented and not abrasive. This also means the members accept that they lack knowledge in any specific instance and do not hesitate to seek help and cooperation to overcome the deficiency.

Involvement and Engagement

The team members of successful scrum teams display a very high degree of engagement and involvement in their work. Focus towards making every attempt successful is visibly present. Daily stand up meetings are seen to be most beneficial besides adopting Scrum and Extreme programming. It has been seen that teams where members are truly engaged following various aspects of Agile manifesto are highly successful as compared to teams where members are 'present' in the team.

Receptive to Feedback

Feedback mechanism is a critical requirement of a successful scrum team. While at leadership level, feedback from the customers, as described elsewhere in this chapter, provides the necessary input to fine tune the performance of the organisation, feedback on the performance of the individuals and the team from both internal and external sources are equally important to make the teams highly result oriented.

Individual and team feedback can be both formal and informal. Formal feedback is received from customers during progress review meetings, engagement feedback surveys and escalations. Internal formal feedback is given during periodical reviews of the projects, performance appraisal of the team members and business reviews. Informal feedback is also equally important to get the not-so-critical-but-equally-important views of the clients and management of the organisation. Ignoring them over a long period of time will result in precipitation of issues and loss of goodwill. The team should have a mechanism to capture the informal feedback also in addition to the formal ones and process to consider, analyse and act on them. The Business Excellence group's support is preferably taken towards this need and analysis of the feedback done to generate actionable.

Empowerment and Collaboration

This is one of the significant enablers for the success of Scrum teams. Empowerment in the Agile world is the ability of the teams to take timely decisions, calculate risks and determine the progress of the work without the deeper involvement of the leadership. There are a few critical roles in the team such as Product Owner and Scrum Master who play roles that support this empowerment. The team members mostly work without any hierarchy or titles. For the team empowerment to be effective, the combined skill levels of the team, both technical as well as soft skills need to be adequate. Thus, it becomes one of the critical responsibilities of the management team in selecting the most appropriate members of the various teams.

Collaborative working goes hand in hand with empowerment. As discussed elsewhere, most Agile teams are cross functional. Every function has a role to play in a team and members representing the various functions should have the broad purpose of the project and their part in it. Thus, whenever there is a need, which is often the case, every team member is aware of his / her preparedness, contribution and hand over requirement to demonstrate the collaborative working. Collaborative working ensures the speed and avoidance of wastages which are critical for the Agile team success.

Generalist Specialists

Given that it is preferable to have small Scrum teams for effective working, it may be essential that we may have a few "Generalist Specialists" in the teams. These people are multi skilled and experienced. While they have their specific assigned responsibilities in one or two areas, for example, Project Manager and Architect, they may also have skills and experience in one or two other areas of the team like, say, Test Design and Process owner. Such a team becomes a "whole" team and essentially self-reliant.

Meta Scrum

Large Agile teams, say of sizes 20 or more people, would require additional features than the typical Scrum teams. There are specific reasons for forming large teams and may evolve from a normal team of 3 – 5 people or may be explicitly formed for the purpose.

Such large teams are generally formed with a few sub teams, each of them focusing one or few of the aspects of the team objectives. The sub teams work under the Scrum framework and have their own stand up meetings. Additionally, a representative from each of the sub teams participate in the stand-up meeting of the larger Agile team. This is called Scrum of Scrums or Meta Scrum. Such teams may have a Product Owners team instead of a Product owner.

Distributed Agile Team

The earlier principles of Agile were based on Co-located teams whose benefits are well known. However, increasingly the business imperatives have necessitated the projects to be developed over geographically distributed teams, either people of the same organisation located in different places or due to the outsourced partnerships. Distributed Agile team was an oxymoron to begin with but slowly became the order of the day. The team dynamics, also known as the team interactions, were subjected to a high degree of stress and inefficiencies in the early distributed agile teams. This had to be overcome in due course the make distributed agile teams work.

Collaborative tools played a big role in realising this provision. Phone and email communications were the primitive tools that helped but as the projects became complex, they are grossly inadequate for the purpose. The emergence of internet based and cloud-based tools served the purpose to a good extent. However, it must be appreciated that the tools are implementations of the basic tenets of Distributed Agile working which are interesting to consider. Listed below are some of the strategies applied in the context of distributed Agile teams.

'One team' mindset is a concept to be developed as soon as the team is formed in multiple locations. Ideally an Agile Coach facilitates this by bringing the mindshare and attention of the team members across locations to the common purpose of the project and working arrangements. Tools and techniques are introduced to make this happen and slowly the geographically distributed teams synchronise with each other.

Coach travels is a strategy for sustaining the initial development of One Team mindset. During the initial days of the project and if needed, for a longer time, the Coach visits various locations the team is dispersed and ensures that they are able to efficiently work together as if they are co-located. The coach also solves any problems the team may have, thus removing the impediments to the progress of the work.

Team ambassadors are representatives in each location that ensure that the objectives and arrangements of Distributed Agile working are accomplished seamlessly by taking additional responsibilities for facilitation.

Personal touch is a psychological safety factor that is very difficult to achieve in distributed teams. However, techniques such as Virtual coffee rooms using collaborative tools, casual discussion groups and one-on-one feedback are used to realise the personal touch factor to a reasonable extent.

Creating a rhythm is another useful strategy in distributed working. The need for constant synch up is avoided and the delays due to dependencies are significantly reduced if not fully eliminated. However, this strategy also has the disadvantage of making the late customer's requirement change quickly adopted in the work which is easily accomplished with co-located teams.

However, there are some challenges the distributed mode of working, especially in the Agile environment, face that may have to be addressed on a case to case basis. Some of these challenges are communication limitations due to significant time zone difference, Requirements misunderstanding, Trust and collaboration and cultural differences.

Measurements to Manage

Just as any other mode of project execution, Agile development and Scrum methods also need appropriate measurement to objectively evaluate the performance against the plan and to determine the status of the project. There are a dozen or more recommended measurements for Agile projects. Some metrics are helpful in understanding the status but a few can be very gainfully used to run the projects very effectively. While the measurements and metrics analysis are the job of the leaders of the project, it is essential that every member of the team clearly understand the purpose of the metrics and use them to their best benefit. This is one of the core modes of working of Self Organising teams which is fundamental to the Scrum framework. Let us consider the typical Metrics plan for Agile programs.

Burndown charts are a display of utilisation of time and effort of the team in completing the work. These charts have the planned scheme of expending the time and team effort and the actual performance is plotted against the plan. As long as the performance is within 10% deviation from the plan at any point in time, the work can continue the way it is progressing. If the deviations are more than 10%, it becomes essential for the team lead / scrum master to analyse the cause for the deviation and determine if any course correction or point action needs to be taken.

The deviations can happen in one-off instances or it may occur more often. In the former case, generally, there will be a special cause for the deviation and the project lead may have to correct it if it is systemic so that such a special cause problem does not occur again. However, if the deviations are seen to be constantly happening, it can be taken that there are some common cause problems in the process or working. They certainly have to be found out, corrections worked out, tried out, fine-tuned and made a part of the operating procedure. This is an essential step which not only involves the lead but also all the team members of the scrum team. As a preparatory work to taking up an Agile engagement, sufficient awareness and knowledge on these aspects will have to be imparted to the team by the coach.

Velocity measurements, control chart and cumulative flow chart serve a similar purpose. Velocity measurement also helps in sizing the team mid-course as well as tune the competency map of the team. A lot of diligence is needed in the leadership team as well as project leads in augmenting the team and/or changing the competency profile. It may be worth remembering the Brook's Law that states that, "Adding more people to a late Agile project, make the project later". Basically, this law conveys that merely adding more resources to a team to speed up a project which is slipping in its schedule compliance is dysfunctional and may result in further slipping of the schedules.

Lead time is another important measure from the perspective of estimation and planning. This is defined as the time duration between the receipt of request of a service to the actual delivery of the service.

Some agile organisations use Value Delivered charts as a key customer facing measurement. While Burndown charts and Flowcharts are more of quantum measures, Value Delivery chart is more of an assessment measure. A program may have a number of deliverables aligned to the various sprints and each sprint a certain number of backlogs would be serviced. Every feature or service designed, implemented and delivered has a commercial and non-commercial value to the client and they are not the same for all the features. There are priorities and dependencies in deciding the product and sprint backlogs and the decision on them are collectively taken along with the client. Thus, every sprint delivers a certain value to the client and tracking the same helps both the organisation and the client in evaluating the Return on Investment (RoI) in the project.

Another important measure is the blocked time. This is the measure of time that went unutilised in carrying out the assigned tasks by the team. It could have a linkage to the deviations in the Burndown charts and is supplemental to the effort overrun reasons. Once again, the project lead and management team need to analyse this measure to determine the actions that need to be taken to progress on schedule, effort and cost plans. Thus, the measure helps in course corrections in terms of team composition, team competency, customer management, Requirement gathering and analysis, infrastructure adequacy and non-human resource planning and availability.

It is also essential to have a certain amount of quality metrics in the metrics plan of the agile engagements. Measures related to Defects, time to fix, Field defects reported by the customers, CSAT are some of the useful measurements.

One of the recent measures introduced in the Software domain is Quality Intelligence. Quality Intelligence helps in determining the quality of software in the recently added code before it is tested. Thus, it helps in determining the quantum of testing required thereby ensuring that the software delivered to the client is of consistently high quality.

Therefore, the Metrics program not only helps in the outcome of the team but also in managing the dynamics of the team both by the self-organising team and the leadership team.

Need to Have Documentation

There is a misconception that Agile programs do not require any documentation. The Agile manifesto also suggests working software (read product) over documentation. However, in practice and the experience of successful and high-performance Scrum teams show that it is highly recommended to have "Need to Have Documentation".

Where and how does documentation in Agile working help? The simple thumb rule is wherever there is an opportunity for misunderstanding of communication, possibility of multiple interpretation, when the right people are not available for explanation, when new members are added to the team who do not get the opportunity to experience the full details of the project from the start and may need to pitch in and be effective as the members who are present in the team from the beginning. Therefore, there is a strong case for sufficient documentation in any Agile project that would meet the above needs.

In such a scenario, what are typically the documents that may be useful? Here are some of them: Requirement Specifications and their interpretations, Oral agreements with the client, Product description and the context of its usage, High Level designs, Reasons for the choice of the design option, Dependencies, Risks and risk management, Design FMEA (Failure Mode and Effect Analysis), Test Strategy and in large teams, the rationale behind the formation of sub teams.

Since this is not a full set of documentation as recommended in conventional projects, the best outcome has to be achieved in an optimised set. It is essential to identify a person in the Scrum team(s) who would have the necessary bandwidth, capability and experience to make such documents. He/she may be assisted by the Product owner and the Scrum Master to ensure that no critical point is missed out.

Since the preparation of 'Need to have documentation' is not a trivial activity, most Agile teams end up either making full documentation as in a conventional project or no documentation at all. Both are dysfunctional to the success of the project.

Failure Modes of Agile Teams and Leadership

The preceding sections detail various aspects of Agile culture, behaviour and practices that management teams and operations teams need to have for a successful and sustained capability to execute Agile programs. It may be relevant to look at some of the considerations that the industry has experienced for Agile to be a failure. By corollary, it may appear that, not doing what have been described in the earlier sections may lead to failure; however, it may be worth considering explicitly certain behaviours and deficiencies in the team and at leadership that lead to the failures.

Broadly, these issues can be categories under System Failures, People Failures and Technical failures. In this section, let us look at People related failure factors along with a few Systemic failure modes.

As has been emphasised elsewhere in this chapter, the commitment of the leadership is the most important factor for an organisation to embrace Agile culture. Studies have shown that the failures have occurred due to the leadership not changing themselves to the new need of Agile working. The change has to begin at the top. An aggressive form of this behaviour is that some of the leaders consider themselves above all of these. They are insulated from the changes required to drive the Agile culture in the organisation. These are sure recipes for failure.

A major cause of failure in new age organisations is the refusal to accept failure by the management. While every effort must be taken and planning done to make the Agile transformation successful, leadership should be tolerant to and be prepared for failure due to factors beyond control or expectation. Many organisations create an environment of fear of failure and that is completely unsuitable for Agile change. The ability of management to think through the failure modes, take care of them in design and planning and counter measures to recover and be on track in case of a precipitation of a risk, is the critical requirement.

The considerations discussed so far are related to the mindset, behaviour and the prerequisites for transforming an organisation to be Agile-ready. There are a few aspects that can fail the organisation during the implementation of the change also.

Every organisation is unique and every transformation, therefore, is unique. While lessons and principles can be learnt from other's experience, it must be realised that designing and implementing the Agile transformation with adequate experimentation is critically needed to ensure a higher degree of success probability. So, adopting someone else's strategy and approach does not work.

Secondly, it must be realised that, to adopt the Agile environment, the organisation must change and the practices should not be tweaked to suit the present way of working of the organisation. This is one of the biggest challenges for the leadership team. Depending on the size, tenure and culture of the organisation, varying degrees of change management activities are required. Some leaders try to circumvent the change with other alternate means which do not work.

Some failed organisations have tried to map the Agile practices to the current practices followed by the organisation for the fear of backlash that an organisational change would bring. This is a certain step for failure. The Agile transformation leader should have the empowerment and be bold enough to make the change the organisation requires without fear.

The organisation changes for Agile adoption will certainly need to look at rethinking on some of the roles of the organisation. Without sacrificing the incumbent members in these roles, the leaders must plan the reskill, redeployment and repositioning of them to contribute to the new organisation aligned to the Agile culture. People who do not wish to change or unable to cope up with the change may have to be eased out.

The change will also bring the necessity to reengineer the performance measurements and metrics plan of the organisation for various functions. The leadership must be able to facilitate this change too.

Experiences show that "Doing Agile" is different from "Being Agile". If the Agile way of working is not entrenched and made a way of working, intentional and unintentional slips are bound to happen while 'doing Agile'. Being Agile is a part of the enculturation of the organisation and the team members have equal responsibilities as the leadership in making this happen.

Thus, the leadership team can make or break the Agile transformation of an organisation.

CONCLUSION

As covered in the Introductory section, the objective of this chapter is to supplement the behavioural and psychological aspects of Leadership and Self-Managed Scrum teams which are adequately researched and well documented, with Structural and Organisational dynamics aspects which are more found in the knowledge base of practising industries. As the Agile mode of working matures, the industry faces a new and fresh set of challenges and solutions are to be found for them on a continuous basis. Often, the solutions are available in the principles and practices of related industries and management principles and by suitably adopting them to the Agile working mode, the challenges can be overcome. Some of the proven behavioural aspects of the team and leadership also require reimagining with the advancement in their respective areas. This chapter has accomplished these purposes, at this point of time and maturity of Agile organisations.

Agility in the organisation is a constant journey; the benefits reaped so far may plateau out or may no longer be available. It becomes the responsibility of researchers and practitioners to constantly look for solutions for unaddressed issues as they arise.

ACKNOWLEDGMENT

The author of this chapter wishes to acknowledge the decade and a half experience of understanding, experimenting, internalising traditional and new age agile modes of working in all its aspects in the organisations he has served as well as in the professional communities that he is part of. These experiences and interactions helped to evaluate, validate and propose the solutions to making an organisation Agile-ready and that formed the basis for the contents of this chapter.

REFERENCES

Aghina, W., Ahlback, K., De Smet, A., Lackey, G., Lurie, M., Muraka, M., & Handscomb, C. (2018, Jan). *The Five trademarks of Agile Organisations*. https://www.mckinsey.com/business-functions/organization/our-insights/the-five-trademarks-of-agile-organizations

Aghina, W., Handscomb, C., Ludolph, J., West, D., & Yip, A. (2018, Dec 20). *How to select and develop individuals for successful Agile teams: A practical guide*. https://mckinsey.com/business-functions/organization/our-insights/how-to-select-and-develop-individuals-for-successful-agile-teams-a-practical-guide

Agile Alliance. (2001). *Manifesto for Agile Software Development. Section: Principles*. www.agile-manifesto.org

Agile CxO. (2017). *The Agile leadership Check book: Leading in a Self-Organising world*. https://agilecxo.org/wp-content/uploads/2017/09/agilecxocheckbookv7.pdf

De Smet, A., Lurie, M., & St George, A. (2018). *Leading Agile Transformation: The new capabilities leaders need to build 21st Century Organisations*. McKinsey & Company.

Denning, S. (2019). *The five biggest challenges facing Agile*. www.forbes.com

Druskat, V., & Wheeler, J. (2001). Managing from the boundary: The effective leadership of self-managing work teams. *Academy of Management Annual Meeting Proceedings*. 10.5465/apbpp.2001.6133637

Goleman, D. (1995). *Emotional Intelligence: Why it can matter more than IQ*. Bantom Books.

Gren, L., Torkar, R., & Feldt, R. (2017). Group development and Group Maturity when building Agile teams: A qualitative and quantitative investigation at Eight large companies. *Journal of Systems and Software, 124*(Feb), 104–119. doi:10.1016/j.jss.2016.11.024

Johnson, J., & Mulder, H. (2017). *Big, Bang, Boom Revisited: Why large projects fail, A case study research of NPAC*. www.standishgroup.com/sample-research-files/BBB2017-Final-2.pdf

Joiner, B., & Josephs, S. (2007). *Developing Agile leaders.* www.researchgate.net/publication/242157752

Kaczor, K. (2019). *Agile leadership in and beyond the Scrum team(s).* Scrum.org white paper.

Kenton, W. (2020). *Hersey – Blanchard Model.* www.investopedia.com

Kortum, F., Klunder, J., & Schneider, K. (2019). Behaviour driven dynamics in Agile Development: The effect of fast feedback on teams. *International Conference on Software and Systems Process*, Montreal, Canada.

Lean, C. X. (2019). *What is Servant Leadership in Agile Project Management?* www.leancxscore.com

Mersino, A. (2018). *Agile leaders' role during an Agile transformation.* www.vitalitychicago.com/blog/what-leaders-role-agile-transformation

Moe, N., Dingsoyr, T., & Kvangardsnes, O. (2009). Understanding Shared Leadership in Agile development: A case study. *Proceedings of 42nd Hawaii International conference on System Sciences.*

Parker, D., Holesgrove, M., & Pathak, R. (2015). Improving Productivity with self-organised teams and Agile leadership. *International Journal of Productivity and Performance Management, 64*(1), 112–128. doi:10.1108/IJPPM-10-2013-0178

Parris, D., & Peachey, D. (2013). A systematic Literature review of Servant Leadership theory in Organisational Context. *Journal of Business Ethics, 113*(3), 377–393. doi:10.100710551-012-1322-6

Pearce, C., & Sims, H. (2002). Vertical versus Shared Leadership as Predictors of the effectiveness of change management teams: An examination of Aversive, Directive, Transactional, Transformational and Empowering leader behaviours. *Group Dynamics, 6*(2), 172–197. doi:10.1037/1089-2699.6.2.172

Riggins, J. (2019). *Three challenges to the new Agile leader.* Aginext Community.

Roning, P. (2019). *Agile Leadership Took kit.* Addison – Wesley.

Srivastava, P., & Jain, S. (2017). A leadership framework for distributed self-organised scrum teams. *Team Performance Management, 23*(7).

Stray, V., Hoda, R., Passivara, M., & Krutchen, P. (2020). *What an Agile leader does: The Group dynamics perspective.* https://www.ncbi.nlm.nih.gov/pmc/articles /PMC7251611/

Vilmate. (2019). *Why communication is a driver of Agile project success?* https://vilmate.com/blog/communication-challenges-in-agile/

Chapter 3
Integrating Agile Teams Into the Organization

Van Goodwin
Van Allen Strategies, USA

James W. Logan
University of New Orleans, USA

ABSTRACT

The purpose of this chapter to is examine the issues involved in the integration of Agile teams into existing organizations that have not previously incorporated Agile teams, and suggest mechanisms that can make the integration process more efficient and effective. Issues and solutions discussed include conflicting environmental viewpoints, differing project end-point definitions, organizational reporting, budgeting and financial performance reporting challenges, and the special challenge of legacy technologies to Agile teams. Methods discussed for successful integration of Agile teams into existing organizations include leadership selection, use of cross-functional team members, appropriate performance measures, funding for the team, and effective communication within and among the organizational members.

INTRODUCTION

An Agile team is ultimately only as effective as the value it brings to the organization. This chapter discusses some of the common problems with integrating Agile teams into existing organizations, and how to increase the effectiveness of Agile teams within existing organizations. An Agile team, even if composed of technically and operationally savvy members, often will not accomplish its original goals unless all affected levels of the organization are clear on how Agile teams will be integrated into the organization. Leadership at all levels of the organization must work together to enhance the congruence of Agile team goals and broad organizational goals in order to effectively bring Scrum and Agile techniques into existing organizations. Support of the Agile team methodology must be signaled from higher leadership not only through words of support, but also through concrete actions and changes in reporting structure and budgeting practices.

DOI: 10.4018/978-1-7998-4885-1.ch003

Copyright © 2021, IGI Global. Copying or distributing in print or electronic forms without written permission of IGI Global is prohibited.

Among the most common issues that arise when introducing Scrum and Agile practices into existing organizations are:

- The iterative and short horizon nature of Agile projects can cause issues conveying current project status to the larger organization that may be built around a system that uses waterfall style linear projects with discrete end dates. Thus, the organizational environmental forces that influence an Agile team may seem very different to an Agile team leader than the overall leader of the division in which the Agile team is placed.
- The value of Agile's nimble abilities frequently conflicts with legacy technical infrastructure and processes that are incompatible with normal sprint planning, particularly in older organizations that may have legal or operational constraints on overall organizational output or changes in method.
- Because an Agile team may have changing members as requirements change, and may not have a fixed timetable or even budget to measure operational success against, often Agile team members may not be evaluated or managed in a manner similar to other organizational members. This can cause conflict and difficulty in recruiting the most effective team members if not addressed at the initial stage of implementation
- Organizations and large subdivisions of organizations tend to have an accounting and budgeting system that reflects the core goals and time horizon of the larger organization. Often, this system will not be optimal to foster effectiveness and efficiency in an Agile team structure.

This chapter will examine these issues, offer more specific guidance for organizational leadership, and discuss how Scrum and Agile team methodology may better fulfill its promise in the management of organizations. Issues and solutions discussed include conflicting environments,

CONFLICTING ENVIRONMENTS

Most Agile teams live in the context of companies that not only predate the methodology but are also in industries removed from software or system development in general. Key differences in cultures, expectations, and constraints often leads to conflict between the Agile team and the broader organization to which it ultimately provides a service. Where the Agile team is focused on continuous product enhancement, its division or company may have its focus and budgetary system built around a manufacturing process or the ROI over 5 years of new products. This difference in focus often causes, particularly in initial integration of Agile teams into existing organizations, difficulty in translating what goals are being accomplished and the total cost of a planned Agile project.

For example, an Agile team might take on a $1.5 million, six-month re-platforming effort that shows clear incremental progress across 12 sprints. In a manufacturing company, however, that initiative might be assessed by the same people and methods evaluating a $150 million, five-year capital improvement project that ends when the first tangible product rolls off an assembly line. In this scenario, the organization may have an excellent method of fostering and assessing its core business and the Agile team may produce an excellent product following the best Scrum practices. But because of differing interpretations of success, and especially the time-frame and end product of success, the Agile team will frequently find itself at a disadvantage, such as:

- A core business that necessarily functions on the traditional, waterfall-based project management backing manufacturing processes does not easily understand the iterative and cyclical nature of Agile sprints.
- The rules around accounting and finance designed for large capital projects make accurate financial reporting difficult or less meaningful for Agile projects broken up into small pieces of work with less defined end dates.
- The deeply integrated legacy systems cannot be updated at a pace (or cost) that keeps up with sprint development timelines.

To address this conflict, organizations should address a few key areas. One of the most basic areas is recognizing differences in how the beginning and ending of a project is defined, specifically as it relates to an iterative and cyclical Agile approach contrasted to the more linear expectations of the broader organization.

Defining the Beginning and Ending

A key challenge Agile teams face is a conflicting definition of end of project or "done" in an environment accustomed to a linear, phased approach to completion rather than an iterative one. In more traditional development of software (and many physical products), development generally follows the path of initiation, planning, development, test, release, and maintenance/support. Agile, however, assumes that all these phases co-exist simultaneously and that all but the last phase happen in recurring sprints of generally two-to-four weeks.

The Project Management Institute (PMI) examined this issue.

The move to greater use of Agile methodologies has at least two accounting issues. First, there is a difference in the completeness of requirements defined up front compared to traditional, phased development. Second, in traditional, phased development, the preliminary phase, the application development phase, and the post-implementation phase are distinct. In an Agile project, it may be hard to disentangle some of the application development and post-implementation phases. (Srinivasan, Quan, & Reed, 2014)

These high-level phases commonly play out in a large organization accustomed to linear software development.

While the last phase is operational with both linear and Agile software development projects, the phases before that occur in an iterative cycle in an Agile project. While a linear software development project may call the product "complete" at the Release stage, Agile instead has many smaller releases, and the product never necessarily has to be considered complete.

Defining "done" can cause confusion inside the Agile team as well. One member of the team may define it as when code on a story is complete, while another defines it as when they have conducted a full regression test.

Before we proceeded, I asked the team what information its estimates included. Did the estimates take into account how long it would take to analyze, design, and code the requirements in the Product Backlog? Did they include time for unit testing... Did the estimates allow time for code reviews, for refactoring, for writing code cleanly and legibly, and for removing unnecessary code? It was important that everyone

Table 1. Typical phases and activities of a linear software development project

Phase	Activities
Initiation	The project is formally proposed, and funding to proceed is approved, typically with a milestone timeline, business justification, planned benefit, and total budget requested
Planning	The project team gathers requirements for the development as a whole and develops a detailed plan to include the project plan, work breakdown structure (WBS), risk/issue logs, and other management artifacts; this is the time when most stakeholder input is incorporated into the product, which is a disadvantage as compared to Agile as is covered later in the chapter
Development	The development team begins software development based on the requirements set in Planning, and drives toward the timeline in the Project Plan; requirements generally remain static, and any major updates to them results in a change order and financial and/or timeline impact
Test	Development is complete, and the team tests the final product before making it available to end-users
Release	The product is formally released to end-users; this will often be referred to as "pushing to the production environment"; there may be a short "hypercare" period immediately following a release where the development team is available if issues arise that were not found in Test
Maintenance & Support	The product goes into a maintenance and support phase, where it is monitored and supported on an ongoing basis, with no changes to the product itself

understood exactly what the estimates allowed for because understanding would prevent people from thinking work was "done" before all of the work taken into account in the estimate was complete... After spending an hour figuring out the impact of this new definition of "done," the team had updated the estimates. (Schwaber, 2004)

While an Agile team finds a number of differences in how it interacts with specific people and departments, much of the conflict is rooted in three questions: " What is 'it', When did 'it' begin, and when does 'it' end?"

These differences do not exist only in the software development area. These key sources of conflict touch areas like reporting to the rest of the organization, accounting for project expenditure, and even human resources where the definition of "done" can greatly impact team member performance measurement.

Reporting

Commonly accepted expectations around reporting are sometimes difficult to provide given how an Agile team functions. In one sense, while the Agile team is delivering a discrete product like a project team, the iterative approach does not always allow for the standard project style reporting metrics such as percent progress to the one "go-live" event. In another sense, the Agile team's iterative approach could be reported more like an operational team, such as the reporting that comes out of a call center. Some of these metrics are not easily understood outside of the Agile team and do not necessarily relate to ultimate business goals, however. For example, a common metric used in Agile is "velocity," whereby the team adds up efforts associated with completed user stories and uses the data as a method to predict project completion timing (What is Velocity in Agile? 2019). This tool for iteratively estimating past performance and revising predictions works well in an Agile setting but does not necessarily translate well to a broader organization that views progress toward completion in more absolute terms.

Leaders can recognize that an Agile team's functioning does not necessarily lend itself well to how the organization consumes reporting and assesses status. A release report or sprint retrospective may provide rich information on development but does not necessarily align with the organization's reporting style or timing expectations. The Agile team and broader leadership can identify the best ways to convey this reporting, but it is important that leadership of both Agile teams and upper management to whom they report have a broad understanding of the issues that may cause conflict and possible resolutions or accommodations that may be necessary.

These disconnects can be more than just inconvenient or inefficient. The inability to communicate status to people who are not actively involved in Agile development can lead to management not thinking they are receiving reliable information, or that the Agile team is hiding status on purpose. It is particularly evident when there is no well-defined minimum viable product (MVP, which can serve as a proxy for communicating "complete" for reporting purposes), or when the Agile team is iterating on a product already in production.

Take the following additional example, based on the author's experience with a client where this disconnect was especially pronounced.

Special Events Flowers (SEF) is one of the larger retail flower distributors targeting special events, such as weddings. SEF has been a dominant player in the national retail flower market for decades, but its e-commerce capabilities had lagged behind over the last several years.

Deciding to invest in their e-commerce site, leadership commissioned a new Agile team to revamp SEF's web sales capabilities and portal completely. One of the most anticipated new features included adding personalization directly into the site's header, which would allow for dynamic marketing explicitly targeted to the individual visitor. The new header's preliminary design was distributed to the different market leads across the business, which generated a buzz throughout the company about the new abilities to market existing SEF products. One market lead had just sent out a press release about some of the new functionality they would demonstrate at a trade show scheduled for the following month. In an internal memo, he circulated a copy of the release and added, "I'm especially excited about the ability to suggest flowers common to the customer's area. I'm seeing an increasing trend to evoke local visuals, and I'm certain that feature coming out next week in the new site header is going to be a huge hit."

On seeing this the Scrum Master thought he should chime in to set expectations on the timing of that feature. "I'm glad you're excited about that feature, we are too," he wrote. "I just wanted to give you a quick heads up that it won't actually be in the header for several more weeks."

The subsequent exchange went something like this:

Market Lead: "The new header is supposed to be on track to come out next week. You reported that just a couple of days ago. Did something change?"

Scrum Master: "Not at all, it's on track to be released with sprint 12 next Thursday! It's just that the local flower suggestions won't be there yet. We have to wait for the geolocation data to be loaded in the flower database, which doesn't happen until sprint 15."

Market Lead: "But this feature was on the designs you distributed at the beginning of the project and that was supposed to be in the header. We already have a press release and marketing material out on this, and my team has started planning for regional displays! Why didn't we know about this sooner?"

Scrum Master: "Sorry for any miscommunication there, the header being released absolutely will be able to accommodate and automatically start using that feature once the integration is giving it that data. We should be able to get you some example mockups to show for different regions. Would that work?"

This example demonstrates one of the key issues commonly seen in communicating progress on Agile products. From the Agile team's standpoint, they accurately communicated the header function's release and were likely excited about the additional iterative functionality that the header *would allow them to expose later*. It was a significant enhancement that no doubt left the Product Owner elated. However, from the standpoint of the business, the team may seem disingenuous about what it said was being released. As with many facets of management, better communication at the initial stages, and understanding of how announcements will impact those to whom they are sent are of primary importance.

Accounting and Finance

Accounting and Finance rules around software development generally work well in Waterfall software development. Activities leading up to and following from the development and testing phases are considered "expensed" (or "opex"), meaning the costs are recognized in that fiscal year. The actual development and testing activities, however, are typically "capitalized" (or "capex"), meaning the costs are recognized over a set period of fiscal years in which they are expected to incur a benefit for the company.

Taking the standard linear example from above, a software development project's typical financial treatment would look something like the below, with some variation on which specific release activities are capitalized.

Table 2. Financial treatment of linear software development projects

Phase	Capex/Opex
Initiation	Opex
Planning	Opex
Development	Capex
Test	Capex
Release	Varies
Maintenance & Support	Opex

In Agile development, however, the distinction of when a product moves from planning to development to operations is not as clear-cut, and consequently, neither is what is defined as a capitalized expense. The financial treatment of a linear software development project assumes that a release or "go-live" means "Complete" and that this is when the product is in Maintenance & Support (and thus considered opex).

While an Agile team developing a brand-new product will have a first release where it is made available to end-users, this often only occurs when the product has reached a level of maturity that it is considered a viable product for them (usually called the "Minimum Viable Product," or MVP). The sprint releases, including planning, development, and testing, happen in multiple iterations both before and after this point.

In an Agile project, all requirements may not be known upfront. However, managers approve the budgeting for the project and know that requirements may be added, removed, or adjusted after each Sprint. In an Agile project, after the approval decision, some activities in the development phase are capitalizable and others are expensed. Capitalizable expenses include design, coding, and testing costs. They also include the purchase and installation of hardware and software, and data conversion to the system. However, some costs cannot be capitalized, such as training costs, auxiliary data conversion, and general, administrative and other overhead costs. (Srinivasan, Quan, & Reed, 2014)

The complexity of choosing what to capitalize vs. expense becomes more complex for Agile projects, as it must adhere to an activity in an iterative cycle rather than a specific milestone. It is not how most corporate financial reporting systems are designed. Instead, they will ask, "With which phase in the project plan was this work associated? Planning, development, or maintenance?" Thus, the Agile team may find financial reporting difficult even if it has done the due diligence to track activities with this level of granularity.

To add additional complexity, the iterative development of a product post-go-live within an Agile team might be considered a new "project" from the company's standpoint. Consider, for example, a product funded for its initial launch, with the understanding that there would be not-yet-funded iterative development after this point. The company will require this new "project" for continuous development to start back at the Initiation phase of the linear software development cycle.

For financial reporting purposes, the Agile team must identify what it considers planning versus development and how this is will be treated by stakeholders who are not familiar with Agile development. Will the team immediately move forward with their standard sprint cycle into the Development phase and completely skip the Planning phase necessary in a Waterfall software development project? Since they are moving directly into development, will they capitalize all expenses as the financial reporting system will assume?

While there are no easy answers, the authors examine some recommendations in the last section of this chapter.

Legacy Technology and External Factors

Agile development teams developing anything of consequence in a large organization will face challenges integrating with existing technologies that are too unwieldy to update within the timeframe of an Agile epic (or perhaps ever). Beyond these established technologies with tentacles throughout the organization, Agile teams find long-established processes and regulations, some of which are simply holdovers from older development methodologies, but many that exist because of legitimate policy or regulatory concerns that impact other parts of the organization, such as legacy data format or legal privacy concerns.

From a technological perspective, Agile teams should bear in mind why an older technology that does not provide a modern API or adhere to other more recent standards still exists. These technologies are typically the result of years or decades of development rooted in long-lost institutional memory and integrated into dozens of other systems used throughout the organization. Updating the legacy system is not necessarily a request built into a few sprints. However, it is instead a development and testing project potentially much larger than the project for which the Agile team would make the request. It likely also necessitates development, testing, and communications planning for other teams around the company, not necessarily related to or even aware of the Agile team. Organizations sometimes choose to make a capital investment in updating or replacing legacy technologies when the revenue justification becomes clear enough (and an Agile team may benefit from building a revenue story to this end).But most often, the organization will choose to find ways to keep some or all of it in place. There are four typical approaches an organization may take:

- *Do nothing. Some applications are too small or too infrequently updated to warrant the investment to modernize.*
- *Wrap and trap. Expose the application's core features and functionality through well-defined interfaces (APIs) while creating new functionality in modern systems.*
- *Re-architect or refactor. Change the application design, including breaking the code base into a series of discrete and independent functional parts and removing hard-coded values.*
- *Replace. Develop a new application using modern architectural patterns such as microservices.*

(Poindexter, Berez 2019)

In established companies in industries that have relied heavily on software for decades, such as finance, travel, and government, this becomes an especially pronounced challenged. Take the following example based on the author's work consulting with clients on this topic. In this example, the Agile team identifies a clear path that it believes will address a business need and involve only a minor change to one system outside of their direct control, the Content Management System (CMS). But because the team did not understand the technical ecosystem of the company, they did not factor in that they would not only face an unexpected technical constraint, but also risk downstream impacts to APIs, telephone support, and ultimately external partners.

Marketing research at a major hotel company identified the need to change the description of the location of the snack machines from "Near elevator," a term initially designed to only be viewed by front desk staff to, "Ideally situated on the way to your room," a term that better resonates with online shoppers now viewing this text on their mobile app. Based on the points assigned to this story, the Agile team estimated that the change would require approximately $3,600 in development costs and could accomplish it in one two-week sprint.

When the Agile team spoke to the team managing the underlying CMS this text would need to be updated. The developers informed them that the field only allowed for 16 characters per its original specifications. It would not accommodate the updated text or most other richer verbiage that Marketing might want to put in the field later. A meeting was called.

At the meeting between the two teams, the CMS developers had good news. They had looked at the database structure before the meeting and determined that it would be an easy change they could potentially make in their next bi-monthly release. The Agile team could simply move the story into later sprints. The CMS team would, however, need to check with teams for some other systems who used the same field accessed through the APIs to their system. They sent an email to the leads for the seven other systems using the API, asking them to validate the change would not adversely impact them.

Most teams did not care, but the first question was about the phone system's Interactive Voice Response (IVR). Would the extended verbiage change the length of the voice messaging customers heard on the phone beyond their standard 20 seconds, should a customer get to the point in the phone tree where this text was inserted?

Another email came back, "Wait, what about Hotwire and all the other online travel agencies? They get that text from our system, and we'd need to make sure the API changes accommodate them."

Four department heads who were not aware of the Agile team were called to a meeting about what was now being referred to as, "the new initiative to change fields in the company's shared CMS."

After approximately six weeks and two or three political flare-ups, the CMS team ultimately determined that implementing the change to their system and the related API would cost approximately $350,000 and would need to wait until after a code freeze for one of the other integrated systems, meaning a release date in approximately nine months.

Given that the update now extended beyond the Agile team's last sprint and would consume a quarter of their total budget, they scrapped this story.

While toward the more extreme end, this example reflects real challenges an Agile team may face for even some of the most straightforward changes. What they expected to be a simple modification impacted departments owning three major underlying systems (CMS, API, and IVR), and relationships with external partners.

To mitigate situations like this, Scrum Masters, Project Managers, Product Owners, and other management supporting the Agile team must work to build relationships across the organization, socialize Agile to outside parties, and think about the end-to-end environment that exists outside of the Agile team, *prior* to implementation of Scrum or Agile practices in an existing organization.

FOSTERING THE TEAM

A Scrum implementation of Agile outlines how the team functions reasonably clearly. Fostering the team according to this tested methodology, however, does not necessarily set it up for success in navigating the broader organizational environment. Champions in senior and executive leadership play a critical role in providing Agile team support for developing the product that helps the organization meet its performance targets. With upper level champions, Agile projects are often difficult, without champions, they are often doomed to fail.

Organizational leaders – meaning individuals such as directors and executives who influence corporate structure – accomplish this in a few key areas. They can ensure managers who directly interact with the Agile team have a deep enough technical background to command the team's respect and represent it to the broader organization. Simultaneously, leadership can build relationships between the team and other areas so that it is in a better position to effectively meet business objectives. And finally, they can evaluate the team's performance in a manner appropriate to the functioning of an Agile team.

Place Leaders with Technology Chops

Agile Scrum teams tend to be small with deep subject matter expertise and skillsets. As with other groups with strong technical backgrounds, leadership within and immediately surrounding an Agile Scrum team garners more respect if they have the hard skills and experience common among those they lead. Similarly, these leaders support and bring in individuals with similar traits, making an Agile Scrum team more effective at task-oriented goal, but often more narrowly focused.

Management outside of the Agile team may grow frustrated at the various disconnects in style between the Agile team and the rest of the organization and, with the best of intentions, seek to put managers they are "more comfortable with" in charge of the Agile team. This will often not yield the expected result. While the organization may start getting the kind of status and financial reporting from the team in line with what it expects, the team's actual performance will suffer without the support of management that understands technology and software development. Instead, leadership should place more technically oriented managers in charge of Agile teams. "Supplanting the business-oriented IT manager is a true engineering manager, with the technical chops to check others' code along with enough business savvy to work closely with product managers and business owners." (Poindexter, Berez 2019)

To address this facet of Agile teams directly, organizations placing someone in charge of an Agile team or collection of teams should consider factoring technical experience as part of the hiring or placement criteria. These positions vary significantly depending on the organization, but they would typically include:

- Product Owners, who also function as part of the Agile team in some cases, especially Scrum implementations
- Product Area Lead, who may engage with multiple Agile teams and focus on a certain area such as Digital Solutions
- Project/Program Managers, who may interface between the Agile team(s) and a traditional PMO

It is often difficult to identify leaders for these areas with the necessary technical background and good organizational management skills that are not being used elsewhere in the organization, or they may seem difficult and expensive to find. However, due to the nature of challenges to the leadership of Agile teams, it is poor economy to put less than the best candidate in charge of an important Agile team.

Use Cross-Functional Teams

While present extensively outside of Agile teams, the use of cross-functional teams can become both more fluid in their makeup and more effective in their contribution to the end product. While the advantages of cross-functional teams are not useful only to Agile, the effective Agile team understands how to use its methodology in a cross-functional setting. One of the most significant advantages an Agile team can use is its ability to continuously obtain feedback and assess issues without being beholden to a strict separation of requirements gathering and implementation. Agile teams can accomplish this by engaging stakeholders from other areas as part of their iterative process, and at times may find opportunities to conversely engage as part of other teams.

When an Agile team realizes it has not included important input, this input can consist of additional feedback in the next sprint rather than a sad story of how requirements were already locked down. When the team needs a key voice from legacy infrastructure because of an unforeseen issue, it has an iterative cycle to include it as soon as the need is recognized.

The table below summarizes concrete examples of leveraging the power of cross-functional teams.

Members of an Agile team can conversely engage in teams across the organization. To foster delivery quality and alignment to overall business objectives, leadership should identify ways to engage the Agile team outside of the software development environment. For example, putting development team members in a more active role as a point of production support encourages accountability for the quality of code. (Poindexter, Berez 2019)

Similarly, engaging the Scrum Master or Product Owner in marketing initiatives increases awareness of how feature releases and press releases are related and can help mitigate miscommunications that result in the organization's public image being tarnished by unclear feature release timelines.

Table 3. Common problems addressed by engaging cross-functional teams

Problem	Cross-functional Solution
Expectations of the completion of a project or milestone are different among the Agile team and other parts of the organization.	Include the business customers within the organization in key sprint review meetings and map releases of functionality to business objectives
Conflicts arise in how expenditure on an Agile project should be categorized with respect to the phase of activity.	Clearly establish a minimum viable product in coordination with business customers and articulate the point at which this product is "released," demarking a move into operational phases.
The complexity of an organization's technical ecosystem is not being factored into sprint planning.	Engage key system owners as part of sprint planning to advise on broader systems implications with respect to sprint planning. And on larger projects, "a good approach is to consider 'full-stack feature teams', where teams are oriented to a product feature, originating end-to-end reduced dependencies on external teams and individuals." (Almeida, 2017)

Basically, anything that can be done to foster cross communication between and among relevant team and organizational members will be useful.

Evaluate Performance Appropriate for the Team

Agile teams typically function in small, collaborative groups with a servant-leader. Many of the normal methods of evaluating performance do not work as well for this kind of team

One suggestion for rethinking how to evaluate success is taking advantage of Agile teams' collaborative nature and move from individual evaluations conducted by a manager to a team-based evaluation.

Developing team-based performance evaluation with indicators tuned to agile attributes... can foster team collaboration and use of agile practices... To make team-based performance evaluation more effective, team members can act as evaluators as well as being evaluated. (Conboy, Coyle, Wang, & Pikkarainen, 2011)

Depending on the level of trust, management may decide to take this a step further and give the Agile team the responsibility of setting its group goals, potentially with shorter timelines to match an Agile environment's more rapid and fluid pace. In this case, replacing a formal evaluation with regular coaching may be appropriate if the organization's larger HR framework allows, though this requires that managers have a skillset to coach well. (Sochova, 2019)

ADVICE FOR THE AGILE TEAM

Much of this chapter has focused on the issues Agile teams face in the context of broader and more traditional organizations. The previous section described how organizational leadership can foster the success of Agile teams. The authors would like to leave the reader with some current research findings and advice to the Agile teams to position themselves for success within the organization.

Align Features and Communications to Business Goals

Agile team leadership, especially Product Managers, must ensure the product roadmap is clearly aligned to specific organizational goals outlined by executive leadership. It makes the product and Agile team more effective and supports more transparent communication with the broader organization. Document how the product backlog supports those goals in concrete terms and use that documentation to guide reporting and communication. With this relationship clearly articulated, the Agile team can communicate in a manner relevant to the business. For example, a sprint report may indicate the successful completion of a feature to "Pre-populate customer data from previous orders."

When communicating this accomplishment, however, consider something more like, "On April 18th, the development team completed enhancements that removed two steps from the online checkout. We anticipate this change will move even more customer contacts via phone and help meet the goal of reducing call center costs by 20% in the next year." A statement like this conveys the value of an incremental sprint rather than a big splash product release, while simultaneously articulating the tangible business value.

Use Differences as Shared Experiences

Technologists often talk like war veterans, and regardless of their industry or software development methodology, they will find similar battles in their past. The story of a simple text change that led to a six-figure enhancement estimate, or of dealing with a non-technical Project Manager, is not specific to Agile. One of the authors, when consulting on a statewide governmental implementation, found that the primary roadblock to project completion was that the base customer data was in a heavily patched COBOL database for which this government agency was the prime employer of COBOL programmers….and thus moving into the future was almost impossible, since the code changes that made the data accessible to the legacy system had not been annotated or recorded. This story, in various versions, is common to almost anyone who has worked with legacy governmental systems and thus is a common point of reference.

Agile teams can leverage collective ownership of their ultimate objective for the product. (Almeida, 2017) They may find it useful to bring the ask *of the business* rather than of the Agile team to the collective technical stakeholders and talk about how both the respective teams function differently and can jointly accomplish the goal they've been given.

Fund the Team and Product Rather than the Project

This chapter has discussed Accounting and Finance challenges in a previous section and did not find conclusive research addressing how Agile teams can overcome these challenges. Further research is needed in this area, and indeed, some of the accounting research into activity based costing holds promise.

However, an Agile team may find it useful to change its financing model to enable iterative development. It can work with organizational leadership to structure financing requests more like an operational rather than a project team, with the operation being enhancements to a product. The Agile team will have its annual budget but can internally measure its financial performance by quarter rather than the fiscal year.

The model also gives the Agile team more freedom to use its short-term development sprint model to meet changing business requirements. Large organizations measure their financial performance by quarter, and there is no reason the Agile team delivering on business needs should have to be any different.

CONCLUSION

While much of this book goes into depth on Agile Scrum, the authors hope that this chapter provides a context of how Agile fits within the broader organization and leaves management, developers, Scrum Masters, and Product Owners in better positions to not only provide value to the business but also foster an effective Agile team. In recognizing the Agile Scrum does not exist in a vacuum and addressing this fact directly, teams are in a better position to use the advantages of Agile to thrive in an organization.

Agile leaders have tools at their disposal to build excitement and leadership support. They can look to sprint plans and backlogs, now aligned to specific business goals, and talk about what is next. It encourages enthusiasm around the Agile team and supports the case for continued funding and the realization that iterative product improvement does not have to have a discrete project with an end date. The Agile team is in a unique position to leave the business always wanting more.

REFERENCES

Aghina, W., Ahlback, K., De Smet, A., Lackey, G., Lurie, M., Murarka, M., & Handscomb, C. (2018, January). Retrieved February 10, 2020, from https://www.mckinsey.com/business-functions/organization/our-insights/the-five-trademarks-of-agile-organizations

Almeida, F. (2017). Challenges in Migration from Waterfall to Agile Environments. *World Journal of Computer Application and Technology,* 1–11. Retrieved from https://pdfs.semanticscholar.org/555d/47e2b9846f38ef66c137afbb3fc0d7bdf3b7.pdf?_ga=2.38570467.1502277820.1576607231-1259273190.1576607231

Birkinshaw, J. (2017). What to Expect From Agile. *MIT Sloan Management Review*. Retrieved from https://sloanreview.mit.edu/article/what-to-expect-from-agile/

Bouray, R. P., & Richards, G. E. (2018). Accounting for external-use software development costs in an agile environment. *Journal of Accountancy*. Retrieved August 12, 2020, from https://www.journalofaccountancy.com/news/2018/mar/accounting-for-external-use-software-development-costs-201818259.html

Burden, A., Ouderaa, E. V., Venkataraman, R., Nystrom, T., & Shukla, P. P. (2018, June 19). *Technical Debt Might Be Hindering Your Digital Transformation*. Retrieved August 12, 2020, from https://sloanreview.mit.edu/article/technical-debt-might-be-hindering-your-digital-transformation/

Conboy, K., Coyle, S., Wang, X., & Pikkarainen, M. (2011). People over Process: Key Challenges in Agile Development. *IEEE Software, 28*(4), 48–57. doi:10.1109/MS.2010.132

Poindexter, W., & Berez, S. (2017). Agile Is Not Enough. *MIT Sloan Management Review*. Retrieved from https://sloanreview.mit.edu/article/agile-is-not-enough/

Schwaber, K. (2004). *Agile project management with Scrum*. Microsoft.

Srinivasan, R., Quan, T., & Reed, P. (2014). *Accounting for agile projects*. Project Management Institute. Retrieved from https://www.pmi.org/learning/library/accounting-agile-projects-9303

What Is Velocity in Agile? (2019, September 26). Retrieved July 23, 2020, from https://www.agilealliance.org/glossary/velocity/

Chapter 4
A Wrinkle in the Promise of Scrum

Aruna Chandrasekharan
Independent Researcher, USA

ABSTRACT

Jeff Sutherland worked on the first Scrum project in 1993, but the framework as we know it now was formally coined by Jeff and Ken Schwaber in 1995. Since then IT divisions have seen the growing adoption of Scrum within their organization. However, this growth has been peppered with poor examples of adoption leading to lackluster results. This chapter explores why there is such a prevalence of "Bad" Scrum and the impact it has on the culture of the organization. This chapter explores the impact of poorly led transformations and will also provide some ways to reconsider how transformations should pivot.

INTRODUCTION

Scrum is a process framework created by Ken Schwaber and Jeff Sutherland to address complex adaptive problems, while productively and creatively delivering products of the highest possible value. Scrum proposes to be a lightweight, simple to understand approach especially for software development (Scrum. org, 2020). It has been in use since the 1990s. It is not a set of definitive techniques but rather a framework within which a person might employ a variety of techniques to continuously improve the product, the team and the environment around the team. It is founded on three pillars of "Transparency," "Inspection," and "Adaptation" which uphold five Scrum values of "Courage," "Focus," "Respect," "Commitment," and "Openness." These pillars and values are the guideposts for the events, artifacts and roles that are found within the framework.

BACKGROUND

Scrum has been widely adopted over the last 15 years and continues to expand its impact not just on software and product development but in other areas as well (ScrumAlliance.org, 2017). However, there

DOI: 10.4018/978-1-7998-4885-1.ch004

Copyright © 2021, IGI Global. Copying or distributing in print or electronic forms without written permission of IGI Global is prohibited.

are plenty of examples of bad Scrum in the industry mostly due to the gross misinterpretations of the intentions embedded within the framework (Chee, 2018; Handscomb et al., 2018). Changing this is a huge task that is not easily undertaken unless enterprises everywhere fundamentally change their understanding of its application. However, as big a task as it is, it is also imperative that the task be undertaken. With Scrum adoption growing year over year, the impact of poorly implemented transformations can have deep and negative consequences for organizations (State of Agile, 2020). This chapter will not discuss Scrum events, roles or artifacts. Rather it will focus on why good Scrum is hard to implement, the consequences of bad Scrum, and its impact on organizational culture. It will end with a call to action to all leaders who are in the midst of a Scrum adoption or are contemplating inviting Scrum through their doors.

REASONS WHY GOOD SCRUM IS RARE

Most Ecosystems do not Allow Scrum Values to Thrive

Values can be defined as broad preferences concerning appropriate courses of actions or outcomes. Personal values provide an internal reference for what is good, beneficial, important, useful, beautiful, desirable, and constructive. Values are one of the factors that generate behavior (besides needs, interests, and habits) and influence the choices made by an individual (Wikipedia, 2020). In other words, values serve as explicit or implicit guideposts that influence the way people within an eco-system comport with each other. When these values are misaligned with that ecosystem, success and satisfaction are at stake. Therefore, in order to understand why we see so much bad Scrum around us, we first need to explore the misalignment of Scrum values within the organizations that Scrum is prevalent in. What are these Scrum values? There are five values that the success of Scrum is founded upon.

Courage: Scrum team members have the courage to do the right thing and work on tough problems. This "courage to do the right thing" takes many shapes. Courage to hold each other accountable to the team, to ask difficult questions that need answers regardless of who needs to be questioned, to hold true to Scrum values even when the environment around the team does not support this.

Focus: Everyone focuses on the work of the sprint and goals of the scrum team. This means that the team is dedicated to the work and have no interruptions or outside expectations which could cost the team productive hours.

Commitment: People personally commit to achieving the goals of the Scrum team. This implies a level of ownership and pride in the team for the work they have taken on for the sprint. In other words, personally committing to something means prioritizing this work over everything else and giving it all the attention that it needs.

Respect: Scrum team members respect each other to be capable, independent people. Respect has many forms and a scrum team exhibits that respect by giving each other space, helping each other grow, holding each other accountable, and fundamentally understanding that each person in the team has an equal voice that will contribute to a great sprint outcome

Openness: The Scrum team and its stakeholders agree to be open about all the work and the challenges with performing the work. Openness implies a trusting environment where the team and stakeholders allow themselves to be vulnerable, to learn from failures and ask for help when needed.

How simple and yet how difficult these values are. Simple in that there is familiarity with these everyday words that are used in everyday language. Difficult in that it is not enough that only one of

Figure 1. Scrum Values (Scrum.org, 2020)

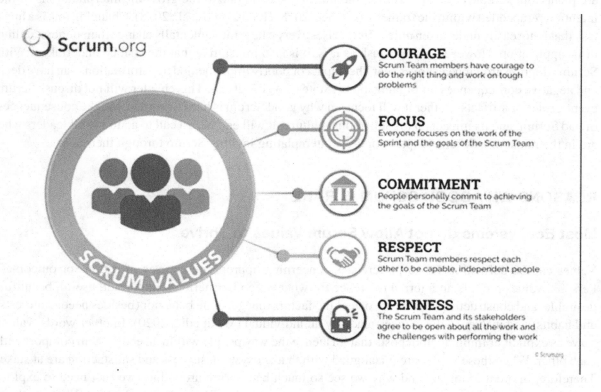

these values exist in an environment that wants to benefit from Scrum. All these values **must coexist simultaneously**. It simply does not work otherwise. Take a moment to let that sink in (Prokopets, 2020).

Let's explore some scenarios where this holds true. Take for example a team that has courage but cannot respect each other. What happens to the productivity of that team? It would be in tatters with all the bickering that would occur whenever a challenge presented itself. Let's take another example of a team that has respect but is unable to commit to the work. They might have tremendous respect for each other but the environment they are in does not have allow for enough respect for their commitment to the sprint. They are pulled in multiple directions with too many other #1 priorities that live outside of the Scrum team. What about when a team has commitment but there is a tangible lack of focus. Their ability to achieve their sprint goal will be severely impacted. Where does this lack of focus come from? It is the environment around them that prevents them from having this focus. Once again when an enterprise is faced with the familiar problem of too many #1 priorities that live outside of the Scrum team, the resulting culture and behaviors trickle down to the Scrum teams as well. Too many conflicting priorities also means too many interruptions in the day. All this context switching can lead to a decline in productivity of almost 80% (Mackay, 2019). When a team has the best of intentions but the environment does not support those intentions, Scrum will fail.

Back to the notion that all these values must coexist simultaneously.

a.   The team must have respect for each other. This respect is fundamental to openness.

b. With respect, the team trusts each other and therefore can be open to each other. The same respect is needed with stakeholders as well. The team must believe that the relationship with the stakeholders is one of mutual respect. That is the only way openness with stakeholders can occur.

c. A relationship that has openness encourages courage as well. The trust that is built with openness is what gives the team the courage to ask the right questions and push each other and others outside the team to do the right thing.

d. Courage is the incentive that a team needs to commit to their work. Commitment is a profound statement. It weaves courage, ethics, honor and beliefs into one single word. Without courage, a team would not be able to commit to anything.

e. Commitment creates the need for focus. Or rather, without commitment there is no incentive to focus. A team that does not commit is in danger of being pulled into many directions. After all, when we are prone to distractions and without an urgency of commitment, distractions will thrive.

These values are closely interwoven. While Scrum has three pillars, these values are pillars in themselves. No single value can be held up without the other four values being in place. Much like a pillar. These values together unlock the intrinsic motivation of people. Environments that interpret Scrum values as they were truly intended, create ecosystems that amplify productivity of teams. Teams in these environments have autonomy, mastery, and purpose which tend to lead to success (Van Der Star, 2017). Had Scrum been implemented at that time and place, the results would have been exceptional.

The issue is that there are not enough ecosystems that support Scrum values. This is, unquestionably, why we don't see enough "Good Scrum." Poor interpretation, understanding, and implementation of these values have now created an enormous challenge for "Good Scrum" or "True Agile" (Peterson, 2019). "Good Scrum" or "True Agile" happens when an individual belongs to a team and an ecosystem where all five Scrum values are part of the norm, ubiquitous and as normal as breathing. Any time any one of those values is off-kilter, the ecosystem will highlight the dysfunctions caused by the imbalance and act on it immediately. Not acting on it would result in a toxic culture and good employees abandoning it. Studies have shown people leaving toxic culture even before they land the next job (Mautz, 2019).

Sustaining the Right Culture is Hard

A culture that allows all five Scrum values to thrive is an exceptional culture indeed. It is exceptional for two reasons. The first and obvious reason is that one gets exceptional results with an exceptional culture. The second reason is that it is extremely difficult to create a culture that is exceptional in so many ways. A better word perhaps is sustain rather than create. We humans can create a culture like that for the short term, but sustainment takes energy, effort, and a lot of intention. There are plenty of examples of great companies that have been able to do this (Bastone, 2018). That's what Scrum values are meant to do. Living those values encourages each one of us to bring the best version of ourselves every day to not only our work but to our personal life as well. That takes a commitment from each individual which must be respected by the ecosystem that surrounds the individual.

The challenge here is sustaining a culture that brings out the best in us. It is a challenge because it requires every individual to value a goal that is higher than their own personal gain. When personal gain gets in the way, the quality of the culture also deteriorates. What does this mean? Merriam Webster defines culture as the set of shared attitudes, values, goals, and practices that characterizes an institution or organization (Merriam-Webster.com, 2020). Those shared attitudes, values, and goals are defined by humans. Humans in turn are defined by a very powerful force. That force is called the "Ego," ergo "Ego" defines and influences everything within our ecosystem. At first glance, this might be too simplistic. But it is deceptively so. It is ego that drives decisions on ecosystem design and impacts the quality of interactions within that design. Ego is fundamental to our identity. If one googles the word "Ego," what comes up is this: "a person's sense of self-esteem or self-importance." If one digs a little deeper about "ID," "Superego," and "Ego" one will get:

According to Freud's model of the psyche (Freud, 1923), the id is the primitive and instinctual part of the mind that contains sexual and aggressive drives and hidden memories, the super-ego operates as a moral conscience, and the ego is the realistic part that mediates between the desires of the id and the superego.

In other words, the "Id" is the most basic part of personality that urges people to fulfill their most primal urges, whilst the "Superego" is the moralistic part of personality that is formed by upbringing and social norms.

The "Ego" has a difficult job to do since it has to find a balance between two competing forces. More often than not, primal urges are too powerful to control (Freud, 1917) and the "Superego" tends to lose to the "Id." When this happens, people subconsciously design structures and interactions that serve them well as individuals but not necessarily others or a greater cause. Let's revisit those five scrum values again: courage, respect, focus, commitment, and openness. Ego can and does prevent a person from summoning the courage to do the right thing especially when that comes at the cost of oneself. Ego must be subservient to a person's desire to give respect which is very hard to do on a consistent basis. Focus and commitment to do the right thing at the cost of ego is extremely difficult to do. Being vulnerable and transparent with others requires one to put their ego aside and let humility take over. This is not to say these values can't win in the short term. It's the long game that counts. If people within an ecosystem do not become hyper aware and intentional about what ego does to their culture, exceptional outcomes will not occur. Living those scrum values produces exceptional outcomes. The magic that these values bring is what makes Scrum successful. Now we begin to understand why we see so much bad Scrum. As it turns out, bad Scrum is more intuitive to us than good Scrum. Bad Scrum is ubiquitous while Good Scrum shines like a precious and rarely seen diamond.

The Prevalence of Fake Speed Creates a Real Threat to Good Scrum

So bad Scrum is intuitive to us. What happens when bad Scrum is ubiquitous to an ecosystem? You will see a lot of movement without quality outcomes. This author identifies movement for the sake of movement as "Fake speed." Fake speed can be further defined as the following:

It is the desire for movement regardless of outcome

It is the compulsion to stay busy without regard to measurable effectiveness

It is the willingness to work around the dysfunctions rather than remove them

It is the focus on tasks rather than outcomes

It is the safety that comes with a false perception of success

Let us explore each one individually.

The desire for movement regardless of outcome. This is what one sees when teams get on the ground before the ecosystem is ready for the team. People are in such a hurry to start writing code that they don't give enough time to the team for it to boot up properly. That means an unwillingness to take the time to be disciplined about the process of ramping up a team. An example of this is getting started even if the team does not have a product owner, or if the team does, that product owner is not dedicated to the team and it is outside his/her day job. But the ecosystem needs the team to get started so after a two-day training session they hop, skip, and stumble along.

The compunction to stay busy without regard to measurable effectiveness. One sees this when a team gets on the ground and starts writing code and starts measuring throughput on a backlog that is full of stories but one cannot pinpoint value. An example of this is a backlog of technical stories written from the developer's point of view and not a value statement from the customer's point of view. Sometimes one does see user/customer-centric stories but they are way down in the backlog that typically integrates all the other layers of code into something that a user can touch and feel. The team feels good because their velocity is high and their ability to build and deploy code is fast and efficient but real effectiveness comes from measuring the value that was developed.

The willingness to work around the dysfunction rather than remove them. Usually when an organization decides to do an "Agile Transformation," they usually start and more of than not, end with Scrum at the team level. This is called "Agile Adoption" and not "Agile Transformation" (Job, 2019). As a result, the team starts working in a Scrum manner and there is an expectation that they will produce an increment of value every sprint. But what is the reality on the ground? The reality is that the rest of the organization is busy being busy and busy doing things they've always done. This means that the rest of the organization still has dysfunctions that surround the team and the team goes through the motions and accepts the dysfunctions. It takes courage to stop and try to remove those dysfunctions. It takes courage to make the scrum framework retell a team's story even if it is a story fraught with challenges and the battle has not yet been won. But courage is hard and sometimes the consequences of courage can be loss of employment. So, teams continue to go through the motions and managers are happy because nothing in their life has been impacted. Manager did not have to disrupt themselves.

The focus on tasks rather than outcomes. This ties back to the notion of a backlog full of technical statements and not from a customer's point of view. Let's take that a little further. The backlog does not only have technical stories, but analysis stories, wireframe stories and design stories as well. The team is busy tracking tasks, measuring throughput on tasks. This is akin to the notion of Vanity metrics. The team should be in the business of measuring outcomes and not tasks, measure outcomes and not outputs.

The safety that comes with the false perception of success. People tend to feel good when they are busy. They feel good because they are in constant motion, going from one meeting to the next. Being able to say that they have 10-hour days with back to back meetings. While they might feel tired, they feel good. The problem here is getting so invested in being busy because one thinks that one's corporate culture values that. That false perception of value gives people job safety. Instead, one should shift one's focus from being busy to being productive.

To Have Effective Speed is Difficult

If there's fake speed, surely there's a concept of effective speed. What is effective speed? This author defines effective speed as the following:

It is the desire for the right type of movement at the right time and at the right place.

It is the courage to push the ecosystem for a better solution.

It is the willingness to remove dysfunctions rather than work around them.

It is the focus on outcomes rather than tasks.

It is the safety that comes with real tangible success.

Let's explore each one individually.

The desire for the right type of movement at the right time at the right place. This means that a team will, with great intention, make the decisions that need to be made even if they are hard ones. They will have the patience to wait for the right time and take the right steps in a disciplined manner in order to win the long game. That is what effective speed is all about.

The courage to push the ecosystem for a better solution. This obviously speaks to the Scrum value of courage. This is truly a difficult thing to do. It means one must challenge the ecosystem to remove the silos that prevent flow of ideas, collaboration, and partnership. Removing silos is not a trivial task and is rarely done at the team level which, as has been stated previously, is where all the adoption happens. Without fighting this difficult battle, effective speed will not thrive.

The willingness to remove dysfunctions rather than work around them. A team that truly wants to live by Scrum values will not live with dysfunctions. They will not mind changing their ecosystem and they will not allow themselves to be hit by the same wall twice. They would much rather stop, take the time to reflect, and then intentionally remove the wall. This is why they become truly effective and this is why they see excellent performance and can drive value faster.

The focus on outcomes rather than tasks. A team that truly understands Scrum values and what Agile principles and values intended will focus on delivering business value to the customer and to their organization. This does not mean they lose their hyper focus on productivity and commitment to getting their tasks completed on time. This just means that they choose not to get sucked into the weeds of metrics that don't bring transparency to outcomes but end up focusing on those tasks. They have their eye on the real prize which is outcomes for the customer.

IMPACT OF BAD SCRUM IS TRANSFORMATION FATIGUE

What happens when fake speed abounds for an extended period of time? One will find disappointment across the organization. Disappointment can be defined as "the distance between expectation and reality" (Author Unknown, Unknown). This author has taken this definition of disappointment and applied it to disappointment that comes from failed transformation. "Transformation Disappointment" is the state of mind evidenced and behavior exhibited when a person, team, leader, or organization does not see the fulfilment of transformation promises made, in their current reality.

So why do organizations find themselves in this situation? They got here because they did what every other organization that is about to start on an Agile journey does. They started Scrum at the team level and stayed there. They had unrealistic expectations about timelines. They focused on processes at the team level but nothing else (Mersino, 2019).

Figure 2. Habits of Change(Chandrasekharan, 2018)

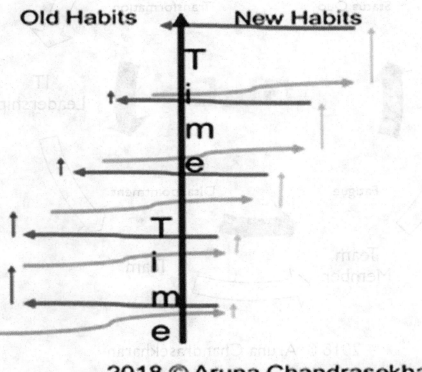

Change is hard (Figure 2) and the change journey is fickle. It takes clarity of vision, faith in that vision, and almost an iron will and tenacity to get through the journey. To add to this, most organizations suffer from what is called "The Circle of Blame" (Figure 3).

There is a long-standing tradition of distrust between business and IT. This distrust makes IT leadership cascade that same sentiment down the chain to teams and team members which circles back up. Transformations start with an "agreement" between business and IT which then leads to disappointment and subsequently fatigue. At that point, the organization is back to where it started.

When one is caught in this vicious cycle, "Transformation Disappointment" changes to "Transformation Fatigue." Merriam Webster defines fatigue as a state or attitude of indifference or apathy brought on by overexposure (as to a repeated series of similar events or appeals) (Merriam-webster.com, 2020).

Figure 3. Circle of Blame (Chandrasekharan, 2018)

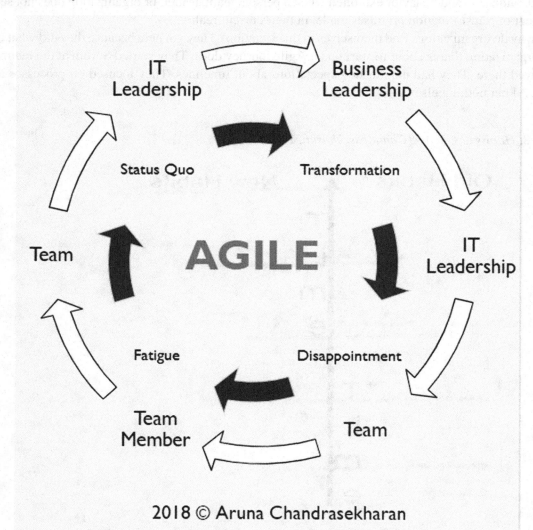

This author defines "Transformation Fatigue" as the state of mind evidenced and behavior exhibited when a person, team, leader, or organization does not see the fulfillment of transformation promises made, in their current reality, *on a consistent and persistent basis.*

One can see this fatigue within multiple levels of the organization. Fatigue can be found at the level of a team member, the team, the organization level and within the transformation change agents who are there to support an organization through its transformation journey (Crosby, 2019; Locke, 2019).

Impact of Different Types of Fatigue

How do we recognize what type we are dealing with when it comes to fatigue? Let's start with team member fatigue. There are several examples that we can cite for team member fatigue. When a team member rolls his/her eyes when the word "Agile" or "Scrum" is heard. Rolling eyes, grimacing or snickering are all negative physical reactions. Here are a few more examples. When a team member simply nods to a change agent's recommendations, there is no action unless the change agent asks for an update and that update is to further delay a more valuable action. The team member will use words like "we do what we have to do," "we are used to it," "that's how it works around here," "no one in my team cares about this," "I have already asked and nothing's changed," when they are challenged about their attitude or inertia. This team member is going through the motions of Scrum or Agile without any appreciation. This team member is tired.

Let's take a team where everyone has the same issue. That's when the team is suffering from fatigue. What type of behaviors are prevalent when this happens? Here's what this looks like. The team has gradually shortened their retrospectives and are not creative in their facilitation of the event or have gone so far as to cancel them all together. There is a general disinclination to rock the boat or hold each other accountable (Scrum values have failed here). At Scrum events, only one or two members engage in entertaining any recommendations at all. The whole team will use words like "we do what we have to do," "we are used to it," "that's how it works around here," "I know that…," "I understand but…"

What does this same apathy look like when it moves from teams to the leaders who are supposed to serve those teams? What behaviors does one see when this happens? These leaders start to cancel coaching events quite frequently. They tend to surf on their phones during those events and tend to make a humorous reference for any anti-pattern that is highlighted as an impediment to a culture that wants Scrum values to thrive. They are willing to facilitate change conversations with their direct reports but are unwilling to rock the boat by leading any change. In other words, all talk and no walk. They only have 30 minutes for any in-depth discussion with a change agent about any change related item. They play the blame game for lackluster performance despite "doing Scrum." They feel that the teams are not performing so the focus should be on teams—that's the best way they can say "NO" to improvements and not have to look in the mirror. They are busy greasing the wheels for the "NOW" and feel good about it—They have no time for what they would call "ideal scenarios" because they obviously live in the real world.

When leaders suffer from this, it is only natural for the organization as a whole to start feeling the same fatigue. How does this happen? Attendance on Enterprise sponsored coaching events like Lunch and Learns and Quality Circles/Communities of Practice is extremely low. There are more frequent questions about what shouldn't be transitioned to a Scrum/Agile approach rather than what should. The C-Suite wants to know the ROI on their transformation investment. This is because they have not seen the results of their investment. Why? Because the organization is drowning in a culture that has subverted Scrum values and is busy being busy.

With all this going, it is only natural that change agents whose sole responsibility is to champion, implement and support transformative changes within these organizations, also experience fatigue. What happens when one goes head to head with an irresistible force? The force that is being referred to here is the inevitable fatigue that has now diseased the organization. The change agent succumbs to the same malaise and shies away from continued exploration and experimentation of different progressive techniques to further those transformative goals.

Options to Combat Fatigue

There are ways to mitigate the damage caused by these different types of fatigue. The mitigation techniques mentioned here take time and patience and are not guaranteed that they will work but they do give one a fighting chance to win. Let's take each of those levels of fatigue and explore how one can do this.

When it comes to a team member there are several things to consider. What is the timing of the desired change? What's happening in this member's personal life? What time of the year, regardless of calendar and fiscal year, is it? Are vacations coming up? Is it the holidays? If the timing is not right and the individual is distracted, perhaps it is better to wait for a time that is more conducive to inspiring them to change. There is no bigger waste than a good intention delivered at the wrong time.

Has the individual been asked to change without presenting a compelling case to trigger their intrinsic motivation—What's In It For Them (WIIFM)? Has an attempt been made to elicit an emotional response to this change from the individual? How will one's life truly change if one lives the Scrum values? If a personal or emotional connection cannot be made, then the change is less likely to happen. Is the desired change something within the individual's sphere of influence and control? More than likely it is outside their control. The ecosystem around them is not living those same Scrum values. When a team member feels powerless, then inaction is the path of least resistance.

Another important thing to consider is the type of employment this person has with the organization. Is this person an employee or a contractor—this influences the power dynamics. Most organizations claim to treat contractors and employees alike with the exclusion of a few items that do not impact the overall quality of their experiences. That may not be the case (Livni, 2018). More often than not, the power lies with the employee and not with the contractor. Add to that the uncertainty of the contract itself and now one really has an unequal balance. Contractors are more than likely not going to hold employees accountable to Scrum values because they fear loss of pay. How does one change this imbalance so that both parties appreciate and hold themselves accountable to building the right culture? That's the journey that is devoid of fake speed and is full of effective speed.

What are some options to consider when dealing with team member fatigue? Is the team member too distracted with whatever is going with them either in their personal or professional life? If that's the case, defer the discussion of change and wait for a better time.

There must be an active attempt to build a relationship with that team member. This could be as simple as going for coffee, enquiring about their weekend or establishing a monthly lunch date where you do not talk about just work. Share stories with each other. Earn their trust before trying to inspire them to change either themselves or their ecosystem. This is very similar to the saying "Physician! Heal thyself." Explore the team member's understanding of the Organization's Transformation Vision—do corrections need to be made? Perhaps they did not understand it all or misunderstood it. Either way, the result is apathy towards the vision and apathy leads to inertia. Inertia implies that the old culture stays and does not allow Scrum values to thrive. It could also be that they understand the organization's vision but can't connect the dots to themselves. What is the impact of this transformation on their career, quality of work, and ability to grow? These are very important gaps that, if they do exist, must be filled in order to progress. Has the leadership been able to connect their vision with their employees at an emotional level that makes them want to own their transformation?

What are some considerations to make when dealing with team fatigue? A common challenge that most teams have is hard deadlines. In other words, too much to do with too little time and money. More often than not, teams that do not change are overwhelmed with too much to do with too little time and caught in a vicious cycle. When you add little or no leadership support to that cycle, then you have a no-win situation. A team that has raised its challenges to its leadership and all they see is inertia from that same leadership, is highly unlikely to be inspired to a different reality. Even though they might intellectually acknowledge that change is important, their immediate and important burdens just prevent them from caring about anything else.

What about their relationship with their product owner? Most instances of Scrum adoption that is prevalent in the industry, show an imbalanced relationship between the development team and the Product owner. The product owner has limited understanding of his/her role in the Scrum framework and tends to command the team. He/She speaks in terms of the development team reporting to them and will say things like "the team needs to get it done," "the team should do more," "this team reports to me." In a situation like this, it is clear to see the nature of the power dynamics between the development team and the product owner. The same dysfunction might be seen in the relationship between the team and the scrum master. Either way, it is a toxic relationship that leads to poor results.

There is another big challenge to consider: the budget challenge. How many times has one seen a team that has been reduced in numbers but the scope has not been reduced to align with that cut? Budget cuts always impact effort but more often than not, they do not impact the amount of work that the team has to do. With such challenges, what are the chances that the organization is going to shift to a culture that respects Scrum values?

Well, there are several options for an organization to leverage in this situation. For one thing, just support the team in their efforts to achieve success within the deadline. This support could come in many ways—deferring difficult discussions until the crisis has passed, buying breakfast and bringing it to the team. Simple acts like this will let the team know that the organization cares and is part of that effort. The team will see the organization as being on their side. If time and budget allow and the team is willing, some kind of offsite team-building trip can also help. Though there is a lot of debate about the value of team building activities and whether they truly help the team or not (Vinje, 2018), in this situation, the team offsite trip is a decompressor. They need to unwind from all the pressure that they are always under. This is the organization's way of trying to help a team forget about their burdens for a little bit of time and come together and just have fun. This affords an opportunity for the team to have great conversations. They will remember those conversations and they will remember the feeling they had when they were in those team building activities. So, it is a relatively low risk experiment for an organization to try.

Inflexible scope is the enemy of a team and is a leading cause for team fatigue. The Business wants the scope in its entirety. They truly and firmly believe that everything on that backlog is important. They must ask for all of it or they might never get it. There's a history of distrust usually between Business and IT. An organization that wants to shift to a better culture should actively help the team by nudging the business to negotiate with the team and find opportunities where value can be achieved by maximizing the amount of work not done. When all else fails sometimes it is best to just leave that team alone and get out of their way. The team would appreciate this more than you know.

Let's talk about leadership fatigue. Change agents are exposed to this a lot more than is productive (Mitchell,2018). A change agent should consider whether the leader in question has respect for them on a personal level. That is probably the most important point to consider. Without respect on a personal basis, no professional relationship can be formed. The next question to ask is do they respect the change agent role. They might have respect for the person but not for the role and the scope it represents in their organization. There are plenty of people who like an individual during happy hour but everything changes once the clock starts at work.

What about the said leader's confidence in their relationship with their boss or even with their direct reports? Do they have trust going either way? What is the inevitable result of an environment that lacks trust? Insecurity is a cancer and can spread rapidly. An insecure leadership culture is a toxic culture where the wrong actions are rewarded while the right ones are punished. Is this leader insecure or simply disillusioned? This is an important distinction. If someone is insecure there's nothing a change agent can do to shift that core fear. Insecurity can only be solved by building trust in the quality of relationship that they have with their seniors or their direct reports. If they are disillusioned on the other hand, there is a chance that with the right incentive and inspiration, they will be ready to forge ahead towards a better future.

What are some options to consider while dealing with leadership fatigue? When one meets leaders who are distracted by budget cuts, or worried about the mission when they're worried about people leaving, or they are worried about deadlines, the best thing to do is to show empathy for their current challenges. Empathizing goes a long way in that situation. Instead of focusing on the leader him/herself and asking for a change it is good advice to shift the focus from them to a situation around them or near them where they feel they can have more power and make more impact. So, shift the focus. The leader is probably not going to change their reality right now in the short term. However, shifting to something in their ecosystem that they can actually help improve will get the real results that are needed in the long run.

Leaders who have transformation fatigue need a thought partner, a trusted advisor, a wing man so to speak, who can advise, guide and coach them either in explicit terms or more subtly. It really depends on the relationship between the leader and the thought partner. They want this person to observe and provide specifics, be their eyes and ears on the ground not as a spy as much as a different perspective. That way they can actually impact change because they get concrete advice from such thought partners. These thought partners can nudge leaders along and help them navigate and change their ecosystem one small step at a time.

What about organization fatigue? Sometimes a change agent must recognize that they cannot win against the tide of organization fatigue. So, one must simply help the organization leverage whichever Agile framework to tell its story however ugly it may be. One thing Agile does really well is highlight the ugly early and often so that it might be removed or changed to something beautiful. When enough ugly stories are told, then the organization must look in the mirror. This groundswell movement is more powerful than one might think. It can shift the inertia. It can convert fake speed to effective speed. Doing this means that as a change agent one needs to get real with one's expectations of the rate of change. It takes a long time and several circular roads before we can nudge an organization towards a better culture. Getting real with this is crucial for a change agent's sanity.

Dealing with all this fatigue can lead to burn out. One way to combat this is to find the company of change champions who continue to inspire people within their ecosystem. Whether these change champions are within the organization or outside does not really matter. This type of stimulus is needed so that others can be inspired to go into their respective organizations every single day hoping that those little tiny nudges that they try to make within their ecosystem is eventually going to shift that company's culture. It will eventually become a place where people are able to thrive and excel.

As the esteemed Edwards Deming said, 85% of the reasons for failure are deficiencies in the systems and process rather than the employee (Deming, 1982). The role of management is to change the process rather than badgering individuals to do better. This is fundamental to why fatigue occurs. This is fundamental to why Scrum values do not thrive, and this is fundamental to why the promise of Scrum has remained a fantasy rather than a reality.

3 KEY RECOMMENDATIONS TO RESET YOUR TRANSFORMATION

How does one remove this wrinkle in Scrum? Where does one start? How does one not try to fix teams but trying to fix everything else around the team? Most software development teams want to do well. Most teams want to come in every day and do great work. The most common reason for disruption to occur at the team level is because they cannot say no to the change(s) being thrust upon them. Teams usually sit at the lowest level of the organization while leadership sits at a much higher level. Leaders have the prerogative to say "No" to change while teams do not. Leaders usually say no to changing themselves but are gung-ho to change teams because if they have to start a change it is so much easier to change someone else. It is this author's belief that the first step to fixing a vicious cycle of failed transformations and the failed promises is to start fixing the ecosystem around the team and leave the team alone. Give the team the right ecosystem and they will do well.

Visualize Work

Visualizing work within the organization brings transparency to the question of where the budget is being spent and who is working on what. When there is transparency to this, higher quality conversations can occur. The organization can be much more intentional about the choices they make and understand what's keeping them busy. They can evaluate whether what's keeping them busy is also providing value and keeping them productive. Understanding what's going on will also control how much is going on. Too much in progress work is what keeps organizations busy and unable to stop and be more intentional. Too much work also spreads teams too thin and it often leads to slower results. Being intentional means working on the right things that allow the right folks to come together for the right initiative and for magic to happen (SAFe, 2019).

Build Resilience

What causes so much work? Besides just trying to keep up with new opportunities, it is the maintenance of the old. Maintenance on legacy systems, legacy business processes, and legacy culture can slow an organization down tremendously. Organizations should build strength within their ecosystem. This strength comes in many forms. Strength in the right platforms, right business processes, right skills, right speed—all these lead to the Agility that enterprises desperately need to survive in today's world. When an organization does all this then it becomes obvious that the organization understands how to walk the walk and not simply be an inane mouthpiece. This is when teams truly thrive because now they have an environment where they can clearly comprehend their purpose and see the value—connect the dots. This organization allows the team to explore their autonomy, become masters of their craft. This organization gives the team the breathing room it needs to grow. When an organization greases the environment so that teams can truly fly then they have earned the right to worry about whether they should do Scrum, Kanban, or You Name It Scaling Framework for teams.

Remove Silos

Lastly, siloes between business and IT and silos even within IT have plagued productivity and in the long run, toxic culture grows and unfortunately stays. Removing these siloes is a journey and is fraught with perceived risks on both sides so it will take not one but several leaps of faith for both parties to work together on a common purpose. Perceived risks are a natural byproduct of a poorly planned transformation. Perceived risks occur when we embark on a transformation journey without thinking through on how to sustain that transformation. Sustainability is tightly coupled with the institutionalized risk and reward system. Change the risk and reward system to encourage new mindset and behaviors. Without changing the risk and reward system of the old ways, implementing new ways is a colossal waste of energy and time. This might take a while and it might make those who want to see changes quickly impatient. However, if one wants to see *sustained* changes, take the time to do it the right way.

You succeed only when you fly with ease

You must first learn new ways to succeed

You must remove noise, to learn

You must have patience, to remove noise

You must go slow, to build patience

You must accept that you must go slow *(Aruna Chandrasekharan,2018)*

REFERENCES

Bastone, N. (2018). *The 29 tech companies with the best company culture in 2018*. Retrieved from https://www.businessinsider.com/best-tech-companies-to-work-at-glassdoor-2018-11

ChandrasekharanA. (2018). *Transformation Fatigue*. Retrieved from https://www.agilealliance.org/resources/sessions/the-inevitability-of-enterprise-agile-transformation-fatigue-how-do-you-reset-2/

Crosby, P. (2019). *How to recognize and prevent Transformation Fatigue*. Retrieved from https://theuncommonleague.com/blog/transformation-fatigue

DemingE. (1982). Retrieved from https://deming.org/quotes

Fe, S. A. (2019). *Principle #6 – Visualize and limit WIP, reduce batch sizes, and manage queue lengths*. Retrieved from https://www.scaledagileframework.com/visualize-and-limit-wip-reduce-batch-sizes-and-manage-queue-lengths/

Freud, S (1917). *A difficulty in the path of psycho-analysis*. Academic Press.

Handscombe, C., Allan, J., Khushpreet, K., Belkis, V., & Ahmad, Z. (2018). *How to mess up your Agile Transformation in 7 easy (mis) steps*. Retrieved from https://www.mckinsey.com/business-functions/organization/our-insights/how-to-mess-up-your-agile-transformation-in-seven-easy-missteps

Holiday, R. (2016). *5 Deadly Kinds of Ego That Prey Upon Your Success*. Retrieved from https://www.entrepreneur.com/article/276972

Hsia, H. C. (2018). *Common Misinterpretations of Scrum*. Retrieved from https://www.scrum.org/resources/blog/common-misinterpretations-scrum

Job, J. (2019). *7 Vital Differences between Agile Adoption and Agile Transformation*. Retrieved from https://responsiveadvisors.com/blog

Livni, E. (2018). *I was a contract worker in Google's caste system—and it wasn't pretty*. Retrieved from https://finance.yahoo.com/news/contract-worker-google-caste-system-144104055.html

Lock, D. (2019). *14 symptoms of change fatigue*. Retrieved from https://daniellock.com/14-symptoms-of- change-fatigue/

Mackay, J. (2019). *Context switching can kill up to 80% of your productive time (here's what to do about it)*. Retrieved from https://blog.rescuetime.com/context-switching/

Mautz, S. (2019). *These 5 Toxic Factors Cause People to Quit Even Before They Have Another Job, According to a Recent Study*. Retrieved from https://www.inc.com

Merriam-Webster.com Dictionary. (n.d.a). *Culture* Retrieved from https://www.merriam-webster.com/dictionary/culture

Merriam-Webster.com Dictionary. (n.d.b). *Fatigue*. Retrieved from https://www.merriam-webster.com/dictionary/fatigue

Mersino, A. (2019). *Most Agile Transformations Will Fail*. Retrieved from https://vitalitychicago.com/blog/most-agile-transformations-will-fail/

Mitchell, I. (2018). *Twenty Top Fails in Executive Agile Leadership*. Retrieved from https://www.scrum.org/resources/

Peterson, O. (2019). *What is Fake Agile? Understanding the Dark Side of Agile and How to Avoid It*. Retrieved from https://www.process.st/fake-agile/?utm_campaign=Submission&utm_medium=Community&utm_source=GrowthHackers.com

Prokopets, M. (n.d.). *The 5 Scrum Values and Why They Matter*. Retrieved from https://usefyi.com

ScrumAlliance.Org. (2017-2018). *State of Scrum Report, Scaling and Agile Transformation*. Retrieved from https://www.scrumalliance.org/learn-about-scrum/state-of-scrum

Scrum.Org. (n.d.a). *Scrum Values*. Retrieved from https://www.scrum.org/resources/what-is-scrum

Scrum.Org. (n.d.b). *What is Scrum*. Retrieved from https://www.scrum.org/resources/what-is-scrum

14. th Annual State of Agile Report. (2020). Retrieved from https://stateofagile.com/#ufh-i-615706098-14th-annual-state-of-agile-report/7027494

UnknownA. (n.d.). Retrieved from https://www.reddit.com/r/quotes/comments/

Van Der Star, A. (2017). *Team Morale and team happiness indicators.* Retrieved from https://www.productowneroftheyear.com/team-morale-and-team-happiness-indicators/

Vinje, N. (2018). *Do Team Building Exercises Really Work?* Retrieved from https://glideconsultingllc.com/team-building-exercises-really-work/

Wikipedia. (2020). Retrieved from https://en.wikipedia.org/wiki/Value_(ethics)

Chapter 5
Integrating Scrum Processes Into SDLC Maintenance and Enhancement Projects

Jacqueline H. Jewkes
Independent Researcher, USA

ABSTRACT

This chapter discusses the steps necessary to incorporate appropriate Scrum procedures into maintenance and enhancement projects on legacy systems, developed and maintained using a systems development life cycle (SDLC). It considers the benefits of introducing a more modular approach to system development, where the characteristics of existing systems have created interdependent modules, functions, and application architecture. Although these systems represent an investment in money, resources, time, and knowledge that make decommissioning them inexpedient, the process can and must be improved and incorporating Scrum procedures and practices will improve the success rate of maintenance and enhancements to these systems.

INTRODUCTION

Since the 1960s, most companies have developed information systems by using a Systems Development Life Cycle (SDLC) project structure, which is a sequential methodology involving planning, requirements analysis, design, development, testing and implementation of software (Ungvarsky, 2019). The SDLC development process brought order to the processes of creating information systems. As new functions were added to these systems the application architecture grew and evolved into large complex systems, with many interdependent modules. This complicated the maintenance and enhancement of these systems to keep up with changing business needs. Replacing these systems with newer more modular approaches is one solution, but incorporating newer methods, like Scrum, into the SDLC process can provide benefits that address some of the issues and improve success rates.

DOI: 10.4018/978-1-7998-4885-1.ch005

Copyright © 2021, IGI Global. Copying or distributing in print or electronic forms without written permission of IGI Global is prohibited.

BACKGROUND

"A legacy system is an information system that is built in the past using technology of that time, and that continues to be used" (Gangadharan et al, 2013). Many institutions are faced with decisions related to decommissioning their existing and still functional legacy systems or of creating process improvements to extend the life of these systems.

The complexity, cost, and time to replace these systems with newer, more modular, approaches can be prohibitive. Gangadharan (2013) suggests "that software characteristics, development methods, dependency of systems, lock-in, system complexity, new technologies and system ownership influence the decision whether to decommission or to maintain a system." These factors associated with decommissioning a legacy system indicate that identifying improvements in project processes may be a more viable option for many companies. Crotty and Horrocks (2017) indicate that in the financial services industry some estimates put system maintenance as high as 75% of IT budgets. Reducing that cost, while increasing the ability to add additional functionality to existing systems is key to extending the life of legacy systems. In order to accomplish this, the issues related to current processes need to be identified.

Historic Issues with Legacy Projects

Legacy project challenges include cost overruns, missed deadlines, requirements changes, and worst of all, project cancelation that means a great deal of resources, time, and money has been completely wasted (Kaleshovska et al., 2015). Khan and Beg (2012) point out the additional issue of poor quality of the resulting products. In more recent years, the challenges of coordinating offshore teams with onshore employees has added to the complexity of all issues. New projects integrated into aging systems and application architecture have impacted cost, deadlines, testing, and risk management. User engagement and involvement has been an issue where a user, mainly concerned with day-to-day issues, finds it difficult to commit to a large project where there may be no visible results for months, or even years. The end results may be disappointing to users who have not been closely involved throughout the process.

Kaleshovska et al. (2015) use the following results from the Standish Group, a Boston based research firm, to illustrate the historic success rates of software projects, between 1994 and 2012. The results from this report consolidate the success/failure rate in software projects in three categories:

> **"Project success** - projects completed on time within the budget approved, containing the functionalities according to specification.
> **Project challenged** - projects completed, but either beyond the budget approved, or longer than planned and/or not fulfilling some of the functionalities initially specified in the scope of the project.
> **Project impaired** - projects that were cancelled at some point in time after commencement." (Kaleshovska et al., 2015).

The results indicate an improvement in project success, but that improvement rate went from 16% to 39%. The project challenged rate went down, but still only reduced the challenged rate from 53% to 43%. The project impaired rate went from 31% to 18% but canceling 18% of projects after they begin is still quite high. Clearly this indicates that the issues with traditional project procedures and processes need to be addressed, by looking at each step of the process to identify issues.

Legacy systems projects traditionally followed a sequential (Waterfall) pattern. This has meant that "organizations rooted in traditional 'Waterfall' software development employed heavy upfront project design and limited changes and feedback during and between project stages" (Mahadevan et al., 2015). The obvious drawback to this approach is that the pace of change at the business and technological level makes the complete and final definition of requirements, before a project begins, an impossible task for a large project. According to Maruping, et al. (2009), changes in business needs "are occurring with increasing frequency and speed in an ever more competitive market environment (Lansiti & Mac-Cormack, 1997)." This may account for the 18% of projects, mentioned above, that are canceled after commencement.

Replacing legacy systems with newer approaches and methods may seem to be the obvious solution, but "legacy systems cannot be simply discarded because they are important for the business they support and encapsulate a great deal of knowledge and expertise regarding the application domain" (Aversano & Tortorella, 2004). By analyzing the SDLC process and the Scrum process we can identify areas where Agile Scrum is able to improve the outcome.

SDLC PROCESS ANALYSIS

The Systems Development Life Cycle (SDLC) is a planned, sequential series of steps that enable the design and development of software systems. "These steps include system planning, system analysis, system design, implementation and deployment, system testing and integration, and system maintenance" (Ungvarsky, 2019). Each step is completed before the next step begins. Dubey et al. (2015) defined the typical stages of an SDLC approach as:

1. "Planning and analysis of requirements.
2. Defining requirements.
3. Designing the software architecture.
4. Developing the product.
5. Testing it.
6. Deployment in market & maintenance."

Planning and Analysis of Requirements

The SDLC process begins with a discussion of user/business requirements. "From top to bottom all the necessities of the system to be developed are captured in this fragment and documented in a prerequisite specification document" (Dubey, et al. 2015). Project estimates of cost and resources are created. It is assumed that user requirements, even for a large project, can be determined at an early stage and will remain static throughout the life of the project. That means cost and timeframes are predictable. Unfortunately, given the nature and volitivity of business needs and, for many industries, regulatory requirements and regulatory changes, determining specifications, cost, and an exact time-frame up-front is unlikely to be successful for most projects. In addition, the results of this process are broad requirements that may be open to interpretation and do not define interim deliverables. As the success rates previously discussed indicate, complete definition of a large project up-front is not often successful.

Designing the Software Architecture

The business requirements provide input to the next phase, the high-level design. The HLD is an area that is costly, requires a lot of time, and assumes complete business requirements at the start of the project. This is an area that is exposed to cost overruns as requirements change, or worse still, the project is canceled. It is also the part of the project that sets expectations for deadlines and project cost

During the HLD phase of a project, the system architects are involved to identify designs that are not compatible with existing architecture and/or the structural changes that will be required within the architecture. For large legacy systems, the system architecture is not limited to external technical, application independent, structure. It includes application structure and an application expert needs to be assigned the role of application architect. The application may involve large numbers of interdependent program modules. This may be one of the greatest obstacles to converting older processes and systems to support new projects and use new procedures.

Traditionally the HLD defines the deliverables for the complete project. By aligning the HLD with the structured business requirements, we have also defined interim deliverables. Following the HLD phase, the detail design is completed.

"The practical development of software design starts in terms of writing program code in the suitable programming language and developing error free executable programs efficiently" (Sharma, 2017). Detail design has always been an expensive and time-consuming phase of any project. In some cases, the detail design goes beyond a description of changes to existing modules, or a design description for new modules, to the level of code or simulated code. The detail design is then reviewed before coding begins. One reason for this approach is the varying level of expertise among technical team members, who may reside in multiple locations.

Developing the Product and Testing It

Coding and unit testing, sometimes called technical testing, are mainly controlled by the programming members of the team. "Module testing (or unit testing) is…a process of testing the individual subprograms, subroutines or procedures in a program. Its purpose is to check if the module contradicts the system internal specifications" (Li, E., 1990). A test region must be maintained to aid module testing and keeping it up-to-date and usable can be a challenge. The testing in this region is module specific but may include tests of module linkage. The use of a separate unit test region is a traditional approach that has value keeping higher test regions clean and identifying issues quickly.

Integration and User Testing

"Also called interface testing, incremental testing or string testing, integration testing is a process of merging and testing program modules to see if they can work correctly as a whole without contradicting the system's internal and external specifications" (Li, E., 1990). Integration and user testing are the final stages of an SDLC project before implementation. Integration testing involves executing modules in an established test system region that can be run in an automated fashion.

JIRA is a software systems package designed to provide defect tracking for software development teams (Li, P. 2015). During integration and user testing, using software developed to track software defects, like JIRA, can help to control the log of issues identified and ensure the correction of identified issues.

It should be noted here that large legacy systems, developed over a period of years, were often customized to meet the needs of new customers, and not in a modular way. This presents unique challenges for testing and when creating a robust test environment. For each new project, the test system process must be reviewed to identify modules and/or functionality that are impacted by this project. Building additional functionality into test systems over time, should provide on-going improvements to the test regions.

In a legacy environment issues related to interdependencies arise. These issues may be related to an interdependency created over time between the modules within the system or to interdependencies with outside systems that provide input to the system or receive data from it. In an SDLC project these issues may not be discovered until integration testing and the impact can be severe. The result may be large cost overruns or even project cancellation, creating a loss of the entire amount of time, resources, and money expended thus far.

User testing is the final stage before implementation. At this point the involvement of the end-user is required. "The newly developed software system is executed in as near the user's operational environment and host computer configuration as possible" (Li, E., 1990). The test environment must be identical, or nearly identical, to the production environment and the end user needs to verify that the product being delivered meets their needs. If communication has been ongoing, there should be no surprises, but in the real world, that is unlikely. In an environment where user involvement occurs at the beginning and end of a project, there will inevitably be surprises and the resolution of these issues may have a major impact on the project outcome.

Shikha Verma (2014) states that the strengths of a waterfall approach are that it is simple, controllable, and is consistent with many technology practices, and the weaknesses are that it is inflexible, does not support iterations, delivers results late in the process, and user feedback is not part of the process until the very end. Scrum addresses these weaknesses.

SCRUM PROCESS ANALYSIS

Scrum is an Agile process that has been used in software development since the 1990s, but the history of Agile approaches goes back further to applications outside the realm of software development. In 1986, an article in the Harvard Business Review identified companies that were using innovative manufacturing techniques to create new products faster and in a more flexible manner than their competitors (Takeuchi & Nonaka, 1986). The authors describe the old methods of production as a relay, or sequential process, while these innovative companies were using a process that involved small select multi-disciplinary teams moving forward together in a flexible environment that allows overlapping phases to continue at the same time, rather than waiting for a hand-off from a prior phase. Takeuchi & Nonaka (1986) describe this approach using the analogy of the rugby approach to a team moving forward as a unit and passing the ball back and forth. The article used Fuji-Xerox, Honda, and Canon as examples of companies that used this approach to bring innovative products successfully to market at a much faster pace than their previous products (Takeuchi & Nonaka, 1986). This flexible adaptive process has been used successfully "for organizing and managing work associated with hardware development, marketing programs, and sales initiatives" (Rubin, 2013). The ability to be used in such varied environments attests to the flexibility of the process.

In 1993, after considerable research into methods used by the Takeuchi article and those used by other companies, Jeff Sutherland, applied the approaches he had studied to a software project. "Sutherland created a new way of developing software; honoring the rugby imagery, he dubbed his approach 'scrum'" (Rigby, Sutherland, & Takeuchi, 2016). Scrum is one of a group of innovative processes developed in the 90s, including extreme programming (XP), and dynamic-systems-development method (DSDM). Together these approaches have been called Agile to represent a new more dynamic approach to software development.

Scrum is not a strict set of procedures to be followed. "Agile development is suitable when there is a high degree of uncertainty and risk in a project that arises from frequently changing requirements and/ or novelty of technology used" (Mahadevan et al., 2015). It is a framework that can be used to create a process that is unique to the company and project to be undertaken. Scrum recognizes that uncertainty and change are inevitable in a large software project, and more so if the project is maintenance or enhancement to an existing legacy system. Business volatility and unknown interdependencies make creating firm project requirements at the beginning impossible. Scrum works with this reality to create usable interim products that are not lost when roadblocks are encountered, or changes are made.

A Scrum project begins with planning at multiple levels. Overall user requirements are used to create a prioritized backlog of functions to be developed. Scrum relies on this prioritized list of desired features and capabilities which allows the development team to always work on the highest priority items and on short daily team meetings to evaluate progress. This process allows small complete deliverables of the most important features. It is an adaptable system that produces usable products in the short term even when priorities or resources prevent the entire project from completing. Daily meetings allow the team to spot issues quickly and the multi-dimensional team allows creative responses to those issues.

Small cross-functional teams work on each prioritized item, performing all the tasks required for designing, building and testing that item. They produce a usable product and multiple teams can be engaged to complete items concurrently (Rubin, 2013). Multiple teams may be developing items from the backlog concurrently.

The team includes a product owner, Scrum Master, and the development team. By having a product owner involved in the team, issues and miscommunication can be minimized. The Scrum Master is well versed in the values and processes of Scrum and acts as a leader and coach to the development team.

Each team will work on a requirement from the backlog broken down into segments that can be completed in two to four weeks. Each of these periods is called a sprint and multiple sprints may be required to create a usable function, ready for deployment. Coding and testing occur within the sprint. The latest releases of JIRA include additional support for Agile/Scrum processes for the tracking of defects and issues (Li, P., 2015).

Deployment in Market & Maintenance

By developing functions in short sprints of 2-4 weeks, reviewing the test results after each sprint, and combining sprints into a release to be installed, the project team can deliver usable results in an ongoing manner. Agile is a flexible approach that can accommodate this situation by developing modules in sprints but installing multiple sprints as a release. The length of sprints and the number of sprints included in a release are flexible.

By keeping a maintenance backlog list, maintenance items can be prioritized within an enhancement project, or can be combined into a maintenance project. These are areas where the flexibility of Scrum design can be adapted to the needs of a system or a project.

SDLC vs. SCRUM

By looking at the project life cycle to determine where another approach, such as Scrum, could create benefits, even for projects that involve enhancing and maintaining existing large systems, a method to extend the life of valuable systems can be found. This analysis will identify processes that lend themselves to Scrum adaptation, and which are not compatible.

The main features of the SDLC process are a sequential organization that requires up-front complete definition of the project and a multi-team structure that sequentially addresses the phases of the project from definition, coding, testing and implementation. The product owner is involved in the definition phase, and then at the end to certify results just prior to implementation.

A Scrum project is structured with a multi-dimensional team that develops deliverables from beginning to end in an iterative process that allows multiple deliverables to be developed simultaneously by multiple teams. End-user participation in the team ensures that the prioritization of project requirements meets the immediate needs of the data owner first, the smaller size of each deliverable, and the daily meetings to evaluate progress provide a more flexible method of systems development. Table 1 identifies the main characteristic differences between SDLC and Scrum.

Table 1. Comparison of SDLC with Scrum

SDLC Process	Scrum
Sequential	Iterative
Entire project definition complete upfront	Small incremental steps defined and implemented
Customer involvement at the beginning and the end	Project customer-driven throughout the life of the project
Separate teams addressing each step of the project	Multi-functional teams work together to create holistic solutions
Teams based on function: Design/Coding/Testing of the entire project	Team members represent all functions and deliver a usable feature of the project in a short time.
Deliverables at the end of the project	Prioritized deliverables progressively throughout the project
Interdependencies may not be recognized until the end of the entire project	Small deliverables will identify interdependencies sooner, with less overall impact

However, it must be considered that "with agile methods, development begins before the requirements are well defined. In complex and/or large projects, this approach is potentially crippling, because important features might be forgotten or misunderstood" (Barlow et al. 2011, p. 28). The introduction of Scrum into the life cycle of a project must done by considering the advantages of Scrum along with the needs of the business unit.

The use of sprints and daily Scrum meetings may address this problem. These meetings identify issues quickly, and defects can be cataloged and tracked. The presence of the data owner on the team allows immediate prioritization of issues, possibly even leading to a change in requirements to prevent the issue. Issues can be addressed in a holistic fashion, not just from a technical view.

"Agile methods seem to be more suitable for new product development projects than maintenance projects" (Ihme, 2012). Recognition of this fact of life may require adjustments to Scrum procedures, particularly in the testing area, to control the level of risk involved in integrating new functions into older systems, but still allow some benefits to be realized. Testing may need to be more extensive in a legacy environment and involve testing functions that may appear outside the scope of the immediate sprint.

The use of Scrum methods does not exclude planning on a project level. An overall plan is required to know if the short sprints/releases are heading in the right direction, and a timeframe estimate is needed to assess progress. Scrum requires a change in thinking about the HLD process that does not consider it as a predictable, static, entity. It must be viewed as a changing process that will be updated as needed. While Scrum anticipates obtaining early usable results by not defining the whole project up-front, the planning, analysis, and estimation phase of an SDLC project cannot be eliminated, nor should it be. Business units expect to maintain the ability to estimate the cost and timeframe of a project, regardless of the structure of the project process. "Such expectations are quite reasonable. But expectations of accountability of software developers are also reasonable and, like it or not, companies will require it" (Armour, 2014). One issue with SDLC processes has been that estimates may be treated as commitments, rather than a range of possibilities based on the risk inherent in the project (Armour, 2014). While companies will, and should require accountability, a realistic view of the estimation process is required whether the system is SDLC or Agile.

It should be noted that "too many waterfall [SDLC] projects failed because they did too much planning and likewise agile projects failed because they had less planning" (Shenoy, 2019). A balance must be struck in the project definition phase. However, the structure of the initial project requirements document can be improved, from the traditional SDLC definition, so that it leads into flexible structured phases later in the project.

Accepting that hard end-dates may be an unrealistic approach is a necessary part of the transition. For regulatory requirements compliance projects, the exposure to penalties for non-compliance need to be mitigated in the initial planning stages. Minimal requirements need to be defined and temporary manual solutions may be needed to bridge the gap between the regulatory deadline and the possibility of incomplete software.

Improving this requirements analysis process involves a change in thinking that accepts that project requirements and priorities do change. "The modern reality of software development is that change is unavoidable and must therefore be explicitly accommodated in the life cycle. It is not an error that must be fixed; it's a natural aspect of system construction" (Laplante & Neill, 2004). Defining requirements in a manner that considers interim short-term deliverables, can ensure that any part of the project that is successfully completed will be a usable product. Part of this process is the prioritizing of these deliverables, so the most needed functionality is produced in the shortest amount of time. This is true whether this project is strictly maintenance and correction of existing issues or is adding new functionality to existing systems.

The view of Maruping et al. (2009, p. 382) is that "the ability to respond to changes is embedded within the specific processes that make up each agile methodology (Conboy 2009, Fowler and Highsmith 2001, Larman 2003)". The whole process of designing and developing a large project by identifying high-priority, short-term deliverables, reduces the impact of the inevitable changes to user requirements. The content and sequence of releases can be adjusted to meet changing client requirements, without negating the releases that have already been implemented.

Project cancellation happens. Historically, this sad occurrence has caused a complete waste of time and money for the company, and a demoralizing impact on the team. By delivering usable products on a short-term release schedule, the cost and time loss for the company is reduced and the impact on team morale is minimized.

Implementing deliverables as frequently as every two weeks may not be desirable in a large legacy system. There is always an element of risk involved in production software installs, due to the interdependence of many modules in older legacy systems, and this can be addressed by combining short deliverables (sprints in Scrum terms) into packages to create a release for production installs. This must be addressed in the testing phases. Testing in a legacy system of interdependent modules must include testing beyond the new functionality to prevent introducing new issues into these modules. Some level of regression testing of existing functions is required. Daily Scrum meetings can be used to provide transparency to other stakeholders and to identify issues quickly.

The variables related to expertise level and multiple locations are not likely to change. A method of controlling system risk, given these factors, is needed. A requirements definition and HLD structure that align with each other and create short deliverables may help. Daily Scrum meetings and a robust test environment may be the keys to a solution. While Scrum teams typically do not have a lead technical developer, it may be necessary to identify a senior technical programmer to guide and assist inexperienced members of the team, particularly if the team members reside in multiple locations.

Scrum Benefits for SDLC Processes

Scrum was designed for small projects, using small teams located in one location. As Hobbs & Petit (2017) point out, "There has been very limited research on the topic of large-scale software development projects using agile approaches (Dyba & Dingsoyr, 2008; Razavi & Ahmen, 2014)". That is particularly true of adding Scrum procedures to maintenance and enhancements projects, on systems that may be both large and aging legacy systems. Incorporating new products into existing systems architecture is an issue, but the nature of maintenance and enhancement projects complicates this further by requiring new or changed functions to integrate with existing application architecture. There are potential benefits to incorporating Agile/Scrum processes, into the SDLC design. Darrin and Devereux (2017) identify the following benefits: customer involvement in the entire project, short-term releases to demonstrate progress, the accommodation of changes, based on those releases, and that this approach allows options for both design and installation of releases and reduces risk.

Perhaps the most important benefit of Scrum, for legacy projects, is user satisfaction. Should priorities change, changing the requirements or even canceling the project will still produce a usable product. The development team benefits from the manageability of small units of work and the satisfaction of seeing short-term results. The lessons learned from previous project releases can improve the project as it progresses, and lower defect rates. Monitoring progress in an Agile environment is changed and improved by measuring success rather than conformity to the plan. In an SDLC project progress is measured based on adherence to the original plan, while in an Agile project progress is measured based on outcomes-usable deliverables (Mahadevan, 2015).

"Agile methods can achieve a high-level of satisfaction among all project stakeholders (users, customers, business managers, developers, and project managers) in terms of productivity, product quality, cost containment, time-to-market, and overall morale" (Waguespack, & Schiano, (2012). The nature of Scrum can improve the management of projects, and the transparency of progress and results, but it should be noted that even selective use of Agile/Scrum techniques will impact all project participants; users, management, technical team, and testers. Scrum processes will be better suited to some elements of the SDLC process than others.

Initial Scrum Training

One of the most important features of Scrum is that it is an iterative process that allows time for reflection on processes, successes, and failures so that learning is on-going, and procedures are adapted to create continuous process improvement. To achieve that valuable benefit, a thorough understanding of the goals of Scrum is required.

The role of Scrum master may be considered somewhat relatable to the traditional role of project manager. A project manager has the role of seeing that the project progresses, deadlines are met, and impediments to progress are removed. Typically, this involves Gantt charts that include detailed tasks with deadlines assigned to each one. Time-consuming status meetings are held to determine whether the dates are being met. The project manager does not have direct control over the team. He can report slippage in schedules, but he cannot dictate specific actions to be taken by team members.

Cohn (2009) indicates that the Scrum master runs the short daily Scrum meetings. While it is his job to remove impediments, he has no authority over team members, only over processes. He can determine that a process change is required in response to sprint failures, perhaps shorter or longer sprints, but he cannot assign a task to a team member. Cohn also considers that choosing a Scrum master based on a previous role may not be the best approach. A SRUM master should have some level of knowledge of the both the business and technical functions of the existing structure and the proposed new functionality. He should also be skillful in persuasion and influencing without authority or control.

By providing adequate Scrum master training, small workable teams can be created, and the Scrum master can train the team in the procedures of Scrum.

Large Legacy System Issues and the Impact of Scrum Procedures

Scrum processes do not emphasize documentation but for many industries, like banking and financial services, documentation and traceability are required, sometimes by law. Periodic audits of IT departments are undertaken by in-house auditors as well as out-side auditors who require complete documentation. This is an issue that must be addressed during project development. This is another area where Scrum processes need to be adapted to the needs of the business and the project.

It is a misconception that Scrum is anti-documentation. The goal in Scrum is to eliminate unnecessary documentation, but that does not preclude producing the required documentation to meet audit or legal requirements. Rubin (2013) considers several reasons for producing documentation in addition to legal requirements, for example, user guides, capturing important discussions, or providing documentation used as training for new team members. Scrum is adaptable.

Management and Employee Education

Integrating Agile Scrum procedures into well-established older systems requires both management and employee education and engagement. Reluctance on the part of management or employees to be open to new ways of thinking and operating can greatly reduce any beneficial effects that might be realized.

Clearly defining the goals of any change in thinking or processing will aid the transition. Starting with the end-user, the ability to see results sooner and the ability to adapt to changes in the business needs and priorities should be explained and emphasized. Strong business analysts can greatly assist in this process. For users with a big vision, adjusting to small incremental steps may be a difficult adjustment. Pointing out the failure rate of prior large projects may help, and the promise of seeing increased functionality, completed quickly, will also make the transition seem logical. Having a long-term plan is necessary to provide direction to the short-term deliverables, but creating short-term deliverables increases the possibility of success, while allowing the ability to react to changes in scope.

At the project team level, it is important the developers and testers involved in the daily Scrum meetings see the value in these meetings and do not just consider them an added annoyance to their daily life. They need to understand and agree to short meetings that encourage progress each day or identify impediments to progress. A Scrum meeting involves just 3 questions:

1.   What did you accomplish yesterday?
2.   What are you planning to do today?
3.   What impediments are preventing you from progressing?

A Scrum should not last more than 10 or 15 minutes. This is not the time for in-depth analysis of project issues or defects. It simply identifies impediments to progress and makes the entire team aware that there are issues. It takes a strong Scrum master to ensure that the meeting doesn't become a traditional status meeting, which would extend the time and lose the benefits of Scrum. It's easy for team members who do not buy-in to the concept, to not pay attention, requiring a lot of repetition of topics and slowing of progress. If the team is in multiple locations, the meeting may happen through video or phone conference calls and each team member needs to avoid distractions in their environment. It's up to the Scrum master to maintain the focus and keep the meeting moving. Other meetings of impacted parties may need to be scheduled to pursue an impediment to progress in greater detail.

For each project, Agile/Scrum activities need to be evaluated to determine which processes will improve the project success rate. If daily Scrum meetings prove to be too frequent, another schedule can be established. If the sprint duration is too short or too long, that can be adjusted. If releases to production of multiple sprints makes sense, that can be done. If addressing defects on JIRA requires a different meeting in a different timeframe and meeting attendees that can go into more depth on the defects, that can be done. "Collective team functioning, where each individual is aware of and invested in the activity of the team as a whole was seen to support feelings of personal security and control; feelings that seem to be absent in many instances of software development in teams" (Whitworth & Biddle, 2007). The team working together to determine these guidelines will increase the buy-in rate.

Employee Benefits, Motivation, and Job Satisfaction

As noted above, benefits to the team and the project also benefit the individual team members. In large legacy companies, issues with project failures have often led to an attempt by management to gain greater control of the process. By creating more forms to fill out and adding more meetings, they hope to create better outcomes. The view of team members is often that these additional procedures will slow a project down, without improving the outcomes. Work becomes tedious and motivation goes down. This, in turn, leads to high turn-over rates which are already a problem when dealing with off-shore contracting firms who control their own employee deployment and may shift people to other projects based on their needs, not the current client project.

Scrum offers the opportunity to increase motivation and job satisfaction. The benefits described above can convince team members that a cohesive, communicating, team can produce results that benefit each participant. There is nothing as motivating as success and experiencing frequent short-term wins benefits every level of the team as well as the whole project. Scrum doesn't eliminate the considerable challenges of adding new functionality to existing large systems, but it provides a holistic way of identifying them and increases the options for dealing with them.

Overhage and Schlauderer (2012) conducted a case study of the long-term use of Agile/Scrum and how well it was accepted by team members. It was conducted by interviewing team members with Scrum for an average of 4.5 years. The results showed that developers viewed Agile methods as improving time-to-market and improving meeting customer needs. They also indicated that the Scrum meetings identified issues quickly and led to team members helping each other to overcome impediments, team cohesion was built. Overall satisfaction was high. They were not satisfied with the up-front process. Scrum doesn't address the initial long-term planning that is needed for a company and a project to produce large quality products. They perceived Scrum as a change of lifestyle requiring a higher level of discipline to keep on-task every day. Developers viewed this as a negative to acceptance.

This was a case study in one company, but it does indicate that long-term acceptance, of Scrum methods, is possible and has advantages for projects and teams. It also pointed out some areas that require attention—initial long-term planning and changing the view of developers that a higher level of discipline is a negative.

SOLUTIONS AND RECOMMENDATIONS

Education

Agile/Scrum methods require a change in thinking. In a company that has been developing software using traditional sequential processes, possibly for decades, this change can be quite difficult. Education must begin at the company level, with management taking the lead in embracing the process. Management must recognize the need for product owner involvement in the entire process. End users need to see the benefits of receiving smaller, complete deliverables, but must also be assured that overall planning and cost analysis is not being abandoned. The product owner drives the process, defines the product, prioritizes the deliverables, and controls the outcome. The product owner cannot control the outcome unless they are involved in the entire process. Finally, the team members need to be educated to the processes that will change and know that they provide input into the structure and functions of the team. At all levels the flexibility to adapt Scrum to the current environment should be emphasized.

Analysis of Current Processes

Analysis needs to be done to determine the points where Scrum methods are feasible. Up front planning and design are still required to satisfy the business need for predictability of costs and functionality and to ensure accountability from the development team. However, these estimates should be treated as a range of possibilities, not an absolute guarantee of an outcome. When the project involves regulatory changes with a hard deadline, an alternate manual process may be needed to bridge the gap until the project can be completed.

Time spent in reviewing the current procedures and determining where Scrum practices would be beneficial and where they would not add value, can make the difference between success and failure.

Scrum is not a one-size fits all approach to software development. One advantage of Scrum is its flexibility, and that makes it possible to adapt it to any environment.

A detailed, prioritized log of deliverables is created, but unlike with SDLC, this need not be a complete list that encompasses all aspects of the overall project, and work can begin as soon as the highest priority items are identified. Care should be taken that this list consists of usable functions that can be implemented in one, or a few, iterations of the Scrum sprint.

Addressing Maintenance and Enhancement Issues

In a maintenance environment, the sprint may uncover interdependencies that were not originally recognized, but the ability to address backlog items and/or to add additional sprints is part of the system.

In the Scrum process, the SDLC functions of coding, technical testing, including integration testing, and user testing all take place at the sprint level and the multi-functional team can identify and resolve issues. In a maintenance environment integration testing is extremely important and the results could conclude that functionality is not worth the expense involved by the impact on other parts of the system or other systems. Unlike an SDLC project, this may mean removing one requirement, without jeopardizing the entire project.

Scrum is performing the same functions that an SDLC project performs, but they are done at a small modular level that produces usable results, even when the requirements change, or the project is cancelled. Multiple items can be in progress simultaneously, but it should be noted that maintenance of legacy systems may involve unexpected interdependencies at the module level. Multiple teams requiring access to the same module, needs to be addressed in the prioritization of the initial log items. The multi-functional team approach can be a benefit by having technical team members working with product owners throughout the process. When issues do arise, a plan can be adapted to the situation, and the identification of these issues related a small deliverable rather than at the end of the entire project is an enormous benefit to incorporating Scrum into maintenance and enhancement of legacy systems.

CONCLUSION

The historical success rate of software projects indicates that changes to the process are essential to meet the speed of change in market factors and technology. Scrum provides a flexible option to achieve both business and technical goals. The customer-driven approach gives control to the data-owner so that changes in requirements based on cost, company goals, regulatory requirements, or competitive market factors can be accommodated.

Decommissioning and replacing functioning legacy systems is a costly process that could cause the loss of a valuable product, and the investment of many years of effort. Adapting Scrum methods to large projects, that involve adding new functionality to existing legacy systems, as well as maintenance projects, is a more economical approach. This is possible even with the unique and interdependent application architecture usually found in large legacy systems. Scrum can be used to enhance the appropriate portions of the SDLC system process for adding new features to existing systems as well as processing maintenance in a more efficient way. Scrum processes are flexible and can be adapted to co-exist and enhance existing project life cycles. Time to market can be improved, and the ability to adapt to changes in requirements can be built into the process. The risk of undertaking a large project is mitigated by frequent usable deliverables, cutting losses. "Scrum is not a silver bullet or a magic cure (Rubin, 2013)," however its adaptability does make it a useful tool to address historic issues with legacy systems.

This study was done based on many years' experience in large banking and financial systems, informal interviews with current Scrum users in that industry, and reviews of relevant literature. Additional studies following companies' use of Scrum over time, for maintenance and enhancement of large legacy systems, are needed to provide definitive answers, but the empirical results so far indicate that Scrum can add value and improvements to these companies and projects.

REFERENCES

Armour, P. G. (2014). The business of software: Estimation is not evil. *Communications of the ACM*, *57*(1), 42–43. doi:10.1145/2542505

Aversano, L., & Tortorella, M. (2004). An assessment strategy for identifying legacy system evolution requirements in eBusiness context. *Journal of Software Maintenance & Evolution: Research & Practice*, *16*(4/5), 255-276.

Barlow, J. B., Keith, M. J., Wilson, D. W., Schuetzler, R. M., Lowry, P. B., Vance, A., & Giboney, J. S. (2011). Overview and guidance on Agile development in large organizations. *Communications of the Association for Information Systems*, *29*, 25–44. doi:10.17705/1CAIS.02902

Cohn, M. (2009). *Succeeding with Agile*. Addison-Wesley Professional. https://learning.oreilly.com/library/view/succeeding-with-agile/9780321660534/?ar=#toc

Crotty, J., & Horrocks, I. (2017). Managing legacy system costs: A case study of a meta-assessment model to identify solutions in a large financial services company. *Applied Computung and Informatics*, *13*(2), 175–183. doi:10.1016/j.aci.2016.12.001

Darrin, M. A. G., & Devereux, W. S. (2017). The Agile Manifesto, design thinking and systems engineering. *2017 Annual IEEE International Systems Conference (SysCon)*, 1-5. 10.1109/SYSCON.2017.7934765

Dubey, A., Jain, A., & Mantri, A. (2015, March). Comparative study: Waterfall v/s agile model. *International Journal of Engineering Sciences & Research Technology*, *4*(3). http://www.ijesrt.com

Gangadharan, G., Kuiper, E., Janssen, M., & Luttighuis, P. (2013). IT innovation squeeze: propositions and a methodology for deciding to continue or decommission legacy systems. In Y. K. Dwivedi, H. Z. Henriksen, D. Wastell, & R. De' (Eds.), *Grand Successes and Failures in IT. Public and Private Sectors. TDIT 2013. IFIP Advances in Information and Communication Technology, 402, 481-494.* Springer. doi:10.1007/978-3-642-38862-0_30

Hobbs, B., & Petit, Y. (2017). Agile methods on large projects in large organizations. *Project Management Journal*, *48*(3), 3–19. doi:10.1177/875697281704800301

Ihme, T. (2012). *Scrum adoption and architectural extensions in developing new service applications of large financial IT systems*. The Brazilian Computer Society. doi:10.100713173-012-0096-0

Kaleshovska, N., Josimovski, S., Pulevska-Ivanovska, L., Postolov, K., & Janecski, Z. (2015). The contribution of SCRUM in managing successful software development projects. *Economic Development / Ekonomiski Razvoj*, *17*(1/2), 175-194.

Khan, P. M., & Beg, M. M. S. (2012). Measuring cost of quality (CoQ) on SDLC Projects is indispensable for effective software quality assurance. *International Journal of Soft computing and Software Engineering*, *2*(9). doi:10.7321/jscse.v2.n9.1

Laplante, P. A., & Neill, C. J. (2004). "The demise of the Waterfall model is Imminent" and other urban myths. *ACM Queue; Tomorrow's Computing Today*, *1*(10), 10–15. doi:10.1145/971564.971573

Li, E. Y. (1990). Software testing in aa system development process: A life cycle perspective. *Journal of Systems Management*, *41*(8), 23–31.

Li, P. (2015). JIRA Essentials: Use the features of JIRA to manage projects and effectively handle bugs and software issues (3rd ed.). Packt Publishing.

Mahadevan, L., Kettinger, W., & Meservy, T. (2015). Running on hybrid: Control changes when introducing an Agile methodology in a traditional "Waterfall" system development environment. *Communications of the Association for Information Systems*, *36*(5). Advance online publication. doi:10.17705/1CAIS.03605

Maruping, L. M., Venkatesh, V., & Agarwal, R. (2009). A control theory perspective on Agile methodology use and changing user requirements. *Information Systems Research*, *20*(3), 377-399.

Overhage, S., & Schlauderer, S. (2012). Investigating the long-term acceptance of Agile methodologies: An empirical study of developer perceptions in SCRUM projects. *45th Hawaii International Conference on System Sciences*. 10.1109/HICSS.2012.387

Read, A., & Briggs, R. O. (2012). The Many Lives of an Agile Story: Design Processes, Design Products, and Understandings in a Large-Scale Agile Development Project. *2012 45th Hawaii International Conference on System Sciences, Maui, HI*, 5319-5328.

Rigby, D. K., Sutherland, J., & Takeuchi, H. (2016). The secret history of Agile innovation. *Harvard Business Review Digital Articles*, 2-5. https://hbr.org/2016/04/the-secret-history-of-agile-innovation

Rubin, K. S. (2013). *Essential Scrum: A Practical Guide to the Most Popular Agile Process*. Addison-Wesley.

Sharma, M. K. (2017). A study of SDLC to develop well engineered software. *International Journal of Advanced Research in Computer Science*, *8*(3).

Shenoy, A. (2019). Common misconceptions about Agile. *PM World Journal*, *8*(10), 1–4.

Takeuchi, H., & Nonaka, I. (1986). The new new product development game. *Harvard Business Review*, *64*(1), 137–146.

Ungvarsky, J. (2019). *Systems development life cycle (SDLC)*. Salem Press Encyclopedia of Science.

Verma, S. (2014). Analysis of strengths and weaknesses od SDLC models. *International Journal of Advance Research in Computer Science and Management Studies, 2*(3). http://www.ijarcsms.com/docs/paper/volume2/issue3/V2I3-0094.pdf

Waguespack, L. J., & Schiano, W. T. (2012). SCRUM project architecture and thriving systems theory. *2012 45*th *Hawaii International Conference on System Sciences*, 4943-4951. 10.1109/HICSS.2012.513

Whitworth, E., & Biddle, R. (2007). Motivation and cohesion in agile teams. In G. Concas, E. Damiana, & M. Scotto (Eds.), Lecture Notes in Computer Science: Vol. 4536. *Agile Processes in Software Engineering and Extreme Programming. XP 2007*. Springer. doi:10.1007/978-3-540-73101-6_9

Section 3
Significant Scrum Organizational Issues

Chapter 6
When Is It a Good Fit to Apply the Scrum Approach to Project Management

Edward T. Chen
University of Massachusetts, Lowell, USA

ABSTRACT

This chapter discusses how the method selected to manage a project can play a role in the success of that project. Certain projects are better suited to particular models of project management. The traditional, or "waterfall," approach; the agile approach; and a more refined agile approach known as Scrum, which will be evaluated. The Scrum approach to project management is gaining a lot of momentum in recent years but all projects may not be well suited for this method. By analyzing the different styles of project management, a discussion of the benefits and pitfalls of each approach will be completed as well as how those characteristics may contribute to risks. An examination of project types, project roles, and project management experience will be completed to provide insight for when the Scrum approach to project management is most appropriate to contribute to the overall success of a project and when it may be best to apply a different management style.

INTRODUCTION

The purpose of this research is to evaluate the traditional, agile, and Scrum approaches to project management, with a focus on Scrum, and assess their risks and benefits as an approach to achieve project success. As a fairly new technique, Scrum is becoming popularized as a project management style. There has been an increasing global trend towards pushing the limits on projects to achieve not only the objectives of the project but to also gain strategic and competitive advantages for the organization and to do so faster and more affordably (Meredith et al., 2018). The growing interest in the agile style of Scrum is no doubt tied to the increase of more complex and unpredictable projects, which aim to achieve more for a business (Fernandez & Fernandez, 2008).

DOI: 10.4018/978-1-7998-4885-1.ch006

Copyright © 2021, IGI Global. Copying or distributing in print or electronic forms without written permission of IGI Global is prohibited.

Adoption of the Scrum method, however, is not appropriate for all projects, and the type of project and the experience of the project management staff can help to steer project managers to the best approach for their efforts. While agile project management and Scrum, in particular, have their benefits and have proven to be a success in many types of projects, they are not without their risks and the use of them cannot always be applied successfully, especially by inexperienced project managers (Birkinshaw, 2018; Repenning et al., 2018; Taylor, 2016). With any project, there are several things to consider and by understanding the different approaches one can take and the benefits, as well as the pitfalls associated with each, organizations and project managers, can be sure to utilize the best method to contribute towards project success (Gonçalves et al., 2017). Further, understanding the objectives which are sought from the project and for the organization can help steer the most appropriate project management style to pursue.

There are several factors against which risks and benefits should be evaluated when deciding upon a project management approach, these include the project team, the company culture, the methods and techniques to be used, the environment in which the project is taking place, and the technology which will be utilized (Ozierańska et al., 2016). These elements are important to evaluate with any strategy, but with a refined model such as Scrum which is still a relatively new approach in project management, these become critical to determining if this framework is well suited to direct you towards project success. Only by understanding the project goals and objectives, the environment in which they will be operating, and the culture of the business which is facilitating the project, can a project manager be properly equipped to select the best approach, gain and retain the appropriate support from upper management, and ultimately deliver a successfully executed project (Aytac et al., 2019; Gupta et al., 2019).

BACKGROUND

Chan & Reich (2007) indicate that the IT environment is decided by the business process, the business side should tell how IT side should do to improve the business, however, Masa'deh et al. (2015) demonstrate that the IT environment and business should be on the same level. IT helps businesses to improve, while the business should also focus on the IT environment in the organization. Dennis et al. (2018) publish a book to discuss the whole steps of developing a system. There are several methodologies to develop the system, such as waterfall, V-Model, iterative development, agile, scrum, etc.

Leau et al. (2012) compare the differences between agile and traditional development methodologies. Meanwhile, Balaji and Murugaiyan (2012) also compare those two methodologies with V-Model. Agile is an advanced development methodology, there is an organization that maintains the standard manifesto of the agile. Highsmith (2002) introduces the agile development methodology. This methodology includes the client to the developing team to reduce the cost of changes to the requirements from the business side. Those changes are quite common in IT projects (Vijayasarathy & Butler, 2016).

Meredith et al. (2018) discuss the project management. In the discussion, Meredith et al. also indicate concepts about project management, such as the iron triangle, and several methods and tools to plan and simulate projects. Garel (2013) goes through the history of project management, form the pre-model to the standard model. Project management begins in the military in the 1980s, and then becomes standard and enters more fields in the mid-1990s. Carr (2003) indicates that "IT doesn't matter." Carr demonstrates that IT should be basic and in an important supportive place, so IT should not use new technology to try to pursue any kind of advantage. Nelson (2007) also demonstrates the new technology is one of the key reasons that led to the failure of IT projects. The rest three reasons are people, process, and product.

Dybå et al. (2014) point out two main objectives that IT projects have are uncertainty and complexity. The uncertainty is the frequent changes in the business side. The complexity is to meet the requirement from the business side. The IT project should be complicated enough to fit the requests. Agile is a flexible and dynamic developing methodology. Although agile methodology reduces the risk of the change from the business requirements, meanwhile, it also increases the complexity. Cockburn and Highsmith (2001) indicate that the agile methodology is actually closely related to humans, so human factors, such as developers and clients should be closely taken care of. Maruping et al. (2009) point out two important areas to control the developing process, one is the user requirement, and the other is the project team itself. Agile methodology has focused on the user requirement, however, project managers should find another way to manage the fast pace of the agile methodology.

Projects by their nature share common characteristics in that they have the same general objectives: a defined scope or set of deliverables, a specified timeline in which to produce those deliverables, and a budget within which they must remain (Meredith et al., 2018). In turn, measures of project success are derived from these three aspects of a project and a successful project is one that fulfills the required deliverables, within the specified timeline, and at or under the costs defined in the project budget (Rahman et al., 2018). To execute a project successfully, however, managers must make ancillary consideration for resource allocation, risk analysis, and project priorities as they relate to the core measures of scope, timeline, and budget (Gonçalves et al., 2016). For this reason, while these primary components of projects will be the focus of the discussion around project management approaches, there will be supplementary considerations put into the ancillary goals which are often tied to projects.

When deciding on the management approach to projects, a project manager must understand the strategic goals of the business as well as evaluate several different styles to project management since the model which is applied can both steer project success and lead an organization to attain a competitive advantage in their market (Mathur et al., 2013; Stoica et al., 2016). To understand the best management approach to utilize, one must first understand the different characteristics which define traditional and agile project management, as well as how Scrum is differentiated from basic agile methods. Taking this understanding of what a project is and how they are generally guided and measured, it is appropriate to describe three of the different approaches which may be utilized in the project management: traditional, agile, and Scrum.

TRADITIONAL APPROACH

The techniques of project management in their modern form were developed and driven by the military (Meredith et al., 2018). The traditional framework that was adopted as part of this modern project management entailed a linear development of a project solution, which would not be exposed until the final stage of a project. Also, there are no feedback cycles included in this approach (Fernandez & Fernandez, 2008). This classic model for project management often described as the "waterfall" approach, utilizes systematic and sequential steps such as planning, designing, development, testing, and deployment (Tanner & Mackinnon, 2015).

Waterfall methodology is a step-by-step methodology. Each step begins with the end of the last one. The deliverable of each step would come to hundreds of pages (Dennis et al., 2018). The largest advantage of this methodology is that all the step has a unified sight. All the steps are based on the deliverables from the last step. Meanwhile, this unification also leads to the disadvantages. When the requirements change, those changes will directly lead to the changes in the working sections (Leau et al., 2012). Because of the high unification of waterfall methodology, the changes will affect the whole steps, that will mess up all the plans of the project. To reduce the cost of rework on the same process, there comes the changed version of the waterfall methodology.

The waterfall framework, described as such for its batch release of product deliverables, has little interaction between the customer and development team after an initial requirement gathering phase (Meredith et al., 2018). Thus, project requirements must be well known and well documented in advance and communicated thoroughly with little to no intent to deviate from the defined project specifications (Williams et al., 2017). The need for detailed project deliverables is imperative as changes to the scope are not welcomed in the traditional approach. With this in mind, the risk assessment should be a primary factor of discussion early in the project and is extensively considered as part of the overall project planning process (Leau et al., 2012; Vijayasarathy & Butler, 2016).

AGILE APPROACH

Agile project management also follows a plan, yet the process is quite different from the traditional model as it takes a more iterative approach. One key difference to the agile approach from traditional methods is the idea of welcoming change into the project at any phase of the project development life cycle. To accommodate this acceptance of change, the framework for an agile strategy involves repeated phases, or sprints, of a partial solution release and includes a feedback loop (Fernandez & Fernandez, 2008). Each phase delivers a particular component of the project, which over time will result in the final collective product.

More emphasis is given to development teams working together to produce working software than following certain processes or entering data in a tool or writing extensive documentation. Processes and documentation are still needed, but the idea is that the methodologies do not drive things by the process or by the tools. Rather, the development team uses processes and tools to help the work of individuals. Documentation is important, especially when the development team is building some complex systems. Without documentation, it is hard to follow for new developers when there are thousands of lines of code. The contract should instead state that the project team is going to work in collaboration to create a working software. The team needs to be able to respond to changes uncovered during the development process than just blindly follow a plan. The main aspects of the agile method are simplicity and speed. Initially, the development team concentrates only on things that are most valuable to business and delivers the product fast. The team then enhances the product in the next iteration based on the feedback received (Stoica et al., 2013; Vijayasarathy & Butler, 2016).

This approach intends to complete a better and more affordable project faster than the traditional model (Tanner & Mackinnon, 2015). Due to the iterative characteristics of the agile approach, regular communication exists between clients and developers as well as project team members (Maassen, 2018). Communication is a driving force to the success of this approach and therefore transparency and shared knowledge must be a priority for all participants. This channel for frequent and open communication in the agile approach is essential to accommodate the flexible assignment of project deliverables (van Ruler, 2019).

SCRUM APPROACH

Scrum is a lightweight framework to manage projects using agile. Scrum is the most popular agile software development model. Scrum relies on self-organized teams. The product owner will identify and prioritize requirements (also called user stories) in the product backlog. The development team will work off the prioritized list of requirements. The development team will estimate and commit to a set of user stories to be delivered in an iteration (sprint). The product backlog is then re-prioritized at the end of an iteration and the next set of user stories are then selected for the next iteration (Almadhoun & Hamdan, 2020).

Scrum at its core is rooted in the agile method. Therefore, it shares many of the same characteristics but is a more refined technique to this model. The Scrum model stands by three elements: transparency, inspection, and adaptation (Schwaber & Sutherland, 2017). To support and facilitate these elements, Scrum sprints incorporate five distinct components: sprint planning, daily Scrums, development work, a sprint review, and finally, a sprint retrospective (Schwaber & Sutherland, 2017). Many of these are comparable to a typical cycle in the agile approach, however, this approach specifically calls for a daily Scrum, or a quick meeting, of the development team to discuss the plans for the next day. These structured daily meetings are a key piece of the Scrum iterative approach, which supports the idea of open communication and collaboration in an ever-developing project (van Ruler, 2019).

Where the traditional approach has a firm scope and approximated schedule, the Scrum approach has a firm schedule and flexible scope (Bick et al., 2018). This difference in the Scrum approach is what allows for a continuous cycle of development and release while incorporating feedback and learning. Another defining difference of the Scrum approach is the lack of a project manager. Within the Scrum model, the project team is comprised of a Scrum Master, a product owner, and the development team (Schwaber & Sutherland, 2017). With this alternative perspective to the team structure and in the absence of a project manager, participants must be self-organized and self-managed to complete their tasks and develop the requested product.

SYSTEM DEVELOPMENT ASSESSMENT

As with any project undertaking, some risks come with the benefits. The same is true of project management styles. Risk management is a critical piece of project management. Therefore, it must be included in the planning process and mapped out appropriately. In the absence of appropriate risk management, there can be any number of unforeseen obstacles to achieving project deliverables on time and the budget. There are tools, which can be utilized to help manage projects and mitigate risks, such as work breakdown structures and project management information systems (Rahman et al., 2018). These tools cannot altogether eliminate risk so this must become an important consideration in project planning. The following discussion will explore how the strengths and weaknesses of each project management approach can either be a source of, or solution for, project risk and why careful consideration must be employed when selecting the most appropriate project management model.

Project Management Using Traditional Approach

With the traditional approach to project management, there are some apparent strengths and weaknesses. Strengths of this approach include a clear definition of resource requirements and a fully mapped project schedule both of which are created at the beginning of the project (Fernandez & Fernandez, 2008). By mapping out the project in detail, business managers are provided the information they need to commit sufficient resources. The project plan ensures project managers have ample time to schedule and coordinate resources appropriately throughout the life cycle of the project. Establishing a full picture of the project early can be a powerful tool for understanding and visualizing how a project will progress throughout its lifecycle. It enables all team members to be on the same page at the start of a project.

Regular face-to-face interactions are not expected when utilizing this approach. By establishing deliverables upfront, team members do not need to be centrally located. Participants know what is expected and can continue to contribute to the project objectives without having to meet in person. This sort of project visualization can be extremely helpful in not only planning the project development process but also in devising a risk management plan for each step of the project. A work breakdown structure can be utilized to map tasks to be completed, assign a budget to those tasks, and develop contingency plans for managing potential risks. This and other project management tools can be especially helpful with a traditional framework so all team members, as well as upper management, can be aware of project expectations and milestones by which to measure project progress (Stoica et al., 2013).

The traditional approach also has its weaknesses and it can present difficult hurdles to overcome. One of the most challenging characteristics of this approach is it provides little room to accommodate a change in the project after the initial planning phase. Any changes to the scope of the project must be managed via a change order, which must be submitted in writing for review and approval by upper management (Meredith et al., 2018). Engagement and approval of such a request can significantly jeopardize a project timeline and budget. Thus, careful evaluation of the costs and benefits of tackling such a change in project deliverables must be weighed to make a responsible decision. With little room for adjustment built into the project budget and timeline, scope changes can be a serious risk for projects following this model. Extra effort must be put forth early in the project during the planning and requirements gathering phase to ensure all aspects of the project have been thought out, resources have been identified and scheduled, and there is a procedure in place to accommodate scope changes should they arrive.

Several tools can be used to help plan and therefore mitigate risks but with project deliverables not being released until the end of the project. This structure makes it difficult to guarantee customer satisfaction without some risk involved. Another strength that could also present itself as a risk is the ability of this approach to accommodate decentralized team members. This disconnect between participants can create a barrier to communication. Customers and developers typically have little interaction after initial planning occurs. It is difficult for customers to know if their expectations were communicated and interpreted correctly to deliver their vision of a successful project. Because regular feedback and communication are not part of this model, customers may find themselves unsatisfied once deliverables are produced during the deployment of a project solution (Vijayasarathy & Butler, 2016).

Project Management Using Agile Approach

This section will look at the agile approach to project management and identify risks and benefits inherent with this framework. One of the major differences between agile and traditional methods is where the traditional approach identifies all deliverables at the beginning of a project. The agile approach allows refinement of the scope as the project evolves (Williams et al., 2017). This ability to delay the finer details of the deliverables is accommodated by frequent, repeated loops of development, and the release of a partial solution. Regular exposure of partial solutions to the client is a major strength of this approach. Keeping clients engaged and allowing them to see the product evolve. This approach provides feedback to ensure that deliverables will meet the expectations of the customer. Project outcomes will be effective in their intended use and will earn value for the organization (Stoica et al., 2013; Williams et al., 2017).

This cycle of delivery and feedback also supports changes to the project scope. Consequently, the agile approach can be adopted knowing there is a reduced risk to the execution of satisfactory project deliverables. This can be an important trait, especially for projects with a potentially high return on investment for both customers and developers. Customers can obtain the desired product to improve their bottom line and the developer may attain a repeat customer. Another strength of this approach is that customers and developers can explore the best technology to apply for their solution. Through this continued evaluation and discovery of technology, team members on both sides are enabled to stay apprised of new technologies and incorporate them into the project solution when possible. Since the path to the final solution does not need to be mapped out at the project inception, the project team is free to explore different options in technology and identify the best tools to achieve optimal results. With software development projects in particular, by incorporating evolving technological advances into the project, and not being forced to define the solution in advance of the final release, companies can significantly reduce the risk of undertaking a project solution at the inception of a project, which may become obsolete by its conclusion (Stoica et al., 2016).

The agile approach and its heightened acceptance of flexibility is not without risk. While a large amount of flexibility has its appeal, this characteristic of the agile approach can also be considered a pitfall. With ample room to allow for changes in project scope, project deliverables cannot always be specified upfront. Therefore, it may be difficult to determine once a solution has been achieved (Fernandez & Fernandez, 2008; Waterman, 2018). With this amount of flexibility included in the project model, it takes a skilled project manager to ensure the team and the project stays on track. With each iteration of the project and each release of a partial solution, there must be an agreement upon what is considered acceptable for targets to be reached and for the project to continue forward. In the absence of established measures of success and acceptable performance standards, the risk of getting stuck and slowing project momentum can be a difficult hurdle to overcome. It can be easy for team members, and especially the customer, to constantly be seeking something more once a partial solution is delivered. There can be an almost infinite amount of refinement that can take place and only with well-defined terms of suitable deliverables at each phase can risks be managed (Lin et al., 2015).

An additional risk with the agile approach can be seen in a lack of managerial support. Where the traditional approach does not encourage change, the agile approach is constantly encountering change and this may be difficult to explain to project sponsors who may want and be more comfortable with, a clearly defined vision of the overall project (Waterman, 2018). Corporate managers may become frustrated with project managers who are continuously asking for more or modified resources to support their ongoing, ever-changing projects. In the absence of support from upper management, however, it can be increasingly difficult for the project manager to avail the team of necessary resources to support development throughout the project lifecycle (Meredith et al., 2018; Stoica et al., 2013).

The agile model facilitates the constant delivery of products while also supporting changes and modifications to scope. Therefore, it can be a challenge for all necessary resources to be identified as straightforward with this framework. The risks that come with poor resource allocation planning can be a serious obstacle to the overall success of any project. A project manager must keep communications current and relevant to upper management to safeguard that necessary resources, human or otherwise, are secure as the project team reaches each new phase of the project. An open line of communication between corporate and project managers is very helpful to support the continual fluctuation in project deliverables. Striking the right balance of planning, delivery, and communication can help to keep managers, project managers, and team members positive about project progress (Maassen, 2018). Retaining the support of not only management but also team members helps to keep project morale high and acts to motivate project participants. By keeping the lines of communication open and sharing relevant and timely updates with upper management, agile projects can continue to receive the support they need to ultimately achieve success (van Ruler, 2019).

Project Management Using Scrum Approach

Finally, this chapter will explore the Scrum approach and discuss the strengths, weaknesses, and associated risks involved with this model. The formal structure of Scrum itself can be a benefit to this refinement of the agile model in that it helps facilitate the adaptive and responsive nature of a changing project, which is not only supported but also valued by this framework (Sibona et al., 2018). As discussed, this highly flexible and responsive structure can be difficult for team members and even senior management to fully accept and adopt as a way of conducting business and it takes skilled participants to implement this approach (Lin et al., 2015). Scrum has specific events including sprint, sprint planning, sprint review, and sprint retrospective, all of which add structure to this free-flowing project approach (Schwaber & Sutherland, 2017).

Sprint Review

The sprint review and retrospective steps in the cycle play important roles to communicate and inspect progress as well as evaluate past performance as a mechanism to improve future development (Ozierańska et al., 2016). This is an important trait of sprints as it is imperative with this approach to not only develop and refine the product as the project progress but also to learn from experiences and evolve techniques for more efficient project development. Additionally, the sprint review provides an opportunity for members to reflect on changes in the marketplace and any potential impact this may play upon the overall outcome of the project (Schwaber & Sutherland, 2017).

During a sprint review, there may be determinations that production values have shifted and new plans may need to be implemented to keep the project relevant. This sort of mid-project change can be hard for businesses that may be more comfortable or familiar with a traditional model. But with agile, it is accepted, and with Scrum, it is specifically tasked as one of the defining elements of the project model. Incorporating the review and evaluation of changing market technologies as part of the Scrum framework ensures that projects following the Scrum approach stay current as they evolve through their life cycle. Another unique characteristic and strength of the Scrum approach is the team structure (Waterman, 2018).

The most notable difference in this model is the role of the Scrum master instead of a project manager and the difficulty of accepting the Scrum approach can be one of the driving forces behind this role (Schmitz, 2018). The Scrum Master is an essential function in this framework. Scrum master is not charged with managing the project but rather with seeing that the principles and theories behind

Scrum are maintained throughout the project life cycle (Srivastava & Jain, 2017). Staying focused on the principles of Scrum is essential if success is to be achieved with this model and is what differentiates it from the typical agile model. Having a skilled team member acting as the Scrum master is key to keep the project in focus.

Scrum Team

Scrum teams are intended to be small and centrally located allowing the Scrum master to more readily control and limit external distractions, which could impede the project progress. Additionally, the size of the team and location of members is meant to forge a path for easier project management concerning communication (Almadhoun & Hamdan, 2020). Communication is an essential part of the Scrum model and is demonstrated with the daily Scrums within a sprint cycle. With the fast-paced cycle of the Scrum approach, good communication stands as a mechanism of providing timely updates and reports, which are important to retain the support of upper management as well as project personnel (. Dybå & Dingsøyr, 2015; Friess, 2019; Meredith et al., 2018).

Another defining element of the Scrum team structure is that they are self-organized. Scrum team members make decisions about what tasks will be accomplished during each sprint based on the product backlog priorities established by the customer (Ozkan & Kucuk, 2016). This sort of empowerment enables participants to construct realistic assignments of work to keep the project progressing towards a final solution. It also acts to engage project participants and get them excited about their work. Each of these elements of Scrum helps to drive this model towards success but must be implemented correctly (Stoica et al., 2016).

Strengths and Risks

Some of the strengths of the Scrum approach can also be sources of risk with this framework. Starting with the autonomous structure, the Scrum team needs to be careful to avoid external interruptions during a sprint cycle. External interruptions can be a major source of risk when using the Scrum approach. Team members must be able to stay on task to accomplish the goals outlined in each sprint cycle. Interruptions may come in a variety of forms and can quickly derail progress on both a sprint and the project as a whole (Tanner & Mackinnon, 2015; Werder & Maedche, 2018).

As part of the Scrum framework, at the start of each sprint, the backlog items to be tackled within that cycle are defined and they are not changed during that cycle without risking project progress. Team members must communicate about their priorities throughout the project life cycle, commit to these tasks, and stay focused on their assignments for each sprint (Srivastava & Jain, 2017). There is a potentially serious risk that also comes from team members who may not be exclusively devoted to the project. If tasks or duties external to the project are demanded of members of the development team mid-cycle, the interruption to the project can again seriously derail progress (Tanner & Mackinnon, 2015).

It is imperative of the Scrum master to keep external obstacles away from project team members to ensure that the project continues forward with little interruption and can be completed successfully (Schwaber & Sutherland, 2017). If the Scrum master loses sight of this task and lets project members become influenced by an external interruption, the risk to project success grows significantly. Lastly, with the Scrum approach, there is a dependence on daily face-to-face meetings to facilitate open communication (Friess, 2019; Werder & Maedche, 2018).

This is a strength that can also present itself as a risk. With a need for in-person communication, Scrum becomes difficult to scale up to larger projects where teams may not be centrally located and virtual meetings are more commonplace (Bick et al., 2018; Ozkan & Kucuk, 2016). Large, more complex projects, even with the most experienced Scrum master, will have a difficult time adopting a truly Scrum approach. This is not to say it cannot be done but risks and challenges will be plentiful. Project members and managers should be aware of this fact (Birkinshaw, 2018; Repenning et al., 2018; Taylor, 2016).

DECISION IMPLICATIONS

After discussing three different approaches to project management and evaluating the strengths and weaknesses of each, it is easy to see that careful consideration must be taken when approaching a project. Regardless of your experiences as a project manager, choosing the wrong management approach for your project can have dramatic implications for your success. Some projects are ideally suited for a particular project management style and that decision can be easily made. For example, construction projects are an excellent candidate for the traditional waterfall approach since project requirements are typically well-known and can be thoroughly defined early (Repenning et al., 2018).

A timeline can be precisely defined and the budget is specifically outlined. The agile approach, on the other hand, is well suited for technology projects where an overall project goal is known but the pathway to achieving that goal is flexible. Scrum, as a more precisely defined model of agile, is well suited to the same types of projects as the agile approach but what makes a project suitable for the use with Scrum may lie more in the culture of the business, experiences of the team members, and scale of the overall project goal (Schmitz, 2018). When considering any particular approach, not only must the characteristics of the project be evaluated, but also the culture of the company and the environment in which corporate management is familiar with operating as each of these plays a role in the ultimate success of a project (Aytac et al., 2019; Gupta et al., 2019; Mathur et al., 2013; Schmitz, 2018).

Elements of Scrum, such as the sprint retrospective and the sprint review, are good models for any agile project as they help the team evolve in their development approach as well as stay in focus with each other during the entire life cycle of a project. The face-to-face daily Scrums involved with this approach may be too constricting to apply to all agile-suited projects, especially those with decentralized teams. While there are many tools available to project managers to help them learn and master the Scrum approach (Sibona et al., 2018), an effective Scrum master is still a challenging role to fulfill. Knowing the skills of your team may be the strongest asset when deciding upon your project management approach (Stoica et al., 2016; Werder & Maedche, 2018).

CONCLUSION

While the Scrum approach has been around for some time and has been growing in popularity as an effective project model, it is still a relatively new approach and the research on this style has plenty of room for growth. As more project managers become educated on the Scrum approach or certified as Scrum masters, there may be adaptions that arise to develop this framework as an even more useful project management technique. One of the appeals of the Scrum approach is that it allows a project to iterate frequently and respond quickly to change.

This is extremely helpful with the fast pace and shifting trends of our growing global economy. However, at this pace, it may only be a short time before another method is discovered or Scrum evolves further to adapt to the high-speed project management world. While there may be any number of projects that are well suited to portions of each of these approaches, it may still be difficult to adopt and effectively implement any of these strategies without incorporating elements of other approaches. Where the Scrum approach holds several strengths to direct a successful project while minimizing project risk, one still must consider both core and ancillary goals before proceeding with a project management style. If the project scope and development approach are well known, if customer feedback is not needed during the development phase, and if the schedule is fairly loose, the traditional approach would be a suitable model to employ.

However, if the specifics of the final deliverables will be defined via iterative communication, if the customer wants or needs to be engaged in the development process to secure market relevance, and if the scope is flexible, Scrum may be an appropriate approach. While this may seem like an easy distinction to make, in the absence of a highly experienced project manager who is well supported by upper management, either of these approaches may still present itself as a challenge and a hybrid approach to project management may be the best solution. While the confines of a specific approach may be more of a hindrance than a facilitator to project success, there are elements of particular models that can be readily assigned to almost any project. For example, applying a primary waterfall approach but accommodating greater customer participation throughout the development process, or incorporating a retrospective element as part of a traditional agile approach but excluding a daily Scrum.

If the application of an agile approach is going to be used to manage a project, it certainly would benefit team members to be familiar with the Scrum method and its defining principles. The specific framework of Scrum can help to guide a project team through an iterative approach and keep them focused on the tasks at hand and isolated from external distractions. The role of Scrum master, while exclusive to the Scrum approach, is a taskmaster of sorts and has principle duties, which play an important role that can be helpful within any agile approach. Where a project manager is responsible for managing the project, a taskmaster who can keep the process in check is equally important. Especially, in the fast-paced project world where the method can be overlooked when the focus gets directed towards project results.

Defining the desired project characteristics is always a helpful tool to steer project managers towards the best project management approach but they must also have a thorough understanding of the company culture in which they are operating. By using information about the company culture and strategic mission in conjunction with project details, a project manager will be able to select the best strategies to apply when proceeding towards successful project management. Through the continued application of the Scrum model along with research on the successes and failures of businesses and project managers who apply this technique, the shared knowledge about what makes Scrum work and when best to utilize this approach will continue to evolve.

REFERENCES

Almadhoun, W., & Hamdan, M. (2020). Optimizing the self-organizing team size using a genetic algorithm in agile practices. *Journal of Intelligent Systems*, *29*(1), 1151–1165. doi:10.1515/jisys-2018-0085

Aytac, T., Dagli, G., Altinay, Z., & Altinay, F. (2019). The role of learning management in agile management for consensus culture. *The International Journal of Information and Learning Technology, 36*(4), 364–372. doi:10.1108/IJILT-02-2019-0017

Balaji, S., & Murugaiyan, M. S. (2012). Waterfall vs. V-model vs. Agile: A comparative study on SDLC. *International Journal of Information Technology and Business Management, 2*(1), 26–30.

Bick, S., Spohrer, K., Hoda, R., Scheerer, A., & Heinzl, A. (2018). Coordination challenges in large-scale software development: A case study of planning misalignment in hybrid settings. *IEEE Transactions on Software Engineering, 44*(10), 932–950. doi:10.1109/TSE.2017.2730870

Birkinshaw, J. (2018). What to expect from agile. *MIT Sloan Management Review, 59*(2), 39–42.

Carr, N. G. (2003). IT doesn't matter. *Harvard Business Review, 81*(5), 41–49. PMID:12747161

Chan, Y., & Reich, B. (2007). IT alignment: What have we learned. *Journal of Information Technology, 22*(4), 297–315. doi:10.1057/palgrave.jit.2000109

Cockburn, A., & Highsmith, J. (2001). Agile software development: The people factor. *IEEE Computer, 34*(11), 131–133. doi:10.1109/2.963450

Dennis, A., Wixom, B. H., & Roth, R. M. (2018). *Systems Analysis and Design* (7th ed.). John Wiley.

Dybå, T., & Dingsøyr, T. (2015). Agile project management: from self-managing teams to large-scale development. *Proceedings of 2015 IEEE/ACM 37th IEEE International Conference on Software Engineering (ICSE)*, 945-946. 10.1109/ICSE.2015.299

Dybå, T., Dingsøyr, T., & Moe, N. B. (2014). Agile project management. In Software Project Management in a Changing World. Springer-Verlag. doi:10.1007/978-3-642-55035-5_11

Fernandez, D., & Fernandez, J. (2008). Agile project management – Agilism versus traditional approaches. *Journal of Computer Information Systems, 49*(2), 10–16.

Friess, E. (2019). Scrum language use in a software engineering firm: An exploratory study. *IEEE Transactions on Professional Communication, 62*(2), 130–147. doi:10.1109/TPC.2019.2911461

Garel, G. (2013). A history of project management models: From pre-models to the standard models. *International Journal of Project Management, 31*(5), 663–669. doi:10.1016/j.ijproman.2012.12.011

Gonçalves, E. F., Drumond, G. M., & Méxas, M. P. (2017). Evaluation of PMBOK and Scrum practices for software development in the vision of specialists. *Independent Journal of Management & Production, 8*(5), 569–580. doi:10.14807/ijmp.v8i5.598

Gupta, M., George, J. F., & Xia, W. (2019). Relationships between IT department culture and agile software development practices: An empirical investigation. *International Journal of Information Management, 44*, 13–24. doi:10.1016/j.ijinfomgt.2018.09.006

Highsmith, J. (2002). What Is agile software development? *Crosstalk, 15*(10), 4–9.

Leau, Y. B., Loo, W. K., Tham, W. Y., & Tan, S. F. (2012). Software development life cycle agile vs. traditional approaches. *2012 International Conference on Information and Network Technology (ICINT 2012)*, *37*, 162-167.

Lin, C. P., Joe, S. W., Chen, S. C., & Wang, H. J. (2015). Better to be flexible than to have flunked. *Journal of Service Management*, *26*(5), 823–843. doi:10.1108/JOSM-08-2014-0201

Maassen, M. A. (2018). Opportunities and risks of the agile software development management in the IT field. Case study: IT companies between 2009-2018. *Review of International Comparative Management*, *19*(3), 234–243. doi:10.24818/RMCI.2018.3.234

Maruping, L. M., Venkatesh, V., & Agarwal, R. (2009). A control theory perspective on agile methodology use and changing user requirements. *Information Systems Research*, *20*(3), 377–399. doi:10.1287/isre.1090.0238

Masa'deh, R., Tarhini, A., Al-Dmour, R. H., & Obeidat, B. Y. (2015). Strategic IT-business alignment as managers' explorative and exploitative strategies. *European Scientific Journal*, *11*(7), 438–457.

Mathur, G., Jugdev, K., & Fung, T. S. (2013). Project management assets and project management performance outcomes. *Management Research Review*, *36*(2), 112–135. doi:10.1108/01409171311292234

Meredith, J. R., Shafer, S. M., & Mantel, S. J. Jr. (2018). *Project management: a strategic managerial approach* (10th ed.). John Wiley & Sons, Inc.

Nelson, R. R. (2007). IT project management: Infamous failures, classic mistakes, and best practices. *MIS Quarterly Executive*, *6*(2), 67–78.

Ozierańska, A., Skomra, A., Kuchta, D., & Rola, P. (2016). The critical factors of Scrum implementation in IT project – the case study. *Journal of Economics and Management*, *25*(3), 79–96. doi:10.22367/jem.2016.25.06

Ozkan, N., & Kucuk, C. (2016). A systematic approach to project-related concepts of Scrum. *Review of International Comparative Management*, *17*(4), 320–333.

Rahman, H., Shafique, M. N., & Rashid, A. (2018). Project success in the eyes of project management information system and project team members. *Abasyn Journal of Social Sciences*, *AICTBM-18*, 1–6.

Repenning, N. P., Kieffer, D., & Repenning, J. (2018). A new approach to designing work. *MIT Sloan Management Review*, *59*(2), 29–38.

Schmitz, K. (2018). A three cohort study of role-play instruction for agile project management. *Journal of Information Systems Education*, *29*(2), 93–103.

Schwaber, K., & Sutherland, J. (2017). *The Scrum Guide*. Retrieved from https://www.scrumguides.org/docs/scrumguide/v2017/2017-Scrum-Guide-US.pdf

Sibona, C., Pourreza, S., & Hill, S. (2018). Origami: An active learning exercise for Scrum project management. *Journal of Information Systems Education*, *29*(2), 105–116.

Srivastava, P., & Jain, S. (2017). A leadership framework for distributed self-organized scrum teams. *Team Performance Management*, *23*(5/6), 293–314. doi:10.1108/TPM-06-2016-0033

Stoica, M., Ghilic-Micu, B., Mircea, M., & Uscatu, C. (2016). Analyzing agile development - from waterfall style to Scrumban. *Informações Econômicas*, *20*(4), 5–14. doi:10.12948/issn14531305/20.4.2016.01

Stoica, M., Mircea, M., & Ghilic-Micu, B. (2013). Software development: Agile vs. traditional. *Informações Econômicas*, *17*(4), 64–76. doi:10.12948/issn14531305/17.4.2013.06

Tanner, M., & Mackinnon, A. (2015). Sources of interruptions experienced during a Scrum sprint. *The Electronic Journal of Information Systems Evaluation*, *18*(1), 3–18.

Taylor, K. J. (2016). Adopting agile software development: The project manager experience. *Information Technology & People*, *29*(4), 670–687. doi:10.1108/ITP-02-2014-0031

van Ruler, B. (2019). Agile communication evaluation and measurement. *Journal of Communication Management*, *23*(3), 265–280.

Vijayasarathy, L. R., & Butler, C. W. (2016). Choice of software development methodologies: Do organizational, project, and team characteristics matter? *IEEE Software*, *33*(5), 86–94. doi:10.1109/MS.2015.26

Waterman, M. (2018). Agility, risk, and uncertainty, part 1: Designing an agile architecture. *IEEE Software*, *35*(2), 99–101. doi:10.1109/MS.2018.1661335

Werder, K., & Maedche, A. (2018). Explaining the emergence of team agility: A complex adaptive systems perspective. *Information Technology & People*, *31*(3), 819–844. doi:10.1108/ITP-04-2017-0125

Williams, M., Ariyachandra, T., & Frolick, M. (2017). Business intelligence – success through agile implementation. *The Journal of Management and Engineering Integration*, *10*(1), 14–20.

KEY TERMS AND DEFINITIONS

Agile: Agile is a software development methodology around the idea of iterative development, where requirements and solutions evolve through collaboration between self-organizing cross-functional teams. Agile enables teams to deliver value faster, with greater quality, predictability, and greater aptitude to respond to change.

Culture: Refers to the entire way of life for a group of people. It consists of the values, beliefs, and norms, which influence the behavior of the group.

Project: A project is a unique, transient endeavor, undertaken to achieve planned objectives, which could be defined in terms of outputs, outcomes, or benefits. Time, cost, and quality are the building blocks of every project.

Project Management: Project management is the application of processes, methods, skills, knowledge, and experience to achieve specific project objectives according to the project acceptance criteria within agreed parameters. Project management has final deliverables that are constrained to a finite timescale and budget.

Risk Analysis: Risk analysis guides where the greatest vulnerabilities lie. Because risk analysis is fundamentally perception-based, the project professional needs to engage stakeholders early to identify risks. To make sense of differing perceptions, it is important to describe risk events clearly, separating causes, from risk events, from effects.

Scrum: Scrum is considered a subset of Agile. It is a lightweight process framework for agile development and the most widely used one. Scrum is most often used to manage complex software and product development, using iterative and incremental practices.

Waterfall Life Cycle: Life cycle offers a systematic and organized way to undertake the project-based work and can be viewed as the structure underpinning deployment. The waterfall life cycle is sequenced into a set of distinct phases, from the development of the initial concept to the deployment of an outcome, output, or benefits. This approach aims to be highly structured, predictable, and stable.

Chapter 7
An Investigation Into Product Owner Practices in Scrum Implementations

Andrew Schwarz
Louisiana State University, USA

Corey Baham
Oklahoma State University, USA

James Davis
Louisiana State University, USA

ABSTRACT

The utilization of the Scrum methodology delineates a separation of roles for a product team, with the Product Owner being responsible for identifying and describing product backlog items and making decisions regarding the priority of these items, ensuring business requirements are being met, and providing feedback throughout the project to the team to ensure that there is success in the deployment of the IT solution. Despite the importance of this role, there is scant research to examine the effectiveness of the Product Owner in the outcomes of the Scrum effort. In this chapter, the authors study and empirically evaluate the efficacy of the Product Owner and the practices and procedures that are inherent to the Scrum methodology, as well as the intervening effects of the challenges of the development process and the changing requirements. They conclude by presenting the results of the analysis and the implications of the findings for future work in Scrum, as well as what the research means for Product Owners within organizations that are employing the Scrum methodology.

DOI: 10.4018/978-1-7998-4885-1.ch007

Copyright © 2021, IGI Global. Copying or distributing in print or electronic forms without written permission of IGI Global is prohibited.

INTRODUCTION

Software development during the 1990s experienced a fundamental shift in respect to the planning and management techniques. With accusations such as the Chaos Report, the field of IT project management was under attack and innovative approaches were emerging from industry (Mulder, 1994). One of the main instigations causing new development approaches was the requirement of substantial upfront planning and the inability of traditional methods to handle frequent changes. In 2001, the *Manifesto for Agile Software Development* was born (Beck et al., 2001) after several thought leaders gathered to discuss better ways of building software to meet the demands of a more globally connected digital economy. By the early 2000s, several agile software development (ASD) methods were created, including eXtreme Programming, Scrum, Dynamic Systems Development Method, Adaptive Software Development, Crystal, Feature-driven Development, and Pragmatic Programming.

Scrum, the most widely used agile approach (Version One, 2018; West, Grant, Gerush, & D's ilva, 2010), has been instituted in many organizations and deeply studied by academicians (Rising and Janoff, 2000; Smits and Pshigoda, 2007; Bannerman and Hossain, 2012; Khmelevsky, Li, and Madnick, 2017). Past studies have examined an array of Scrum-related topics such as how Scrum works in local and distributed development environments, organizational transitions from individual to self-managing teams, inter-team coordination dynamics, perceptions of sustainability, Scrum adaptations in practice and the classroom, and the overall impact of Scrum practices on project outcomes (Rising and Janoff, 2000; Sutherland et al., 2007; Moe et al., 2010; Overhage and Schlauderer, 2012; Paasivaara et al., 2012; Hron et al., 2018; Masood et al., 2018). The Scrum framework consists of roles, artifacts, and events that guide teams in developing products for customer needs (Scrum Alliance, 2020). One central aspect of Scrum that is said to be critical for producing targeted outcomes is working in close collaboration with the customer or customer representative (i.e., Product Owner). However, despite the attention that Scrum has received from researchers, the Product Owner role that represents customer needs has received much less attention. While the extant literature describes the responsibilities and ideal skillset of a Product Owner (Cohn, 2010; Sutherland & Schwaber, 2016), many organizations struggle with determining who should assume the Product Owner role and integrating Product Owner practices in existing work practices, as these organizations don't know how to relate this new role to existing roles in the organization (Oomen et al., 2017). Recent studies suggest a gap between the activities performed by Product Owners in industry and those commonly found in the agile literature (Sverrisdottir et al., 2014; Bass et al., 2018). Of the dearth of studies that examine the Product Owner role, most focus on the expectations of the Product Owner role from the team's point of view (Unger-Windeler Schneider, 2019), such that few studies provide a perspective from actual Product Owners (exceptions include Schlauder and Overhage, 2013; Sverrisdottir et al., 2014; Matturro et al., 2018). Given that the Product Owner is said to maximize the value of the product (Deemer et al., 2012; Sutherland & Schwaber, 2016), understanding the role and the impact of its practices on outcomes yields helpful insights to both research and practice. While there are countless studies focusing upon the role of the IT staff in projects, we suggest that the literature surrounding the Scrum framework and project success is naïve in that much less research has been given to the Product Owner role or the perspective of Product Owners (Schlauder and Overhage, 2013). The objective of this chapter is to examine the nature of Product Owner practices and their impact on (the Product Owner's) perceptions of project success. In the next section, we provide a brief overview of Scrum, the Product Owner role.

BACKGROUND

Prior to the agile project management movement, the process for developing software applications was dominated by models with sequential activities (Krasner & Iscoe, 1988). Most notably was the software development lifecycle (SDLC) known as 'Waterfall'. In his seminal paper on software development, Winston (1970) formally describes the Waterfall model. In the Waterfall method, also referred to 'Traditional' project management, application development is conducted in sequential phases with each phase dependent on the deliverables of the previous phase. Borrowing from the manufacturing and construction industries, the traditional project management method relied on a predictive paradigm where stakeholder requirements can be known and resources can be predicted (Sutherland, 2014). Interestingly, Winston's paper (1970) includes a discussion to "do it twice" when creating a software application. The first version would be a rapid development to "quickly sense the trouble spots in the design" and the following version benefiting from lessons learned resulting in fewer errors.

Scrum

Jeff Sutherland and Ken Schwaber, the co-creators of the Scrum framework, sought to create a software development framework that embraced change. Borrowing from the sport of Rugby where interlocked teams attempt to move the ball down the field, the term 'Scrum' was first used by professors Hirotaka Takeuchi and Ikujiro Nonaka in their seminal 1986 Harvard Business Review paper "The New New Product Development Game." Building on the observations of Takeuchi and Nonoka, Sutherland and Schwaber codified several new agile practices in their 1995 presentation at the Association of Computing Machinery research conference (Verheyen, 2019). Thus, the 'inspect and adapt' foundation of Scrum was born. Sutherland and Schwaber's Scrum framework has only three roles. Team members are either: (a) a worker, or a project team member responsible for creating the product, (b) the Scrum Master, or a servant leader in charge of removing impediments and facilitating teamwork, or (c) the Product Owner, the individual in charge of laying out the vision and prioritizing work (Schwaber & Sutherland, 2012). The subsequent sections of this paper will focus on the Product Owner and the importance of the Product Owner's role to project success.

The Product Owner Role

The Product Owner is one of the main roles prescribed by the Scrum framework. Scrum guides describe the role and responsibilities of the Product Owner (Sutherland & Schwaber, 2016; Mike Cohn 2010; Scrum Alliance, 2020), including:

- identifying and describing product backlog items.
- making decisions regarding the priority of the product backlog items.
- ensuring that business requirements are understood.
- determining whether a product backlog item was successfully delivered.
- providing useful feedback throughout the project.

As the title may imply, the Product Owner 'owns' the product by setting the vision for the product and the direction for the team along with ensuring a valuable result. Reflecting on his past experiences with software development, Sutherland (2014) articulates the need for a team role that focuses on marketing plans, engages with stakeholders, and product strategy. He compares the notion of a Product Owner to Toyota's Chief Engineer system, which provides direction and vision for their product line. In Scrum, the Product Owner role provides a connection to the customer. While the Scrum Master and team are focused on quality and speed, the Product Owner is a conduit that renders the team's effort into value. The Product Owner is expected to understand the market, competing technologies, and stakeholder expectations. As a fighter pilot flying missions over Vietnam, Sutherland (2014) likens the Product Owner's vision of the product to the pilot's ability to "see" the enemy from far away and maintain his or her situational awareness. According to Sutherland, the design of an aircraft's canopy was of the utmost importance and allowed the winning pilot to get inside of, figuratively and literally, an enemy's decision loops. He called this "observation translated into action".

Although developing and sharing a vision can be difficult, one way that the Product Owner balances immediate and future product needs is by managing the product backlog. A Product Backlog is a list of all the features needed to make the vision a reality. It is an evolving roadmap that spans the life of a project (Leffingwell 2012). The Product Owner role is tasked with prioritizing the Product Backlog or ordering the features from most important to least important. Scrum development is conducted in time-boxed work increments, called Sprints, usually between 1 – 4 weeks. Immediately before it begins, the team selects features from the top of the Product Backlog that will be completed during the Sprint. This ensures that the most valuable features are completed sooner than lesser value features. This also maximizes the value produced by the team during each Sprint (Sutherland, 2014).

In software development, there is a non-scientific observation that 20% of the features provide 80% of the value for a product (Sutherland, 2014). As an example, there are hundreds of features in Microsoft Excel, yet few of these features are used by most users. The goal of articulating this 80 / 20 observation in to focus development toward the minimally viable version of a product, or MVP. The purpose of an MVP is to put your product in front of users and receive feedback sooner rather than later (Schwaber, 2009). With Scrum, the framework comes with a built-in feedback loop. Each Sprint ends with a ceremony called the Sprint Review. During the Sprint Review, the team openly demonstrates the completed features as a working increment of the Product Owner's vision (Sutherland, 2014). Stakeholders are welcome to attend the Sprint Review and provide feedback on the features and the status of the product. As part of the feedback loop, the Product Owner evaluates the value created, incorporates reactions, and continually grooms the Product Backlog with the most valuable features (re)prioritized at the top (Law and Larus-dottir, 2015). Sutherland describes this change embracing process and getting "your change for free".

Beyond the stated responsibilities (Schwaber & Sutherland, 2012; Sutherland & Schwaber, 2016), there are emerging complexities concerning the implementation of the Product Owner role. For instance, the nature of the customer that the Product Owner serves can vary depending on the scope of a software development project. On the one hand, a Product Owner can be assigned to develop software for a local client who is known to the Product Owner in the development of a specific solution. On the other hand, a Product Owner can be assigned to develop software for a mass market where there is no specific known customer. In this study, we focus on the former case, which is in line with the assumptions of most Scrum guides and the recent academic literature on customer representatives in agile software development. Prior empirical studies note the relevance of customer integration in new product development (Slaughter, 1993; Hippel and Krogh, 2003) and the importance of accurate system requirements (Rosenkranz et al., 2014; Vitharana et al., 2016). Leadership is needed in requirements analysis to manage requirements changes and avoid project delays, cost overruns and unwanted functionality (Vitharana et al. 2016). In practice, researchers have found that the customer representative role (i.e., Product Owner in Scrum) that is central to several agile methods contains implicit responsibilities in addition to the stated responsibilities found in practice guides (Maruping and Matook, 2014) examine. Thus, some organizations struggle with understanding the Product Owner role and integrating its practices in existing work practices (Oomen et al., 2017). Recent studies investigate a gap between the activities performed by Product Owners in industry and those commonly found in the agile literature (Sverrisdottir et al., 2014; Bass et al., 2018). As with most new practices, the Product Owner role and its practices should be situated to solve problems in a particular context in order to facilitate its long-term success (Dougherty, 2001). Because Product Owner practices such as ensuring that business requirements are understood are dynamic, continuous, and require heavy team interaction, we conceptualize the practice of Product Ownership as a consisting of both judgments (e.g., determining whether a product backlog item was successfully delivered) and interactions (e.g., providing useful feedback during team meetings). This is supported by recent research that examines additional "soft skills" that impact the effectiveness of the Product Owner role such as the amount of time that the Product Owner spends with the team and the degree to which the Product Owner showed a vested interest in the success of the software application to understand their impact on project success (Matook and Maruping, 2014; Matturro et al., 2018; Baham, 2019). Thus, we develop our hypotheses and measures of Product Owner practices in line with this conceptualization, as described in the next sections.

HYPOTHESES DEVELOPMENT

The Product Owner is a key stakeholder who is responsible for working with the Scrum team to ensure product increments are delivered to the satisfaction of the business customer. Desirable Product Owner characteristics include someone who is empowered to make decisions, available to the team, understands the interest of the business it represents, and able to communicate effectively. Product Owners that work in close collaboration with the development team can inspire confidence in their team's understanding of evolving business requirements and assure the team that the product backlog items under completion are of high importance to the customer. Thus, the Product Owner is said to maximize the value of the product resulting from the work of the development team for the lowest number of working hours (Deemer, Benefield, Larman, and Vodde, 2012; Sutherland and Schwaber, 2016). By minimizing rework, the development team can spend more time testing and refactoring to ensure higher code quality. Given the duel objective of agile methodologies, adapting to change and producing high quality code (Maruping et al., 2009), the Product Owner role brings the team closer to the root of change and allows the team to confirm the legitimacy of its software changes using several customer acceptance tests. Thus, Product Owners that employ the practices outlined for the Product Owner role (Sutherland and Schwaber, 2016) are well-positioned to aid the development team in producing high quality code. We hypothesize:

Hypothesis 1: Product Owner practices will have a positive influence on software project quality.

Although user requirements are gathered up front, they often undergo changes during the software project. Several factors can contribute to these changes, such as the customer desiring additional features to an overall change in a business's strategy. In response to industry needs, agile methods were developed to suit a more dynamic software development approach by embedding processes that enable responsiveness to requirements changes (Conboy, 2009; Fowler and Highsmith, 2001; Larman, 2003). Whereas requirements changes were found to negatively impact project quality using waterfall methods (Curtis et al., 1988; Nidumolu, 1995), requirements changes were found to positively impact the relationship between agile methods use and software quality (Maruping et al., 2009). Although prior research acknowledges the centrality of the Product Owner role, the Product Owner role and its practices have received much less attention than the roles of Scrum master and development team member in past research (Oomen et al., 2017). Similar to measuring the impact of agile practices related to the development team such as pair programming and automated tests, the Product Owner role and its practices need to be examined for their potential effect on software quality. Understanding the impact of specific Product Owner practices under requirements changes may help some organizations extract more value out of the Product Owner role. Moreover, recent studies acknowledge the complexity of the role and its success being impacted by organizational factors such as culture, team dynamics, and management (Sverrisdottir et al., 2013). Despite its challenges, having a liaison between business and IT helps to address the longstanding alignment issue and forges a mutual understanding between business and IT in the software development context. The execution of Product Owner practices should translate business requirement changes and their priority to the development team. Because the effectiveness of Product Owner practices depend on a collaborative effort in responding to change, an increase in Product Owner practices under high requirements changes should help Scrum teams to pull together and clarify changing user requirements, ultimately leading to a more focused effort on the business's needs. With Product Owner practices in use, a high degree of requirement changes should heighten the development team's situation awareness and focus their efforts on delivering high quality software. We argue that the relationship between Product Owner practices and software quality will be more positive when requirements changes are high.

Hypothesis 2: The positive relationship between Product Owner practices and software project quality is moderated by requirements change.

Although we expect Product Owner practices to positively impact software quality, one factor that has been known to impact software quality is task/software complexity (Curtis et al., 1979; Banker et al., 1998). Large and complex software projects may involve more lines of code, a larger team or multiple teams, and more dependencies and interactions between systems. Such complexities increase uncertainty and decrease the utilization of prior knowledge as a team is presented with new challenges. These complexities may also require additional organizational support to help teams manage the development process and deliver quality software in a timely manner. Therefore, high task/software complexity may have a negative impact on software quality.

Hypothesis 3: Software complexity will have a negative impact upon software quality

The results of our theoretical development are found in Figure 1 below.

RESEARCH METHOD

Our first step in the testing of our model was the development of items to correspond to each of our constructs. Pre-existing items from previous studies were included for the constructs of requirements

Figure 1.

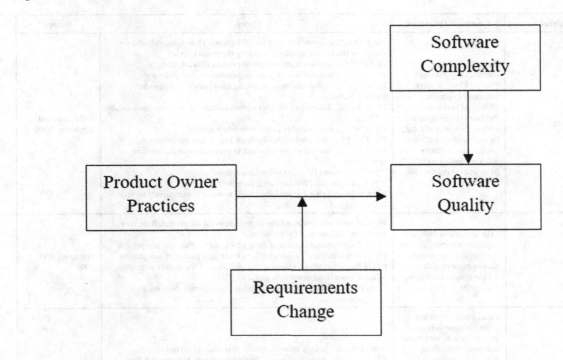

change, task complexity, and software quality. To measure Product Owner practices, the behaviors outlined by Sutherland and Schwaber (2016) were adapted to the context of the Product Owner. After analyzing these constructs, we separated the behaviors into two categories: practices where a Product Owner made a judgment and practices where a Product Owner interacted with the team. We, therefore, conceptualized Product Owner practices as a second-order construct. We have outlined the measures that we utilized for our study below in Table 1.

DATA COLLECTION

We collected data from Product Owners recruited through Amazon Mechanical Turk (or MTurk). Previous studies within the information systems literature (e.g., Steelman et al., 2014 and Lowry et al., 2016) have validated the approach of using MTurk survey participants. To screen out our respondents, we placed two questions at the beginning of our survey: (1) Have you been a Product Owner on the development of an IT solution for an organization in the past 12 months and (2) Has the application that you were a Product Owner of been implemented? To participate in the study, subjects had to answer affirmatively to both questions. There was a total of 69 subjects who qualified for the study, 55 of which were male and 14 females. The respondents reported that, on average, the project teams consist of 12.4 individuals.

Table 1. Research Items Used in Study

Construct	Construct Definition	Items	Source
Product Owner Practices	Behavioral norms introduced to standardize Product Owners' work processes (Mintzberg 1980) and to direct Product Owners towards company-wide goals, e.g., by encouraging software engineers to focus on software quality right from writing the first line of code.	We want to know your role as a Product Owner. How frequently did you engage in the following activities during the project cycle? PRAC1(*) … identified and described product backlog items. PRAC2(*) … ensured that business requirements were understood. PRAC3(**) … made decisions regarding the priority of the product backlog items. PRAC4(*) … determined whether a product backlog item was successfully delivered. PRAC5(*) … was available to the team when needed. PRAC6(**) … provided useful feedback throughout the project. PRAC7(*) … showed a vested interest in the success of the software application (*) Items measure Product Owner Interactions (**) Items measure Product Owner Judgements Items measured on a 7-point Likert scale from very infrequently to very frequently	Sutherland and Schwaber, 2016
Requirements change	"The extent to which user requirements changed over the course of a software development project from start to finish" (Maruping et al. 2009, p. 386).	We now want to know about the requirements for the project. Rate your agreement with each of the following. REQ1 Requirements fluctuated quite a bit in early phases of this project. REQ2 Requirements fluctuated quite a bit in later phases of this project. REQ3 Requirements identified at the beginning of the project were quite different from those toward the end. Items measured on a 7-point Likert scale from strongly disagree to strongly agree	Maruping et al., 2009
Task Complexity	Task complexity refers to the characteristics of the software development tasks that make them difficult to understand and change (based upon software complexity refers to the characteristics of the data structures and procedures within the software that make it difficult to understand and change (Curtis et al. 1979; Banker et al. 1998))	Concerning the last six months, you or your team faced tasks: TASK1 … for which there was a clearly known way how to solve them. TASK2 … for which the team's pre-existing knowledge was of great help to solve them. TASK3 … for which the team's pre-existing work procedures and practices could be relied upon to solve them. Items measured on a 7-point Likert scale from very infrequently to very frequently	Schmidt et al., 2014; Banker et al., 1998; Curtis et al., 1979
Software Quality	The degree to which having a Product Owner allowed the team to meet the specified requirements and expectations of the user and is free of errors.	We want to know about your view of your role as a Product Owner in the quality of the software. Rate your agreement with each of the following. OUT1 Having a Product Owner allowed you or your team to enhance the functionality of applications that you build. OUT2 Having a Product Owner allow you or your team to decrease the number of errors in the systems/software products you build. OUT3 Having a Product Owner allow you or your team to improve the quality of the systems/software products you build. OUT4 Having a Product Owner allow you or your team to be more conscious of software quality. Items measured on a 7-point Likert scale from strongly disagree to strongly agree	Senapathi and Srinivasan, 2014; Mendoza et al., 2019

DATA ANALYSIS AND RESULTS

We analyzed the data from our study utilizing structural equation modeling. Given our focus upon the early stages of theory building (Chin 1998), we selected the partial least squares (PLS) approach, specifically Smart PLS (Ringle et al., 2005) software. We will begin with a discussion of our measurement model.

Measurement Model

The first step in a PLS analysis is the analysis of the measurement (or outer) model. Using the repeated indicators method (Chin, Marcolin, and Newsted, 2003; Lohmöller, 1989; Wold, 1982), we estimated the Product Owner practices model. First, following a molecular approximation, we created first-order latent constructs and related them to their corresponding items. We then created the second-order constructs by the repeated use of the manifest variables of the first-order latent constructs. The paths between the first and the second-order constructs can be assessed as second-order loadings (see Table 2 below). We began by examining the loadings and cross-loadings of all items to ensure that they each loaded on their respective constructs and that all the loadings were higher than the prescribed threshold of 0.70 on their respective construct. Based upon this analysis, we determined that the first outcome item, the first business practice item (i.e., …identified and described product backlog items.), and the first requirement item (i.e., Requirements fluctuated quite a bit in early phases of this project) did not meet the threshold. All the remaining loadings were greater on the intended construct than on any other constructs and were therefore included in the analysis.

Table 2. Loading and Cross-Loading Analysis

	Complexity	**Outcomes**	**Scrum Practices**	**Interactions**	**Judgements**	**Requirements**
COMPLEX	**1.000**	0.443	0.482	0.441	0.389	0.187
OUT2	0.331	**0.779**	0.298	0.127	0.344	0.198
OUT3	0.297	**0.775**	0.269	0.257	0.199	0.285
OUT4	0.398	**0.798**	0.505	0.393	0.471	0.024
PRAC2	0.363	0.511	**0.750**	0.421	**0.812**	0.044
PRAC3	0.469	0.272	**0.633**	0.796	0.345	0.231
PRAC4	0.427	0.359	**0.781**	0.546	**0.833**	0.120
PRAC5	0.297	0.256	**0.698**	0.756	0.523	-0.000
PRAC6	0.141	0.218	**0.670**	0.421	**0.808**	0.036
PRAC7	0.295	0.296	**0.718**	0.824	0.474	0.035
REQ2	0.037	0.122	0.028	0.022	0.021	**0.805**
REQ3	0.243	0.202	0.135	0.136	0.106	**0.933**

Using the loadings from the constructs in the model, we estimated composite reliabilities for the constructs in the model. Table 3 presents average variance extracted and the correlations between the constructs. A comparison of the square root of the average variance extracted (i.e., the diagonals in Table 3 representing the overlap of each construct with its measures) with the correlations among constructs (i.e., the off-diagonal elements in Table 3 representing the overlap among constructs) indicates that, on average, each construct is more highly related to its own measures than to other constructs. Our findings are also consistent with the recommendation of Fornell and Larcker (1981) that the average variance extracted should be larger than the square of the correlations (i.e., equivalent to a monotonic power transform of numbers in the table). Moreover, all average variances extracted are well above the .50 recommended level. In summary, these results support the convergent and discriminant validity of our constructs.

Table 3. Discriminant Analysis

	Composite Reliability	AVE	Complexity	Interactions	Judgments	Moderating Effect	Outcomes	Requirements	Scrum Practices
Complexity	1	1	1.000						
Interactions	0.835	0.628	0.441	0.793					
Judgements	0.858	0.668	0.389	0.569	0.818				
Moderating Effect	1	1	-0.227	-0.175	-0.155	1.000			
Outcomes	0.827	0.615	0.443	0.347	0.449	0.004	0.784		
Requirements	0.863	0.760	0.187	0.106	0.084	0.303	0.194	0.872	
Scrum Practices			0.482	0.864	0.900	-0.182	0.475	0.107	

Structural Model

Figure 2 shows the results of our PLS estimation. Using a bootstrap of 5000 samples, our results indicated that the first-order constructs of interactions and judgments were significantly related to Scrum practices ($\beta = 0.900$ and 0.874, $p < 0.001$, respectively) and that Scrum practices predicted software quality outcomes ($\beta = 0.350$, $p < 0.05$), with an r-squared of 0.307. The remaining path loadings were insignificant based upon our analysis.

DISCUSSION

This study investigated the role of the Product Owner practices in managing a Scrum project and the corresponding benefits that derive from their involvement. Our findings suggest that there is empirical evidence to support the assertion that Product Owner practices do result in higher software quality outcomes. Furthermore, the lack of empirical support for the role of task complexity and requirements changes further illustrates the role that Product Owners have in a Scrum project.

Our interpretation of the lack of empirical support is that, regardless of task complexity or requirements changing, the strength of the path between Product Owner practices and outcomes overshadows these paths. In other words, a Product Owner who engages in the types of behaviors outlined by the Scrum methodology and observed in the successful implementation of Scrum will be able to help shape project outcomes even if these issues arise. This differs from the findings of prior studies that examine the impact of software development practices on project outcomes under requirements changes and complexity. Past findings suggest that agile software development practices were able to harness change and thrive under specific conditions of uncertainty (Maruping et al. 2009; Schmidt et al. 2014). Focusing on the Product Owner role, the findings of this study demonstrate the resilience of the Product Owner role

Figure 2. Structural Model Results

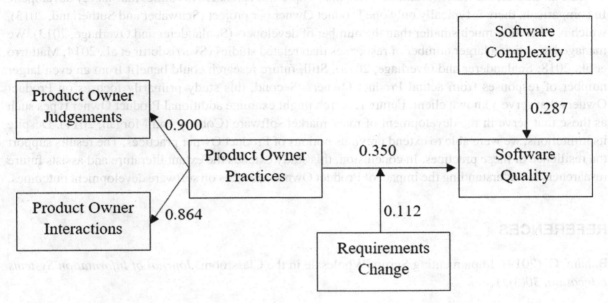

and its practices on software quality, which was not found to change under previously tested conditions. The resilience of the Product Owner role may yield insights concerning the long-term impacts of agile on organizations. Future research should extend this notion by testing whether the impact of Product Owner practices hold over time (e.g., consecutive projects).

This study contributes to the dearth of empirical research on the Product Owner role in several ways. First, this study extends prior work that examines the gap between theory and practice of the Product Owner role by not only identifying activities that Product Owners perform (Bass et al., 2018; Matturro et al., 2018) but measuring their effect on software outcomes (i.e., software quality). Because our study involves a larger sample of Product Owners than prior studies, which tend to be limited (i.e., N < 10), we were able to develop and test our model quantitatively. Second, this study complements prior work that examines factors that influence a Product Owner's acceptance of Scrum (Schlauder and Overhage, 2013) and the knowledge and skills needed to fulfill the Product Owner role (Matook and Maruping, 2014; Oomen et al., 2017) by instantiating Product Owner skills into actionable activities that influence outcomes. Whereas prior studies provide competencies that can be used by IT and human resources managers to assess a person's relative fit for the Produce Owner role, this study provides key insights into a Product Owner's own self-reflection and assessment of their impact on the software product.

The implications of our findings suggest that the Product Owner plays a key role in stabilizing the Scrum team. As requirements changes occur over the course of a project, the Product Owner role can help the team resist the negative effects of uncertainty by clarifying and reprioritizing requirements. Our findings suggest that organizations that adopt agile methods should not remove roles and practices that liaison between IT and business such as Scrum's Product Owner and XP's on-site customer, especially under high levels of uncertainty. As both research and practice tend to tailor agile use by selecting agile practices in an a la carte fashion (Tripp et al. 2018), careful consideration should be given to the impact of the Product Owner role in each context.,

Like all studies, ours has limitations. First, the sample size is relative to studies that survey developers. In comparison, there is typically only one Product Owner per project (Schwaber and Sutherland, 2013), which is inherently much smaller than the number of developers (Schlauderer and Overhage, 2013). We managed to solicit a larger number of responses than related studies (Sverrisdottir et al., 2014; Matturro et al., 2018; Schlauderer and Overhage, 2013). Still, future research could benefit from an even larger number of responses from actual Product Owners. Second, this study primarily focuses on Product Owners that serve a known client. Future research might examine additional Product Owner types such as those that serve in the development of mass market software (Conboy and Morgan, 2011). Despite its limitations, we were able to extend previous notions of Product Owner practices. The results support the resilience of these practices. In conclusion, this study extends the extant literature and assists future researchers in understanding the impact of Product Owner practices on software development outcomes.

REFERENCES

Baham, C. (2019). Implementing Scrum Wholesale in the Classroom. *Journal of Information Systems Education, 30*(3), 1.

Banker, R. D., Davis, G. B., & Slaughter, S. A. (1998). Software development practices, software complexity, and software maintenance performance: A field study. *Management Science, 44*(4), 433–450. doi:10.1287/mnsc.44.4.433

Bannerman, P. L., Hossain, E., & Jeffery, R. (2012). Scrum practice mitigation of global software development coordination challenges: A distinctive advantage? *2012 45th Hawaii International Conference on System Sciences*, 5309–5318.

Bass, J. M., Beecham, S., Razzak, M. A., Canna, C. N., & Noll, J. (2018). An empirical study of the Product Owner role in Scrum. *Proceedings of the 40th International Conference on Software Engineering: Companion Proceeedings*, 123–124. 10.1145/3183440.3195066

Beck, K., Beedle, M., van Bennekum, A., Cockburn, A., Cunningham, W., Fowler, M., Grenning, J., Highsmith, J., Hunt, A., Jeffries, R., Kern, J., Marick, B., Martin, R. C., Mellor, S., Schwaber, K., Sutherland, J., & Thomas, D. (2001). *Manifesto for Agile Software Development*. Retrieved March 9, 2018, from https://agilemanifesto.org/

Conboy, K. (2009). Agility from first principles: Reconstructing the concept of agility in information systems development. *Information Systems Research, 20*(3), 329–354. doi:10.1287/isre.1090.0236

Conboy, K., & Morgan, L. (2011). Beyond the customer: Opening the agile systems development process. *Information and Software Technology, 53*(5), 535–542. doi:10.1016/j.infsof.2010.10.007

Curtis, B., Krasner, H., & Iscoe, N. (1988). A field study of the software design process for large systems. *Communications of the ACM, 31*(11), 1268–1287. doi:10.1145/50087.50089

Deemer, P., Benefield, G., Larman, C., & Vodde, B. (2012). A lightweight guide to the theory and practice of ScrumScrum. *Ver, 2*, 2012.

Fowler, M., & Highsmith, J. (2001). Agile methodologists agree on something. *Software Development*, *9*, 28–32.

Hron, M., & Obwegeser, N. (2018). Scrum in practice: an overview of Scrum adaptations. *Proceedings of the 51st Hawaii International Conference on System Sciences*. 10.24251/HICSS.2018.679

Khmelevsky, Y., Li, X., & Madnick, S. (2017). Software development using agile and Scrum in distributed teams. *2017 Annual IEEE International Systems Conference (SysCon)*, 1–4. 10.1109/SYSCON.2017.7934766

Larman, C. (2003). *Agile and Iterative Development: A Manager's Guide*. Addison-Wesley.

Law, E., & Larusdottir, M. (2015). Whose Experience Do We Care About? Analysis of the Fitness of ScrumScrum and Kanban to User Experience. *International Journal of Human-Computer Interaction*, *31*(9), 584–602. doi:10.1080/10447318.2015.1065693

Leffingwell, D. (2012). *Agile Software Requirements: Lean Requirements Practices for Teams, Programs, and the Enterprise*. Pearson Education.

Maruping, L., & Matook, S. (forthcoming). The Multiplex Nature of the Customer Representative Role in Agile Information Systems Development. *Management Information Systems Quarterly*.

Maruping, L. M., Venkatesh, V., & Agarwal, R. (2009). A control theory perspective on agile methodology use and changing user requirements. *Information Systems Research*, *20*(3), 377–399. doi:10.1287/isre.1090.0238

Maruping, L. M., Venkatesh, V., & Agarwal, R. (2009). A control theory perspective on agile methodology use and changing user requirements. *Information Systems Research*, *20*(3), 377–399. doi:10.1287/isre.1090.0238

Masood, Z., Hoda, R., & Blincoe, K. (2018). Adapting Agile Practices in University Contexts. *Journal of Systems and Software*, *144*, 501–510. doi:10.1016/j.jss.2018.07.011

Matook, S., & Maruping, L. (2014). A Competency Model for Customer Representatives in Agile Software Development Projects. *MIS Quarterly Executive*, *13*(2). https://aisel.aisnet.org/misqe/vol13/iss2/3

Matturro, G., Cordovés, F., & Solari, M. (2018). role of Product Owner from the practitioner's perspective. An exploratory study. *Proceedings of the International Conference on Software Engineering Research and Practice (SERP)*, 113–118.

Mendoza, I., Kalinowski, M., Souza, U., & Felderer, M. (2019, January). Relating verification and validation methods to software product quality characteristics: results of an expert survey. In *International Conference on Software Quality* (pp. 33-44). Springer. 10.1007/978-3-030-05767-1_3

Moe, N. B., Dingsøyr, T., & Dybå, T. (2010). A teamwork model for understanding an agile team: A case study of a Scrum project. *Information and Software Technology*, *52*(5), 480–491. doi:10.1016/j.infsof.2009.11.004

Mulder, H. (1994). *The Chaos Report*. Academic Press.

Nidumolu, S. (1995). The effect of coordination and uncertainty on software project performance: Residual performance risk as an intervening variable. *Information Systems Research, 6*(3), 191–219. doi:10.1287/isre.6.3.191

Oomen, S., De Waal, B., Albertin, A., & Ravesteyn, P. (2017). How can Scrum be succesful? Competences of the ScrumScrum Product Owner. *Proceedings of the European Conference on Information Systems*.

Overhage, S., & Schlauderer, S. (2012). Investigating the long-term acceptance of agile methodologies: An empirical study of developer perceptions in Scrum projects. *45th Hawaii International Conference on System Sciences*, 5452–5461. 10.1109/HICSS.2012.387

Paasivaara, M., Lassenius, C., & Heikkilä, V. T. (2012). Inter-team coordination in large-scale globally distributed Scrum: Do Scrum-of-Scrums really work? *Proceedings of the ACM-IEEE International Symposium on Empirical Software Engineering and Measurement*, 235–238. 10.1145/2372251.2372294

Rising, L., & Janoff, N. S. (2000). The Scrum software development process for small teams. *IEEE Software, 17*(4), 26–32. doi:10.1109/52.854065

Rosenkranz, C., Vranešić, H., & Holten, R. (2014). Boundary interactions and motors of change in requirements elicitation: A dynamic perspective on knowledge sharing. *Journal of the Association for Information Systems, 15*(6), 2.

Royce, W. (1970). Managing the Development of Large Software Systems. *Proceedings of IEEE WESCON*, 26.

Schlauderer, S., & Overhage, S. (2013). *Exploring the customer perspective of agile development: Acceptance factors and on-site customer perceptions in Scrum projects*. Academic Press.

Schmidt, C., Kude, T., Heinzl, A., & Mithas, S. (2014). How Agile practices influence the performance of software development teams: The role of shared mental models and backup. *Proceedings of the International Conference on Information Systems*.

Schwaber, K. (1995). *ScrumScrum Development Process*. OOPSLA'95 Workshop on Business Object Design and Implementation, Austin, TX.

Schwaber, K. (2009). *Agile Project Management with ScrumScrum*. Microsoft Press.

Schwaber, K., & Sutherland, J. (2012). *Software in 30 Days: How agile managers beat the odds, delight their customers, and leave competitors in the dust*. John Wiley & Sons. doi:10.1002/9781119203278

Scrum Alliance. (2020). *Overview: What is Scrum?* Retrieved July 27, 2020, from https://www.Scrumalliance.org/about-Scrum/overview

Senapathi, M., & Srinivasan, A. (2014). An empirical investigation of the factors affecting agile usage. *Proceedings of the 18th International Conference on Evaluation and Assessment in Software Engineering, 10*. 10.1145/2601248.2601253

Slaughter, S. (1993). Innovation and learning during implementation: A comparison of user and manufacturer innovations. *Research Policy, 22*(1), 81–95. doi:10.1016/0048-7333(93)90034-F

Smits, H., & Pshigoda, G. (2007). *Implementing Scrum in a distributed software development organization. Agile 2007 (AGILE 2007), 371–375.*

Sutherland, J. (2014). *ScrumScrum: The Art of Doing Twice the Work in Half the Time.* Crown Publishing.

Sutherland, J., & Schwaber, K. (2016). *The Scrum Guide: The Definitive Guide to Scrum: The Rules of the Game.* Academic Press.

Sutherland, J., Viktorov, A., Blount, J., & Puntikov, N. (2007). Distributed Scrum: Agile project management with outsourced development teams. *2007 40th Annual Hawaii International Conference on System Sciences (HICSS'07),* 274a-274a.

Sverrisdottir, H. S., Ingason, H. T., & Jonasson, H. I. (2013). The role of the Product Owner in Scrum-Scrum comparison between theory and practices. *Proceedings of the 27th IPMA World Congress.*

Tripp, J., Saltz, J., & Turk, D. (2018, January). Thoughts on current and future research on agile and lean: ensuring relevance and rigor. *Proceedings of the 51st Hawaii International Conference on System Sciences.* 10.24251/HICSS.2018.681

Unger-Windeler, C., & Schneider, K. (2019). Expectations on the Product Owner Role in Systems Engineering-A Scrum Team's Point of View. *2019 45th Euromicro Conference on Software Engineering and Advanced Applications (SEAA),* 276–283.

Verheyen, G. (2019). *Scrum: A Pocket Guide* (2nd ed.). Van Haren Publishing.

Version One. (2018). *12th Annual State of Agile Report.* Retrieved June 15, 2018, from https://www.stateofagile.com/#ufh-i-423641583-12th-annual-state-of-agile-report/473508

Vitharana, P., Zahedi, F., & Jain, H. K. (2016). Enhancing analysts' mental models for improving requirements elicitation: A two-stage theoretical framework and empirical results. *Journal of the Association for Information Systems, 17*(12), 1. doi:10.17705/1jais.00444

West, D., Grant, T., & Gerush, M., & D'silva, D. (2010). Agile Development: Mainstream Adoption has Changed Agility. *Forrester Research, 2*(1), 41.

Chapter 8
Software Testing Under Agile, Scrum, and DevOps

Kamalendu Pal
https://orcid.org/0000-0001-7158-6481
City, University of London, UK

Bill Karakostas
Independent Researcher, UK

ABSTRACT

The adoption of agility at a large scale often requires the integration of agile and non-agile development practices into hybrid software development and delivery environment. This chapter addresses software testing related issues for Agile software application development. Currently, the umbrella of Agile methodologies (e.g. Scrum, Extreme Programming, Development and Operations – i.e., DevOps) have become the preferred tools for modern software development. These methodologies emphasize iterative and incremental development, where both the requirements and solutions evolve through the collaboration between cross-functional teams. The success of such practices relies on the quality result of each stage of development, obtained through rigorous testing. This chapter introduces the principles of software testing within the context of Scrum/DevOps based software development lifecycle.

INTRODUCTION

The world is witnessing a tremendous influence of software systems in all aspects of personal and business areas. Software systems are also heavily incorporated in safety-critical applications including manufacturing machinery, automobiles operation, and industrial process controls. In these applications, software failure can cause injury or loss of life. The correct behaviour of software is crucial to the safety and wellbeing of people and business. Consequently, there is an increasing requirement for the application of strict engineering discipline to the development of software systems.

DOI: 10.4018/978-1-7998-4885-1.ch008

Copyright © 2021, IGI Global. Copying or distributing in print or electronic forms without written permission of IGI Global is prohibited.

The human being, however, is fallible. Even if they adopt the most sophisticated and thoughtful design techniques, erroneous results can never be avoided *a priori*. Consequently, software products, like the products of any engineering activity, must be verified against its requirements throughout its development.

One fundamental approach to verification is experimenting with the behaviour of a product to see whether the product performs as expected. It is common practice to input a few sample cases *(test cases)*, which are usually randomly generated or empirically selected, and then verify that the output is correct. However, it cannot provide enough evidence that the desired behaviour will be exhibited in all remaining cases. The only testing of any system that can provide absolute certainty about the correctness of system behaviour is exhaustive testing, i.e., testing the system under all possible circumstances.

In addition, new improved methods and tools for software development are the goals of researchers and practitioners. The procedure of software development has evolved over the decades to accommodate changes in software development practice. Many methods and modelling techniques have been proposed to improve software development productivity. Also, software engineering has gone through an evolution in its conception by the business world in the 1960s to recent day application development methodologies (Pal, 2019).

Software practitioners employ software development methodologies for producing high-quality software, satisfying user requirements, effectively managing the software development cost, and ensuring timely delivery. In this way, software development methodologies play an important role to provide a systematic and organized approach to software development (Sommerville, 2019). According to Kevin Roebuck (Roebuck, 2012), a traditional Software Development Life Cycle (SDLC) provides the framework for planning and controlling the development or modification of software products, along with the methodologies and process models are used for software development.

According to researchers such as (Beck et al., 2001), the Waterfall Modell (Royce, 1970) was proposed to the information processing industry, as a way in which to assess and build for the users' needs. It starts with an end-user requirements analysis that produces all required input for the next stage (software system design), where software engineers collaborate with others (e.g. database schema designers, user interface designers) to produce the optimal information system architecture. Next, coders implement the system with the help of specification documents, and finally, the deployed software system is tested and shipped to its customers (Beck, 1999).

This process model (work practice) although effective from a theoretical perspective, did not always work as expected in real life scenarios. Firstly, software customers often change their minds. After weeks, or even months, of gathering requirements and creating prototypes, users can still be unsure of what they want – all they know is that what they saw in the produced software was *not* quite "it". Secondly, requirements tend to change mid-development, however, it is difficult to stop the momentum of the project to accommodate the change. The traditional process models (e.g. Waterfall, Spiral) start to pose problems when change rates of requirements are relatively high (Boehm, 2002) because coders, system architects, and managers need to introduce and keep up to date a huge amount of documentation for the proposed system, even for small changes (Boehm, 1988). The Waterfall software process model was supposed to fix the problem of changing requirements once and for all by freezing requirements and not permitting any change once the project starts. However, it is a common experience that software requirements cannot be pinned down in one fell swoop (Beck, 1999).

In recent decades, the software industry has moved its production mechanism from traditional software development practice to agile methodologies, to mitigate the ever-increasing software complexity and globalization of software design and development business. Many industries have started to adopt new software development methodologies, known as *Agile methodologies*, for their software development purpose (VersionOne, 2011). Agile methodologies are premised on the values expressed in the Agile Manifesto (Cunningham, 2001), a statement from the leaders of the agile movement. In short, Agile methodologies are a reaction to traditional ways of developing software and acknowledge the "need for an alternative to documentation driven, heavyweight software development process" (Beck et al., 2001). The main purpose of these methodologies is to keep close customer collaboration, to provide business value as quickly as possible in an incremental manner, and to respond promptly to changing customer requirements (Barlow et al., 2011) (Cockburn, 2003).

However, large software projects are more problematic to tackle and often fail to satisfy stakeholders' expectations. While agile methods have been received with interest in the software industry, there is insufficient investigative research regarding their architecture and their mode of adoption within a large scale environment involving outsourcing, multiple programs, projects and methodologies – currently seen as a major challenge in the industrial problem-solving context (Rodriguez et al., 2012) (Lee & Young, 2013). It is widely agreed that there can be no single methodology that can be universally applied to all projects; thus, all agile and non-agile methodologies need to be tailored and integrated to support software development (Mahanti, 2006) (Boehm & Turner, 2003) (Gill, 2014). Hence, the trend to adopt agility in non-agile elements for architecture context-aware hybrid adaptive methodologies.

Scrum is one of the most widely used Agile methodologies in the industry (VersionOne, 2011). Scrum provides a lightweight process framework that can be described in terms of *roles* (product owner, scrum master, team), *process* (planning, iteration, review), and *artefacts* (product and sprint backlogs, burndown charts) (Schwaber & Sutherland, 2009). Scrum projects progress through a series of definitive (e.g. 30 days long) time-based iterations called *sprints*. At the start of each sprint, the team determines the amount of work it can complete during that sprint. Work is selected from a prioritized list called the *product backlog*. The work the team believes it can complete during the sprint is moved onto a list called *sprint backlog*. A brief daily meeting, the *daily scrum*, is held to allow the team to inspect its progress and to adapt any change, as necessary. Software testing is part and parcel of all Scrum activities.

In addition, contemporary software development is complex, and all the manual operations are moving towards automated solutions. The accelerated software delivery is a key to success in business. The increased business demand for continuous software delivery and the interwinding of development and operations has resulted in the concept of DevOps. DevOps has been adopted by prominent software and service companies (e.g. IBM) to support enhanced collaboration across the company and its value chains. In this way, DevOps facilitates uninterrupted delivery and coexistence between development and operation facilities, enhances the quality and performance of software applications, improve end-user experience, and help to the simultaneous deployment of software across different platforms.

Moreover, software testing is a very costly part of the software development process, estimated to make fifty per cent of the whole process development cost (Pal, 2020). In addition, testing in Scrum projects is different from traditional testing because of the continuous and integrated nature of testing in the project lifecycle from the very beginning (Crispin & Gregory, 2009) (Lindvall et al, 2004) (Talby et al, 2006). Furthermore, because every iteration aims to deliver a "potentially shippable" product, the development functionality within every iteration should be tested and validated to assure that risks are covered. Although the conceptual differences between Agile testing and traditional testing are several, the test types and techniques that are applied in Agile testing are not different from those applied in traditional testing (van Veenendaal, 2010) (van Veenendal, 2009), as after all, the goal of testing in Scrum is still to verify that requirements are met.

This chapter examines the importance of effective testing strategies in the context of the aforementioned paradigms of agile software development/Scrum and DevOps, for efficient software delivery. The chapter focuses on the importance of software testing in Agile methodologies such as Scrum, often practised in a DevOps environment.

The rest of this chapter is structured as follows. Section 2 describes background information on software design, agile methodologies, and particularly Scrum-based application development practice. Section 3 explains the basic concepts of testing in the software development process. Finally, Section 4 concludes the chapter with final remarks and future research plans.

AGILE/SCRUM BASED SOFTWARE DEVELOPMENT

This section describes Scrum, an Agile methodology, for software development business processes. Scrum was conceived by Ken Schwaber and Jeff Sutherland in the early 1990s, who published a research paper (Schwaber & Beedle, 2002) to describe the processes. The term "Scrum" is borrowed from the game of rugby to stress the importance of teams, and illustrates some analogies between team sports like rugby, and being successful in the game of product development.

As discussed in the previous section, the demand for rapid delivery of software is booming, due to stiff competition in the business domain and the premise that accelerated deliver the key to success. Many organisations believe that the solution to rapid delivery is DevOps. DevOps focuses on the long run of the software with shorter feedback, quick integrations, and rapid deliveries.

The literature suggests that Scrum is the best methodology to be used as an Agile practice. The success of Scrum is based on the integration of the flow throughout the software development process. Scrum, however, does not place a priority on the quality of all produced artefacts. As a result, one drawback of Scrum is that the developers may have not delivered the most optimal implementation, focusing for example on 'quick and dirty' solutions.

An incremental process is one in which software is built and delivered in real-world applications. Each piece or increment represents a complete subset of functionality. The increment may be either small or large, perhaps ranging from just a system's login screen on the small end to a highly flexible set of data management screens. Each increment is fully coded and tested, and the assumption is that the work of an iteration will not need to be revisited. In the Scrum world, instead of providing complete detailed descriptions about how everything is to be done on a project, much of it is left up to the software development team. This is because it is assumed that the team will know better how to solve any problem they are presented with. The approaches to projects that agile teams pursue are diverse. A team can be dedicated to a single project or be part of another larger project. Every project, every team and sometimes every iteration is different. How a software development team solves problems depends on the requirements, the people involved, and the software tools that the team will use.

Today, agile approaches promising rapid delivery and time to market have started to dominate the software industry, removing traditional approaches such as Waterfall from the mainstream (Schwaber & Beedle, 2002). Agile introduces key four principles i.e:

(1)   Individuals and interactions over processes and tools.
(2)   Working software over comprehensive documentation.
(3)   Customer collaboration over contract negotiation.

(4)   Responding to change over following a plan.

The above concepts do not directly fit to the conventional software development lifecycle which include deriving the specification, design and development evaluation and evolution. As a result, several methodologies have been evolved from the basic principles of the Agile concept, with Scrum, Extreme Programming, Lean, Kanban the main examples. Scrum is used as an Agile software development practice (Schwaber & Beedle, 2002) (Hneif & Ow, 2009). It comprises project management as part of its practices. Scrum creates a product backlog about the pending development.

Scrum is both an iterative and an incremental process-based development methodology. An iterative process is one, which makes progress through successive refinement. A development team takes the first approach at a system, knowing it is incomplete or weak in some (perhaps many) areas. They then iteratively refine those areas until the product is satisfactory. With each iteration, the software is improved through the addition of greater detail. For example, in a first iteration, a search screen might be coded to support only the simplest type of search. The second iteration might add additional search criteria. Finally, a third iteration may add error handling.

Scrum is one of the more widely used Agile methodologies in the industry (VersionOne, 2011). Scrum provides a lightweight process framework that can be described in terms of roles (product owner, scrum master, team), process (planning, iteration, review), and artefacts (product and sprint backlogs, burndown charts) (Schwaber & Sutherland, 2009). Scrum projects progress through a series of definitive (e.g. 30 days) time-based iterations called sprints. At the start of each sprint, the team determines the amount of work it can complete during that sprint. Work is selected from a prioritized list called the product backlog. The work the team believes it can complete during the sprint is moved onto a list called sprint backlog. A brief daily meeting, the daily scrum, is held to allow the team to inspect its progress and to adapt, as necessary.

Scrum relies on a self-organizing, cross-functional team. The Scrum team is self-organizing in that there are no overall team leaders who decide which person will be doing which task and how the problem will be solved. In other words, Scrum is a project management framework that applies to any project with aggressive deadlines, complex requirements, and a degree of uniqueness.

When describing the Scrum framework, it is easy to split it into three main areas. They are:

- Roles, which include the product owner, Scrum Master, and Scrum team.
- Ceremonies, which include the sprint planning meeting, sprint review, and sprint retrospective meetings.
- Scrum artefacts, which include the product backlog, sprint backlog, and the burndown chart.

The product owner is a project's key stakeholder and represents the users for whom the developers are building the solution. The product owner is often someone from the product management, a key stakeholder, or a user of the system. It is quite common for a business analyst with the domain experience to take on the product owner role of the development team who will engage regularly with the customers.

A diagrammatic representation of a Scrum-based software life cycle is shown in Figure 1.

The Scrum Master is responsible for making sure the team is as productive as possible and achieves this by removing impediments to progress, by protecting the team from outside, and so on. Their role is very much facilitating the team to steer their product to completion, and they act very much as a servant leader, fulfilling the needs of the team. The typical Scrum team has between five and nine people. A

Figure 1. Diagrammatic representation of the Scrum process

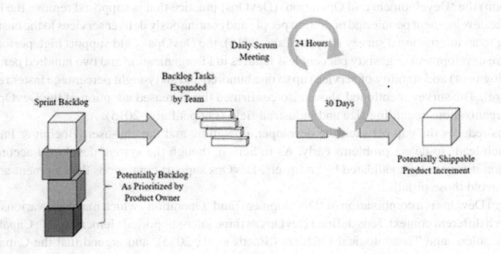

Scrum project can easily scale into the hundreds; however, Scrum can easily be used by one-person teams and often is.

The Difference Between Agile and Scrum

Agile is a concept comprised of principles that guide through the iterative approach for software processes. Agile management is a set of methodologies for software development that are incremental and iterative. Agile management apart from Scrum includes the rational unified process (RUP), extreme programming (XP). Agile processes result in need and outcome evolution made possible because of the collaboration between teams. Agile teams are cross-functional and self-organizing. The analysis, documentation, and development of a new project go hand in hand. Advancement occurs with every iteration. This approach offers ease of accommodation of changes. It also results in better scalability. The flexibility of operations and processes increases. There are certain rules that testers must follow in an agile environment. This set of rules is called Scrum, therefore, Scrum needs to be part of an Agile framework, as a technique used to address complex issues and deliver high-quality products simultaneously.

Scrum with DevOps

Typically, a software development process addresses the following activities: (i) Requirements Analysis and Specification, (ii) Software architecture and Implementation, (iii) Testing and Documentation, and (iv) Training, Support and Maintenance. Software maintenance was considered as a separate subprocess and developers focus on the rest of the process activities. This has created a crucial gap between the developers, the production, and operations staff, which is leading to challenges such as process cost overheads.

However, the pressure derived from the ever-changing business environment (e.g., competition, technology, market conditions), an increasing number of software companies are adopting (or considering adoption) the 'Development and Operation' (DevOps) practice that is supposed remove the barriers between the development people and operation people and continuously deliver services to the customers. According to an international survey (Puppet Labs, 2015), the DevOps could support high performance for software development (e.g. sixty per cent less failures in IT organization and two hundred percentage faster deployment) and stability of service (up to one hundred and sixty-eight percentage faster recovery from failure). The survey mentioned above also confirmed the increased adoption of the DevOps in all types of organizations regarding size and industrial field (Puppet Labs, 2015).

DevOps reduces the gap between the developer, operation, and the end-user (Boehm & Papaccio, 1988) which leads to detect problems early. As in Scrum, though the system developed according to specification it may not get validated by end-users. DevOps support continuous development and integration to avoid those pitfalls.

The term DevOps is a combination of 'Development' and 'Operation', which may have various definitions under a different context. Jens defined DevOps as three inter-supported elements – i.e., Capabilities, Cultural Enablers, and Technological Enablers (Smeds et al., 2015), and argued that the Capabilities is the main DevOps aspect, which includes capabilities such as continuous planning, collaborative and continuous development, continuous integration and testing, continuous release and deployment, continuous infrastructure monitoring and optimization, continuous user behaviour monitoring and feedback and service failure recovery without delay, etc. To strengthen these capabilities requires process improvement in various aspects. However, process improvement usually means different things to different companies due to the unique issues they are facing. To this end, a relatively thorough understanding of the performance of the current process and effective guidance for future process improvement is thus needed.

However, DevOps, does not incorporate a software development framework or process (Boehm & Papaccio, 1988). To become stable DevOps should have a complete software process model, which supports specification, design and development, evaluation, and evolution phases. The deployment flow between Scrum and DevOps cannot be achieved without addressing the missing components. To identify gaps, it is needed to check the role and the requirements of Scrum and DevOps in different stages of the software lifecycle. The Scrum methodology covers the first three stages of the software lifecycle, i.e., up to the development and release stages only. The final stages of (i) Planning (ii) Execute (iii) Inspect and adapt, and (iv) Operation and support, are not covered at all by the Scrum process.

DevOps cannot therefore be combined directly with the current Scrum. To understand the gaps and missing components, first, it is required to understand the industry need to minimize the time to market while maintaining the stability of the product. in addition, the industry needs to attend the production issues as fast as possible to achieve customer satisfaction and retention.

SOFTWARE TESTING

Software Testing is the execution of code using selected combinations of input and state, to reveal bugs. Software testing can be viewed as a systems engineering activity, i.e. as the design and implementation of a special kind of software system: one that exercises another software system with the intent of finding errors (Binder, 2000). In software testing, a program with well-designed input data is run to observe errors (Ipate & Holcombe, 1997; Mall, 2006; Jalote & Jain, 2006). In other words, software testing addresses the problem of effectively finding the difference between the expected behaviour given the system specification, and the observed behaviour of the implemented system (Binder, 2000). Testing of software also helps to find errors, gaps, or missing requirements. This can be done either manually or with automated tools.

The testable artefacts can be requirements and design specifications, modules of code, data structures, and any other objects that are necessary for the correct development and implementation of the software.

Software testing, on average, accounts for a large percentage of total development costs and increases in accordance with the size and complexity of software (Myers, 2004). As systems grow larger and more complex, testing time and effort is expected to increase. Therefore, the automation of software testing has become an urgent practical necessity to reduce test cost and time. Also, defining complete test case sets plays an important role in software testing, and the generation of test cases has generally been identified as an important research challenge. In recent years, researchers presented the results of an informal survey in which researchers in testing were asked to comment on the most notable achievements of the research effort and the open challenges in the field. The most common keywords in the experts' answers are the word "generation", which, together with a few other terms such as "tools" and "practice", confirms the importance of the topic of test generation approaches, which must be accompanied by good tool support to cover practical needs.

Modern software development is a knowledge-intensive activity. Process models, development methods, technologies, and development tools are part of the toolbox of the modern software designer, which includes several toolkits, configuration management tools, test suites, standards, and intelligent compilers with sophisticated debugging capabilities, just to name a few. The software engineer's vision of carefully crafting language statements into a work program is outdated and gives way to the use of a variety of tools and techniques that support the coordination of work and the creation of systems that conform to the complexity of the concept demanded by users of modern software.

Much of the development cycle is spent on debugging, where the programmer performs a long, failure trace and tries to locate the problem in a few lines of source code to clarify the cause of the problem. In this way, testing among software quality assurance techniques is one of the commonly used techniques in practice. Consequently, testing is also extensively studied in research. An important aspect of testing that is receiving a lot of attention in the issue of generating reusable test cases.

Software testing has been the most widely used software quality assurance technology for many decades. Due to its successful practical application, considerable research effort has been made to improve the effectiveness of tests and to scale the techniques for dealing with increasingly complex software systems. Therefore, automation of test activities is the key factor for improving test effectiveness. Automation involves four main activities: (i) generating tests, (ii) performing these tests on the system under test, (iii) evaluating the results of test procedures, and (iv) managing the results of test executions.

Software Testing Types

Below are the main types of software tests addressing different stages of the software development lifecycle:

- Collaborative testing involving developers, testers, and other QA professionals
- User acceptance testing- involving actual software users test the software to make sure it can handle required tasks in real-world scenarios, according to specifications
- Exploratory testing- an approach that involves simultaneous learning, test design and test execution

- Usability testing- evaluating a product or service by testing it with representative users
- Pairwise testing- a test case generation technique that is based on the observation that most faults are caused by interactions of at most two factors

Testers test performance, data migration, infrastructure, stress, and load. Other aspects include security to ensure authentication. The product should have preventive measures for hacking and attacks. Scalability is another factor tester undertake.

Automatic Test Case Generation

The software industry needs to perform testing by a systematic and practical approach and to address complete test coverage. This testing criterion attempts to group elements of the input domain into classes such that the elements of a given class behave in the same way. This way, the software testing group can choose a single test case as representative of each class. If testing group divide the input domain into disjoint classes, they say the classes constitute a partition or an equivalence partitioning of the domain, then there is no particular reason to choose one element over another as a class representative. As in any other engineering disciplines, it is important to document the design of software products, from the initial development through the maintenance period that follows. Documentation is used in design reviews, to guide the programmers, to guide the users and to save cost when the software must be extended or modified. The software development team needs to perform testing on developed software product to provide quality assurance to the ultimate users of the software. In this way, testing needs to be a systematic and practical approach that cover all aspects of the software product and commonly known as complete coverage principle.

This testing principle tries to group elements of the input domain into classes such that the elements of a given class behave in the same way. This way, one can choose a single test case as representative of each class.

Test case generation is a critical step in testing. A test case species the pretest state of the product under test and its environment, as well as the test inputs or conditions. A test suite is a collection of test cases, typically related by a testing goal or implementation dependency.

The test case generation can generate not only input to exercise the software, sometimes the properties of the corresponding output can be specified too. In this thesis, only the generation of input data is concerned. However, the method and algorithm, as well as the tool developed in this chapter, can be easily extended to determine whether an <input, output> pair satisfies the relation described by the specification.

An analysis of black-box testing techniques is described in, such as boundary-value analysis. Later binomial method was proposed, and a tool based on this method was developed. While our method is selecting test cases randomly within a partition, they select test data according to rules-based upon certain assumptions. Both of these are complementary to but different from, the work described in this chapter.

The equivalence partitioning is usually regarded as black-box testing. However, because tabular expressions can be used to document all the software documentations involved in all stages of software life cycle, including software requirements as well as module internal design and implementations, this method can also be used to test system specification, i.e., consistency, and to test module internal design.

A recent survey (Anand et al., 2013) covers test-case and test data generation techniques that include various techniques like symbolic execution, model-based testing, combinatorial interaction testing, adaptive random testing, and search-based testing. Relevant work includes that of Mayrhauser's (Mayrhauser et al, 2000), approach is an attempt to design a system that can use the idea of test case generation. In their work, a new method of test case generation is proposed to improve the reuse of test cases through domain analysis and domain modelling. Also, research into the reuse of test cases has been proposed, mainly divided into two categories: the generation of reusable test-cases and the management of reusable test cases.

Xu and colleagues (Xu et al., 2003) advocated a theoretical model for generating and executing patterns, making the test cases independent of the software under test and achieving the goal of reusing tests. Wang has focused on a test-case generation approach based on ontology. To describe the test case precisely and accurately, Guo and his colleague (Guo et al., 2011) pointed to an ontology-based method widely used as the basis for the sharing and reuse of knowledge in information science. Xiao-Li and collaborators (Xiao-Li et al., 2006) developed a test case library and discussed the model of test case management. To aid effective reuse of tests, Shao and collaborators (Shao, Bai & Zhao, 2006) proposed a software test design model based on the analysis of reusable test assets and their relationships.

Comparison of Traditional and Agile Software Testing

Traditional software development uses a phased approach (e.g. requirement elicitation, specification, coding, testing, and release). Testing takes place at the end of the software development, shortly before the release. This is shown schematically in the upper part of Figure 2. The diagram describes an ideal situation because it gives the impression that there is just as much time for testing as for coding. However, this is not the case with many software developments projects. Testing is 'squeezed' because coding takes longer than expected and the teams end up going through a code-and-fix cycle. Traditional testing was the mainstream, but efficiency increases when an enterprise makes a shift from traditional to agile testing.

Traditional testing aims to understand user needs and develop a product. After development, testers test the product and report bugs before deployment. The development team then works on them and fixes any errors using the best possible solution. Traditional testing works on the assumption that the processes are repetitive and predictable.

The concept is that the team can get the processes in control during the SDLC. A hierarchy ensures stability at different levels. It standardizes procedures by allotting different tasks to people according to their skills. But while the traditional model seems clear, it lacks flexibility. The procedure is time-consuming as the team completes tasks in a fixed sequence.

In contrast, Agile testing seeks to correct the rigidity of traditional testing. It is a team-based approach that, unlike traditional testing, is interactive and dynamic. As a result, the delivery time shortens. Agile testing is iterative and incremental. This means that the testers test each code increment as soon as it is complete. An iteration can only take a week or a month. The team builds and tests a bit of code to make sure it is working properly, and then proceeds to the next part that needs to be created. Agile software development is shown in the lower part of Figure 2. The label 'A', 'B', 'C', 'D', 'E', and 'F'- represent block or unit of code in a software system.

In comparison, in the Waterfall model, the testing process is more structured and there is a detailed description of the testing phase. Agile testing is well suited for small projects. On the other hand, Waterfall testing can be adopted for all sorts of projects. As testing begins at the start of the Agile project, errors can be fixed in the middle of the project. In the waterfall model, however, the product is tested at the end of the development. For any changes, testing must start from the beginning.

There is very less documentation required for agile testing. In contrast, the testing in the waterfall approach requires elaborate documentation.

Figure 2. The difference between traditional software development model and agile model

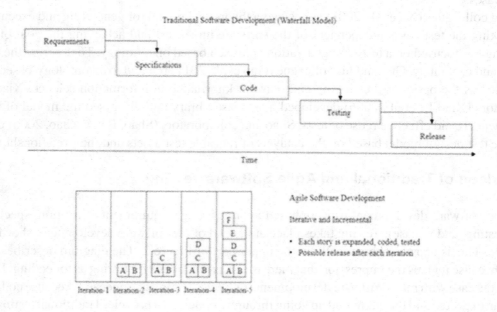

In the Agile approach, every iteration has its own testing phase. The regression tests can be run every time new functions or logic are released. In the waterfall approach, testing begins only after the completion of the development phase.

In agile testing shippable features of the product are delivered to the customer at the end of an iteration. In the waterfall approach, however, all features developed are delivered altogether after the implementation phase.

While testers and developers work closely in Agile testing, they work separately under a waterfall approach. User acceptance is performed at the end of every sprint but can only be performed at the end of the project in waterfall projects.

While in Agile, the testers need to establish communication with developers to analyze requirements and planning, developers are not involved in analyzing the requirements and planning process under a waterfall approach

Agile testing, therefore, is characterized by the following:

- *Testing is continuous*: Agile team tests continuously because it is the only way to ensure continuous progress of the product.
- *Continuous feedback*- Agile testing provides feedback on an ongoing basis and this is how your product meets the business needs.

- *Tests performed by the whole team*: In a traditional software development life cycle, only the test team is responsible for testing but in agile testing, the developers and the business analysts also test the application.

The resulting benefits can be summarized as:

- *Decreased time of feedback response*: Because the business team is involved in each iteration feedback is continuous and the time of feedback response is shortened.
- *Simplified & clean code*: All the defects which are raised by the agile team are fixed within the same iteration, which helps in keeping the code clean and simplified.
- *Less documentation*: Agile teams focus on the test instead of the incidental details.

Agile Testing Methods

There are various agile testing methods as follows:

- Behavior Driven Development (BDD)
- Acceptance Test-Driven Development (ATDD)
- Exploratory Testing

Behavior Driven Development (BDD)

Behavior Driven Development (BDD) improves communication amongst project stakeholders so that all members correctly understand each feature before the development process starts. There is continuous example-based communication between developers, testers, and business analysts.

The examples are called Scenarios that hold information on how a given feature should behave in different situations with different input parameters. These are called "Executable Specifications" as it comprises of both specification and inputs to the automated tests.

Acceptance Test-Driven Development (ATDD)

ATDD focuses on involving team members with different perspectives such as the customer, developer, and tester. Meetings are held to formulate acceptance tests incorporating perspectives of the customer, development, and testing. The customers focus on the problem that is to be solved, while the developers focus on how the problem will be solved, whereas testing is focused on what could go wrong. The acceptance tests are a representation of the user's point of view and they describe how the system will function. It also helps to verify that the system functions as it is supposed to. In some cases, acceptance tests are automated.

Exploratory Testing

In this type of testing, the test design and test execution phase go hand in hand. Exploratory testing emphasizes working software over comprehensive documentation. The individuals and interactions are more important than the process and tools. Customer collaboration holds greater value than contract negotiation. Exploratory testing is more adaptable to changes. In this tester identify the functionality of an application by exploring the application. The testers try to learn better determination of issues through daily meetings.

Test Plan for Agile

In agile testing, the test plan is written as well as updated for every release. A test plan in agile includes:

- The scope of the testing, consolidating new functionalities to be tested
- Types of testing/Levels of testing
- Performance & load testing
- Consideration of infrastructure
- Risks Plan
- Planning of resources
- Deliverables & Milestones

Iterative Testing Cycle in Agile Methods

The agile testing life cycle includes the following 5 phases:

- Impact assessment
- Agile Testing Planning
- Release Readiness
- Daily Scrums
- Test Agility Review.

The iterative cycles make changes according to consistent customer communication and feedback.

The first step is to check the quality of the code. The testers give immediate feedback. Then, based on the feedback, the developers carry on with their tasks. These tasks include unit testing and component architecture testing. The former refers to checking a coding unit to see if it fulfils the requirement, which is often done by the developers. The latter is to ensure that the pieces of code work when integrated.

Both the testers and developers get the requirement. Both carry out their respective tasks keeping business objectives in mind. That includes testing possible scenarios. Testers must perform prototype and wireframe testing while keeping user experience in mind.

Automation testing evaluates the product usage. Despite the product development being incomplete, tests are run. The scheduled demos ensure that development is going on according to business goals. These are the five stages the third quadrant covers:

Challenges of Agile Testing

Since the methodologies are different in traditional and agile testing, there are many challenges testers must face. These include:

- Sharp deadlines

- Learning the development procedure and programming languages
- Sudden changes requested from the stakeholder
- Need for impeccable coordination between teams

However, these challenges are counteracted by huge learning opportunities for the testers.

Agile Testing Automation Tools

Test automation is software that automates any aspect of testing of an application system. It includes capabilities to generate test inputs and expected results, to run test suites without manual intervention, and to reveal pass/no pass. The aim is to run the tests in a timely and efficient manner.

The aim is to automate testing as much as possible. Automated testing offers many significant advantages such as (Binder, 2000):

- Every time the software is changed, the automated test can be generated accordingly. On the other hand, manual testing is not repeatable, and rewriting is time consuming, tedious and errors prone.
- The test process information produced by manual testing is often inconsistent and fragmentary.
- An automated test is the only repeatable way to generate a large quantity of input and to evaluate a large quantity of output.
- The randomly generated test can greatly improve tester productivity.
- The cost of test automation is typically recovered after two or three projects from increased productivity and the avoided costs associated with buggy software.

Regression testing. automation tools to speed up testing include **Selenium WebDriver**, **HP UFT**, and **Appium**. **JUnit**, **Cucumber**, **Pytest**, **JBehave**, are some testing tools relevant to Agile testing.

Additionally, Project Management Tools such as **Slack**, **JIRA**, and **Mantis** can be used, apart from identifying bugs, for efficient collaboration and project management.

CONCLUSION

This chapter has addressed the important challenge of testing in a Scrum/DevOps software development environment. The adoption of agility at a large scale often requires the integration of agile and non-agile development elements in a hybrid adaptive methodology. The challenge is to determine which elements or components (agile and non-agile) are relevant to develop a hybrid adaptive testing methodology and framework. Making a move from traditional to agile testing can be overwhelming for testers at first, however, it offers potential for broadening the learning scope and an opportunity for enhancing their skills and professional growth. In agile processes like Scrum/DevOps, strong customer involvement demands techniques to facilitate the requirements acceptance testing. Additionally, test automation is crucial, as incremental development and continuous integration require high efforts for testing. In test-driven development, tests are written before the code, with developers adopting a short cycle of test-code-test-code and so on. During the test phase, the rule is that no operational code may be written except in response to a failing test.

The benefits of the agile testing approach can be summarized as follows: (i) it saves time and money, (ii) agile testing reduces documentation, (iii) it is flexible and highly adaptable to changes, and (iv) it provides a way for receiving regular feedback from the end-user.

As the size of developed software systems increases, agile testing will need to increasingly rely on software testing tools to solve challenges and speed-up the release of feedback from stakeholders. Such test tools and environments will need to incorporate collaboration features, automated and customized reporting and ways to avoid repeated efforts. Additionally, such tools will need to co-exist and integrate with other Agile lifecycle development environments.

REFERENCES

Ananda, S., Burke, E. K., Chenc, T. Y., Clark, J., Cohene, M. B., Grieskampf, W., Harmang, M., Harrold, M., Phil, J., & McMinn, P. H. (2013). An orchestrated survey of methodologies for automated software test case generation. *Journal of Systems and Software*, *86*(8), 1978–2001. doi:10.1016/j.jss.2013.02.061

Barlow, J. B. (2011). Overview and Guidance on Agile Development in Large Organizations. Comm. of the Ass. for Inform. *Systems*, *29*(1), 25–44.

Beck, K. (1999). Embracing change with extreme programming. *Computer*, *32*(10), 70–77. doi:10.1109/2.796139

Beck, K. (2003). *Test-Driven Development: By Example*. Pearson Education.

Beck, K., Cockburn, A., Jeffries, R., & Highsmith, J. (2001). *Agile manifesto*. http://www.agilemanifesto.org

Binder, R. V. (2000). *Testing Object-Oriented Systems: Models, Patterns, and Tolls*. Addison-Wesley.

Boehm, B. (1988). A spiral model of software development and enhancement. *IEEE Computer*, *21*(5), 61–72. doi:10.1109/2.59

Boehm, B. (2002). Get Ready for Agile Methods, with Care. *IEEE Computer*, *35*(1), 64–69. doi:10.1109/2.976920

Boehm, B., & Papaccio, P. (1988). Understanding and controlling software costs. *IEEE Transactions on Software Engineering*, *14*(10), 1462–1477. doi:10.1109/32.6191

Boehm, B., & Turner, B. (2003). *Balancing Agility and Discipline: A Guide for the Perplexed*. Addison Wesley Pearson Education.

Boehm, R., & Turner, B. (2003b). Using risk to balance agile and plan-driven methods. *Computer*, *36*(6), 57–66. doi:10.1109/MC.2003.1204376

Cockburn, A. & Williams, L. (2003). Agile software development: it's about feedback and change. *IEEE Computer, 36*(6), 39–43.

Crispin, L., & Gregory, J. (2009). *Agile Testing: a Practical Guide for Testers and Agile Teams*. Addison-Wesley Professional.

Cunningham, W. (2001). *Agile Manifesto, 2001*. http://www.agilemanifesto.org

Gill, A. Q. (2014). Hybrid adaptive software development capability: An empirical study. *Journal of Software*, 9(10), 2614–2621. doi:10.4304/jsw.9.10.2614-2621

Guo, S., Tong, W., Zhang, J., & Liu, Z. (2011). An Application of Ontology to Test Case Reuse. *International Conference on Mechatronic Science, Electrical Engineering and Computer*.

Ipate, F., & Holcombe, M. (1997). An integration testing method that is proved to find all faults. *International Journal of Computer Mathematics*, 63(3-4), 159–178. doi:10.1080/00207169708804559

Jalote, P., & Jain, G. (2006). Assigning tasks in a 24-hours software development model. *Journal of Systems and Software*, 79(7), 904–911. doi:10.1016/j.jss.2005.06.040

Jilin, C., Hneif, M., & Ow, S. H. (2009). Review of Agile Methodologies in Software Development 1. *International Journal of Research and Reviews in Applied Sciences*, 1(1), 2076–73. doi:10.1109/MEC.2011.6025579

Labs, P. (2015). *State of DevOps 2015 Report*. IT Revolution Press. https://puppet.com/resources/white-paper/2015-state-of-devops-report

Lee, S., & Young, H. (2013). Agile Software Development Framework in a Small Project Environment. *Journal of Information Systems*, 9(1).

Lindvall, M., Muthig, D., Dagnino, A., Wallin, C., Stupperich, M., Kiefer, D., May, J., & Kahkonen, T. (2004). Agile Software Development in Large Organizations. *IEEE Computer Society*, 4(12), 26–34. doi:10.1109/MC.2004.231

Mahanti, A. (2006). Challenges in Enterprise adoption of agile methods – a survey. *Journal of Computing and Information Technology – CIT*, 197-206.

Mall, R. (2006). *Fundamental of Software Engineering* (2nd ed.). Prentice Hall.

Mayrhauser, A., France, R., Scheetz, M., & Dahlman, E. (2000). Generating test-cases from an object-oriented model with an artificial-intelligence planning system. Reliability. *IEEE Transactions on.*, 49, 26–36. doi:10.1109/24.855534

Myers, G. J. (2004). *The Art of Software Testing* (2nd ed.). John Wiley & Sons.

Pal, K. (2019). Markov Decision Theory Based Crowdsourcing Software Process Model. In Crowdsourcing and Probabilistic Decision-Making in Software Engineering: Emerging Research and Opportunities. IGI Publication.

Pal, K. (2020). Framework for Reusable Test Case Generation in Software Systems Testing. In Software Engineering for Agile Application Development. IGI Global Publication.

Rodriguez, P., Markkula, J., Oivo, M., & Turula, K. (2012). Survey on agile and lean usage in finnish software industry. *Proceeding of ACM-IEEE international symposium on Empirical software engineering and measurement*, 139-148. 10.1145/2372251.2372275

Roebuck, K. (2012). *System Development Life Cycle (SDLC): High-impact Strategies – What You Need to Know: Definition, Adoption, Impact, Benefits, Maturity, Vendors*. Emereo Publishing.

Royce, W. W. (1970). Managing the Development of Large Software Systems. *Proceedings of IEEE WESCON, 26*(August), 1–9.

Schwaber, K., & Beedle, M. (2002). *Agile Software Development with SCRUM*. Prentice-Hall.

Schwaber, K. & Sutherland, J. (2009). Scrum guide. Scrum Alliance, Seattle. *Journal of Mini-Micro Systems, 27*, 2150-2155.

Sommerville, I. (2019). *Software Engineering*. Addison Wesley.

Talby, D., Keren, A., Hazzan, O., & Dubinsky, Y. (2006). Agile Software Testing in a Large-scale Project. *Software, 23*(4), 30–37. doi:10.1109/MS.2006.93

van Veenendaal, E. (2009). Scrum & Testing: Back to the Future. *Testing Experience, 3*.

van Veenendaal, E. (2010). Scrum & Testing: Assessing the risks. *Agile Record, 3*.

VersionOne. (2011). State of Agile Survey 2011 - The State of Agile Development. *Journal of Computational Science, 33*, 290–291.

Xu, R., Chen, B., Chen, B., Wu, M., & Xiong, Z. (2003). Investigation on the pattern for Construction of Reusable Test Cases in Object-oriented Software. *Journal of Wuhan University, 49*(005), 592–596.

KEY TERMS AND DEFINITIONS

Agile Software Methodology: An evolutionary and iterative approach to software development with focuses on adaption to changes.

Critical Software Systems: Software whose failure would impact safety or cause large financial or social losses.

DevOps: Development and operations (DevOps) has been adopted by prominent software and service companies (e.g., IBM) to support enhanced collaboration across the company and its value chain partners. In this way, DevOps facilitates uninterrupted delivery and coexistence between development and operation facilities, enhances the quality and performance of software applications, improving end-user experience, and help to simultaneous deployment of software across different platforms.

Scrum: An agile process framework for managing knowledge work, with an emphasis on software development.

Software Engineering: The application of engineering to the development of software in a systematic method.

Software Life Cycle Processes: It provides a framework for the sequence of activities to be performed for software projects.

Software Process Standards: It presents fundamental standards that describe activities performed as part of the software life cycle. In some cases, these standards also describe documents, but these represent plans for conducting activities.

Software Quality: Software engineering standards, if sufficiently comprehensive and if properly enforced, establish a *quality system*, a systematic approach to ensuring software quality, which is defined as (1) the degree to which a system, component, or process meets specified requirements; and (2) the degree to which a system, component, or process meets customer or user needs or expectations.

Software Quality Assurance: Software quality assurance is defined as follows: (1) a planned and systematic pattern of all actions necessary to provide adequate confidence that an item or product conforms to established technical requirements; and (2) a set of activities designed to evaluate the process by which products are developed or manufactured.

Software Testing: Software testing provides the mechanism for verifying that the requirements identified during the initial phases of the project were properly implemented and that the system performs as expected. The test scenarios developed through these competitions ensure that the requirements are met end-to-end.

Verification and Validation: The process of determining whether the requirements for a system or component are complete and correct, the products of each development phase fulfil the requirements or conditions imposed by the previous phase, and the final system or component complies with specified requirements.

Waterfall Model: A sequential design, used in software development processes, in which progress is seen as flowing steadily downwards (like a waterfall) through the phases of Requirements, Specifications, Coding, Testing, and Release.

Chapter 9
Human Resource Management in Agile Scrum Processes

Matthew Zingoni
University of New Orleans, USA

ABSTRACT

The value agile scrum process can generate is not guaranteed simply by mere adoption. Rather the process creates an opportunity for improvement in the development process. Mismanagement of the approach by an organization can reduce the potential added value or in extreme situations have a negative impact. Therefore, appropriate management procedures are necessary to realize the full potential of the agile scrum approach. This chapter focuses on the human resource challenges the agile scrum approach creates for an organization. The dynamic pace, cross-functional composition, and self-directed team approach requires special consideration in the development of most human resource functions. In particular, the authors will review changes to the employee selection, performance management, and learning and career development processes. These changes will better align these functions with the values and principals of the agile scrum approach and help organizations manage this sometimes chaotic approach to innovation without constraining it.

INTRODUCTION

The benefits of an Agile Scrum process have been well established in the software development field (Rigby, et. al., 2016) and other organizations have taken notice. Today an Agile Scrum process approach can be seen applied to fields beyond information technology such as marketing and financial (Oprins, et al., 2019; Sherman, et. al., 2017). Essentially an Agile Scrum process approach is increasingly being applied to situations where innovation is needed to respond to rapidly changing customers' demands (Rigby, et. al., 2018). This creates a challenge to organizations to not only implement an agile scrum approach but to also create processes and procedures to manage the Agile Scrum process and also cultivate the proper organizational climate needed to realize its full benefit in a sustainable manner (Mahajan, 2013; Rigby, et. al., 2016).

DOI: 10.4018/978-1-7998-4885-1.ch009

Copyright © 2021, IGI Global. Copying or distributing in print or electronic forms without written permission of IGI Global is prohibited.

Like previous process innovations such as total quality management, the Agile Scrum approach offers an opportunity for a competitive advantage but not a certainty. In what has been described as a chaotic approach to innovation (Rubin, 2012) the Agile Scrum approach to development generates several challenges for organizations to overcome. Just like a sailor cannot control the wind but instead must try to direct and harness it, managers must direct Agile Scrum teams without containing the sometimes-chaotic process of innovation. This chapter will address some of the human resource challenges an organization must overcome to successfully implement the agile scrum approach to innovation and other dynamic endeavors in a sustainable manner. Specifically, this chapter reviews and offers recommendations for an organization to consider in the areas of talent acquisition and management, which are vital to implementing an Agile Scrum approach effectively (Gilles & van der Meer, 2017).

Human resource management addresses who works for an organization and how work gets done. In particular human resource processes (i.e. employee selection, performance management, talent deployment, and employee career development) play an essential role in the acquisition and cultivation of the main raw material needed to utilize the agile scrum approach, which is the individual. The Agile Scrum approach requires a cross functional team to self-navigate a demanding, fast pace, dynamic environment (Beck, et. al, 2001; Rubin, 2012; Rigby, et. al., 2016). The Agile Scrum approach has a set of values and principles that human resource functions need to be aligned with to be successful. Specifically, agile processes are built around people over process and tools, emphasize working prototypes over excessive debate, respond to change than follow a plan, and focuses on customer collaboration instead of structured contracts (Beck, et. al, 2001; Rigby, et. al., 2016). It is important that organizations have human resource practices that reflect these values and principals so the Agile Scrum approach can be effectively managed but not constrained. However, human resource practices have traditionally been slow to involve (Cappelli, 2015) at the organizational level so it is important that organizations make adjustment to the procedures used to manage employees directly involved in the Agile Scrum approach to innovation. This will allow the organization to maximize the benefit of the Agile Scrum approach and develop human resources practices that may be suited to be expanded company wide. In short organizational level human resources changes may be slow to evolve but if companies can successfully create human resource practices to accommodate their Agile Scrum involved employees it could lead to a more agile approach to human resources at an organization wide level.

This chapter will review the major aspects of human resources that will need to be adjusted to accommodate the Agile Scrum approach. First, it will review adjustments needed to the hiring process for employees who will directly participant in work utilizing the Agile Scrum approach. Next, it will review how changes to the performance management procedures an organization uses will be necessary for employees to make the corrective changes in their work behavior that is required by such a dynamic process. This in turn will transition to a discussion on talent deployment which is how an organization should determine what Agile Scrum team an employee should be involved with next. A review of the changes to how an organization handles career development of their Agile Scrum involved employees will then follow. Lastly. it will discuss how adjusting human resource practices used to manage Agile Scrum involved employees will assist in the evolution of a more agile approach to human resources at the organizational level. During these discussions examples not only from the technology field but also other innovation focused industries such as the entertainment industry and fashion industry will be used.

Employee Selection in an Agile Scum Context

All aspects of human resources are interdependent and therefore equally important. However, employee selection is the human resource function that gets the most attention as it directly determines who joins an organization. Due in part to this attention, employee selection procedures have greatly evolved from the days of solely relying on a single job interview. This evolution has included organization trying to assess applicants fit at multiple levels such as, person-job, person-group, and person-organization (Kristof-Brown, et. al., 2005) and the increased use of psychological assessments and situational judgements test (Chamorro-Premuzic, 2015). When selecting employees to work in an agile scum approach a radical departure from these advancements is not necessary but adjustments, particularly to how each selection tool is weighted in the hiring decision and who should be involved in the selection process, is needed (Gilles & van der Meer, 2017). Furthermore, the qualities desired in an employee are difficult to directly measure so organization need to take steps to utilize multiple selection tools to indirectly measure these qualities in candidates.

The job interview has always been and will continue to be the cornerstone of employee selection in business. In particular, the structure interview approach, where a predetermined set of questions are developed to measure desired qualifications and are consistently asked across all applicants, is vital to any selection process. This of course remains true for employee selection for positions that will have a role in an agile scrum approach. However, during the question development process an emphasis on measuring not only technical knowledge but also person-group fit, emergent leadership, and broad competencies is important.

Focus on fit between an employee and a potential job, group, and or organization is vitally important to all hires (Kristof-Brown, et. al., 2005). However, due to the cross functional team composition of the Agile Scrum process group-fit becomes a priority. Group-fit focuses on the match between and individual and their work group (Kristof-Brown, et. al., 2005). In an interview setting a panel interview with existing team members is considered a best practice. However, due to revolving number of team memberships a new employee will be part of in an agile scrum approach, team members will not be a constant. Therefore, a panel interview with experienced proven members of ongoing agile scum process should be conducted. Even though these panel members will not always directly work with the applicant their perspective and input will be valuable. For example, GE utilize a cross functional team to assist in all hiring requisitions (Cappelli & Tavis, 2018).

Although not specifically established in the "fit" literature it would be valuable to try to measure person-approach fit. That is does the applicants competencies match the unique demands of the Agile Scrum approach. This is particularly true if the applicant does not have previous experience working on an Agile Scrum development team. In fact, a lack of experience is one of the most significant challenges in implementing the Agile Scrum approach (Cappelli & Tavis, 2018). For example, the dynamic nature of Agile Scrum work creates a level of uncertainty that may be uncomfortable for some employees. Uncertainty has a significant negative relationship with performance for both students and professionals (Taipalus, et. al., 2018). Therefore, assessing an applicant's tolerance for ambiguity (Frenkel-Brunswik, 1948) would be valuable. Tolerance of ambiguity is often used to indicate how comfortable someone is with change. Furthermore, tolerance for ambiguity has been found to have a significant relationship to creativity (Zenasni, et. al., 2008) Tolerance for ambiguity is the combination of three factors (Budner, 1962). First factor is novelty, which is how comfortable someone is with new information and processes. Second is complexity, which is how comfortable some is with complex problems that change often. The last component is insolvability, which is how comfortable people are working on problems that do not have a clear or perfect solution. Overall, these components reflect agile scrum processes and therefore someone high in tolerance for ambiguity will likely be a better fit for the agile scrum approach.

In addition to the panel interview, contextual questions such as situational judgement test should be utilized as well. Situational judgement questions are a selection tool that presents an applicant a relevant challenging situation they are likely to encounter (Chamorro-Premuzic, 2015). Often the applicant is then given several choices of action to which they are to select what they feel is the most effective approach. Having an applicant complete a series of situational judgement questions and then discuss their responses with a panel would be the best course of action for hiring potential Agile Scrum team members.

A focus of the structure interview and situational judgment tests should be if the applicant reflects an emergent leadership style. In a New York Times article Google executive stated that emergent leadership and humility are more valuable the traditional leadership traits in a dynamic environment (Friedman, 2014). Emergent leadership does not only include the ability and motivation to step up and lead a group when the situation calls for it but also the ability to take a step back and let others lead when appropriate (Anderson & Wanberg, 1991). This is vital in a self-managed team like the ones used in Agile Scrum process because as objectives change during each sprint it is important for employees to be able to lead at times but also be a good follower at other times. Emergent leadership is a form of contingency or situational leadership models that are found to be the most useful in self-managed teams such as agile scrum teams (Anderson & Wanberg, 1991; Przybilla, et. al., 2019).

The use of assessments as a selection tool has steadily increased over the past decade. To the point where fortune 500 companies use assessments for over half of their entry level positions and almost three quarters of their upper management positions (Chamorro-Premuzic, 2015). These assessments offer another means to measure qualities we attempt to gauge in the structured interview process. As situational judgement test with a panel interview, as described above, can help measure person-group fit. Assessments could further this examination by assessing other traits and abilities valuable for dynamic team-based work. For example, certain dimensions of the Big Five personality dimensions as described below may be valuable.

- **Extroversion**: Sociable and outgoing
- **Neuroticism**: Stability in emotions
- **Openness to experience:** Being flexible and curious
- **Agreeableness**: Being courtesy and caring
- **Consciousness**: Detailed and achievement oriented

Specifically, of the Big Five personality dimensions agreeableness, being courtesy and caring, is vital for person group fit. Furthermore, openness to experience, being flexible and curious, also vital for a dynamic team structure particularly one that requires constant learning and adjusting (Barrick & Mount, 1991). In addition, emotional intelligence would be another important assessment to utilize in the selection process. Emotional intelligence is one's ability to be aware their emotion and keep them under control. Along with recognizing emotions in others and responding appropriately. Emotional intelligence is a vital ability for employees to not only respond to feedback appropriately but also giving feedback to others (Chamorro-Premuzic, 2015). Furthermore, emotional intelligence has been found beneficial in agile processes particularly regarding the dynamic nature and resulting time compression (Wilding, 1999).

In summary the selection process for employees needs to be refocused if the employee is going to be part of an Agile Scrum development team. The use of panel interviews, a focus on group-fit, and supporting assessments (i.e., agreeableness, openness to experience, emotional intelligence) are useful in most if not all hiring situations. However, these qualities are more relevant to the Agile Scrum process and therefore greater emphasis and weighting should be place on these selection tools.

Performance Management

Performance management is a systematic evaluation to ensure that employee's behavior is align with assigned responsibilities and organizational goals. Changes in performance management have been slower to evolve than that of other aspects of human resources. The traditional approach to performance management consist of an annual review, where a formal evaluation is conducting and discussed with the employee. In addition, corrective action is discussed along with any compensation decisions. This annual meeting is supported by shorter less formal coaching sessions throughout the year. Recently there has been movement away from this approach towards a more flexible process (Cappelli & Tavis, 2018). However, for employees participating in Agile Scrum development teams breaking away from this traditional approach is vital.

Performance management for employees involved in the Agile Scrum approach to development needs to take three major questions into consideration.

- **How often?** Focus on frequency and timing
- **Who to involve?** Stakeholders and information sources
- **Where it takes place?** Not location but organizational climate

First focus is on the "how" that is how often performance management should be conducted. When managing an Agile Scrum development teams, the timing and frequency of performance management efforts need to reflect the flow of work and not a predetermined day on the fiscal calendar. Specifically, once a project is completed a formal evaluation should be done to discuss the employee's contributions during the project and future assignments. Therefore, this conversation is not only serving a performance management purposes but also addresses deployment and development issues as well. Second, is the "who", that is who should be involved in the performance management process. When managing an Agile Scrum development teams, feedback needs to be conduct in a 360-degree format, with an emphasis on team member input. Due to the interdependent nature of Agile Scrum work it is challenging to determine individual contributions, so team member input is vital. Third is the "where", that is the environment or culture the feedback is given in. A culture of learning and improvement through effort is needed to avoid employees becoming defense and ensure employees are receptive to feedback (Murphy & Dweck, 2010).

Changing the timing and frequency of performance evaluation to match the flow of work is a change that is starting to be adopt in the greater business community. This approach can now be seen in fields that specialize on project-based work like business consulting and the entertainment industry. The approach's value can be best seen through the lens of Reinforcement Theory of motivation (Skinner, 1953). Reinforcement theory is a theory on how to change behavior and essentially discusses how an individual learns how to behave and not behave. According to reinforcement theory consequence for behavior dictates individual's future behavior in either a positive or negative direction. If an individual receives a positive consequence (i.e. reward) after a behavior the behavior will be repeated. If an individual receives a negative consequence (i.e., punishment) after a behavior the behavior will not be repeated. A key tenement to reinforcement theory is the timing of the consequence. The closer the consequence, either positive or negative (i.e., punishment or reward), to the behavior the stronger the directed influence will be on future behavior (Luthans, & Stajkovic 1999). Therefore, according to reinforcement theory, if a project is completed in June but the employee does not receive a full evaluation till the annual designated time in January the evaluation is less effective than one done immediately afterwards in July.

As reinforcement theory informs us on how to best time performance conversation it also holds true for compensation as far as pay for performance decisions. Performance conversation and compensation need to be aligned for both to be effective. The rewards aspect of receiving positive feedback is much strong if any financial reward is also given at the same time (Rigby, et. al., 2018). Therefore, any adjustment to the timing of performance conversations should have a corresponding adjustment to compensation decisions (Cappelli & Tavis, 2018). Also in regards to compensation, organizations need to focus on group level pay for performance policies not just individual level as agile scrum employees are producing a product or service that requires an interdependent group (Darrell, et. al., 2016; Rigby, et. al., 2018).

Frequency of feedback is also important to the performance management of employees participating in an agile scum approach to development. Frequent feedback during a project serves two major purposes. The first is it allows for the opportunity for corrective action by the employee. This approach reflects the workflow of Agile Scrum, which is incremental improvement of a series of iterations or sprints. Therefore, in an Agile Scrum approach the outcomes is constantly being incrementally improved so must the employee behavior who is directly producing the outcome. The second benefit of frequent performance conversations is managing expectations. It is natural for employees to have a positive bias in their perception of their own work contributions leading to inaccurate expectations of their performance level. This can be true about their intangible contributions and interpersonal behavior, which are better viewed from the eyes of team members. Realistic expectations about their performance level is vital to the success of the post project evaluation session. Employee are less defensive when personal information is predictable or anticipated and therefore more responsive to feedback.

Of course, having frequent performance management conversations and timely formal evaluation sessions can be a heavy time burden for any manager regardless of their good intentions. This is particularly true when incorporating feedback from all team members in a 360-degree fashion. In theory, frequent feedback from all stakeholders sounds great. However, the time burden makes it a daunting if not impossible task. Even if an Agile Scrum team accomplished this feat the time committed to it and away from directly working on their project could lead members to resent the performance management process and disengage from it. To avoid this fate, it is important that the performance management process be not only effective but efficient. This is especially true for feedback conversations that take place during an ongoing project.

Creating an efficient and effective performance management process is not solely about forms and procedures but also reflection of team and organizational culture and environment. A company's culture not being aligned with the values of the agile scrum approach is often seen as the most significant challenge to effectively implementing the agile scrum approach (Cappelli & Tavis, 2018). Therefore, discussion about performance need to be routine and a natural part of the organizations culture. For example, at the company Netflix feedback discussion are done frequently and are project driven, like recommended above. The frequent feedback conversations are done in person in a group setting. The conversation is a simple three statement approach about each team member. Please *start* doing this. Please *stop* doing this. Please *continue* doing this (McCord, 2014). This "start, stop, continue" approach is efficient and predictable for employees and not difficult to make a requirement. However, team and organizational culture must reflect a respectful and forgiving environment also referred to as a learning culture (Murphy & Dweck, 2010). Creating an organization and team with a learning culture is the real challenge to using this approach and the right people go a long way in creating it.

Netflix contributes having this such environment to their rigorous selection process. Simple stated if you hire the right people implementing progressive human resource policies are possible (McCord, 2014). As recommended early in the chapter incorporating potential team members into the selection process in the form of panel interviews sets the right tone for the development of a learning culture. Having potential teammates involved in the selection process signals to an applicant that teammates are a valuable source of information and their feedback is respected.

Of course, creating a learning culture requires more than hiring the right people and involving them in the process. This alone handle the "who" part of human resource management, but steps still need to be taken to address the "how" question. The above recommendation of efficient quick feedback conversation addressing the "start", "stop", and "continue" questions are a significant step towards addressing the "how". However, supplying training that briefly describes how to formulate an effective feedback message is particularly important even in brief exchanges. Focusing on the behavior and subsequent problem not the person is essential. Behavior and problems are controllable where personal characteristics are harder to change and, in some cases, not possible at all. There is a big difference between saying "Stop being stupid because it is creating a problem" and "stop this stupid behavior because it is creating a problem".

Essentially a learning environment focus on improvement through effort (Murphy & Dweck, 2010). This approach is referred to as reflecting a growth mindset and is vital for innovation. Innovation and learning inherently involve mistakes and corrective action but always moving forward through effort and the desire to improve. When feedback focuses not on effort and process but instead on solely just the outcome produced it cultivates what is called a fixed or entity mindset (Dweck & Leggett, 1988). This type of mindset creates an environment that is less forgiving and therefore instills a fragile sense of confidence. Innovation natural involves mistakes and setbacks so when the inevitable setback occurs those with a fixed mindset respond poorly. Specifically, they will become defense and not be receptive to feedback. On the other hand, those with a growth mindset, who view effort to improve future performance, will be more resilient in the face of setbacks and more receptive to feedback (Dweck & Leggett, 1988). The Agile Scrum approach to development is focused on consistent incremental improvement in response to customer's feedback. This is best executed when the employees are also focused on making consistent incremental improvements to their own behavior in response to team member's feedback.

This growth mindset is not only valuable for employees in their response to feedback about themselves but also in the way they give feedback and coach others. Specifically, managers with a more growth mindset, more accurately recognized a change in employees' performance, both positive and negative, from an initial performance level (Heslin, et. al., 2005). Furthermore, managers with a growth mindset, engage in more extensive developmental coaching of their employees, compared with, managers with a fixed mindset (Heslin et al., 2006). This increase in coaching behavior, along with the more accurate performance appraisals mentioned earlier, has led to managers with a growth mindset to also be viewed as more procedural just or fair, by their employees (Heslin & VandeWalle, 2010). Thankfully, research has shown the growth mindset can be cultivated in employees with the proper training (Heslin, et. al., 2005) or presenting them with the proper evidence (Aronson, et. al., 2002).

A culture that is aligned with the values and principals of the Agile Scrum process is important to achieve the highest level of performance (Cappelli & Tavis, 2018). A learning culture, which is one that focuses on effort and incremental improvement (Murphy & Dweck, 2010), is an important component of an aligned organizational culture. Another component an organization should consider is the feedback environment they create. Originally feedback environment just referred to the perceived availability of feedback by employees (Herold & Parson, 1985). However, this concept has been expanded on to include several dimensions supplied by both supervisors and coworkers. These dimensions include, but are not limited to, feedback source and availability, feedback quality and delivery, and promoting feedback seeking behavior (Steelman, et. al., 2004). The recommendations in this chapter positively influence all these components. By directly involving team member in the feedback process both informally and formally on a frequent basis improves both feedback source credibility and source availability. Focusing feedback on effort and controllable behaviors will improve both feedback quality and feedback delivery. Finally, cultivating a learning environment will promote feedback seeking behavior (see Kluger & DeNisi, 1996 for summary of feedback findings). Taken together, these recommendations would improve the feedback environment leading to stronger Agile Scrum team output.

In summary, in an Agile Scrum context an organization needs to address three major characteristics to properly implement effective performance management. First is the question of how and specifically "how often". Moving away from a formal evaluation given at a designated day on the fiscal calendar is necessary. Instead formal evaluations at the time of project completion is the more effective approach. In addition, smaller informal feedback conversation should occur which will allow for corrective action and better manage employee's performance expectations. Furthermore, focusing on effort and controllable behavior will decrease the chances of employees being unreceptive and defensive to feedback. Regarding who, it is important that all team members contribute to the informal feedback conversations in person and give input to the formal evaluation session conducted at project completion. Finally, the "where" question focuses the attention on the environment and team/organizational culture where the feedback is given in. Cultivating a learning/growth culture not only at the team level but also company level will in time create a more resilient agile scrum team that will not only focus on incremental improvement on team outcomes but also incremental improvements in their own actions and behaviors. All these recommendations will positively affect the feedback environment leading to more effective performance management and high-quality outcomes from agile scrum teams.

Learning, Deployment and Career Development

Career advancement opportunities are essential for employee's engagement particularly for talented employees likely to be a part of Agile Scrum development team. Organization need to establish procedures and strategies to reduce employee turnover and cultivate a strong internal labor supply. The traditional components of a development program are job experience, education, and interpersonal relationships. These components are organized to move people up a define career path commonly referred to as the corporate ladder. Where the corporate ladder reflects career progress as a ridged progression directly up the corporate hierarchy. While this approach has been effective for years and still commonly used today it is not appropriate for Agile Scrum team members. The corporate ladder approach is not appropriate for Agile Scrum team members because job titles have less significance and hierarchical levels are fewer (Rigby, et. al., 2018). Instead for Agile Scrum team members these same components must be combined in a different manner that better reflects the dynamics of the Agile Scrum approach to work. Specifically companies need to view career advancement as developing an Agile Scrum members competencies so they can better expand their influence and increase their recognition (financial and non-financial) all while increase their value to an organization (Rigby, et. al., 2018) .

The learning component needs to be more customized to the individual employee's needs with a focus on the competencies required to be an effective Agile Scrum team member. This is achieved through direct coaching conversations with a manager along with self-directed education opportunities. As described above a performance management process that reflects the workflow of Agile Scrum development teams is important. These processes should include formal evaluation at the completion of a project and frequent performance conversation along the way that allows for corrective action. This performance management approach plays an important role not only for employee's performance on current projects but also assist employees in being better prepared for their next assignment. It is important that there is a distinction in these conversation about evaluation of past performance and a development conversation on how to be better equipped for future assignments.

When it comes to learning opportunities, it is vital that the subject matter reflects the unique demands of the Agile Scrum approach to development. To be an effective member of an Agile Scrum development team you need to have more than just technical knowledge but also the competencies that meet the demands created by cross-functional self-directed teams (Fernandez-Araoz, 2014). Therefore, training topics such as conflict resolutions and suppling critical feedback are essential for developing Agile Scrum team members.

All employees have different developmental needs, but this is particularly true for Agile Scrum team members. It is important that the training opportunities are flexible to reflect the unique background of Agile Scrum members. Flexible training programs that empower employees are becoming more popular, being used by companies such as AT&T (Donovan, & Benko, 2016), on a companywide basis. Regarding Agile Scrum employees IBM offers a good example as they have a long history of effectively using Agile Scrum teams. Their success is partially due to the well-developed learning and training program for their Agile Scrum members. The training interface reflects how information is more commonly consumed today. Diane Gherson, IBM's head of human resources, describes there learning and development interface as "tailored by role, with intelligent recommendation's that are continually updated. It is organized like Netflix, with different channels" (Burrell, 2018). The intelligent recommendations are unique to each Agile Scrum team member's developmental needs. These needs are identified not only through each employee's formal performance evaluation but also frequent "spot checks" by team leaders regarding each team member. These "spot checks" replace time consuming skill inventories that were traditionally utilized (Burrell, 2018). Overall, this process allows for employee empowerment in learning decisions that is informed by input from a variety of stakeholders through the team leader. This allows for an optimal level of customization and a shared feeling of accountability.

Job experience is another component of employee development that often reflects career advancement as well. As mention above the corporate ladder approach is not effective for members of an Agile Scrum development team due to its unidirectional conception of career advancement. In an Agile Scrum context career advancement is not a unidirectional ladder but a multiple directional lattice where career progress can be achieved in a variety of ways. This is a new challenge regarding Agile Scrum development but has been a long-standing challenge for industries that rely on innovation for a sustainable competitive advantage. One such industry is the fashion industry and their management of talent in their design department (Shipilov & Godart, 2015). The fashion industry has moved away from predefined career path due to the need for innovation, unique employee skill set, and lack of hierarchical levels. All these characteristics are like that found in an agile scrum team environment. To address this fashion industry has no set career path as the inherent structure could constrain innovation. In fact, career development strategies are often not disclosed to employees even if selected for development. Instead once an employee is identified as having potential worth development the organization will use experience through job rotation to cultivate experience and verify potential (Shipilov & Godart, 2015). This allows the organization to identify a more natural fit between employee's talents and future assignments. Employees in fashion industry using this approach realize career progress not by steps in a formal program but the fashion brands (i.e., customer) they are assigned to, prestige of location of work, and scope of project.

Organizations utilizing Agile Scrum teams could benefit from using a similar approach to that of the fashion industry. A traditional formal development program requires predicable advancement steps to be achieved over time. This stability does not exist in Agile Scrum teams. Instead Agile Scrum team member are constantly reassigned, often referred to as deployed, to new teams after project completion based off current customer needs and not steps in the employee handbook. In an Agile Scrum environment team assignment becomes an important step in employee development and in turn career advancement. This process of deployment should be guided by employees' current competencies along with customer needs. Furthermore, it should incorporate team member's input from their previous teams.

The company Netflix utilize a project team approach to their content development projects. In addition, their performance management process reflects the one described above. That is evaluation on project completion that incorporates feedback from all team members. In addition to the "start doing this"; "stop doing this"; and "continue doing this" approach to performance evaluation they also ask, "Would you select this employee for your next team and why? (McCord, 2014)" This feedback on deployment reflects a source, their former team members, which has the best perspective to evaluate not only their knowledge but their ability to be a good team member. Of course, this approach is only effective if an organization selection process is effective enough to identify not only strong technical talent but individuals that also have the team orientated competencies required to be an effective Agile Scrum team member.

A sense of career progression is important and without defined steps in career development advancement might not be clear to an Agile Scrum team member. Once again, like the fashion industry, the customer may be the best indirect source to signal this to an employee. There are two customer driven indicators that employees may be sensitive to. First, is regarding the customer's image or reputation. In client-based project importance of a project is derived from the value the client relationship has to the organizations business strategy. This value can be financial assessed or based of the client's reputations. Simply put some clients may be perceived as more important because of who they are. The second indicator will be derived from the substance of the work in the form of complexity or novelty. An Agile Scrum employee assigned to a client who requires a complex outcome or an outcome that is unique may view the assignment with greater importance and in being part of the team tasked to complete the assignment as career progress.

In summary, establishing processes for employees' learning, deployment, and career development present some significant challenges in an agile scrum team context. Although the components are the same as in more traditional systems these components need to be combined and used in a different fashion to be aligned with the dynamics of the Agile Scrum approach. The coaching conversations outlined earlier in the chapter establish an important foundation of continuing improvement. User friendly training programs that focus on both technical knowledge and the competencies need for Agile Scrum work helps build on this foundation. Customized suggestions based off the input of team leaders allows for a directed freedom that encourages engagement and accountable on the part of the employee. Finally, a strategic approach to team deployment allows for an organic multidirectional career path to emerge.

CONCLUSION AND THE FUTURE OF AGILE HUMAN RESOURCES

As described in this chapter human resources do not have to be completely recreated to accommodate the Agile Scrum approach. The main components of human resources (i.e., selection, performance management, and learning and development) remain the same as do their objectives. However, how these components are carried out need to be modified to accommodate the Agile Scrum approach. In this chapter I have offered suggestions on how to modify these components of human resources to help manage but not constrain the Agile Scrum approach.

The selection process should involve potential Agile Scrum team members, not only in a panel interview but also in the development of the job posting and structure interview question formation. A focus on broad competencies not just task specific skills is important. The unique competencies demanded by Agile Scrum work should be assessed to determine not only person-group fit but also person-approach fit. These competencies such as emotional intelligence and tolerance for ambiguity can me measure not only through structured interview question but also psychological assessments and situational judgement tests.

Regarding performance management organizations must modify the "how", "who", and "where" aspects. That is how often feedback is given, who is involved in the process, and where the feedback is given about team climate. Specifically, feedback should be given more frequently and timed with Agile Scrum team's workflow. The focus of feedback should be effort and controllable behavior and generated in a 360-degree manner. Furthermore, cultivating a learning or growth mindset and culture will not only help employees respond to feedback but also improve their ability to give feedback to their team members. All these factors will help cultivate a positive feedback environment that will improve overall team performance.

Learning and development will build on the foundation of performance management utilizing customized learning systems. These learning systems should offer guidance based on specific feedback and performance evaluations but still allow the employee to self-direct to a degree to improve engagement and accountability. Most important, due to the lack of hierarchical levels and less significance of positional titles, a multidirectional view of career advancement is needed. Specifically companies need to view career advancement as developing an agile scrum members competencies so they can expand their influence and increase their recognition (financial and non-financial) all while increase their value to an organization (Rigby, et. al., 2018).

These modifications are needed to effectively manage Agile Scrum team members and should be done when the agile approach is used. However, in today's business environment companies are increasing relying on innovation and rapid response to customers' demands to create their sustainable competitive advantage. Therefore, a more agile approach to human resources in general is likely needed in the future (Cappelli, & Tavis, 2018). It is possible to change over significant organizational operations to an agile approach all at one time like ING did in 2015 (Barton, et. al., 2018). However, this drastic approach is hard to successfully achieve and therefore a slow transition to agile work overtime is more common. This allows the organization to completely understand the principals and values of the agile process and determine where in the organization the agile approach is appropriate (Rigby, et. al., 2018). This chapter hopefully not only assist organizations with the immediate need of managing Agile Scrum teams but also get a head start on the long-term evolution of human resources to a more agile approach.

REFERENCES

Anderson, S. D., & Wanberg, K. W. (1991). A convergent validity model of emergent leadership in groups. *Small Group Research*, *22*(3), 380–397. doi:10.1177/1046496491223006

Aronson, J., Fried, C., & Good, C. (2002). Reducing the effects of stereotype threat on African American college students by shaping theories of intelligence. *Journal of Experimental Social Psychology*, *38*(2), 113–125. doi:10.1006/jesp.2001.1491

Barrick, M. R., & Mount, M. K. (1991). The big five personality dimensions and job performance: A meta-analysis. *Personnel Psychology*, *44*(1), 1–26. doi:10.1111/j.1744-6570.1991.tb00688.x

Barton, D., Carey, D., & Charan, R. A. M. (2018). One Bank's Agile Team Experiment "How ING Revamped its Retail Operation. *Harvard Business Review*, *96*(2), 59–61.

Beck, K., Beedle, M., Van Bennekum, A., Cockburn, A., Cunningham, W., Fowler, M., ... & Kern, J. (2001). *The agile manifesto*. Academic Press.

Budner, S. (1962). Intolerance of ambiguity as a personality variable. *Journal of Personality*, *30*(1), 29–50. doi:10.1111/j.1467-6494.1962.tb02303.x PMID:13874381

Burrell, L., & Gherson, D. (2018). Co-creating the Employee Experience: A Conversation with Diane Gherson, IBM's Head of HR. *Harvard Business Review*, *96*(2), 54–58.

Cappelli, P. (2015). Why we love to hate HR… and what HR can do about it. *Harvard Business Review*, *93*(7/8), 54–61.

Cappelli, P., & Tavis, A. (2018). HR goes agile. *Harvard Business Review*, *96*(2), 46–52.

Chamorro-Premuzic, T. (2015). Ace the assessment. *Harvard Business Review*, *93*(7/8), 118–121.

Donovan, J., & Benko, C. (2016). AT&T's talent overhaul. *Harvard Business Review*, 68–73.

Dweck, C. S., & Leggett, E. L. (1988). A social-cognitive approach to motivation and personality. *Psychological Review*, *95*(2), 256–273. doi:10.1037/0033-295X.95.2.256

Fernández-Aráoz, C. (2014). 21st Century Talent Spotting. *Harvard Business Review*, *92*(6), 46–56. PMID:25051855

Frenkel-Brunswik, E. (1948). Intolerance of ambiguity as an emotional perceptual personality variable. *Journal of Personality*, *18*(1), 108–143. doi:10.1111/j.1467-6494.1949.tb01236.x

Friedman, T. L. (2014). How to get a job at Google. *The New York Times*, 22.

Gieles, H., & van der Meer, W. (2017). *Talent management as the beating heart of an Agile Organization*. Academic Press.

Hastie, S., & Engineer, C. K. (2004). The Agile Mindset: what does it take to make this stuff work? Software Education Associates Ltd.

Hayat, F., Rehman, A. U., Arif, K. S., Wahab, K., & Abbas, M. (2019, July). The Influence of Agile Methodology (Scrum) on Software Project Management. In *2019 20th IEEE/ACIS International Conference on Software Engineering, Artificial Intelligence, Networking and Parallel/Distributed Computing (SNPD)* (pp. 145-149). IEEE.

Herold, D. M., & Parsons, C. K. (1985). Assessing the feedback environment in work organizations: Development of the job feedback survey. *The Journal of Applied Psychology*, *70*(2), 290–305. doi:10.1037/0021-9010.70.2.290

Heslin, P., Latham, G., & VandeWalle, D. (2005). The effect of implicit person theory on performance appraisals. *The Journal of Applied Psychology*, *90*(5), 842–856. doi:10.1037/0021-9010.90.5.842 PMID:16162058

Heslin, P., Vandewalle, D., & Latham, G. (2006). Keen to help? Managers' implicit person theories and their subsequent employee coaching. *Personnel Psychology*, *59*(4), 871–902. doi:10.1111/j.1744-6570.2006.00057.x

Heslin, P. A., & VandeWalle, D. (2010). Performance appraisal procedural justice: The role of a manager's implicit person theory. *Journal of Management*, *12*, 1201–1214.

Kluger, A. N., & DeNisi, A. (1996). The effects of feedback interventions on performance: A historical review, a meta-analysis, and a preliminary feedback intervention theory. *Psychological Bulletin*, *119*(2), 254–284. doi:10.1037/0033-2909.119.2.254

Kristof-Brown, A. L., Zimmerman, R. D., & Johnson, E. C. (2005). Consequences of Individuals'' Fit at Work: A Meta-Analysis of Person–Job, Person–Organization, Person–Group, and Person–Supervisor Fit. *Personnel Psychology*, *58*(2), 281–342. doi:10.1111/j.1744-6570.2005.00672.x

Lei, H., Ganjeizadeh, F., Jayachandran, P. K., & Ozcan, P. (2017). A statistical analysis of the effects of Scrum and Kanban on software development projects. *Robotics and Computer-integrated Manufacturing*, *43*, 59–67. doi:10.1016/j.rcim.2015.12.001

Luthans, F., & Stajkovic, A. D. (1999). Reinforce for performance: The need to go beyond pay and even rewards. *The Academy of Management Perspectives*, *13*(2), 49–57. doi:10.5465/ame.1999.1899548

Mahajan, A. (2013). *The importance of HR in agile adoption*. Scrum Alliance. https://www.scrumalliance.org/community/articles/2013/january/the-importance-ofhr-in-agile-adoption

McCord, P. (2014). How Netflix Reinvented HR: Trust People, Not Policies. Reward Candor and Throwaway the Standard Playbook. *Harvard Business Review*, *90*(3), 71–76.

Murphy, M. C., & Dweck, C. S. (2010). A culture of genius: How an organization's lay theory shapes people's cognition, affect, and behavior. *Personality and Social Psychology Bulletin*, *36*(3), 283–296. doi:10.1177/0146167209347380 PMID:19826076

Oprins, R. J., Frijns, H. A., & Stettina, C. J. (2019, May). Evolution of Scrum Transcending Business Domains and the Future of Agile Project Management. In *International Conference on Agile Software Development* (pp. 244-259). Springer. 10.1007/978-3-030-19034-7_15

Preston, G., Moon, J., Simon, R., Allen, S., & Kossi, E. (2015). The relevance of emotional intelligence in project leadership. *Journal of Information Technology and Economic Development*, *6*(1), 16.

Przybilla, L., Wiesche, M., & Krcmar, H. (2019). Emergent Leadership in Agile Teams--an Initial Exploration. *SIGMIS-CPR '19*.

Rigby, D. K., Sutherland, J., & Noble, A. (2018). Agile at scale. *Harvard Business Review*, *96*(3), 88–96.

Rigby, D. K., Sutherland, J., & Takeuchi, H. (2016). Embracing Agile. *Harvard Business Review*, *94*(5), 40–50.

Rodríguez, G., Soria, Á., & Campo, M. (2016). Measuring the impact of agile coaching on students' performance. *IEEE Transactions on Education*, *59*(3), 202–209. doi:10.1109/TE.2015.2506624

Rubin, K. S. (2012). *Essential Scrum: A Practical Guide to the Most Popular Agile Process*. Addison-Wesley.

Sherman, M., Edison, S., Rehberg, B. & Danoesastro. (2017). *Taking agile way beyond software*. Boston Consulting Group. https://www.bcg.com/enau/publications/2017/technology-digital-organization-taking-agile-way-beyondsoftware.aspx

Shipilov, A., & Godart, F. (2015). Luxury's talent factories. *Harvard Business Review*, *93*(6), 98–104.

Skinner, B. F. (1953). *Science and Human Behavior*. Macmillan.

Steelman, L. A., Levy, P. E., & Snell, A. F. (2004). The feedback environment scale: Construct definition, measurement, and validation. *Educational and Psychological Measurement*, *64*(1), 165–184. doi:10.1177/0013164403258440

Taipalus, T., Seppänen, V., & Pirhonen, M. (2018). Coping with uncertainty in an agile systems development course. *Journal of Information Systems Education*, *29*(2).

Wilding, R. (1999). The Role of Time Compression and Emotional Intelligence in Agile Supply Chains. *Supply Chain Practice*, *1*(4).

Zenasni, F., Besancon, M., & Lubart, T. (2008). Creativity and tolerance of ambiguity: An empirical study. *The Journal of Creative Behavior*, *42*(1), 61–73. doi:10.1002/j.2162-6057.2008.tb01080.x

KEY TERMS AND DEFINITIONS

Deployment: The assignment of employees to new assignment-based employees' capability to meet the future demands of the assignment.

Feedback: Communicating to an employee how a stakeholder views their work behavior.

Learning Mindset: A belief that improvement is possible though increase effort.

Performance Management: Process of informed evaluation and feedback of an employee's work behavior and its alignment with organizational goal.

Person-Group Fit: How a person's values and attitude match with those of a work group.

Person-Job Fit: How a person's skills and abilities match the demands of a job.

Talent Acquisition: The process of identifying, recruiting, and hiring of highly qualified employees.

Chapter 10
Traditional or Agile Contracting for Software Development:
Decisions, Decisions

Dinah Payne
University of New Orleans, USA

ABSTRACT

As the use of software is present in so many activities today, it is important for business in particular to be aware of challenges that may seem different today than before the prevalence of software in our lives. Agile project management is one example: this more recent and nimble approach to software development presents its own challenges. Fortunately, the guiding legal principles related to traditional contract formation and execution are based in principles of fairness and equity, making the customization of legal principles to Agile contracting a reasonable endeavor. This chapter presents basic contract law and such law as it more specifically relates to contracts dealing with Agile software development.

INTRODUCTION: WHY DOES THE CONTRACT MATTER?

According to the Legal Executive Institute, United States (U. S.) companies spend approximately 40% of their revenues on legal services (2017). This is an astonishing number and considerably more than companies in other venues. Miller (2015) reports that CEOs and CFOs spend a great deal of their time on legal matters, from educating outside counsel about the business and the issues it confronts, to seeking to find information requested as a result of legal action, and to preparing for and complying with requests for discovery (depositions, interrogators and requests for documents). These managers must help prepare expert witnesses acting on behalf of the firm and attend hearings or go to trials. Litigation, then, is very expensive and time consuming. "Litigation …will reach deep into the business and the company needs to prepare for and accept that a number of different and valuable people will be taken away from big parts of their day jobs to assist with the (legal) effort (Miller, 2015)." One way to reduce the amount of time and energy wasted on legal disputes is to obviate their occurrence and one way to do this is to fashion carefully researched and crafted contracts. This is no less true for Agile contracting than it is for

DOI: 10.4018/978-1-7998-4885-1.ch010

Copyright © 2021, IGI Global. Copying or distributing in print or electronic forms without written permission of IGI Global is prohibited.

any other business contracting. While Agile contracting may involve a higher degree of collaboration than tradition contracts, the need for trust and the need for as much specificity as possible, even in light of the existence of known uncertainties, is critically important. Software developers and owners must accept that there will be disputes arising out of their contracts: the best way to reduce the negative effects of these disputes is to anticipate as much as possible of what might be points of contention.

There is not yet a great deal of litigation involving project management using the Agile approach, so the development of this material is based on general contract law, which we will see is based on legal principle that works for traditional or Agile contracting. However, in 2019, there was an instance of a dispute that resulted in a split decision by a Texas court (Raysman and Brown, 2019). In *Polar Pro Filters Inc v. Frogslayer, LLC* (2019), the dispute arose from a software development agreement that ran significantly over the original cost estimate and over the revised cost estimate. Further, fraud was claimed as a result of the non-delivery of the software in a viable form. The developer did not receive what he considered to be his full payment and the owner did not receive a viable product. The claims in the case were all based on traditional contract law even though the subject matter was a contract for software development wherein iterations were to be used. The point is that, although traditional contract and Agile contract may focus on, for example, different kinds of payment schedules or different visions of what should be delivered at what times, what installments or iterations are due/owing, the law used to generate a fair and equitable resolution to the dispute is well-established contract law. As Agile contracts become more frequently used and as more litigation develops, it is certainly possible that specific rules will be developed for Agile contract attributes that warrant different treatment. At this time, however, as evidenced by the *Polar Pro* case, traditional notions of contract essentials like fraud and breach of contract have served Agile contracting as well as traditional contracting.

In every successful business relationship, the parties must have agreed as to the purpose of the relationship. Each party must have a reasonably definite concept of what his obligations are under any contract he enters into: this is axiomatic in business and in business law. In traditional contracts, there is certainly enough litigation to make the retention of an attorney a good idea to give the parties a path to redress alleged transgressions, as well as to assure pro-active work to prevent any legal conflict via a well-written contract.

In Agile contracts, the pro-active nature of the work is even more important, as the relationship between the owner of the project and the software developer is far more collaborative than unilaterally providing goods between the buyer and seller. "The unprecedented rate of change in business and technology has made it increasingly difficult for software teams to determine user requirements and respond to their changes…Agile development approaches differ from the traditional, plan-driven, structured approaches as the former put more emphasis on lean processes and dynamic adaptation than on detailed front-end plans and heavy documentation (Lee and Xia, 2010: 88)." This description of Agile project management itself is a description of the root of the difference in contract law between traditional contracts and Agile contracts: as the word denotes, agile means to move quickly and easily (Dictionary.com, n.d.).

The Agile form of project management, designed to be rapid and easily coordinated, is represented by a framework for organizing and managing work in iterative stages. This differentiates Agile contracts from others in a number of ways, not the least of which is that, by their nature, the structure and stability generally found in contracts alerting the contracting parties as to their obligations is not possible: since the work is done on an "as we go" basis, iteratively, concepts of performance, for example, are different between traditional contract law and the contract law associated with Agile. We present here basic elements of contract law and provide insights as to how to contract for Agile projects. In this process, it is important to note that the attorneys with whom the client and project owner is working are advocates for negotiating the best terms for their clients: thus, an important element of Agile contracting means having a lawyer who understands how Agile project management works. As Bhoola and Mallik (2014: 96) summarily describe the point of Agile project management and, by derivation, Agile contracts: "the highest priority (in Agile) is to satisfy the customer through early and continuous delivery of valuable software." As the whole point of Agile project management is to satisfy the customer, so should the contract to provide Agile project management work to identify and pro-actively manage points of contention, to avoid time and energy wasted in disputes that might easily have been avoided with careful contracting, so satisfying all customers.

FACILITATOR OR ADVERSARY: ATTORNEYS INVOLVED IN AGILE CONTRACTING

While courts are interested first and foremost with the ultimate fairness in contract dispute resolution, the roles of the parties' attorneys, however, is not to be "fair" to the opposing party, but to be adversarial if there is a contract dispute. Attorneys are charged with protecting their client's interests competently and zealously (American Bar Association, 2020). Arbogast, Larman and Bode (2010) express concern that attorneys dealing with Agile contracts are too concerned with protecting the client at all costs and that they should rather protect the project success. They describe the Agile attorney as in need of a crash course in uncertainty, inherent in Agile contracting, as differentiated from traditional contracts. In fact, everyone's attorney should be fully capable of grasping the issue of uncertainty in the nature of iterative projects; no attorney should accept any case the subject of which he does not or is not capable of understanding, whether it is a traditional contract or an Agile contract. Additionally, the attorneys for Agile project management should be able to make connections between principles of fairness and equity regardless of the contract being a traditional one or an Agile contract.

In their article comparing legal project management to Agile contracting, Hassett and Burke (2017) interestingly make the case that lawyers themselves, with their firms, can utilize principles of Agile contracting. They describe waterfall contracting, a more traditional approach to project management. This involves the "analysis, design, implementation, testing and evaluation (Hassett and Burke, 2017: 8-9)" of a legal (any) project. They suggest that Agile contract considerations associated with planning, documentation, expectation consistency, etc. are different from traditional waterfall contracts. For example, upfront planning, documentation and project manager control is lower for Agile contracting than traditional contracting, while consistency of expectations, response time to changes in requirements, reassessment of tasks, client involvement and team member autonomy is higher for Agile contracting. Friess (2019: 131) describes a waterfall approach as "each sequential aspect of a project was to be fully competed by specialists, such as designers or developers, before being handed off to the next specialist in line." She also notes that "upfront planning and control" was required, allowing little room for the project to develop organically. Many elements to contracting traditionally or for Agile projects have similar underpinning principles, like planning, but areas to be aware of are also highlighted regarding the differences of approaches (Siddique and Hussein, 2016). Table 1is a simple presentation of major contract issues that both more traditional and Agile contracts must adhere to and with which attorneys for all parties should be familiar with. This material will be presented with greater detail as this chapter proceeds.

Table 1. Waterfall vs. Agile Contracting: The Names Have Changed, but the Principles Remain the Same

Formation of a Valid Contract Requires/ May Require:	Waterfall (Traditional) Contracts	Agile Contracts
Agreement	More certain/well defined responsibilities/ outcomes	More fluid responsibilities as iterations take shape
Consideration	Fixed price with installment payments or at contract conclusion Time and material basis	Iteration payments at end of each iteration Target cost: fixed price and time and material cost pricing
Capacity	One must understand the terms of the contract	One must understand the terms of the contract
Legality	Contract terms and performance must be legal	Contract terms and performance must be legal
A Writing	Depending on the time for performance, the contract must be in writing to be enforceable	If iterations are discrete contracts, a writing is less likely to be required

The attorneys for both the software developer and the owner must be cognizant of the issues prevalent in Agile project management, hall marks of which are trust and collaboration among the parties. Since "fault is a pervasive element in contract law (Eisenberg, 2009: 1414)," the mindset of attorneys tends towards trying to determine fault. Since Agile's iterative processes may be more or less productive per iteration, determining fault is not as important as moving forward to completion of the entire project. Eisenberg notes that litigation is very expensive; it would be better to achieve "performance of contracts through the internalization of the moral norm of promise keeping, which is very inexpensive (p. 1430)." This notion of promise keeping is the essence of contract, regardless of whether it is an Agile project or not. Further, it is the essence of Agile contracting: reliance on the trust and good faith of collaborators in software development is a central characteristic of Agile project management.

WHAT IS A CONTRACT?

Choice of Law

Contract law has developed over millennia across many cultures and with regard to many types of performance. The source of commercial, or contract, law in the U. S. is three-fold: common law contract, the Uniform Commercial Code and Louisiana's conventional obligations law. Common law contract, in effect in 49 states in the U. S., is derived from case law rather than legislative mandate. Courts have developed legal positions that have been followed or reversed in a cycle of continuous development, review and redevelopment of principles of law deemed to be most equitable by society as a whole. Common law contract covers anything not covered by the Uniform Commercial Code (UCC), i.e., sales of services, real estate, etc.: the Restatement of the Law of contracts (American Law Institute, 2020), devised by the American Law Institute, is a complete reference work used by courts to form and support legal opinions.

The Uniform Commercial Code (UCC; Legal Information Institute, 2002) is the second source of commercial law in the U. S. It has little relevance for Agile contracts as the nature of UCC contracts is sales and leases of goods, rather than services. Software developers provide the services of development, but no movable and tangible goods are generated in such development. While the UCC is perhaps less relevant to Agile contracting, it might also be worth a look from the standpoint of a contract template. It contains many provisions that parties might consider in forming an Agile contract; for example, reference may be made to industry standards, which the UCC allows to be used in the resolution of contract disputes. Again, however, the overall use of the UCC will be less helpful than common law contract.

Finally, civil law in Louisiana was developed as a result of Hammurabi's Code via the Napoleonic Code: Hammurabi's Code was "the world's first known set of laws (Marriott, 2016: 16)." The State of Louisiana is the only state in the U. S. to have adopted the Civil Code (Louisiana Civil Code, n.d.), which is based in articles of law deemed to be the set standard. Contract law in Louisiana is based on the Civil Code and is called the Law of Conventional Obligations and Contracts. While common law and civil law use a different vocabulary for many concepts, the principles remain the same or are similar, as are the basic rules of sales and leases law: courts are interested in the ultimate fairness of contracting regardless of the law invoked. This is also true for traditional or Agile contracts: while the contents of the Agile contract may be different from traditional contracts, the equitable principles are the same. In developing the contract for the software development, the parties should educate themselves as to which of these laws they would find most appropriate: the choice of law to be used in a dispute can then be included in the contract.

The Environmental Context of Agile Contracting

The nature of what a traditional contract is is not hugely different from an Agile contract in many principles. A contract is basically an agreement between two or more parties that a court will enforce. Contracts provide stability and structure within which business can be conducted more efficiently; the private law of contract protects promises that have been made between the parties. A contract is a legally binding promise or a set of promises for the breach of which the law gives a remedy, or the performance of which the law in some way recognizes as a duty. These parties can agree to perform some act now and/or refrain from performing some act now and/or perform some act in the future and/or refrain from performing some act in the future. A fundamental truth about contract law, either traditional or Agile, is that the parties are entitled to contract with regard to whatever they want to contract with regard to, as long as the subject matter of the contract is legal, the parties have legal capacity and each party knowingly and willingly enters into the contract.

In Agile contracts, the idea of performing some act in the future is key: each successive iteration is envisioned at the time of contract, but iteration scope, specificity and number can be unknown. Since each iteration of the process could be considered its own contract and each of these "contracts" foresees a cumulative end at the completion of the project, Agile contracting fits within these constraints of contractual performance obligations. Larusdottir, Cajander and Gulliksen (2014: 1118) note that the idea of iterative software development grew out of an acknowledgement that "it is difficult to fully specify systems beforehand." Thus, contracts regarding future software development with Agile terms/ conditions satisfies the need to "address the perceived limitations of (the) more established, plan-driven processes" of traditional contracting. Exhibit 1 provides a list of major legal and managerial concerns surrounding Agile projects and contracts. To offset sources of conflicts like those listed, Siddique and Hussein (2016) make several suggestions; see Exhibit 2.

Exhibit 1: Contracting Process Management Environmental Conditions (Siddique and Hussein, 2016)

- ◦ Environmental context: knowledge and experience of Agile projects and contracting.
- ◦ Identification of causes of contract disputes.
- ◦ Formal documentation of what is due, expected dates of completion, etc.
- ◦ Unequal sharing of risk, i.e., the developer not getting paid if the owner is dissatisfied.
- ◦ Waterfall contract approach or Agile contract approach.
- ◦ Fixed scope vs. fixed objectives.
- ◦ Inadequate owner/developer collaboration: the blame game.
- ◦ Unsatisfied customers.
- ◦ Conflicts regarding roles and responsibilities of owners and developers.
- ◦ Unpaid efforts resulting from owner dissatisfaction.
- ◦ Early termination of projects.
- ◦ Delays and increased costs.

Exhibit 2: Contracting Process Management Strategies (Siddique and Hussein, 2016; Friess, 2019)

- ◦ Clarity in obligations.
- ◦ Capacity.
- ◦ Planning.
- ◦ Kick-off.
- ◦ Trust.
- ◦ Choosing the right contract format.
- ◦ Maintenance.
- ◦ Having a frequent-delivery option.
- ◦ The use of gainsharing rather than risk-sharing.
- ◦ Focusing on functionality above budget.
- ◦ Flow management.
- ◦ Customer involvement.
- ◦ Iteration execution.
- ◦ Forecasting.
- ◦ Consciously proactively seeking conflict resolution strategies.

Generally, in contract, an offer is a promise that can be met with acceptance: "a definite undertaking or proposal made by one person to another indicating a willingness to enter into a contract (Mann and Roberts, 2013: 195)." Again, Agile contracting can follow the basic contract model, but with the caveat that the definite nature of the undertaking also includes a significant understanding that uncertainty is a hallmark of Agile project management. This does not mean that such offers cannot be met with acceptance; it means that the parties to the contract understand and incorporate the uncertainties into the contract. As one of the first, most fundamental elements of contract is that the parties exercise good faith, the notion that Agile projects should be completed in collaboration between the owner of the project and the software developer presumes and requires good faith performance. Arbogast, Larman and Bode (2010) and Ward (2019), for example, both suggest that a collaborative effort between the owner of the project and the software developer is a defining characteristic of Agile. Such collaboration would necessarily entail the use of good faith in the performance of the contract: again, traditional notions of contract law are suitable concepts for application to Agile project contracting. Bhool and Mallik (2014: 96) note that "Moving from a traditional software methodology to the agile is very challenging due to the nature of software projects which are adapting to the changing environments, business dynamics, and continuous process improvement." One could replace software methodology with contracting process and have a good idea of the environment in which Agile contracts must be crafted and concluded. Exhibit 3 represents a list of contractual issues that should be considered when drafting an Agile contract. It is very clear that critically thoughtful care should be given to the drafting of the contract: while it might be more time-consuming to think about all these things ahead of time, knowing only that trust and collaboration are the chief characteristics of the nature of the contract, in the final analysis, such planning might actually be the solution to possible legal disputes.

Exhibit 3: Upfront Planning Elements for Agile Contracting (Lukasiewicz and Miller, 2012)

- Configuration management.
- Measurement and analysis.
- Project monitoring and control.
- Process and product quality assurance.
- Managerial requirements.
- Decision analysis and resolution.
- Integrated project management.
- Product integration.
- Requirements development.
- Risk management.
- Technical solution.
- Validation.
- Verification.

Parties to An Agile Contract

Perhaps the most onerous burden in developing the contractual provisions is on the offeror: the offeror is the person who makes the offer/proposal or undertaking to the offeree. It is immaterial as to whether the owner/customer or the developer is the offeror or offeree. The offeror is the "master of the offer," who can include or not in the offer whatever terms, provisions, deadlines, payment provisions, etc. are legally allowable and desirable. Offerors and offerees also take on roles of obligors, those obligated to perform the contract, and obligees, those to whom obligations to perform contractual provisions are owed. Each party is both an obligor and an obligee: the owner, the obligor, is obligated to pay for what the developer, the obligee, provides, while the developer is the obligor who owes the performance of software development to his obligee, the owner. Regardless of who the offeror is in Agile contracting, the owner or the software developer, the offeror is in control and must guide the negotiations in the collaborative endeavor.

Bhool and Mallik (2014) offer definitions of the parties to the contract. Product owners represent all stakeholder interests in the project and the finished system, as well as maintaining the backlog (the prioritized list of desired requirements and capabilities coupled with an estimated timeline for completion (Rubin, 2013)). The team (software developer) is described as a cross-functional, self-managing and —organizing group and is responsible for achieving the desired requirements: they are accountable for getting the job done successfully in terms of product and timeliness. Other parties to the contract are numerous in terms of executing the contract. Exhibit 4 offers a list of possible parties. See also Table 2 for a review of parties and their primary roles. When considering the parties and their responsibilities, keep in mind that Agility is defined as "a software team's ability to efficiently and effectively respond to user requirement changes (Lee and Xia, 2010: 88)."

Exhibit 4: The Parties (adapted from Larusdottir, et al., 2014: 1123; Friess, 2019)

- Product Owner
- The Scrum Manager: responsible for identifying and prioritizing the needs of the owner.
- Team Members: responsible for delivering the iteration by designing, developing and testing the software; it can include an IT engineer, architect, …
- Usability Specialists: providing requirements analysis, interaction design and evaluation, etc.
- Business Specialists: providing analysis of software requirements during pre-studies.
- Security Engineer
- Technical Writer

Good Faith

Contracts are presumed to be entered into in good faith, without being unconscionable (so unfair to one of the parties that the contractual unfairness "shocks the conscience"). Again, these concepts are not far off of what is necessary in Agile contracts: each party understands that each iteration of the project brings significant uncertainty, i.e., a client will discover that they did not even realize that they needed some other software development to be included in the project until the first, second, third, etc. iterations are complete. Since the best way to approach Agile software development is collaborative, the requirement of good faith is imminently reasonable, as is the prohibition against very unfair contractual provisions. Further, each party to the contract must seriously intend to be bound by the contractual provisions. In the Agile context, presumably each party would understand what the vision of the project would be (Moore, 1991) and, in good faith, anticipate that he can fulfil his contractual obligations satisfactorily in good faith.

For a comparison between traditional contracts and Agile contracts of relevant law, the attorney's role in the Agile contracting process, and several other basic elements to contracting, see Table 2.

CONTRACT CLASSIFICATION

Fully legally enforceable contracts are called valid contracts. A valid contract has four parts: agreement (the manifestation of the parties' intent regarding the substance of the contract, including offer constraints and acceptance), consideration, capacity, and legality. An agreement consisting of offer and acceptance must exist and be supported by legally sufficient consideration. The parties to the contract must have legal capacity to enter into the contract and the contract must be made for a legal purpose or object. These parameters for traditional contracts are likely to be the same in form and function as Agile contracts: the parties in Agile must have entered into an agreement, even if the agreement contains uncertainty, i.e., how many iterations will there be. Much has been written about payment for Agile software development; we will address this shortly. The issues of capacity and legality, too, are fairly straightforward for Agile contracting. For example, entering into an Agile contract with a minor is highly unlikely; again, we will

Table 2. The Preliminaries (Derived from Arbogast, Larman, Mallik, 2012; Baham, 2019; Edwards, Bickerstaff and Bartsch, n.d.; Bhool and Mallik, 2015; Lee and Xia, 2010; Berstein, 2015)

Element	Traditional Sales and Services Contracts	Agile Contracts
Attorney's role and perception of contractual process	Adversarial if necessary. Potential silo mentality with focus only on one's own client/needs.	Mediator encouraging trust and collaboration. Systems/holistic approach focusing on the project's completion rather than individual parties' needs.
Parties and their responsibilities	Offerors and offerees, like buyers and sellers of goods. Obligors and obligees. Responsibilities are more certain: contract performance is specified and the parties are responsible for fulfilling their promises. Focus is on project management (Bhoola and Mallik, 2015), highlighting the accountable person.	Offerors and offerees, like owners/customers and suppliers. Obligors and obligees. Responsibilities can be less certain as each iteration could change in direction from the last iteration, the owner could decide to terminate the project if his needs are satisfied, etc.: owners/customers will need to continuously assess and reassess what they want out of each iteration, the whole project, when to end the project, etc. (Bernstein, 2015). Focus is on team dynamics, possibly diffusing point of responsibility contact; this is prevented by identification of the product owner, who is "responsible for maximizing the value of the product and the work of the Development Team (Baham, 2019: 142)." The development team should be identified and the owner should be given the right to decline membership of team proposals (Edwards, Bickerstaff and Bartsch, n.d.).
Offer	More specific obligations are known: structure and stability are assured.	Inherently uncertain, but initially expected obligations are known within the scope of the project.
Acceptance	More specific obligations are known: structure and stability are assured.	Inherently uncertain, but known within the scope of the project.
Party knowledge of contract subject matter Bernstein	Both parties need to know enough about the nature of the thing they are contracting relative to, i.e., when one wants a mare to breed, one can trust the seller to provide him with one capable of breeding without knowing the lineage of the horse or even much about breeding horses: the buyer is relying on the seller to sell him a horse suitable for breeding purposes (warranty for a particular purpose).	Owner should be educated in Agile principles, i.e., that the process is iterative, that each iteration can have an impact on each other iteration and the course of the project, that the owner's and suppliers must develop a relationship of trust and collaboration: the "we are in this together" approach. The owner's and developer's attorneys should be sufficiently knowledgeable about the Agile process itself to be able to anticipate where disputes might arise and how best to prevent those disputes.
Good faith	Each party needs to feel trust in the other party's good faith promise of performance.	Each party must feel trust in the other party's good faith performance, but also fully engage in a collaborative relationship.
Unconscionability	Extreme unfairness.	Relative ignorance of one contracting party granting an unfair advantage to the other party.

address this element more subsequently. It is equally unlikely that either owner/customers or software developers would both agree to engage in contract performance that was actually illegal.

Voidable and Voidable Contracts

Voidable contracts are valid contracts that reflect the lack of a minor element of contract; a prime example of such a contract would be when an adult enters into a contract with a minor. In this instance, the contract would be voidable at the option of the party who lacked capacity, an unlikely event in Agile contracting, but nevertheless worth confirming each party's capacity. A void contract is equally unlikely in relation to Agile contracting. Void "contracts" are not even really contracts, as there is a major element of contract missing, rendering the "contract" completely invalid and unenforceable by either party. A good example of this would be when one party defrauds another party. Recall that a fundamental tenant of contract law is that each party must knowingly and willingly enter into the contract; when fraud is perpetrated, one of the parties intentionally deceives the other party as to some major element of the contract. While this would certainly be possible in Agile contracting, it would seem unlikely that this would be significantly different from fraud as instigated by any other contracting party. Presumably, too, since iterations are concluded rapidly, fraud would be "found out" quickly and the partnership accordingly resolved or dissolved.

Executed or Executory Contracts

One classification of contract that may have extra meaning for Agile contracting is the classification of whether the contract is executed or executory. An executed contract is one that has been fully performed by all parties, i.e., in a real estate contract, all promises of the seller and buyer have been fulfilled and the title to the land has changed. An executory contract, on the other hand, is one that has not been fully performed by all parties, i.e., a sale of real estate is only an executory contract until the title of the real estate changes from the seller to the buyer. Thus, from the time the contract to sell the real estate is entered into and the time of the closing, this is merely an executory contract. In Agile contracting, the question of substantial performance may come up: if the contract isn't fully and completely performed, the contract may be classified as either executed or executory, depending on circumstances. Such circumstances could be dictated by the "completion" of an iteration: if the iteration does not provide the owner with the desired deliverables, but it still works to some extent, the question could arise as to whether full payment should be made by the owner who is dissatisfied with the iteration's performance. If the contracting parties contracted in good faith and in a collaborative spirit, this problem is less likely to occur, but must be acknowledged as a possible problem.

Express, Implied and Quasi Contracts

Another contract classification that is debatably different for traditional and Agile contracting is the nature of a contract as an express or implied contract. Express contracts are simply those that are fully and explicitly stated, either in writing or orally, at the time the contract is entered into. The only issue here is whether words are actually used. Implied contracts (implied in fact) are contracts implied by the behaviors of the parties. The source of the potential issues here speaks to fundamental Agile contracting tenants: good faith trust and collaboration. Agile creates a double-edged sword: good faith, trusting and collaborative parties want a reasonable amount of uncertainly, so don't want to put everything into words, but leaving contractual provisions to be interpreted by the behaviors of the parties is equally problematic. Having to express all the contractual provisions in words does not acknowledge the effervescent, rapidly changing nature of Agile development. In fact, implied contracts are not valid contracts when the subject matter of the contract is of a unique or personal nature because there is no way to reference what the parties might have wanted in the event of a dispute: there is no standard, which could very easily be a hallmark of Agile development.

If the parties to an Agile (any) contract chose to employ an implied contract model, several requirements must be met for a dissatisfied party: first, the injured party must have provided some service (or property) to the other party. Second, the injured party expected to be paid for the service and the other party did know or should know that the injured party expected payment. And, finally, the alleged transgressor had a chance to reject the services, yet did not do so. In an Agile contracting situation, it is not inconceivable that a software developer would work on an iteration, present that finished product only to have the owner proceed with the project with another software developer. Again, trust, good faith and close collaboration should ameliorate or eliminate this kind of dispute, but only if the parties to the Agile contract know about this sort of dispute.

If there is a dispute and implied contract principles did not result in a fair outcome, *quasi* contract may provide an avenue for relief. In this type of "contract," which is not a real contract because some element of contract is missing, the courts crafted this equitable relief. *Quasi* contracts are fictional contracts created by courts, imposed on the parties in the interests of fairness and justice (implied at law); they are judicial remedies aimed at preventing unjust enrichment when no contract actually exists. For this claim to succeed, some element of contract is lacking, but not to impose a contract would be to treat one of the parties very unfairly or inequitably. The doctrine of unjust enrichment applies: no one should be allowed to profit/enrich themselves inequitably at others' expense. Regarding Agile contracts, the same logic applies to the use of this equitable remedy as to the remedy of an implied contract. One party, for instance the developer, expends time and materials generating software pursuant to a contract found by a court to be unreasonably indefinite, yet produces a product that the owner says does not meet his needs. The developer could assay the equitable remedy of *quasi* contract.

Another element of contract that could differ between traditional contracts and Agile contracts is the necessity for knowing exactly what the terms of the contract are: to what is each party obligating himself? The terms of offers must be reasonably definite to assure seriousness of intent as to the obligations of the parties, i.e., parties to the offer should be identified, the subject matter and/or quantity of the offer should be identified, the consideration due between the parties should be identified, and the time for performance should be identified. Under the Restatement of Contracts, the concept of "reasonably definite terms" was created, allowing for a bit more latitude: this is essential in Agile contracting. For example, the courts can supply a missing term if a reasonable one can be implied from the behaviors of the parties or the circumstances under which the contract is to be completed. Given the nature of the Agile contract as one of trust and collaboration, the court can look at all the circumstances of the contract negotiation, initiation and course of performance to make appropriate determinations at to equitable remedies.

TERMINATION OF THE OFFER BY THE PARTIES

Traditional contract offers can be terminated in three ways: rejection, counter-offer and revocation. This is not going to be the real problem-maker in Agile contracting. Rather than the offer being the source of the dispute, it is more foreseeable that the performance and termination of the contract itself as a whole is at issue. However, briefly, in rejection, the offeree says "no" to the offer in some way. Counter-offer is first and foremost a rejection of the original offer and the communication of a new offer by the original offeree, while revocation is the withdrawal of the offer by the offeror.

ACCEPTANCE OF THE OFFER

Acceptance is voluntary agreement by the offeree to be bound by the offer terms: an objective indication of present intent to be bound. Clear, unambiguous, unequivocal words or conduct must be used in signifying acceptance. Again, for Agile contracts, this is less likely to be a source of friction than the performance of the contract, but nevertheless could constitute a problem. The nature of the problem for Agile contracts is simply that the "clear, unambiguous words" may not exist as in the traditional contract sense. Since performance of the project and each iteration is by nature unknown to some extent, the parties will have to grapple with language that is as clear as can be under these circumstances. This is a perfect instance in which to rely on the concept of good faith: the parties, in good faith, believe that they know what each is offering and what each is agreeing to. As iterations can shift with desired features and requirements, so can words of acceptance be crafted to acknowledge and accept such uncertainties. See Table 3 for a review of issues associated with the agreement.

CONSIDERATION

In binding contracts, each party must exchange something of legal value for the other party's promise: this is the principle behind the concept of consideration. Giving someone a birthday present is not a bargained-for exchange as the recipient did not bargain for the birthday present: the promisor therefore receives no consideration and the "contract" is not binding. Consideration is exchanged for each party's promise (whatever that promise is): the parties bargain about what the consideration is, with each party getting something valuable they bargained for. Consideration can be an act, not acting or even a promise to act or not to act if it is bargained for and there is some measurable value (by contracting parties' standards). This last element of the concept of consideration is key for Agile contracting. For example, the developer will expect to be paid a fair amount for fair work; he will also understand, by the nature of Agile contracting, that some original requirements specified in a contract may be altered or dispensed with. Thus, consideration for Agile contracting is very suitable in the sense of "not acting or…a promise not to act." Whether the contract is a traditional one or an Agile one, there must be a legal detriment to the promisee or legal benefit for the promisor. Legal detriment is one of two things: a promise to do something that one has no prior legal duty to do is consideration or refraining from doing something that one has a legal right to do. Legal benefit occurs when the promisor obtains something that he had no prior legal right to obtain from the promisee. The *Hamer v. Sidway* (1891) case, though obviously about a traditional contract (1891), is a landmark case related to the value of legal rights, but also contains language apropos to Agile contracting. "Courts 'will not ask whether the thing which forms consideration does in fact benefit the promisee…or is of any substantial value to any one.' It is enough that something is promised, done, forborne or suffered by the party to whom the promise is made as consideration…: Thus, it is clear that courts believe that adequacy of consideration is in "the eye of the beholder." It is up to the parties to say what they value at what amount if there is truly legal detriment or benefit. Courts don't like to second guess the parties to the contract regarding their estimation of what something is worth (unless an element of fraud, duress, undue influence… exists). Since Agile contracts are uncertain relative to the number of iterations, for example, or the alteration of desired features or requirements, courts will not want to question the parties' estimations of what the contract should be worth (unless, of course, there is some claim of unconscionability, fraud, duress, etc.). Specifically pertinent to Agile contracts, because

Table 3. The Agreement (Derived from Arbogast, Larman and Mallik, 2012; Bernstein, 2015; Scully, 2014; Edwards, Bickerstaff and Bartsch, n. d.; McGregor and Doshi, 2018; Siddique and Hussein, 2016; Legal Insight, 2014; Bhool and Mallik, 2014)

Agreement Issue	Traditional Sales and Services Contracts	Agile Contracts
Offer and acceptance, con't.	Contract obligations must be reasonably definite	Agile projects "rarely start from a fully defined specification (Bernstein, 2015: 21)."
Complexity	Relatively predictable (Arbogast, Larman and Vodde, 2012); except that multiyear, multi-layered contracts can be very complex	Contracts here are less predictable though not necessarily more complex in terms: the complexity is a result of the inherent increased uncertainty Edwards, Bickerstaff and Bartsch (n.d.: 6): "exiting templates and contracting approaches cannot be easily adapted to properly reflect and support the requirements and philosophy of the Agile model."
Scope of work/vision	Reasonably definite "Contracts are written to contain every detailed specification of the requirements before the contract is signed (Siddique and Hussein, 2016: 53)"	Reasonably indefinite, which can cause friction in defining services to be provided; insightful, careful planning/identification of desired outcomes can reduce this source of friction Working software over comprehensive documentation (Scully, 2014; McGregor and Doshi, 2018) "(R)equirements can change during the development process; therefore it is not possible to state the exact scope of the work at the start of the project (Siddique and Hussein, 2016: 53)."
Start-up time: forming, storming, norming, performing, adjourning	With more specific contract requirements already specified, less time is needed to develop working relationships, particularly of trust, leaving less room for "storming (process of agreement on details)" and "norming (process of establishing standards)"	With less obligation specificity, more time is needed to determine the scope of project, build trust, assure transparency and the creation of a collaborative environment, particularly regarding "storming" and "norming" "(P)rojects that work well are generally those where customer and supplier both have experience of working in an agile way – and ideally with each other (Bernstein, 2015: 23)." Responding to change over following a plan is a hallmark of Agile contracting (Scully, 2014; McGregor and Doshi, 2018)
Environmental time to market constraints	Waterfall contracts (Chand, 2016; Bernstein, 2015) don't recognize rapidly needed software or rapidly evolving software needs	Recognition should be developed that services are subject to rapid evolution, product definition may be uncertain early in the process, and the ability to test for success may be diminished by time constraints Accept the parts of the contract that are agile, that is, subject to flexibility and those that are not, i. e., how payment will be made (Legal Insight, 2014)
Contractual provision comprehensiveness	Include as many foreseeable conditions of performance as possible	It is not possible to provide a comprehensive list of contractual provisions, but provisions that are within the scope of the project vision should be provided The use of "iteration reviews/demos" practices can help manage change to satisfy owner requirements (Bhool and Mallik, 2014)
Use of boilerplate language (industry standard language)	Can be appropriate (UCC Sales and Lease contracts)	More "industry standard" language is recommended against: the uncertainties in what the parties want as iterations proceed is prohibitive of language that is too standardized
Negotiations	Shark: "I win, you lose" approach	Owl: "I win, you win" approach "Agile development values individuals and interactions over processes and tools, working software over comprehensive documentation, customer collaboration over contract negotiation, and responding to change over following a plan (Lee and Xia, 2010: 89)." Customer collaboration over contract negotiation (Scully, 2014; McGregor and Doshi, 2018)

a contract has a cancellation clause in it, however, does not mean that it is an illusory promise lacking consideration and therefore validity: if the contract's cancellation clause puts limits on the cancellation of the project, time constraints on the cancellation or notice requirements for cancellation, it is not an illusory promise, i.e., "I can cancel after performance has begun with 30 days' notice" is not illusory.

CAPACITY, LEGALITY AND GENUINENESS OF ASSENT

All parties contracting in valid contracts must have capacity, the ability to understand the nature of the obligations they are committing. Perhaps with Agile contracts, one of the players in the contractual design, the lawyer who drafts the contract, is the one we must make sure has "capacity," not only legal capacity, but also the capacity to understand the similarities and differences between traditional contracts and Agile contracts. Attorneys less familiar with Agile projects should access literature such as the Agile Primer (Arbogast, Larman and Vodde, 2012) and other sources, to ease concern that the lawyer is the only player in the game that doesn't understand the nature of Agile contracting or how to properly construct such a contract that relies heavily on trust and collaboration between the parties. He should be able to design a contract that is written to reduce possible legal friction, but that acknowledges that disputes arise: suitable solutions can then be discussed/anticipated.

Legality

An agreement is illegal and thus legally unenforceable if either its formation or its performance is criminal, tortious, or opposed to public policy: in these cases, the courts will "leave the parties as they found them" and grant no relief to either party. Contracts contrary to statutory law, such as price fixing, are illegal, as is usury, selling things on days which prohibit the sale, etc. Unconscionable contracts are also illegal, as noted previously and below. It is hard to conceive that businesses associated with Agile development, either owners and developers, would enter into any contract that would violate public policy or be illegal. However, one example is good to highlight the possible issue: if the project development has begun and, before it is concluded, the law of the venue changes to prohibit such project use, the nature of the contract would be illegal and so would the contract be. This just means that the parties to any contract should be aware of the business and political environment in which they do business.

Unconscionable contracts would be a more reasonable problem to find in Agile contracts than illegal ones. An unconscionable contract is so one-sided, with one party having great bargaining power over the other, who had no other choice but to contract, allowing the powerful party to dictate the terms of the contract, that it will not be enforced. This principle is designed to protect the party with the less favorable or advantaged bargaining position. It can be applied to the process by which the unconscionable contract was entered into (i.e., bullying a small software developer into providing a better deal than is reasonable in business: procedural unconscionability) or to the terms of the contract (i.e., the price to be paid for software development: substantive unconscionability). This last is more likely to be in dispute simply because of the uncertainty of the progression of the iterations and the possibility of changes in feature and requirement specifications. Courts finding unconscionability may not enforce the contract, not enforce the unconscionable element of the contract or limit the unconscionable element of the contract.

Genuineness of Assent

Genuineness of assent occurs when the parties have a meeting of the minds: that is to say, when each party understands what they are obligating themselves to. Everyone understands and voluntarily agrees to be bound to the terms of the agreement. Contracting requires parties to knowingly and willingly enter into contracts. Such "knowing and willing" acceptance of obligations can be interrupted in several ways: mistake (unilateral, bilateral and mutual), fraud, duress or undue influence. In Agile contracting, the two failures of genuineness of assent that are easiest to envision are mistake and fraud, both of which concerns should be reduced as a result of the trust and collaborative nature of the relationship between the owner and developer.

In one case of bilateral mistake in which both parties to the contract were mistaken, *Flo-Products Co. v. Valley Dairy Farms Co.*, Flo-Products gave a phone quote of fifteen thirty six to a farm for some machinery: the company meant $1,536 but the Farm thought it was for $15.36. There was no "meeting of the minds" since both parties were mistaken as to the real amount of the contract in the other parties' eyes. The contract was not enforced. Again, the possibility of this problem should be at a minimum given level of trust and collaboration required in Agile project development.

Fraud is a misrepresentation of a material fact or an omission of material fact by words or actions. A material fact is one that might have changed one's mind. Intent to deceive is also a necessary element to proving fraud. Intent to deceive, scienter, is guilty knowledge. In this case, a party knows a fact is not as stated, a party makes a statement that he believes is not true or makes a statement with reckless disregard for the truth or a party says or implies that a statement is made on some basis, such as personal knowledge or investigation, when it is not. Reliance by the other party on misrepresentation and injury are the two other elements to proving fraud. In Agile contracts, the likelihood of substantial damages as a result of fraud is unreasonable, again, because of the nature of the contract and relationships. The contracting parties will be able to find out very soon in the performance of the contract if either party is engaged in fraud: when the first iteration does not go as planned. Thus, the specter of fraud is reduced in Agile contracts in comparison to traditional contracts. Statements of opinion or future facts are not actionable as fraud: this, too, is as applicable to Agile contracts/disputes as to traditional contracts. For example, the developer believes in good faith that the iteration will be complete by a certain date but is wrong: this is not actionable as fraud since the parties did not intend to deceive. On the other hand, negligent misrepresentation is carelessness or using reckless disregard for the truth and is actionable as fraud in either traditional contracting or Agile contracting. If the developer continues to assure the owner that viable iterations will indeed be forthcoming, though in a longer time frame than originally anticipated, and the developer is lying to continue to receive payment for working on the iteration, this would result in actionable fraud: knowledge of falsity is key.

A WRITTEN CONTRACT?

Some contracts must be in writing to be enforceable. The contract more likely to be required to be in writing in Agile contracting is a contract that cannot, by its own terms, be complete within a year. This is far more likely to be an issue than contracts, for example, involving interests in real estate or the promises to pay the debt of another, but they are, by the iterative nature of Agile contracting, not reasonably likely to create an issue. That Agile contracting is founded on short-term deliveries, at the presentation of one delivery, if the parties are satisfied with the project, the project is extended. If the customer is not satisfied, the contract can be terminated. Thus, by the very nature of performance time, Agile contracts won't be subject to this writing requirement. However, if the parties do have a writing, which is recommended, they can include any provision they would like to, in a knowing and willing way, as to what would constitute a writing and how the parties will be bound to the contract. Generally speaking, the contract must be signed by the party against whom enforcement is sought (not the one suing). The writing must contain the essential elements of the contract, i.e., the scope of the project. Further, contracts in general will be interpreted as a whole, not in parts. With Agile contracts, the agreement can be seen as an installment contract, with each iteration an "installment," all of which would be considered in reviewing the entire contract.

PERFORMANCE

Installment Contracts

In fact, an example of a legal concept that exhibits reassuring similarities between traditional contracting and Agile contracting can be seen in installment contracts. Traditional contracts called installment contracts are in the nature of iterative contracts in that they are contracts for separate lots of goods to be delivered and accepted over the course of the contract performance: each month, for example, six loads of aggregate will be delivered to the purchaser, who uses up each delivery in making concrete to build the foundation of a structure. Like Agile contracts, installment contracts are specialized contracts wherein the iterative, installment element of the performance is a defining characteristic of the contract. Again, like Agile iterations (Sprints) which don't meet the scope of work as agreed upon by the parties, an installment contract can be repudiated if any installment substantially impairs the value of the entire contract. Installment contracts and Agile contracts do differ, however, in that it would not be possible for the impairment of the value of the entire contract to be evident only at the completion of the last iteration. Since each iteration in an Agile contract could be considered a separate contract, rather than as a part performance of the whole contract, impairment in the value of the "entire" contract would be evident much more quickly than in an installment contract among good faith parties.

Conclusion of Performance

The parties can perform the contract and thus discharge their obligations in a variety of ways. First, they can discharge by performance: do what one is supposed to do under the contract. Discharge by substantial performance (with minor deviations) requires the parties to do most of what one is supposed to do. Discharge by agreement happens when the parties agree that the contract has been completed and that the contractual relationship is ended. Accord and satisfaction reflects the idea that the obligation between the parties may change, but the parties themselves will continue to work on the contract, while in novations, the parties change, but the obligation remains the same: to complete the original contract. Covenants not to sue are merely contractual provisions that reflect that the parties have agreed that they will not sue one another over contract disputes. Finally, commercial impracticability is the acknowledgement that the contract should not proceed as performance would be too expensive for good faith parties.

Of all of these ways to discharge contracts, many of these ways would be most reasonable for the Agile contract to be terminated. For example, if the parties agree that there are no more iterations needed, they can stipulate that that contract has been performed or substantially performed. If the parties agree to go in a different direction with subsequent iterations, they can agree that the original obligations under the contract have changed, resulting in completion of the first part of the contract by accord and satisfaction. Again, as we have noted throughout, many of the principles guiding traditional contracting and Agile contracting are similar.

The parties should also consider the provision of warranties as to a variety of things. Warranties are a seller's express or implied promise that the goods meet certain standards. An express warranty is one wherein the seller affirms that the goods meet certain standards of quality, description, performance or condition by written/oral words or conduct. Although the warranty of merchantability was developed in the law on UCC sales of goods and clearly software is not a movable, tangible good, the principle again carries over. Goods should be fit for the ordinary purposes for which they were intended/designed. They should conform to any promise or affirmation the developer makes about the software's performance. Finally, at the very least, the developer should warrant that the code used to create the software was open-source code or that he was granted permission to use any proprietary/copyright protected software during the development process.

Breach of Contract

Breach of any contract is a result of failure of performance in some way. This fear is reduced given the relatively short time periods each iteration is expected to be provided. Such fear can also be reduced if the parties clearly understand the consequences of breach: the inclusion of liquidated damages in the agreement can aid in that understanding. Liquidated damages are those agreed-upon in the contract at the initiation of the contract: the parties agree as to what each party will pay, at what triggers/times, in the event of a perceived breach of contract. Since the parties agree ahead of time to what they will pay the aggrieved party, the uncertainty as to what can be assessed as damages is either reduced or eliminated.

Another pro-active approach the parties can take to reducing damages is the use of anticipatory breach: a party who fears that performance will not be timely alerts the other party/ies that breach is imminent. At the very least, this alerts the damaged party that the performance he expected at a certain time will not be forthcoming, possibly giving him time to find other solutions to provide the software he had anticipated receiving. Rescission, wherein the parties back out of the contract for some reason, is also possible: perhaps the software developer comes to the conclusion that he is not the best suited to develop the software; he can go ahead, then, and request rescission, to simply back out of the contract. Finally, specific performance is an equitable remedy wherein the parties are required to complete performance specifically as listed in the contract. This remedy is usually reserved for things that are unique, which the Agile contract could be considered, but the remedy is not a reasonable solution from the perspective that the specificity of the contract requirements is by nature uncertain/unknown. Table 4 provides a thumbnail review of issues associated with performance and breach.

OWNERSHIP RIGHTS TO THE SOFTWARE

A final question unrelated to the way a contract is formed, but closely related to the nature of Agile software development is about ownership of the software that is ultimately developed. One way to deal with this question of ownership is to define the software as "works for hire." Works for hire happen when one of two things occur: first, an employee is paid to create a copyrightable work, in which case the employer retains the ownership of the work. Second, an independent contractor is hired to create a copyrightable work, i.e., the software, in which case the independent contractor retains the ownership of the work as its author. After the parties determine who the owner of the software is, either the customer or the developer, other questions are prompted. If the developer is the owner, specification of the time/

Table 4. Issues Associated with Performance and Breach (Derived from Chand, 2016; Edwards, Bickerstaff and Bartsch, n.d.; Bernstein, 2015; Bhool and Mallik, 2014; Rubin, 2012; Brightwell, 2017)

Time of delivery	As contractually specified As determined by a reasonable time period (which can be dictated by the subject of the contract: fireworks should not arrive at the stand on July 5th	Each iteration should have a set time for performance (Edwards, Bickerstaff and Bartsch, n.d.) Avoid timeboxes (deadlines) to "focus experimentation and avoid waste," but also provide clarity with regard to "how far an engineer should go before they check to see if the direction (they are taking) is still correct (McGregor and Doshi, 2018)"
Performance appraisal timeliness	Liability for contract breach on a re-active basis	Iterative: specter of massive failure (liability for contract breach) is reduced Each iteration could represent a full "contract"
Course corrections	Installment contracts	Iterative delivery Each team member should act with appropriate levels of care and skill, reliance upon which should be made in relation to length of time for performance, reasonableness of iteration success (Edwards, Bickerstaff and Bartsch, n.d.) The team's iterations should be "minimally viable experiments (McGregor and Doshi, 2018)"
Change management	Less flexible	More flexible within ranges/limits Review meetings can re-evaluate priorities, features to be incorporated into further iterations, etc. "Developing the requirements just before each new iteration allows the project to evolve despite changing circumstances (Dutton, 2018: 35)."
Risk acceptance, assessment, and apportionment	Contract provisions will address more certainty of risk and apportionment among the parties	Nature of contract increases uncertainty with each new iteration "Find ways of managing and mitigating risk rather than resisting it or trying to push it where it doesn't belong (Bernstein, 2015: 22)."
Damages	Full breach Anticipatory breach	Lesser damages could be possible with smaller "contracts" of each iteration Establish what will happen if the project "goes wrong (Edwards, Bickerstaff and Bartsch (n.d.: 7)."
Mitigation of damages	Courts are in favor of plaintiff attempts to lessen their damages	Provision of customer right to terminate the contract on an iteration basis Provide incentives for performance Set communications standards to effect transparency in completion issues Keep track, in writing or orally (recorded), of what the parties agree to on a set schedule and/or at the end of an iteration
Liquidated awards or penalties	These clauses provide incentives to timely and correct contract conclusion	Recommended against: the uncertain and iterative nature of the project precludes against penalties particularly Recommended for: the contract can stipulate that late or poor iteration performance is grounds for stipulated penalties (Dataitlaw, 2019)
Payment model/cycles	At agreed-upon intervals (i.e., installment contracts) At performance completion Fixed price per iteration or unit of work (Siddique and Hussein, 2016; Arbogast, 2012): price, scope and time are included and risk is with the supplier Time and material basis (costs of time and materials to date) for a minimum viable product and risk is with the customer (Bernstein, 2015; Siddique and Hussein, 2016)	Innumerable: as agreed upon by contracting parties Payment due at iteration completion with set limits for cost associated with each iteration Pay-per-use of software (Arbogast, 2012) Target cost contracts is a combination of fixed price and time and materials contracts: both parties understand that "software project requirements are uncertain and that they must work collaboratively to attain the goals. If the price of the project exceeds the estimated price, the two parties will share it, and if there is profit in the project (by delivering it for less than the agreed cost), it will also be shared between the customer and supplier (Siddique and Hussein, 2016: 54)." Use of Function Points (Brightwell, 2017) which are units of measure to express the functionality of the iteration
Ease of termination	Can be contractually specific Breach could be a problem if the contract termination is not allowed or if the contract is wrongfully terminated	What possible consequences could accrue from termination? (Dataitlaw, 2019) Clearly state each parties' right to terminate Clearly state at which point in the iteration presentation a contract can be terminated
Time constraints of termination	Is performance complete?	Is iteration complete and is that point a good termination point for the project? Can each iteration trigger termination of the project? Each party should be given the right to terminate the project without liability with identified triggers (Edwards, Bickerstaff and Bartsch, n.d.)
Early termination	See liquidated damages	See liquidated damages
End product	More certain	Iteratively
"Definition of Done"	Performance completion	Iteratively; "Done criteria are a set of rules that are applicable to all user stories in a given (iteration). (Such criteria) include …completed unit testing…, completion of quality assurance tests, completion of all documentation…, (assurance that) all issues are fixed, (and) successful demonstration to stakeholders/business representatives (Bhool and Mallik, 2014: 100)."
Warranties	Implied warranty of merchantability	Granted on each iteration Products should be free from defects, comply with their descriptions, have time limits for imposition, refer to use of open source software and relate to virus protection: warranties of merchantability
Focus on specificity in all terms	Yes	Designate the purpose of the project and how the project is to be established, rather than using rigid terms/performance criteria (Edwards, Bickerstaff and Bartsch n.d.)
Successful contract	Winning a lawsuit	Providing a good project
Intellectual property rights	Shop right, works for hire (Bernstein, 2015)	Shop right, works for hire (Bernstein, 2015)
Dispute resolution	Litigation Alternative dispute resolution	Parties should be aware of litigation as a dispute resolution process, but also of alternative dispute resolution methods, such as arbitration, mediation and negotiation: these alternatives could be very useful in Agile contracting, given that those helping to resolve the dispute would have knowledge and understanding of pertinent law, but, more importantly, of Agile practices as they relate to contract law

trigger for ownership to change hands should be noted in the contract. The rights of the developer relative to the use of the customers' data should also be reviewed (Dataitlaw, 2019).

CONCLUSION

While it is true that lawyers may present as adversarial in zealously representing his client, such adversarially zealous representation is not only mandated by the legal canons of professional responsibility, but also by clients when a contract fails for some reason. Arbogast, Larman and Mallik (2012) seem to suggest that the lawyers are the enemies in Agile contracting because they are basically ignorant of the uncertain nature of the project in terms of what the parties want, how success is defined, when the project will be finished, etc. The only time anyone wants a lawyer is when he needs a lawyer: to mitigate the harm caused by any contract dispute, both the lawyer and the client should have an understanding of the fundamental aspects of the contract, any contract, like the uncertainties inherent in Agile contracts. Such understanding will obviate the need of a lawyer in an adversarial role. "The job of a technology lawyer is to protect clients from undue risk arising from relationships they form in the course of their business, or at least to flag that risk so they can make informed decisions (Sinclair, 2015: 15)." If all the parties to the contract are aware of these fundamentals, including the lawyers, there should be no more contractual contests on Agile contracts than on any other contract. In the final analysis, Kanth (2009: 20) sums up both the best and most challenging aspects of Agile software development that make it worth the efforts: "quality is never an accident, it is always the result of high intention, sincere effort, intelligent direction and skillful execution: it represents the wise choice of many alternatives." In fact, this is not just a description of Agile development principles, but also a description of how to craft an Agile contract. "A well drafted software development agreement benefits both parties and should define success, failure, remedies and an expedited resolution path (Costa, 2020)."

REFERENCES

American Law Institute. (2020). *Restatement of law, second, contracts.* Retrieved February 11, 2020, from https://www.ali.org/publications/show/contracts/

Arbogast, T., Larman, C., & Mallik, B. (2012). Agile contracts primer. *Practices for Scaling Lean & Agile Development: Large, Multisite, & Offshore Product Development with Large-Scale Scrum.* Retrieved February 5, 2020, from https://agilecontracts.org/agile contracts primer.pdf

Baham, C. (2019). Teaching tip: Implementing Scrum wholesales in the classroom. *Journal of Information Systems Education, 30*(3), 141–159.

Bernstein, A. (2015, Aug. 25). How to write supplier contracts for agile software development. *Computer Weekly,* 21-24.

Bhoola, V., & Mallik, D. (2014). Determinants of agile practices: A Gini index approach. *Vilakshan, XIMB. Journal of Management, 11*(2), 95–114.

Brightwell, I. (2017). *Is a 'fixed price' agile contract possible?* Retrieved February 5, 2020, from http://web.b.ebscohost.com/ehost/detail/detail?vid=7&sid+afafbb04-744b-4f89-a249-1523bfdd2f41%sessionmgr102&bdata=JnNpdGU9ZWhvc3QtbG12ZSZzY29wZT1zaXR1#AN=124565087&db=bth

Chand, K. (2016). *What is Agile contracting methodology?* Retrieved February 5, 2020, from https://www.lexology.com/library/detail.aspx?g=b96675c0-6e23-47cb-be8b-e3cc0966250e

Costa, C. (2020). *Software development agreements: Polar Pro Filters Inc. v. Frogslayer LLC.* Retrieved August 17, 2020, from http://ccosta.com/index.php/2020/05/03/software-development-agreements-polar-pro-filters-inc-v-frogslayer-llc-2/

Dataitlaw. (2019). *5 basic legal issues of agile software development.* Retrieved February 4, 2020, from https://www.dataitlaw.com/5-basic-legal-issues-of-agile-software-development/

Definition of Agile. (n.d.). Retrieved February 11, 2020, from https://www.dictionary.com/browse/agile?s=t

Dutton, G. (2018). Choosing the right agile strategy. *Training (New York, N.Y.)*, 34–36. Retrieved February 10, 2020, from http://pubs.royle.com/publication/?i=482831&p=36#{%22page%22:%2236%22,%22issue_id%22:482831,%22publication_id%22:%2220617%22}

Edwards, I., Bickerstaff, R., & Bartsch, C. (n.d.). *Bird & Bird & contracting for agile software development projects.* Retrieved February 6, 2020, from https://www.twobirds.com/~/media/pdfs/brochures/contracting-for-agile-software-development-projects.pdf?la=en

Eisenberg, M. A. (2009). The role of fault in contract law: Unconscionability, unexpected circumstances, interpretation, mistake, and performance. *Michigan Law Review*, *107*, 1413–1430.

Flo-Products Co. v. Valley Farms Dairy Co. 718 S.W. 2d 207 (Ct. Appl. MO.).

Friess, E. (2019). Scrum language use in a software engineering firm: An exploratory study. *IEEE Transactions on Professional Communication*, *62*(2), 130–147. doi:10.1109/TPC.2019.2911461

Hamer v. Sidway 124 N.Y. 538, 27 N.E. 256 (Ct. App. N. Y.).

Hassett, J., & Burke, E. (2017). Why the agile approach is so important to law firms. *Of Council*, *36*(10), 6-9.

Kanth, S. K. (2009). Agile methodology in product testing. *Journal of the Quality Assurance Institute*, *23*(1), 18–23.

Laakkonen, K. (2014). *Contracts in agile software development.* Aalto University School of Science.

Larusdottir, M., Cajander, A., & Gulliksen, J. (2014). Informal feedback rather than performance measurements – User-centred evaluation. *Behaviour & Information Technology*, *33*(11), 1118–1135. doi:10.1080/0144929X.2013.857430

Lee, G., & Xia, W. (2010). Toward Agile: An integrated analysis of quantitative and qualitative field data on software development agility. *Management Information Systems Quarterly*, *34*(1), 87–114. doi:10.2307/20721416

Legal Executive Institute, & Reuters, T. (2017). *US companies vastly outspend rest of the world on legal services, Acritas study shows*. Retrieved August 11, 2020, from https://www.legalexecutiveinstitute.com/acritas-legal-services-spending-study/#:~:text=US%20companies%20spend%20a%20whopping,new%20study%20by%20Acritas%20Research

Legal Information Institute. (2002). *UCC article 2 – Sales*. Retrieved February 11, 2020, from https://www.law.cornell.edu/ucc/index.html

Louisiana Civil Code. (n.d.). *Title iv – Conventional obligations or contracts*. Retrieved February 11, 2020, from https://lcco.law.lsu.edu/?uid=73&ver=en

Lukasiewicz, K., & Miler, J. (2012). Improving agility and discipline of software development with the Scrum and CMMI. *Institute of Engineering and Technology*, 6(5), 416–422.

Mann, R. A., & Roberts, B. S. (2014). *Business law and the regulation of business* (11th ed.). Southwestern, Cengage Learning.

Marriott, E. (2016). *The history of the world in bite-sized chunks*. London, UK: Michael O'Hara Books Limited.

McGregor, L., & Doshi, N. (2018). Why Agile goes awry – and how to fix it. *Harvard Business Review*. Retrieved February 10, 2020, from https://hbr.org/2018/10/why-agile-goes-awry-and-how-to-fix-it

Miller, S. (2015). *Ten things you need to know as in-house counsel*. Retrieved August 11, 2020, from https://sterlingmiller2014.wordpress.com/2015/07/07/ten-things-explaining-litigation-to-the-board-and-the-ceo/

Moore, G. (1991). *Crossing the chasm*. HarperCollins Publishers.

Polar Pro Filters Inc. v. Frogslayer, LLC No. H-19-1706, slip op. (S. D. Tex. Oct. 22, 2019).

Raysman, R., & Brown, P. (2019). Software development agreement dispute produces a split decision. *New York Law Journal Online*. Retrieved November 8, 2019, from https://www.law.com/newyorklaw-journal/2019/11/08/software-development-agreement-dispute-produces-a-split-decision/

Rubin, K. S. (2012). *Essential Scrum: A practical guide to the most popular agile process*. Addison-Wesley.

Scully, J. (2014, Jan.). Agile HR delivery. *Workforce Solutions*, 8-11.

Siddique, L., & Hussein, B. A. (2016). Grounded theory study of the contracting process in agile projects in Norway's software industry. *The Journal of Modern Project Management*, 53-63. Retrieved February 10, 2020, from https://www.researchgate.net/publication/303336244_Grounded_Theory_Study_of_the_Contracting_Process_in_Agile_Projects_in_Norway's_Software_Industry

Sinclair, C. (2012). How to guide your lawyers in brokering agile software contracts. *Computer Weekly*, 23-29. Retrieved February 5, 2020, from http://web.b.ebscohost.com/ehost/pdfviewer?vid=8&sid=afafbb04-744b-4f89-a249-1523bfdd241%40sessionmgr102

Ward, D. B. (2019). *8 do's and dont's of agile contract*s. Retrieved February 3, 2020, from https://telegraphhillsoftware.come/8-dos-donts-agile-contracts-v2/

Section 4
Education

Chapter 11
Learning Scrum:
A LEGO®–Scrum Simulation

Simon Bourdeau
ESG-UQAM, Canada

Alejandro Romero-Torres
ESG-UQAM, Canada

Marie-Claude Petit
ESG-UQAM, Canada

ABSTRACT

The LEGO®-Scrum simulation-based training (SBT) described here shows how LEGO® bricks can help professionals learn first-hand about Scrum methodology, an Agile approach to software development projects. The chapter's objectives are 1) to present the modalities of the LEGO®-Scrum SBT, 2) to demonstrate how LEGO® bricks can help professionals learn, first-hand, about Scrum, and 3) to illustrate how this learning can be relevant and impactful for participants. Based on observations, interviews, and a data collection by questionnaire carried out with 198 participants, the proposed SBT appears to provide a significant, relevant, and valuable learning experience. In addition, four experienced Scrum masters and IT project managers, who played key roles in the SBT, argued that the LEGO®-Scrum SBT provides a realistic representation of real-world Scrum projects; that it is dynamic, complex, challenging, and motivating; and that participants' learning is evocative and relevant, since they learn by doing.

INTRODUCTION

In recent years, the Agile Manifesto (Beck et al., 2001) and agile software development approaches, such as Extreme Programming (XP), Kanban, Crystal and Scrum (Boehm, 2002; Meyer, 2018), have spread and changed how software is developed and how projects are realized. From these various agile approaches, Scrum is the most common approach used by agile practitioners and by project managers (68%) (Allisy-Roberts, 2017). In this context, graduate students enrolled in computing and engineering

DOI: 10.4018/978-1-7998-4885-1.ch011

Copyright © 2021, IGI Global. Copying or distributing in print or electronic forms without written permission of IGI Global is prohibited.

disciplines, as well as practitioners who need to understand and implement Scrum should be exposed to and learn the opportunities and challenges associated with this key agile methodology. Students and practitioners should understand what the main characteristics of Scrum are and its impact on, for instance, project phases, team dynamics, relationships with clients, and on roles and responsibilities, etc. Today, as information technologies (IT) are more and more prevalent in organizations (Ko & Kirsch, 2017), it becomes essential that both students and practitioners in IT and in software development be trained to cope with and develop competencies in Scrum, as this agile approach is the most used in organizations and has a positive impact on projects' success (Hayat, Rehman, Arif, Wahab, & Abbas, 2019).

In both the academic and practitioner literature, different approaches for teaching agile methods have been proposed (e.g. McAvoy & Sammon, 2005; Sharp & Lang, 2019), while a limited number focused on teaching the Scrum framework (e.g. Rodriguez, Soria, & Campo, 2015; Von Wangenheim, Savi, & Borgatto, 2013). Furthermore, even if the idea of using LEGOs for teaching and learning is not new, and it has been used in a variety of teaching contexts (e.g. Cantoni, Botturi, Faré, & Bolchini, 2009; Freeman, 2003; James, 2013; Paasivaara, Heikkilä, Lassenius, & Toivola, 2014; Peabody & Noyes, 2017; Pike, 2002), the idea of using LEGOs to teach Scrum has been used to a limited extent (City, 2009; Krivitsky, 2017; Paasivaara et al., 2014) and, to the authors' knowledge, no study has evaluated the relevancy and usefulness of using LEGOs to teach and learn Scrum.

To enhance the acquisition of Scrum-related competencies, a LEGO®-Scrum simulation-based training (SBT) was developed. A SBT is a teaching/learning method defined as "any synthetic practice environment that is created in order to impart competencies (i.e., attitudes, concepts, knowledge, rules, or skills) that will improve a trainee's performance" (Salas, Wildman, & Piccolo, 2009, p. 560). SBT are developed to reproduce realistic representation of "real-world" contexts in which participants realized various tasks, play different roles and learn by doing (Stainton, Johnson, & Borodzicz, 2010). Thus, as a SBT unfolds, participants analyze the simulation's context and objectives, solve problems, collaborate with each other, make decisions, and take actions. Typically, during and/or after a SBT, periods are devoted to sharing experiences between participants and for debriefing on the decisions made, the actions taken and, finally, for making links with theoretical concepts (Tiwari, Nafees, & Krishnan, 2014). Several researchers have shown that experiential learning approaches, such as SBTs: 1) offer realistic, complex, and challenging learning environments; 2) let reality be simplified and manageable; 3) bridge the gap between the "real world" and the classroom; 4) provide a risk-free and safe environment, 5) engender greater motivation; 6) improve team development and; 7) render the understanding, integration, and retention of knowledge more profound than so-called traditional methods (Clem, Mennicke, & Beasley, 2014; Dekkers & Donatti, 1981; Léger, 2006; Salas et al., 2009; Tiwari et al., 2014).

In this context, students enrolled in computing and engineering courses, as well as practitioners who need to learn and use Scrum, must be sensitized to the challenges, difficulties, and key elements of the Scrum framework (Vinaja, 2019; Schwaber & Sutherland, 2017). To support the development of Scrum-related competencies and introduce students and practitioners to the challenges associated with Scrum, the authors developed and evaluated a LEGO®-Scrum SBT. More specifically, their main research question is: "What pedagogical approach can be deployed to help beginners in Scrum develop Scrum-related competencies?" Two sub-questions flow from this main question: (1) "How can instructors increase novices Scrum awareness of, and sensitivity to, how the method works?" (2) "Can an SBT approach, combined with the affordances of LEGO®, create an impactful learning experience for novices in Scrum?"

The chapter presents an experience report of five LEGO®-Scrum SBTs that took place with 198 undergraduate and graduate students. Four experienced professionals were also involved in one of the five-SBT sessions to participate and to provide their feedback and suggestions. During the SBT, participants had to develop, using LEGO bricks, models of the facilities for the next Olympic summer games using the Scrum framework. Three complete Sprints—including planning, review, and retrospective—were realized. The chapter's objectives are: 1) to present the modalities of the LEGO®-Scrum SBT; 2) to demonstrate how LEGO® bricks can help participants learn, first-hand, about the Scrum framework, and; 3) to illustrate how this learning can be relevant and impactful for participants since they learn by doing. In the first section of this chapter, the Scrum framework and the concept of active learning are presented, as well as explanations as to why LEGO® bricks are used in the SBT. Then, a detailed description of the SBT's modalities is presented. Afterwards, based on interviews and a survey, observations and impressions from the participants as well as from professionals, are provided and discussed.

THEORETICAL BACKGROUND

Scrum

When compared to traditional "command and control" IT project management approaches, Scrum is quite different. First, Scrum is not a method per se, but rather a framework in which individuals can address complex adaptive problems, while creatively and productively delivering valuable services and products (Schwaber & Sutherland, 2017). Second, implementing Scrum requires important organizational changes such as, for example, adapting management styles, modifying the nature of client relationships, changing office layouts, transforming team members' mentality, among others (Rola, Kuchta, & Kopczyk, 2016). Third, Scrum software development projects adopt incremental approaches which include a series of short development iterations, i.e. "Sprints" (Schwaber & Sutherland, 2017). In Scrum software development projects, teams are usually self-organized in terms of planning, scheduling, assigning tasks, and making decisions. In addition, Scrum teams are usually collocated to enable fluid and constant collaboration as well as to facilitate direct, face-to-face communication among team members (Rising & Janoff, 2000).

Scrum teams are usually formed of 4 to 12 individuals and there are three main roles: 1) the *product owner* (PO) represents the eventual users of the system and is responsible for managing the product backlog; 2) the *development team* is formed of individuals who work on delivering a potentially releasable increment of "Done" product at the end of each Sprint (Schwaber & Sutherland, 2017) and is responsible for managing the Sprint backlog, and; 3) the *Scrum master* is the person in charge of ensuring that every individual involved in the project is adhering to the Scrum practices and rules (Castillo, 2016).

Scrum software development projects revolve around five key events which are: 1) the *Sprint*, a time-box of one month or less during which a "Done," useable, and potentially releasable product increment is created; 2) the *Sprint planning*, a time-boxed period where the next Sprint plan is established by the development team; 3) the *daily Scrum*, a short time-boxed period used by the team members to synchronize their activities and create short-term plans; 4) the *Sprint review*, a time-boxed period where the team presents the product's increment to the PO and other interested stakeholders to get their feedback and make adjustments for the next Sprint and; 5) the *Sprint retrospective*, a time-boxed period, after the Sprint review, but before the next Sprint planning, where the development team reflects on what and how things have been done in the last Sprint, and which improvements should be carried out in the next Sprint (Castillo, 2016; Schwaber & Sutherland, 2017).

Scrum projects have three key artefacts: 1) the *product backlog*, a list of all the user stories, which represents the requirements needed in the end product; 2) the *Sprint backlog*, which is a set of the product backlog items that have been prioritized and will be realized in the next Sprint and; 3) the *increment*, which represents all the product backlog items realized in a Sprint. Finally, in Scrum projects, various tools and practices are used to plan and monitor the work that has been done, such as *burn-down charts*, a graphical project monitoring tool representing work left to do versus time; *story points*, an abstract and relative amount of effort/time required to complete a task, and; *velocity*, a measure of work or items realized during a period of time (Castillo, 2016; Schwaber & Sutherland, 2017).

Since Scrum is part of the agile movement, it is characterized by an incremental and iterative project management style, centered on the autonomy of individuals involved in the specifications, production, and validation of an integrated and continuously tested product. It is based on these "practical" realities, and not on a general or structuring theory, that agile and Scrum have been developed. Thus, agile and Scrum are practice-oriented. The challenge for educators and instructors is how to teach agile methodology, and how to get students and practitioners to learn about Scrum's "practical" reality in terms of roles, events, artefacts, and practices. One interesting approach is to get students and practitioners to learn actively through SBT, as this type of simulation makes it possible to recreate "real-world" environments mimicking "practical" realities (Devedzic, 2011; Salas et al., 2009; Smith-Daniels & Smith-Daniels, 2008).

Active Learning

Active learning is a learning method in which participants are engaged in their learning and/or are experientially involved in various learning activities, such as class discussions, collaborative learning groups, debates, or simulations (Smith-Daniels & Smith-Daniels, 2008). This learning method can be defined as "the process of having students engage in some activity that forces them to reflect upon ideas and how they are using those ideas. Requiring students to regularly assess their own degree of understanding and skill at handling concepts or problems in a particular discipline. The attainment of knowledge by participating or contributing. The process of keeping students mentally, and often physically, active in their learning through activities that involve them in gathering information, thinking, and problem solving" (Michael, 2006, p. 160).

Active learning integrates working practices such as collaboration, co-operation, and problem-solving (Prince, 2004). As mentioned previously, SBT incorporates key elements of active learning, as simulations provide realistic and dynamic environments which can help students and practitioners improve teamwork and decision-making (Jeong & Bozkurt, 2014). Various approaches and objects have been used by both researchers and practitioners to develop games and simulations to teach agile (McAvoy & Sammon, 2005) and, more specifically, Scrum, such as card games (Fernandes & Sousa, 2010), software simulations (Cubric, 2013; Gkritsi, 2011; Martin, 2000; Von Wangenheim et al., 2013), balls (May, York, & Lending, 2016), role playing (Medeiros, Neto, Passos, & De Souza Araújo, 2015), and LEGO® bricks (City, 2009; Krivitsky, 2017; Paasivaara et al., 2014). Of these games and simulations, those using LEGO® bricks seem the most interesting because of the LEGO® brick materiality (Taylor & Statler, 2014) and its underlying affordances (Faraj & Azad, 2012). The articles and books that present Scrum simulations using LEGO® bricks, do not explain the added value of using LEGO® in terms of active learning.

LEGO® Bricks: Recreate "Real-Life" Situations

Developing an effective SBT can be challenging since it must accommodate different learning styles, let participants retain some control over their learning, and recreate a real-life Scrum project. Additionally, SBTs are usually costly and time-consuming (Bell, Kanar, & Kozlowski, 2008; Salas, Rosen, Held, & Weissmuller, 2009). A key choice when developing SBTs is to identify the types of tasks performed by participants and the tool used so that they can rapidly immerse themselves in an active learning mode (D. A. Kolb, 2014; Michael, 2006). Thus, to recreate an immersive "real-life" situation where students can live a Scrum project, LEGO® bricks were used, since most participants were familiar with LEGOs, having played with such bricks in childhood. Even though the bricks are usually associated with children's learning activities, they are being used more widely in adult learning activities because they constitute a practical tool for reflecting, discussing, and learning (Steghöfer, Burden, Alahyari, & Haneberg, 2017; Taylor & Statler, 2014).

Creating LEGO® models requires little preparation or planning, so it is fast, as the bricks can easily be interconnected in numerous and unexpected ways, even with little skill (Gauntlett, 2007). Moreover, LEGO® bricks are characterized by low floor, high ceiling, and wide walls, because it is easy for less experienced participants to get started (i.e., low floor); construction becomes progressively as more complex and sophisticated models can be built (i.e., high ceiling); and students' imagination can take a project in countless directions (i.e., wide walls) (Resnick & Silverman, 2005).

LEGO® bricks were used in the LEGO®-Scrum SBT because they allowed one to rapidly create an affordable and flexible experiential learning environment where participants could apply concepts or skills they learned, learn new ones, and reflect on their decisions and actions. Experiential learning is a particular form of learning from life experiences, often distinguished from classroom learning and lectures (D. A. Kolb, 2014). The LEGO®-Scrum SBT tried to recreate a "real-life" Scrum project with LEGO® bricks, where the hands-on, practical situation experienced by participants served as a springboard to reflect, discuss, and learn about Scrum (Schwaber & Sutherland, 2017). By manipulating bricks, participants become immersed in an active state that stimulates various learning modes and allows them to go through Kolb's (2014) full learning cycle: active experimentation, concrete experience, reflective observation, and abstract conceptualization. Thus, the LEGO®-Scrum SBT allows participants to encounter two elements often missing in traditional classroom settings: active experimentation and concrete experience (A. Y. Kolb & D. A. Kolb, 2005).

LEGO® bricks were also used because, when participants manipulate these bricks, they activate brain regions that help to anchor knowledge and skills in a deeper, more meaningful way. This result follows from the "hands-on, minds-on" connections stimulated by LEGO® bricks (Kristiansen & Rasmussen, 2014). In addition, by working with LEGO® bricks, participants create and recreate their own knowledge because this action stimulates the formation of connections between new and existing knowledge (Papert, 1990). Finally, LEGO® bricks were used in the LEGO®-Scrum SBT because of their playful aspect, which, in a learning context, can increase participants' engagement, stimulate curiosity and motivation, reduce habits and prejudices and, ultimately, help them develop new competencies (A. Y. Kolb & D. A. Kolb, 2010; Webster & Martocchio, 1993).

Finally, the playful dimension of the LEGO®-Scrum SBT helps to increase participants' involvement resulting in making them more likely to "relax" certain prejudices and habits (Brown & Vaughan, 2010; A. Y. Kolb & D. A. Kolb, 2010). The SBT presented here is part of the "serious play" movement, which promotes active learning, innovation, and creativity (James & Nerantzi, 2019; Roos, Victor, & Statler,

2004; Statler, Heracleous, & Jacobs, 2011), and Krivitsky's (2017) idea of using LEGO bricks to learn Scrum was used as a source of inspiration to create the LEGO®-Scrum SBT presented here. Although Krivitsky's idea is relevant, the activities proposed are laborious and relatively long to deploy. In addition, the effectiveness and relevance of these activities, in terms of learning, have not been demonstrated. Thus, the authors chose to recreate the simulation scenario, i.e. the phases, the durations, the instructions, the context, the support material, the evaluations, the feedback periods (i.e. double-loop learning (Argyris, 2002)), and the roles. In addition, they created a set of basic user stories (see Appendix 1), which could be used during the three sprints. Furthermore, in the second and third sprints, the POs can add user stories.

LEGO®-Scrum SBT Learning Objectives, Context, and Phases

The LEGO®-Scrum SBT's objective is to stimulate students and practitioners' learning and thinking regarding the opportunities and challenges associated with the Scrum framework. After having participated in this SBT, students and practitioners should be able to understand and appreciate Scrum's (Garud, 1997):

1. **Know-how**, i.e., its "processes," its main characteristics, e.g., events, roles and artifacts, as well as the specificities of client-PO-team interactions.
2. **Know-what,** i.e., identify ideal contexts to deploy Scrum, as well as to recognize the opportunities and challenges associated with Scrum projects.
3. **Know-why**, i.e., principles underlying Scrum projects and behaviors/attitudes to adopt.

The general context of the LEGO®-Scrum SBT is that the city mayor and his executive committee wish to analyze the possibility of organizing the summer Olympic Games in to taken place 10 years from now. Thus, the first step is to develop models of the major infrastructures needed. The participants have been mandated to deliver, in teams and using Scrum's framework, six key Olympic sites: athletes' residence, train and subway central stations, a tennis complex, an Olympic stadium, a gymnasium, and an Olympic pool.

Even if each team builds a single site, they are not competing one against the other. For each site, 17 different "user stories" have been prepared. Briefly, user stories are descriptions of the future product features, such as a building or software, and they provide enough information so that the team can estimate the effort needed to implement it. Examples of users' stories are provided in Appendix 1.

The final product is a set of sites required for the summer Olympic games. The infrastructure models have to be mainly built using LEGO® bricks, even if any additional material is used, such as pencils or paper. Table 1 presents the LEGO®-Scrum SBT phases and their descriptions. Table 2 provides pictures showing a LEGO®-Scrum simulation based-training.

METHODOLOGY

The authors conducted the LEGO®-Scrum SBT with graduate and undergraduate participants (N = 198) enrolled in the "Information Technology Project Management" course at a North American university. Since the simulation in which the participants took part was part of their course, no official recruitment was carried out. In addition, participation was voluntary, as the results of this simulation did not count towards the participants' final grades. During the simulation, the main incentive for the students was to

Table 1. LEGO®-Scrum simulation based-training phases and descriptions

Phases (160 min)	Phases Descriptions
1. Introduction to the simulation process (10 min.)	1. Context and backlog overview presentation. 2. Explanation of Scrum "processes," i.e., high-level Sprint planning, Sprint planning, Sprint, Sprint review, Sprint retrospective, and members' roles.
2. Teams formation and Scrum Master Selection (15 min.)	1. Instructor recall Scrum Master's role and interpersonal skills required. 2. Team members introduce themselves to each other and select a Scrum Master while they remain members become developers. 3. Product owners (PO) are presented to the team.
3. Detailed backlog presentations (10 min)	1. PO presents main required functionalities based on the user stories and define priority levels for each functionality using story points, i.e., 1, 2, 3, 5 or 8.
4. High-level Sprint planning (15 min)	1. Teams evaluate user stories' complexity levels and identify a strategy to assess priorities. 2. Plan which features will be developed in each Sprint based on user stories and on discussions/agreements with the PO. 3. Scrum Master animates this ceremony and PO approves the result.
5.1. Sprint planning (3 min)	1. Team members choose user stories to deliver during next Sprint + Position in corresponding Sprint column (see Picture 1 – Table 2). 2. PO approves results.
5.2. Sprint (7 min)	1. Developers perform scheduled tasks, i.e., build the infrastructure models using mainly LEGO® bricks (See Picture 2 – Table 2).

5.3. Sprint review (5 min)	1. Models are presented to PO and/or clients.
	2. Feedback and/or additional features are provided by PO and/or clients to the team (see Picture 3 – Table 2).
	    a. Elements partially completed are not presented.
	    b. PO/clients validate items that are 100% functional.
	    c. Non-functional returns to the backlog.

5.4. Sprint retrospective (5 min)	1. Scrum Master animates this ceremony: team discussion about what worked and what can be improved for the next Sprint in terms of teamwork and time management. 2. Discussion should not focus on models, but on the team dynamic.
5.5. Questions period (5-10 min)	1. Participants ask for clarification from the instructors on Scrum: project phases, team dynamics, relations with clients, PO, roles and responsibilities, team processes, and dynamics, etc.
6. Sprint cycle #2 (20 min)	1. A second sequence is played: Sprint planning ® Sprint ® Sprint review ® Sprint retrospective.
7. Sprint cycle #3 (20 min)	1. A third sequence is played.

8. Group debriefing (40 min)	1. Instructor animates debriefing by:
	    a. Having a stand-up feedback activity where all participants share their first impression by saying two words describing: first, how they experienced the simulation and second, what they go home with (see Picture 4 – Table 2).
	    b. Asking questions such as: "What do you remember?" "What has marked you?" "To what extent do you think this simulation will help you in your future career?"

be able to experiment with, and reflect on, the Scrum framework they had read about in their preparatory readings. Unlike a "serious game," there is no winning team and no participation points are awarded during the simulation since the emphasis is on learning rather than competing.

The LEGO®-Scrum SBT was deployed five times with five different groups. In each group, participants were split into six teams, and a PO was designated for each team. For each SBT session, two of the authors were present in the classroom. One of the authors played the instructor role, i.e., prepared and presented LEGO®-Scrum SBT, gave the instructions, answered participants' questions, animated the debriefing and discussion, etc. The other author played the observer role during the LEGO®-Scrum

Table 2. Pictures of LEGO®-Scrum simulation based-training

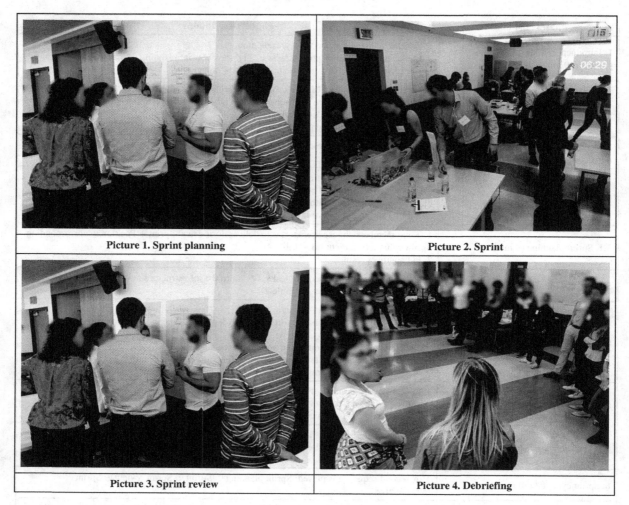

Picture 1. Sprint planning	**Picture 2. Sprint**
Picture 3. Sprint review	**Picture 4. Debriefing**

SBT, i.e., walked throughout the classroom during the simulation without intervening or commenting; took notes of observations using the educational validity framework (Stainton, Johnson, & Borodzicz, 2010), conducted post-activity interviews with participants, etc. Finally, for one of the simulations, two experienced Scrum Masters and two professional IT project managers participated as product owners. Their role was to provide feedback to participants, but also to comment on and formulate areas of improvement for the LEGO®-Scrum SBT. The objective here was to obtain their feedback and interview them after the SBT. The simulation was pre-tested with the research team, the two experienced Scrum Masters, and eight participants. Adjustments regarding time boxing, instructions, and physical organization of the room were made to the SBT scenario.

To assess the extent to which the LEGO®-Scrum SBT was relevant and impactful for participants as well as to evaluate the extent to which the SBT provides a realistic representation of "real-life" Scrum software development projects, three data collection methods were used: observations, questionnaires, and interviews. First, during the group debriefing, the words mentioned by participants to characterize their experience were noted by one of the authors. Second, a questionnaire was developed using existing measures, to evaluate the participants' experiential learning perception (Clem et al., 2014), the quality of their team experience (McCreery, 2003), as well as the teams' dynamic and their satisfaction level (Barki & Hartwick, 2001). It also included opened-end questions. Participants completed the questionnaire directly after the workshop. Finally, interviewswere conducted with 15 participants, the two Scrum Masters. and the two IT project manager professionals. The participant's interviews lasted approximately 25 minutes, and interviews with the professionals lasted approximately an hour each. An interview guide was employed, which focused on the following aspects: their positive and negative impressions of the LEGO®-Scrum SBT; their learning experience; the perceived advantages and disadvantages of using LEGO bricks to learn, and the benefits of such simulation for individuals and for groups. Furthermore Stainton's et al. (2010) educational validity framework was used to develop the interview guides. According to these authors, a simulation's educational validity depends on the quality of its design/implementation and should be evaluated in terms of three key dimensions, which are:

1. **Representation:** The extent to which the simulation: "provides a realistic representation of the real-world business environment (p. 717)", is sufficiently challenging and complex without being confusing, and is strategic and competitive enough so that participants are motivated by what they must accomplish.
2. **Content**: The extent to which the simulation is broad enough to stimulate motivation; integrates double-loop learning (Argyris, 2002); topics are relevant, multifaceted and meaningful for participants; allows participants to expand their knowledge and learning and; satisfies the participants' needs for achievement.
3. **Implementation**: The extent to which the simulation allows participants to apply their knowledge to enhance their cognitive processes; links the decisions made by participants to their performance; supports, "learning by doing"; is affectively rewarding and enjoyable; is experiential so participants could reflect on what they learned, and; is dynamic and problem solving oriented.

RESULTS

In this section, data collected during and after the LEGO®-Scrum SBT is presented. First, during the stand-up feedback activity, participants shared their first impressions by using two words to describe their experience; Table 3 presents the participants' responses.

Table 3. Words used by participants to describe their experience

Words Describing Participant Experience	Words Describing What Participants Learned (Brought Home)
Adaptation, Collaboration, Communication, Condensate, Curiosity, Destabilizing, Discovery, Emotional, Energizing, Exchange, Fast, Learning, Memory, Pleasure, Relevant, Shaking, Sharing, Stimulating, Stressful, Tension, and Useful.	Adjust, Clarify understanding, Delivers a viable solution, Diversity, Fail fast, Fast iteration, Flexibility, Focus on essentials, Focus on people, Listening, Momentum, Mutual aid, Prioritize, Problem identification, Quick feedback, Role sharing, and Team spirit.

In the questionnaire, Clem' et al. (2014) self-reported instrument was used to measure participants' perceptions of the "meaning or value of experienced-based instruction (p. 493)." This instrument has 28 items (see Table 4), grouped into four scales, where each scale can be scored by averaging the answers from the individual items and be interpreted separately. Scoring utilized a 7-point Likert scale, where 1 = Strongly Disagree and 7 = Strongly agree.

When looking at the combined scores for each of the four scales, i.e., *authenticity*, which refers to the way information is provided to participants, had a mean score of 5.78; *active learning*, which refers to participants' engagement level with the learning material, had a mean score of 5.97; *relevance*, which refers to the internalization and reflection of the experience lived by participants to connect new and old knowledge, had a mean score of 6.11; and; *utility*, which refers, to the connections participants make between the experience lived and future opportunities, had a mean score of 5.73. These results show that the participants agree that this learning process has significant value.

In addition, to assess the quality of the team experience, McCrery's (2003) scale was used. It was calculated as a composite score by averaging the score of the individual items. The composite score had a means of 5.65 on a 7-point scale. Finally, in terms of teamwork satisfaction (Barki & Hartwick, 2001), the composite score had a mean of 3.83 on an 11-point scale, where -5 = Very unsatisfied and 5 = Very satisfied. The complete list of the questionnaire's construct items and their descriptive statistics are presented in Table 4. Finally, the post-simulation questionnaire asked four open-ended questions; participant responses are presented in Table 5.

Interviews were also conducted with participants and practitioners to obtain their feedback, impressions, and improvement suggestions, as well as to evaluate the simulation's educational validity (Stainton et al., 2010). Tables 6 through 10 present quotes extracted from both participant and practitioner interviews.

DISCUSSION

The results presented in this chapter lend support to the educational validity (Stainton et al., 2010) of the LEGO®-Scrum SBT and show that LEGO® bricks can help participants learn, hands-on, about Scrum. First, as presented in the previous section, participants who have participated in this SBT reported their learning experience to be intense, emotional, engaging, pleasant, memorable, and shaking. The questionnaire's results also showed that the participants lived an authentic, engaging, relevant, and useful experience (Clem et al., 2014). Indeed, Clem's et al. (2014) Experiential Learning Survey measured the "students' perception of value of an experiential learning activity" (Clem et al., 2014, p. 503) using four dimensions: authenticity, active learning, relevance, and utility. As shown previously, the scores on the four dimensions were positive, ranging from 5.72 to 6.11 on a 7-point scale.

Regarding authenticity (5.78) and utility (5.73), the positive results mean that participants felt that the learning experience they had with the LEGO®-Scrum SBT helped them better understand how Scrum framework works as well, as the challenges underlying Scrum. They also believed it would also help them in the future, and they saw value in this learning experience. In terms of active learning (5.97), the results indicate that students were stimulated by what they were learning, that they were emotionally engaged, and that the LEGO®-Scrum SBT was sufficiently challenging enough to put them in a flow state (Csikszentmihalyi, 1990). Moreover, the students seemed to have found the LEGO®-Scrum SBT relevant (6.11), meaning that it made sense to them, they could identify with the learning experience and that they cared about what they had learned. In short, the positive results show the relevance and usefulness of such a simulation in order to gain hands-on experience with Scrum projects.

Table 4. Constructs items and descriptive statistics

Experiential Learning Perception (28 items) (Clem et al., 2014) Each item is measured using a 7-point Likert scale where 1 = Strongly	Av.	S.D.	Min.	Max.
Authenticity Subscale Items (5 items)	**5.78**			
1. The setting where I learn helps me understand the material better.	6.01	1.09	1	7
2. I expect real-world problems coming up during this learning experience.	5.76	1.65	1	7
3. The environment I learn in does not enhance the learning experience (**Reverse**).	5.25	1.66	1	7
4. The learning experience requires me to interact with people other than students and teachers.	5.75	1.25	1	7
5. I expect to return to an environment similar to the one where this learning experience occurs.	6.12	1.13	1	7
Active Learning Subscale Items (7 items)	**5.97**			
6. I am stimulated by what I am learning.	5.92	1.20	1	7
7. The learning experience requires me to do more than just listen.	5.87	1.20	1	7
8. The learning experience is presented to me in a challenging way.	6.25	0.98	1	7
9. I find this learning experience boring (**Reverse**).	5.84	1.53	1	7
10. I feel like I am an active part of the learning experience.	5.91	1.16	1	7
11. The learning experience requires me to really think about the information.	6.04	0.91	1	7
12. I am emotionally invested in this experience.	5.94	1.12	1	7
Relevance Subscale Items (9 items)	**6.11**			
13. I care about the information I am being taught.	6.15	1.20	1	7
14. The learning experience makes sense to me	6.16	1.32	1	7
15. This learning experience has nothing to do with me (**Reverse**).	6.01	1.40	1	7
16. This learning experience is enjoyable to me	6.13	1.14	1	7
17. I can identify with the learning experience.	5.59	1.78	1	7
18. This learning experience is applicable to me and my interests.	6.65	0.76	1	7
19. My educator encourages me to share my ideas and past experiences.	6.29	1.32	1	7
20. This learning experience falls in line with my interests.	6.16	1.11	1	7
21. I can think of tangible ways to put this learning experience into future practice.	5.86	1.71	1	7
Utility Subscale Items (7 items)	**5.73**			
22. This learning experience will help me do my job better.	5.70	1.69	1	7
23. This learning experience will not be useful to me in the future (**Reverse**).	5.25	1.51	1	7
24. I will continue to use what I am being taught after this learning experience has ended.	5.75	1.44	1	7
25. I can see value in this learning experience.	5.84	1.39	1	7
26. I believe this learning experience has prepared me for other experiences.	5.9	1.59	1	7
27. I doubt I will ever use this learning experience again (**Reverse**).	5.93	1.46	1	7
28. I can see myself using this learning experience in the future.	5.77	1.5	1	7
Quality of Their Team Experience (9 items) (McCreery, 2003) Each item is measured using a 7-point Likert scale where 1 = Strongly Disagree and 7 = Strongly agree	**Av.**	**S.D.**	**Min.**	**Max.**
Quality of the Team Experience (9 items)	**5.65**			
1. The workload was fairly balanced across all team members.	5.46	1.34	2	7
2. Team members cooperated well throughout the exercise.	6.15	1.04	1	7
3. Our team worked through the exercise in an efficient manner.	5.89	1.21	2	7
4. Team members all participated equally in the team decision-making process.	4.95	1.50	1	7
5. Our team maintained a pleasant working atmosphere.	6.15	1.12	2	7
6. Our team worked out disagreements in an equitable manner.	5.05	1.62	1	7
7. Team members were highly motivated to perform well in the exercise.	5.55	1.58	1	7
8. Overall, I am satisfied with my team experience.	6.05	1.12	1	7
9. I would be willing to work with my team on an actual project in the future.	5.64	1.55	1	7
Teamwork satisfaction (4 items) (Barki & Hartwick, 2001) Each item was measured using an 11-point scale, where –5 = Very Unsatisfied and 5 = Very Satisfied.	**Av.**	**S.D.**	**Min.**	**Max.**
Teamwork Satisfaction (4 items)	**3.83**			
Your level of satisfaction with...				
1. ... the composition of the team.	4.25	1.39	-2	5
2. ... to the functioning of the team.	3.76	1.54	-4	5
3. ... how the work was managed.	3.71	1.7	-2	5
4. ... the model that has been developed.	3.61	1.77	-3	5

Table 5. Quotes derived from the post-simulation questionnaire

Questions	Quotes
Q1 - In your opinion, what are the advantages of this LEGO®-Scrum simulation?	– *"Speed of the Sprints is stimulating + LEGO® bricks help to stay focused."* – *"Emotional learning = Emotional remembrance."* – *"Practical application of theoretical learning."* – *"Experiences, discovery of the agile environment."* – *"Practice and demystification of Scrum and the various roles."*
Q2 - In your opinion, what are the disadvantages of this LEGO®-Scrum simulation?	– *"It is very demanding and engaging."* – *"Better define the process and description of the roles at the outset."* – *"Not representative of the real-life. In real life, Sprints are longer and there are real stakes of power, interests, and social dynamics."* – *"Very fast, but final debriefing and feedback a little too slow."*
Q3 - What is your level of satisfaction with the simulation you have just experienced?	– *"100%, because I know this will be useful as part of my job."* – *"High active participation of all."* – *"Satisfied to see the evolution and improvement between each Sprint."* – *"Very good, allowed to experience different roles."* – *"High! Amazing experience. Learning a lot of new knowledge."*
Q4 - What did you learn from this workshop that you could practice in your professional or academic activities?	– *"Communication, autonomy, team management to satisfy the customer."* – *"Importance to clarify needs and roles. Team spirit."* – *"Adaptability, the importance of listening and collaboration."* – *"Prioritization, focus and customer respect."* – *"Communication, equality within the team, collaboration, mutual aid."* – *"Listening, flexibility, adaptability, and validating client needs."*

Participants also had the impression that they learned meaningful and useful elements on the Scrum framework, such as the roles and responsibilities, the team-client relationship, the continuous iterative mode, and the various Scrum events. In addition, they also learned about team dynamics in Scrum projects (McCreery, 2003), such as the importance of listening, collaborating, sharing, validating, adjusting, focusing, and adapting. Thus, with this SBT, the participants performed two key elements that are often missing in the traditional classroom setting: experiencing and acting (A. Y. Kolb & D. A. Kolb, 2005).

Secondly, based on the observations and the remarks made by the professionals who participated in the LEGO®-Scrum SBT, the SBT seems to be educationally valid in terms of its representation, content, and implementation (Stainton et al., 2010). Indeed, the interviewed Scrum Masters and the IT project

Table 6. Quotes related to the "representation" dimension of educational validity

– *As the simulation progressed, the clients became more and more at the center of the project, which is a key characteristic of agile.*
– *The proposed environment is quite like what is found in a "real" work environment.*
– *I am convinced that using LEGO® to learn and experience Scrum is the right way to do it since LEGO® bricks materialize the project. It becomes something real, something concrete.*
– *The simulation provides a good dose of realism and reflects real Scrum project constraints such as clients' involvement, iterations, and time-boxed activities.*
– *There was also a relatively high level of competition. I think all participants had the desire to do well and learn. You could feel the energy in the room.*
– *When you're at university, you do a master's degree, you have good grades, you learn concepts, and you think everything's fine. You have not been confronted yet with the real professional environments. The simulation takes participants out of their bubble and sensitizes them to what is happening "outside." It helps them become aware of the real-world challenges and helps them develop more adaptable/flexible skills and know-how.*
– *In practice, I have seen things very similar because the simulation creates an environment where participants should collaborate and, as in real life, some conflicts arise between participants.*
– *To learn agile approaches, you must feel it and you must live it, and this is what the simulation does.*

Table 7. Quotes related to the "content" dimension of educational validity

---
– *Participants learned, in addition to the Scrum knowledge and know-how, how to behave, how to interact, and what attitude to adopt in Scrum teams. This is key since an important part of Scrum project success is due to team members' attitudes.*
– *One advantage of LEGO® bricks is that they allow participants to create an array of structures quickly and simply without being experts. In this kind of simulation, it's ideal because you want participants to think and focus on how to organize a Scrum project, how Scrum operates, who does what in the team, how to run Scrum projects, etc., but to not take three hours to build a model.*
– *I think participants experiment Scrum's key elements such as continuous iteration mode, client involvement, and constant and quick adjustments based on clients' feedback during Sprint reviews, etc.*
– *Considering the time limits [3 hours], I consider the simulation a good exercise in which participants experience the main characteristics of Scrum. After the workshop, many participants came to me [i.e., one of the Scrum masters] because they wanted to learn more about agile approaches. For me, it shows the impact of this simulation.*
– *I think the participants learned the spirit of Scrum, what it is, what it means to work in an agile way, what are the values, and what are the challenges of collaborating.*
– *It is not just about results. I think that, through the simulation, they also reflected on: with whom, how to coordinate, how to exchange, how to discuss, how to receive comments, and how to handle conflicts.*
– *Participants accomplished the five Scrum values [i.e., focus, courage, openness, commitment, respect]. For instance, I think everyone has remained respectful, even though there have been difficulties. Also, no participant "dropped out" of the simulation.*

Table 8. Quotes related to the "implementation" dimension of educational validity

---
–
– *This simulation has a real potential to transmit knowledge, while enabling participants to experience a reflexive experience.*
– *Using LEGO® was, for this kind of simulation, an excellent idea because the participants had to realize physical models and were forced to think about concrete and practical aspects. It would have been possible to realize the simulation using Post-it or other material, but the result would have been too cerebral, too intellectual. Thus, since it is concrete, it becomes a "real" problem for participants.*
– *LEGO® bricks force you to think differently. They force you to work with your hands and your brain, to build real things, and to collaborate concretely with others rather than to work and communicate through a keyboard. It also stimulates parts of the brain that are generally unsolicited.*
– *LEGO® also add a playfulness aspect, which probably contributes to the simulation's success.*
– *They definitely learned how to work collaboratively and be more tolerant. Participants realized that you could do things very well in a collaborative spirit without, however, adopting a "command and control" approach, which is more associated with Waterfall project management. With Scrum, you use less "command and control" tools" and you start to do things.*
– *Participants were very passionate about building. This usually happens with objects like LEGO® bricks. It was impressive to see how they wanted to move forward and learn.*
---

managers highlighted the fact that the SBT, with its users' stories and its sprint cycles, recreated realistic "real-world" Scrum software development projects, and that these projects are challenging, complex, and stimulating enough without being too overwhelming and/or confusing. They also appreciated the fact that, throughout the simulation, participants received feedback and had the possibility to adjust (Argyris, 2002). Participants also had the opportunity to reflect on different elements of the Scrum framework,

Table 9. Quotes related to improvement suggestions

– *More time should have been devoted at the outset for contextualizing the simulation as well as for clarifying roles and responsibilities to ensure that participants clearly understood.*
– *I think that if participants are to play the clients in future simulations, it will be essential that they be well prepared and that they replace, modify, and/or bring new user stories in Sprints #2 and #3.*
– *For each Sprint review, I would add a minute and a half or two to enable the relationship with the client to develop and to have more feedback.*
– *The simulation's phases and constraints were well thought out to learn Scrum and its framework in three hours. On the other hand, with more time, it would have been necessary to add disruptive events to affect the team's dynamics and the products to be delivered.*
– *During debriefing, I would have put more emphasis on the roles of each and discuss in this groups, because to learn, you must confront the visions and experiences of others.*

Table 10. Quotes related to participant's appreciation

> – I appreciated the simulation because it mobilized participants. They were very happy with their experience. They lived a very emotional and intense moment.
> – So, I would encourage very, very strongly that the simulation be continued and repeated for both undergraduate and graduate participants. It creates a craze, it is certain.
> – This simulation is evidence-based because you see improvements at each Sprint. For me, it is a key indicator. Participants' engagement increased, communication improved, as well as collaboration and velocity.
> – To sum up, the simulation is an excellent exercise to facilitate Scrum learning. Working with LEGO® bricks stimulates participants' creative thinking and it's way more interesting than using Post-it notes.
> – Building something in such a short time and succeeding in getting through a process, even if it is not perfect, it's quite an accomplishment. Listen, it's undeniable that the results were there. Then, in terms of behavior, I saw a lot of people at the end of their iteration clapping hands, saying, "Well done, we did it, we succeeded."

as well as on the team dynamics. Thus, with this simulation, participants learned, in addition to the Scrum framework, how to behave in Scrum teams, how to interact, and what attitude to adopt in Scrum projects. In terms of implementation, the professionals mentioned that participants really learned by doing (Stainton et al., 2010); that the simulation was concrete and focused on solving problems and; as one Scrum Master stated, "the simulation had a real potential to transmit knowledge, while enabling participants to experience a reflexive experience."

Bell et al. (2008) argued that to develop effective experiential learning environments, the instructional features of an SBT should be evaluated along four dimensions: content, immersion, interactivity, and communication. In terms of content and communication, the LEGO®-Scrum SBT's instructional features are relatively rich (e.g. various user stories and role descriptions provided) and offer two-way, synchronous communication between all participants. This context enables the instructor to evaluate participants' progress in real time and provide real-time guidance. As for interactivity, the simulation's instructional features are rich, as participants can interact with one another and with the instructor. These frequent interactions throughout the exercise can be motivating and help students to learn by exchanging in feedback with other individuals. Finally, the LEGO®-Scrum SBT provides students with an environment simulating "real-world" Scrum projects that prompts the essential underlying psychological processes relevant to the Scrum framework.

The LEGO®-Scrum SBT presented here should help students learn and become aware of the opportunities and challenges associated with the Scrum framework. It is aligned with Whetten's (2007) call to develop more "learning-centred" course activities in which participants' learning objectives are focused on remembering, understanding, applying, and analysing. From a review of participants' comments and the questionnaire results, those four learning objectives appears to have been achieved here. Moreover, the manipulation of LEGO® bricks allowed students to immerse themselves in "real-world" Scrum projects; the bricks served as a metaphor to represent reality (Morgan, 2006). The participants mentioned that using LEGO® bricks helped them anchor the concepts of the Scrum framework, which, otherwise, might have been too theoretical and abstract for them.

The LEGO®-Scrum SBT illustrated that the intrinsic physical properties of LEGO® bricks—the affordances provided by these properties—combined with the key characteristics of SBT, can positively affect students' engagement levels and learning processes (Taylor & Statler, 2014). Indeed, when students are emotionally engaged in what they are doing, they learn more effectively (Taylor & Statler, 2014). The study's results appear to support Taylor and Statler's argument, since the students' level of engagement and learning experiences were high and positive. Thus, these results show that the pedagogical approach developed and tested here—combining an active learning technique, SBT, with LEGO® bricks—can support students in developing Scrum-related competencies.

Finally, the use LEGO® bricks in a SBT seemed to be of great support for the participants' active learning (Prince, 2004). As reported by the participants and the practitioners, LEGO® bricks "force" participants to think with their hands, which inevitably leads them to think and act differently. According to one Scrum Master, LEGO® bricks also "stimulate parts of the brain that are generally unsolicited." By manipulating LEGO® bricks, abstract/intellectual problems and concepts become concrete; they become real. Also, LEGO® bricks add a playfulness aspect, which increases participants' curiosity and involvement, as well as helps them to let go of certain habits and prejudices. Finally, with LEGO® bricks, participants can build structures and models quickly without being experts, which is ideal for an SBT, since participants do not have to think too much and lose time on building the models, and can instead focus on how to organize a Scrum project, how Scrum operates, who does what in the team, and how to run a Scrum project, etc.

LIMITATIONS AND FUTURE RESEARCH DIRECTIONS

This study has certain limitations that should be acknowledged. First, due to its simplicity and its limited scope, the LEGO®-Scrum SBT does not reflect all of the stakes affecting real, complex Scrum projects. However, it does reflect the uncertainty, interactions, interdependencies, collaborative nature, and framework of real-world Scrum projects (Vinaja, 2019; Schwaber & Sutherland, 2017). In addition, the sprints developed within the LEGO®-Scrum SBT are artificial in their time scale, which does not reflect the long-term temporal character of real Scrum projects. However, the SBT provides a useful context for participants to have contact with Scrum, learn how it works hands-on, and develop or improve their competencies.

Moreover, the questionnaire was distributed and completed by the students at the end of the simulation. Thus, there is a possibility that students over-reported desirable attributes and under-reported socially undesirable ones. Several techniques were used to minimize social desirability bias (Nederhof, 1985), such as phrasing questions to show that it is acceptable to answer in a way that is not socially desirable, asking indirect or neutral questions, and utilizing a self-administered questionnaire. Indeed, students were clearly informed that the questionnaires were anonymous, they had no obligation to answer the questions, and that the questionnaires would have no effect on their grades. In addition, the questionnaires were distributed and collected by one of the students who volunteered to do so. During this period, both the instructor and the observer left the classroom to allow the students to complete their questionnaires with a minimum of influence from their social environment.

Finally, for teachers or practitioners wishing to use the LEGO®-Scrum SBT, not just in project management courses, but also in more technical courses, it could be possible to use computer tools (e.g. Trello or Jira) and add further constraints (e.g. interdependencies between teams, access to limited resources, using Scrum in matrix organization) to cover the technical aspects of Scrum, such as for burndown charts, bug management, user stories/epic modifications, etc.

In a future study, it would be interesting to measure students' Scrum knowledge and competencies before and after the LEGO®-Scrum SBT to capture the improvements triggered by the simulation. Another possibility would be to compare different groups, some using the LEGO®-Scrum SBT and others learning Scrum via more traditional approaches, such as lectures and paper-based individual exercises. Finally, the quantitative data collected could be used to develop a research model and research hypotheses.

CONCLUSION

The LEGO®-Scrum SBT presented here should help both students and practitioners to learn and be sensitized to the opportunities and challenges associated with the Scrum framework. Participants in the SBT experienced three complete Sprint cycles wherein they learned and experimented with: Scrum phases, team dynamics, the team-client relationship, the roles/responsibilities and, the general Scrum mindset. Between each Sprint, improvement, in terms of participants' engagement, communication, collaboration, and velocity, were observed. Moreover, the use of LEGO® bricks allowed participants to immerse in "real-world" Scrum projects, as the bricks served as a metaphor to represent a "real-world" environment (Morgan, 2006). One challenge faced by several educators and instructors was to get participants to appropriate and internalize both theoretical and practical concepts. The participants in the LEGO®-Scrum SBT highlighted that using LEGO® bricks helped them anchor theoretical concepts and facilitated their understanding of the Scrum software development framework, which, otherwise, might have been too intellectual, too abstract, for them.

Thus, the chapter's objective is to contribute to the conversation on the challenges and opportunities related to teaching and learning Scrum in training rooms, as well as to show that the use of LEGO® bricks and SBT teaching/learning methods can support the development of innovative, evocative, and relevant learning experiences.

REFERENCES

Allisy-Roberts, P., Ambrosi, P., Bartlett, D. T., Coursey, B. M., DeWerd, L. A., Fantuzzi, E., & McDonald, J. C. (2017). The 11th Annual State of Agile Report. *Journal of the ICRU*, *6*(2), 7–8. doi:10.1093/jicru_ndl025

Argyris, C. (2002). Double-loop learning, teaching, and research. *Academy of Management Learning & Education*, *1*(2), 206–218. doi:10.5465/amle.2002.8509400

Barki, H., & Hartwick, J. (2001). Interpersonal conflict and its management in information system development. *Management Information Systems Quarterly*, *25*(2), 195–228. doi:10.2307/3250929

Beck, K., Beedle, M., Van Bennekum, A., Cockburn, A., Cunningham, W., Fowler, M., … Kern, J., R. (2001). *Manifesto for agile software development*. Academic Press.

Bell, B. S., Kanar, A. M., & Kozlowski, S. W. (2008). Current issues and future directions in simulation-based training in North America. *International Journal of Human Resource Management*, *19*(8), 1416–1434. doi:10.1080/09585190802200173

Boehm, B. (2002). Get ready for agile methods, with care. *Computer*, *35*(1), 64–69. doi:10.1109/2.976920

Brown, S., & Vaughan, C. (2010). *Play: How it shapes the brain, opens the imagination, and invigorates the soul*. Penguin.

Cantoni, L., Botturi, L., Faré, M., & Bolchini, D. (2009). Playful holistic support to HCI requirements using LEGO bricks. In *International Conference on Human Centered Design* (pp. 844-853): (pp. 844-853). Springer. 10.1007/978-3-642-02806-9_97

Castillo, F. (2016). Agile-Scrum Project Management. In *Managing Information Technology* (pp. 199–210). Springer.

City, S. L. (2009). *Scrum Lego City*. Retrieved from https://www.agile42.com/en/training/scrum-lego-city/

Clem, J. M., Mennicke, A. M., & Beasley, C. (2014). Development and validation of the experiential learning survey. *Journal of Social Work Education*, *50*(3), 490–506. doi:10.1080/10437797.2014.917900

Csikszentmihalyi, M. (1990). *Flow: The Psychology Of Optimal Experience*. Perennial Modern Classics.

Cubric, M. (2013). An agile method for teaching agile in business schools. *International Journal of Management Education*, *11*(3), 119–131. doi:10.1016/j.ijme.2013.10.001

Dekkers, J., & Donatti, S. (1981). The integration of research studies on the use of simulation as an instructional strategy. *The Journal of Educational Research*, *74*(6), 424–427. doi:10.1080/00220671.1 981.10885343

Devedzic, V., & Milenković, S. R. (2011). Teaching agile software development: A case study. *IEEE Transactions on Education*, *54*(2), 273–278. doi:10.1109/TE.2010.2052104

Faraj, S., & Azad, B. (2012). The materiality of technology: An affordance perspective. *Materiality and organizing: Social interaction in a technological world*, 237-258.

Fernandes, J. M., & Sousa, S. M. (2010, March). Playscrum-a card game to learn the scrum agile method. In *2010 Second International Conference on Games and Virtual Worlds for Serious Applications* (pp. 52-59). IEEE. 10.1109/VS-GAMES.2010.24

Freeman, L. A. (2003). Simulation and role playing with LEGO® blocks. *Journal of Information Systems Education*, *14*(2), 3.

Garud, R. (1997). On the distinction between know-how, know-what, and know-why. *Advances in Strategic Management*, *14*, 81–102.

Gauntlett, D. (2007). *Creative exploration—New approaches to identities and audiences*. Routledge. doi:10.4324/9780203961407

Gkritsi, A. (2011). *Scrum Game: an agile software management game* (Doctoral dissertation). University of Southampton.

Hayat, F., Rehman, A. U., Arif, K. S., Wahab, K., & Abbas, M. (2019). The Influence of Agile Methodology (Scrum) on Software Project Management. In *2019 20th IEEE/ACIS International Conference on Software Engineering, Artificial Intelligence, Networking and Parallel/Distributed Computing (SNPD)* (pp. 145-149). IEEE.

James, A. (2013). Lego Serious Play: a three-dimensional approach to learning development. *Journal of Learning Development in Higher Education*, (6).

James, A., & Nerantzi, C. (Eds.). (2019). *The Power of Play in Higher Education: Creativity in tertiary learning*. Springer. doi:10.1007/978-3-319-95780-7

Jeong, K.-Y., & Bozkurt, I. (2014). Evaluating a project management simulation training exercise. *Simulation & Gaming*, *45*(2), 183–203. doi:10.1177/1046878113518481

Ko, D.-G., & Kirsch, L. J. (2017). The hybrid IT project manager: One foot each in the IT and business domains. *International Journal of Project Management*, *35*(3), 307–319. doi:10.1016/j.ijproman.2017.01.013

Kolb, A. Y., & Kolb, D. A. (2005). Learning styles and learning spaces: Enhancing experiential learning in higher education. *Academy of Management Learning & Education*, *4*(2), 193–212. doi:10.5465/amle.2005.17268566

Kolb, A. Y., & Kolb, D. A. (2010). Learning to play, playing to learn: A case study of a ludic learning space. *Journal of Organizational Change Management*, *23*(1), 26–50. doi:10.1108/09534811011017199

Kolb, D. A. (2014). *Experiential Learning: Experience as the Source of Learning and Development*. FT Press.

Kristiansen, P., & Rasmussen, R. (2014). *Building a better business using the lego serious play method*. John Wiley & Sons.

Krivitsky, A. (2017). *lego4scrum 3.0 - A Complete Guide to lego4scrum - A great way to teach the Scrum framework and Agile thinking*. https://leanpub.com/

Léger, P.-M. (2006). *Using a Simulation Game Approach to Teach Enterprise Resource Planning Concepts*. HEC Montréal, Groupe de recherche en systèmes d'information. Retrieved from http://proxy2.hec.ca/login?url=http:// proquest.umi.com/pqdweb?did=1211107151&Fmt=7&clientId=10342&RQT=309&VName=PQD

Martin, A. (2000). A simulation engine for custom project management education. *International Journal of Project Management*, *18*(3), 201–213. doi:10.1016/S0263-7863(99)00014-9

May, J., York, J., & Lending, D. (2016). Play ball: Bringing scrum into the classroom. *Journal of Information Systems Education*, *27*(2), 1.

McAvoy, J., & Sammon, D. (2005). Agile methodology adoption decisions: An innovative approach to teaching and learning. *Journal of Information Systems Education*, *16*(4), 409.

McCreery, J. K. (2003). Assessing the value of a project management simulation training exercise. *International Journal of Project Management*, *21*(4), 233–242. doi:10.1016/S0263-7863(02)00026-1

Medeiros, D. B., Neto, P. D. A. D. S., Passos, E. B., & De Souza Araújo, W. (2015). Working and playing with Scrum. *International Journal of Software Engineering and Knowledge Engineering*, *25*(06), 993–1015. doi:10.1142/S021819401550014X

Meyer, B. (2018). Making sense of agile methods. *IEEE Software*, *35*(2), 91–94. doi:10.1109/MS.2018.1661325

Michael, J. (2006). Where's the evidence that active learning works? *Advances in Physiology Education*, *30*(4), 159–167. doi:10.1152/advan.00053.2006 PMID:17108243

Morgan, G. (2006). *Images of Organizations*. Sage Publications.

Nederhof, A. J. (1985). Methods of coping with social desirability bias: A review. *European Journal of Social Psychology*, *15*(3), 263–280. doi:10.1002/ejsp.2420150303

Paasivaara, M., Heikkilä, V., Lassenius, C., & Toivola, T. (2014). Teaching students scrum using LEGO blocks. *Companion Proceedings of the 36th International Conference on Software Engineering*. 10.1145/2591062.2591169

Papert, S. A. (1990). *Mindstorms: Children, computers, and powerful ideas*. Basic Books.

Peabody, M. A., & Noyes, S. (2017). Reflective boot camp: Adapting LEGO® SERIOUS PLAY® in higher education. *Reflective Practice*, *18*(2), 232–243. doi:10.1080/14623943.2016.1268117

Pike, C. (2002). Exploring the conceptual space of LEGO: Teaching and learning the psychology of creativity. *Psychology Learning & Teaching*, *2*(2), 87–94. doi:10.2304/plat.2002.2.2.87

Prince, M. (2004). Does active learning work? A review of the research. *Journal of Engineering Education*, *93*(3), 223–231. doi:10.1002/j.2168-9830.2004.tb00809.x

Resnick, M., & Silverman, B. (2005, June). Some reflections on designing construction kits for kids. In *Proceedings of the 2005 conference on Interaction design and children* (pp. 117-122). 10.1145/1109540.1109556

Rising, L., & Janoff, N. S. (2000). The Scrum software development process for small teams. *IEEE Software*, *17*(4), 26–32. doi:10.1109/52.854065

Rodriguez, G., Soria, Á., & Campo, M. (2015). Virtual Scrum: A teaching aid to introduce undergraduate software engineering students to scrum. *Computer Applications in Engineering Education*, *23*(1), 147–156. doi:10.1002/cae.21588

Rola, P., Kuchta, D., & Kopczyk, D. (2016). Conceptual model of working space for Agile (Scrum) project team. *Journal of Systems and Software*, *118*, 49–63. doi:10.1016/j.jss.2016.04.071

Roos, J., Victor, B., & Statler, M. (2004). Playing seriously with strategy. *Long Range Planning*, *37*(6), 549–568. doi:10.1016/j.lrp.2004.09.005

Salas, E., Rosen, M. A., Held, J. D., & Weissmuller, J. J. (2009). Performance measurement in simulation-based training: A review and best practices. *Simulation & Gaming*, *40*(3), 328–376. doi:10.1177/1046878108326734

Salas, E., Wildman, J. L., & Piccolo, R. F. (2009). Using simulation-based training to enhance management education. *Academy of Management Learning & Education*, *8*(4), 559–573.

Schwaber, K., & Sutherland, J. (2017). *The Scrum Guide: the definitive guide to scrum: The rules of the game*. Retrieved from www.scrum.org

Sharp, J. H., & Lang, G. (2019). Agile in teaching and learning: Conceptual framework and research agenda. *Journal of Information Systems Education*, *29*(2), 1.

Smith-Daniels, D. E., & Smith-Daniels, V. L. (2008). Trade-offs, biases, and uncertainty in project planning and execution: A problem-based simulation exercise. *Decision Sciences Journal of Innovative Education, 6*(2), 313–341. doi:10.1111/j.1540-4609.2008.00177.x

Stainton, A. J., Johnson, J. E., & Borodzicz, E. P. (2010). Educational validity of business gaming simulation: A research methodology framework. *Simulation & Gaming, 41*(5), 705–723. doi:10.1177/1046878109353467

Statler, M., Heracleous, L., & Jacobs, C. D. (2011). Serious play as a practice of paradox. *The Journal of Applied Behavioral Science, 47*(2), 236–256. doi:10.1177/0021886311398453

Steghöfer, J.-P., Burden, H., Alahyari, H., & Haneberg, D. (2017). No silver brick: Opportunities and limitations of teaching scrum with lego workshops. *Journal of Systems and Software, 131*, 230–247. doi:10.1016/j.jss.2017.06.019

Taylor, S. S., & Statler, M. (2014). Material matters: Increasing emotional engagement in learning. *Journal of Management Education, 38*(4), 586–607. doi:10.1177/1052562913489976

Tiwari, S. R., Nafees, L., & Krishnan, O. (2014). Simulation as a pedagogical tool: Measurement of impact on perceived effective learning. *International Journal of Management Education, 12*(3), 260–270. doi:10.1016/j.ijme.2014.06.006

Vinaja, R. (2019). The Scrum Culture: Introducing Agile Methods in Organizations. Springer Nature.

Von Wangenheim, C. G., Savi, R., & Borgatto, A. F. (2013). SCRUMIA—An educational game for teaching SCRUM in computing courses. *Journal of Systems and Software, 86*(10), 2675–2687. doi:10.1016/j.jss.2013.05.030

Webster, J., & Martocchio, J. J. (1993). Turning work into play: Implications for microcomputer software training. *Journal of Management, 19*(1), 127–146. doi:10.1177/014920639301900109

Whetten, D. A. (2007). Principles of effective course design: What I wish I had known about learning-centered teaching 30 years ago. *Journal of Management Education, 31*(3), 339–357. doi:10.1177/1052562906298445

ENDNOTE

[1] Due to space limitation interview guides are not presented, but can be provided on demand.

Appendix 1 – User's story examples

Athletes' Residences	
As an: Athlete **I want**: A relaxation and massage therapy room **To**: Recover before and after the sports events **Priority**: 8	**As a**: Future Resident **I want**: A playground for children **To**: Have a safe place for kids to play **Priority**: 1
As the: Olympic Committee **I want**: The residences painted with the Olympic colors **To**: Strengthen Olympic brand image **Priority**: 5	**As an**: Environmentalist **I want**: A minimum of 5 trees on the site **To**: Avoid urban heat islands **Priority**: 5
Train and Subway Central Station	
As the: City Mayor **I want**: A central station to connect all sites optimally **To**: Reduce the number of streetcars **Priority**: 8	**As a**: Spectator **I want**: A roof protecting docks of the train station **To**: Enjoy outdoor even if it rains **Priority**: 5
As a: Resident **I want to**: Get to the city center quickly **To**: Have an integrated transportation service **Priority**: 5	**As the**: Head of Transportation **I want**: A garage near the main station **To**: Maintain and repair equipment **Priority**: 8
Tennis Complex	
As a: Player **I want to**: Play on a court respecting ATP'S standards **To**: Get used to the tennis court's surface fast **Priority**: 8	**As the**: City Mayor **I want**: Ticketing office adjacent to the complex **To**: Facilitate sale tickets **Priority**: 5
As a: Player **I want**: An interior cloakroom **To**: Shower and change after each match **Priority**: 5	**As a**: Player **I want**: A tram station in proximity **To**: Get back quickly to the residences **Priority**: 3
Olympic Stadium	
As a: Spectator **I want**: Covered bleachers **To**: Protect me from elements (i.e. rain, sun) **Priority**: 8	**As an**: Olympian **I want**: An 400-m athletic track with 8 corridors **To**: Perform at the central stadium **Priority**: 8
As the: Olympic Committee **I want**: to emphasize Olympic rings in the design of the Stadium **To**: "Shine" the event on television broadcasts **Priority**: 8	**As the**: City Mayor **I want**: 150,000-spectator capacity stadium **To**: sell many tickets **Priority**: 5
Gymnasium	
As a: Promoter **I want**: To respects the construction standards **To**: Be sound and regulatory **Priority**: 8	**As an**: Organizer **I want**: To have garage type doors **To**: Transport the material easily **Priority**: 8
As a: Promoter **I want**: Two separate gymnasiums **To**: Accommodate different events in the future **Priority**: 8	**As a**: Spectator **I want**: Platforms all around the stadium **To**: Have a better visual on the athletes **Priority**: 5
Olympic Pool	
As a: Spectator **I want**: Platforms in the basins areas **To**: Be closer to athletes and hear the water **Priority**: 8	**As the**: International Swimming Federation **I want**: A 50-m swimming pool with 9 corridors **To**: Respect the Olympic standards **Priority**: 8
As an: Olympic Athlete **I want**: A Jacuzzi near the basins **To**: Relax after my performance **Priority**: 5	**As the**: City Mayor **I want**: Large changing rooms for men and women **To**: Subsequently into a recreational complex **Priority**: 8

Chapter 12

Integrating Scrum With Other Design Approaches to Support Student Innovation Projects

David Parsons
https://orcid.org/0000-0002-9815-036X
The Mind Lab, New Zealand

Kathryn MacCallum
https://orcid.org/0000-0003-3844-7628
University of Canterbury, New Zealand

Hayley Sparks
https://orcid.org/0000-0002-6685-7280
The Mind Lab, New Zealand

ABSTRACT

Students who are innovating in a project-based context need appropriate frameworks to support applied research that is easily understandable, flexible to different contexts, and appropriate to their needs. Such support is particularly important when the research involves the development of a technology-related artifact, where students need empirical methods for the design and evaluation of that artifact, in addition to guidance in meeting the academic requirements of their courses. This chapter describes a Scrum-based approach for supporting innovations in learning contexts, extending previous proposals in the literature. The context of the research is two academic programs where students undertake innovative technology-based research projects. The new research model is designed to provide a better support- ing framework to assist them to effectively manage their projects by integrating the adaptive cycles and ceremonies of the Scrum agile method with complementary concepts and phases from Design Thinking, Design Science, and Design-Based Research.

DOI: 10.4018/978-1-7998-4885-1.ch012

Copyright © 2021, IGI Global. Copying or distributing in print or electronic forms without written permission of IGI Global is prohibited.

INTRODUCTION

For emerging researchers, an understanding of research methods, paradigms and approaches is still developing. Students working in technology innovation are often coming from either the initial stages of higher education or the professional world, where the focus has been on developing artifacts. When translated into an educational context, artifacts are created by students as an outcome of a course of instruction and therefore are similar to the concept of products, which are the outcome of a Scrum process. In an agile software development context, the key outcome is working software (Beck et al., 2001), but in an educational context the set of artifacts is broader, and may include a range of outputs used for assessment, such as designs, reports, strategies, plans etc. Students undertaking this type of study have often not been exposed to the concept and application of research and often have little understanding of how research and product development fit together. They therefore struggle with framing their research, and understanding where the development of the artifact fits within the research process.

The various strands of design research (in both information systems and education) have been developed to help link artifact development with an empirical process, with a focus on rigor in both the development of the artifact and its evaluation. We use the broad term "design research" here to include both design science (also known as design science research) and design-based research, as described later. However, for emerging researchers, the link is not always clear between the development methodology and the research contribution. Design research methods can work well in more substantial research projects (such as doctoral projects) which are significantly longer and can support multiple full-cycle iterative designs, but are not ideal for the scale and learning focus of smaller student projects that may only take one semester.

The focus of this chapter is to outline the development of a guiding framework for emerging researchers so that they can balance the relevance of product development with the rigor of research within the constraints of short, learning-focused projects. This framework is based on iterative Scrum cycles supported by a Design Thinking phase and some complementary techniques drawn from design research. The development of this framework has arisen from the need to provide students with a process that would guide them when undertaking a research project focused on artifact development. Two different contexts of student research have been used as the motivation and testing ground for the ideas that have been incorporated into the framework presented in this chapter.

Background Context

The background context of this study is two higher education programs in different institutions that focus on technology innovation. In both cases, students work on substantial projects that are based on new and disruptive technologies, so their learning is constructionist in nature. In one context, the students are postgraduates with a diverse background, many with industrial experience. In the other context, the students are undergraduates working with industry clients to develop systems. In both cases, the students are focused on the creation of new technology products and typically have little concept of research when they enroll on their programs.

Context 1 is a private graduate school which offers a Master's program in technological futures. This program is focused on an applied project. The students are required to develop an innovative product (artifact) situated in a real-world context using emerging technologies and appropriate research methods. The students within this Master's are typically mature students who have come from an industry background, with many wanting to undertake a program that will help them start a new venture or scale an existing one focused on new and emerging digital technologies. Since this program was developed for professionals, helping them situate research alongside the development of artifacts was needed. Many of these students had finished their undergraduate programs many years previously, or had entered postgraduate study through professional pathways, and had little research and academic background. Therefore, tying in industry concepts with a research method that was focused on strengthening their existing knowledge was necessary.

Context 2 is a regional polytechnic offering mostly vocational programs. The program considered here is an undergraduate degree in computing. Within that program is a pathway for students developing an artifact which is industry-focused, with a specific industry client. The challenge for these students is to ensure that while they are focusing on creating a specific product for an industry client, they are also meeting the academic requirements for their qualification, to ensure that they are both research-informed and producing material that is suitable for academic assessment.

This chapter outlines a framework which marries innovations with reflective knowledge development and dissemination, suitable for student research projects. The focus is to develop a process that can be easily followed, and which adopts robust and systematic methods for the development and evaluation of innovative products. This can better support student project work by recommending a specific research process suitable for innovative learning. By drawing together ideas from agile methods, Design Thinking, and design research the proposed process could be followed to guide students developing a practical project framed by research.

The following sections begin by introducing some observations around the common challenges faced by research students from less academic backgrounds, and what is needed from a supporting framework that can assist them in successfully managing their innovation projects. This is followed by a discussion about how design research, Scrum and Design Thinking might each contribute to a new framework, while acknowledging that none of these approaches was intended for students individually undertaking course-based research in limited timeframes and therefore cannot be adopted uncritically. The next section develops some theoretical ideas around how different aspects of the various approaches being discussed have been combined in previous research, and how their synergies may be interpreted in the context of this study. The chapter then describes the framework that has been developed from these various theoretical strands to help support students in implementing their projects, which is intended to be used as part of a student guide to research in innovation projects. The chapter concludes with some reflections on the current status of the framework and outlines future work.

ISSUES IN INNOVATIVE STUDENT RESEARCH PROJECTS

In observing students working through their projects the researchers have, despite project and student diversity, identified several common factors where better support is required.

Time management is unsurprisingly essential. Students need a framework to structure their research timelines and milestones and manage multiple workflows at the same time to ensure timely completion, while integrating planning as a continuous process (Peters et al., 2012). However, many students try to start at the solution and do not understand the importance of process, or of having an iterative approach and openness to exploring a range of different approaches / processes.

Students in the two contexts being investigated often work on projects independently but usually within real contexts and need to factor in engagement with stakeholders and/or experts when required. In addition to managing this time, students need support in how they engage with these stakeholders. In most cases, these stakeholders are product end-users, where engagement is required to ensure that the product meets their needs. However, in cases where projects are embedded in an industry with a specific client, students also need to balance clients' expectations and to ensure that projects are suitably scoped to meet the needs of the client as well as their own learning outcomes. In these cases, students are often supported by the supervisor of the program to ensure that managing scope and changes in requirements can be balanced to still ensure that a successful outcome can still be reached, even if the outcome is not the final version but just a proof concept or minimum viable product. Since a core concept of agile methods is that scope has to be traded off when new requirements arise, academics need to support students by allowing for flexible assessment criteria that are able embrace change in an agile manner. This requires an awareness of the different metrics needed for student projects and aspects of continuous assessment (Bai et al., 2018).

Students also need to understand that the main required output of a research process in an academic context may not necessarily be the product or technological artifact they are basing their research around but could be a theoretical contribution disseminated as a research article or whitepaper. They struggle with integrating research methodology into a product development context, often focusing on the development of the artifact and developing little understanding of the empirical rigor and robust data collection needed in research.

A flexible and adaptive process is important given the diversity of project foci and possible outputs, and because plans often change considerably. Students who are unable to adapt run out of time, particularly if they are working at the same time as studying. They need to be flexible about potentially having multiple different outcomes that may or may not all become final products or outputs depending on how other aspects of the process play out.

Students also need to be able to begin the substantive part of the process at different points depending on the project (idea, context, level of existing background knowledge). Some projects can be related to well-understood challenges and opportunities and therefore less background research is required, while others might be related to less well-understood challenges and opportunities and therefore more initial research is required. Similarly, they need to be able to restart the process or begin again at a particular point in the process in case of pivots in projects. Although an adaptive and iterative process is required, time constraints limit the number of iterations that can be accommodated.

The context of student research based on practical projects that create useful artefacts is typically addressed by the field of Design Science Research within the Information Systems discipline. The generalized stages within a design science research approach are the identification of a relevant problem, the development of an artifact that addresses the problem, evaluation of the artifact, articulation of its value, and an explanation of the implications (March & Storey, 2008). However, there are many different interpretations in the literature of how design science should be implemented, and many are highly academic and unsuited to industry focused courses. The researchers' experience with students working on applied projects has suggested that design science research has much to offer to academic study but does not help students to develop contemporary skills in an industry that is increasingly based on agile processes.

As an alternative approach, this chapter proposes that Scrum provides a suitably adaptive and flexible framework to address some of the problems outlined above by supporting iterative feedback loops with meaningful milestones without over-emphasizing the various philosophical intricacies of different design science approaches. However, there remain some issues that Scrum alone does not clearly address, such as assisting student engagement with stakeholders and the evaluation of multiple options. In these areas, Design Thinking has shown promise. Design thinking is generally defined as an analytic and creative process that engages a person in opportunities to experiment, create and prototype models, gather feedback, and redesign (Razzouk & Shute, 2012). We believe that it provides a strong complement to a Scrum-based research process, as outlined later in this chapter. In addition, we recognize that there are elements of design science research might be integrated with these more industry-focused approaches to ensure that academic rigor is retained in an educational context. In addition, the field of Design-Based Research, which is similar to design science but focused on education, is also considered for possible contributions to a revised model of what a more agile student project process might look like. The current state of progress of developing a Scrum-based design approach for student innovation projects that integrates concepts from Design Thinking, Design Science and Design-Based Research is described in this chapter.

DESIGN SCIENCE RESEARCH IN INFORMATION SYSTEMS AND EDUCATION

The intention of adopting the approaches embedded within design science (research) is that the creation of a technology artifact can be managed through a rigorous and repeatable research process that creates not only an artifact relevant to its context but also a contribution to the knowledge base. Design science was initially rooted in technology products, but educators saw the value of a design science of education to enable the introduction of new learning technologies. This work has grown into the field of design-based research, which focuses on the learning sciences. There is, however, no single model for how such research can be undertaken, with multiple approaches to both design science and design-based research, with many different emphases on iterative step sequences and adaptation to context, as outlined in the following sections.

Design Science Research Frameworks

Design science research in Information Systems focuses on the design and creation of technology artifacts in an iterative process. There are several design science frameworks, each with their own particular structures and emphases. One of the earliest was the Design Cycle by Takeda et al. (1997). They described an iterative logical process to assist in designing outcomes that cannot be fully known upfront and introduced abduction and deduction phases to acknowledge this challenge.

The Design Cycle forms the basis (along with other early models) of Vaishnavi and Kuechler's (2011) Design Science Research Cycle (developed from work first published online in 2004). The first two steps in their process ("awareness of problem" and "suggestion") establish a project as research, followed by deductive stages of development, evaluation, and conclusion. The cycle is explicit about there being multiple iteration points – at any stage, the cycle may return to further developing awareness of the problem. The circumscription process that takes place during the main body of the cycle (prior to reflection) emphasizes the way that specific acts of construction generate understanding that is contextualized to that research process, so theory cannot predict validity in advance.

Design Science in Information Systems Research (Hevner et al., 2004) was developed around the same time as the Design Science Research Cycle but provides a somewhat different set of key concerns. It emphasizes the necessary balance between relevance and rigor, and the importance of research projects adding not only to the knowledge base but also to be applied in the appropriate environment of people and organizations. There is an expectation that the creation of an artifact also creates improvements or extensions to theories or methods. Although the model includes a cycle of assessment and refinement, there is no concept of multiple entry or exit points in the process. In summary, this model is more concerned with the broader research contexts and outcomes than the mechanics of the design science research process.

The Design Science Research Methodology for Information Systems Research (Peffers et al., 2007) has a similar approach to Vaishnavi and Kuechler's model of iterating back to the original problem space from various points in the cycle. However, it also includes multiple entry points to the research, and the process iteration concludes with communication. The method goes through a series of iterations with explicit sequential steps: Identify the problem and motivate, define the objectives of the solution, design and development, demonstration, evaluation, and communication. Like Hevner et al. it emphasizes the contribution aspect of the design science research, with "disciplinary knowledge" being the final outcome.

Design-Based Research

Although design science was initially rooted in technology products, as early as 1992 Collins was proposing a design science of education (commonly referred to now as design-based research) to enable the introduction of new technologies. A key concept was that the innovation being evaluated could be much broader than a single artifact (Collins, 1992).

Kelly (2004) further elaborates on the outcomes or products from design-based research studies. These may be about models of practice, or learning, or the design and use of a new software tool or learning environments. The main message is that design always leads to an artifact, but that artifact could be a non-tactile outcome such as a new theory. Cobb et al. (2003) reinforce this idea that it is a theory-oriented enterprise, where the theories do real work in practical educational contexts. This idea also emphasizes the links to design science by stating that such design experiments are extended (iterative) and interventionist (innovative and design-based).

Van Den Akker et al. (2006) provide a further set of criteria for design-based research, that it should: 1) aim at designing an intervention in the real world; 2) incorporate a cyclic approach of design, evaluation, and revision; 3) focus on understanding and improving interventions; 4) measure the merit of a design by its practicality for users in real contexts, and 5) be based on, and contribute to, theory. Amiel and Reeves (2008) also highlight the need for a systematic approach to producing research that makes a difference, but also suggests the importance of collaborative methods of investigation.

Unlike design science research in information systems, the design-based research community has not developed extensive frameworks for the process. For example, Brown's (1992) model is a simple construct of inputs to engineering a working environment, and subsequent interactions with theory, outputs and dissemination. The most developed model for education design research is probably McKenney and Reeves' (2013) generic model, with an iterative cycle of analysis / exploration, design / construction, evaluation / reflection and intervention / understanding. The iterative model includes returning to any previous stage from intervention / understanding.

Despite the broad variations in all these examples, from design science and design-based research, there are some common themes that emerge. All of these models are iterative, though there are some variations in where and when these iterations might take flight. They all take into account that the research process goes through different phases and that outputs of the process may be theoretical as well as based on creating an artifact. The overall process is on focusing initial uncertainty through adaptive cycles of learning and a final phrase that focuses on the communication of outcomes. One model, at least, also emphasizes collaboration.

In the context described in this chapter, the aim is to assist student-researchers to manage very diverse innovation projects that may emphasize either product or theory by providing an explicit process that acknowledges the common threads of design science and design-based research while also ensuring that these projects meet the program schedule. A model is needed that is suitably lightweight for small scale, short term student projects, though one that could be expanded, if necessary, to be applied for a longer time scale. The published models discussed above are essentially too focused on process rigor, when many students need to produce output relevance. With this in mind, agile methods (Scrum in particular) have been explored as an alternative model for such projects as being industry relevant, adaptive, simply explained and easy to follow.

AGILE METHODS AND SCRUM

In the 1980s, innovative product companies were shifting from linear to integrated approaches that stimulated new kinds of learning and thinking in breadth (Takeuchi & Nonaka, 1986). By the late 1990s, software development methods were becoming increasingly integrated and iterative by leveraging new technologies and a greater understanding of the development process to embrace change. In 2001, the developers of these new ways of thinking got together to create the Manifesto for Agile Software Development (Beck et al., 2001), which outlined the key values and principles of this approach to building applications. Since then, agile methods have become the predominant global approach to the building of software.

The idea that methods developed from the processes and techniques of the software industry, particularly agile thinking, can be applied to teaching and learning in other domains has become increasingly popular (Parsons & MacCallum, 2019). Software developers were the first to articulate the properties of effective team design, but agile approaches are not particularly tied to software development and can easily be applied to other domains (Cockburn, 2008). Agile approaches, which are founded on continuous learning and improvement, supported by regular reflection and collaboration, seem to hold much promise for education.

The most popular agile method, and the one most focused on within a project management context (as opposed to software engineering), is Scrum (Schwaber & Sutherland, 2017). The concept of Scrum comes from research on innovative product development companies (Takeuchi & Nonaka, 1986) where traditional methods of development were characterized as being like a relay race, a siloed process where each step is separated from the next, while new approaches were more team-based with everyone moving forward together - hence the analogy with the team game of rugby, from which the term "Scrum" comes. In this sense, Scrum is ideal for collaborative student projects but can also be a suitable framework for individual projects, since all projects have to involve stakeholders.

The Scrum framework emphasizes transparency, inspection, and adaptation, which its authors claim makes it an empirical process, and can provide useful guidance for applied educational research projects. The Scrum process of creating a backlog of items that feeds into multiple timeboxed sprints, each producing a meaningful incremental product and followed by a review and retrospective, can be an effective way of keeping research projects on track. A Scrum-based approach has been applied to some programs in the context under discussion to support iterative progress and reflective practice for the development of learning artifacts (products). However, experience suggests that Scrum alone does not provide suitable scaffolding for the early phases of research, nor take account of the nature of academic outputs.

The main problem with using Scrum as a framework for student research is that the Scrum framework was designed with the needs of the software development community in mind. For software projects, the Scrum guide (Schwaber & Sutherland, 2017) assumes that there is a product owner who is able to bring requirements from the customer into the team. It does not provide details on how this original backlog building process takes place since it focuses on the development cycle, not on the gathering of requirements. At the other end of a project, the output from a Scrum software development process is simply a software product to be delivered to the customer. As we have seen from design research frameworks, one of the important considerations is how the output of a project is represented, given that this output may not be any kind of product but could perhaps just be theoretical. Therefore, Scrum is a valid approach to the central series of iterations of a project, where the work is actually done, but students need more structure to the development of an initial backlog for a Scrum-style process of sprints to begin. They also need more support in the process of generating a final output and disseminating it to the relevant stakeholders, which might be, for example, examiners or publishers as well as clients

DESIGN THINKING

Given the issue of how to create a suitable project backlog for a Scrum style process, any series of sprints needs to be preceded by a suitably investigative and creative way to develop a research-focused backlog. One approach that can be used for this purpose is Design Thinking, "an inventive process, through which problems are identified, solutions proposed and produced, and the results evaluated…Succinctly stated, it is purposeful, problem solving thought and action." (Norman, 2001).

As innovative product companies started shifting from linear to integrated approaches in the 1980s, which later led to the Agile movement, Design Thinking also arose. In one of the earliest books on the topic by Peter Rowe, published in 1987, Design Thinking originated within the industrial design and engineering sector (Kimbell, 2011). Design Thinking sprang from the need to develop a process that would help reconceptualize and comprehend problems that were otherwise complex or ill-defined. A significant part of the problem-solving process in Design Thinking involves the ability to synthesize knowledge from various sources as well as take the design of a solution from a user-centered orientation (Koh et al., 2015). Due to this user-centered nature, Design Thinking has been extremely popular within education contexts, as it provides a structure for students to creatively solve the complex problem through the application of ideation and prototyping (Melles et al., 2015). Design Thinking has also been adopted within a formal research context, with some researchers claiming that its adoption within Action Research can provide stronger outcomes (Romme, 2004).

Design Thinking has no single model, and each model tends to vary quite significantly in the terms that it uses, but the model used in the context discussed in this chapter is a customized version of the

Stanford d.school model of empathize, define, ideate, prototype and test (Stanford, 2019). This adapted model of design thinking adds "reflect" and "iterate" stages to the end of the d.school design thinking process to make it more compatible with an academic research context and to more clearly integrate it with the iterative nature of Scrum. Unlike most of the models looked at so far in this chapter, Design Thinking puts a strong emphasis on upfront discovery and ideation based on empathizing with the customer. This raises important questions about the definition of "customer" in an academic student project, which broadens to encompass a range of stakeholders beyond the normal design context, including supervisors, examiners, and publishers.

INTEGRATING PROCESS MODELS

Given that this discussion has drawn on multiple process models, it is important to acknowledge that some of these models have previously been integrated by others. This study is not the first to suggest that agile approaches can be combined with the concepts of design science / design research. For example, Keijzer-Broers and de Reuver (2016) describe developing a health and well-being platform using an approach that combines the distinct stages of a design science process with the concept of a series of agile sprints. This does capture what is perhaps the key difference between an agile process and design research, which is that design science research recognizes that there are explicit phases in the overall process, whereas agile methods do not make explicit distinctions between the types of activity taking place in the sprints, with the exception perhaps of "sprint zero" which initializes the process. The danger with this interpretation is that it removes the iterative revisiting elements from design research models that recognize the specific tasks within each stage, and also the broader flexibility of agile methods that do not dictate what happens in each sprint, and leans more towards a waterfall style process (Royce, 1970).

Conboy et al. (2015) have proposed the Agile Design Science Research Methodology. Based on Peffers et al. (2007). The main feature of this model is that it loses nothing of the existing design science research structures and process. However, this also means that the additional contribution is limited to some elaboration of each stage and an initial "problem backlog" stage. The additional "hardening sprint" is focused on rigor rather than any specific enhancements to the model, so does not provide any fundamental rethinking of design research from an agile perspective. These issues suggest that attempting to add agile methods to a design research process is ineffective because of the sequential structures of these processes, which have more in common with pre-agile iterative frameworks. A better approach may be to wrap an agile Scrum process within additional features from other design processes, which could preserve the adaptive nature of Scrum while bolstering it with a theoretical foundation and outcomes.

Design Thinking and agile methods have also been integrated by some authors, for example, Gurusamy, et al. (2016) map requirements, design and evaluation in agile sprints to different parts of the Design Thinking cycle, while IBM (2018) integrate the discovery aspect of Design Thinking with the delivery aspect of agile methods. This other work suggests that there is a useful role for Design Thinking in agile processes, specifically as a necessary precursor to building a project backlog.

DEVELOPING AN INTEGRATED SCRUM-BASED RESEARCH FRAMEWORK

This section provides a brief comparison of the main process models previously introduced, then presents how these can be integrated. This integrated process draws from multiple sources to address the particular requirements of the programs for which it is designed. This process is described as a Scrum-based research framework since it is primarily based on the artifacts and ceremonies of Scrum. However, it also draws on some ideas from design research and elements of Design Thinking. Table 1 summarizes the key process stages and notable features of the main frameworks that have been considered in this chapter. These include the main concepts from these different sources that have been carried forward into the proposed process model that is shown in Figure 1.

Table 1. Concepts from various models

Model	Key Process Stages	Notable Features
Design Science Research Cycle (Vaishnavi & Kuechler, 2011)	Awareness - suggestion - development – evaluation - reflection	Multiple iteration points, circumscription to context - begins with awareness
Design Science in Information Systems Research (Hevner et al., 2004)	Environment & knowledge base - construction - assess & refine - evaluation - contribution	Focus on contexts and contribution rather than process detail - emphasizes the environment and knowledge base
Design Science Research Methodology for Information Systems Research (Peffers et al., 2007)	Identify problem - define objectives - design & develop - demonstrate - evaluate - communicate	Multiple entry points and emphasis on communication
Design Science of Education (Collins, 1992).	Multiple innovations - objective evaluation - prioritize candidate technologies - multiple expertise - systematic variation - flexible design revision - multiple evaluations.	Introduction of new technologies. Innovation could be much broader than a single artifact
Design Experiments (Brown, 1992; Cobb et al., 2003)	Inputs - working environment - contribution to theory - dissemination	Focus on contribution and dissemination
Generic Model for Educational Design Research (McKenney & Reeves, 2013)	Analysis/exploration - design/construction - evaluation/reflection - intervention/understanding	Potential iterations back from final stage to any previous stage
Scrum (Schwaber & Sutherland, 2017).	Backlog - sprints - review - retrospective Multiple timeboxed sprints	Sprints, empiricism, ceremonies and artifacts
Design Thinking (Stanford, 2019)	Empathize - define - ideate - prototype - test - reflect - iterate	Ideation of multiple options upfront, prototypes and iteration

The Scrum-based research framework (Figure 1) is primarily informed by a need to provide a more explicit process framework to research students while maintaining the agile sprint cycles that have proved beneficial thus far. It is also deliberately simple and so does not present a large number of optional pathways.

The main concept is that the series of iterative sprints that comprise the main "Scrum Cycle" phase are pre-scaffolded by a "Pre-Scrum" phase and followed by a "Post Scrum" phase in a structure that draws ideas from the other process models included in Table 1. The following sections step through each of these three phases before summarizing how the whole framework is intended to support iterative development.

Figure 1. A Scrum-based research framework for innovation-based projects

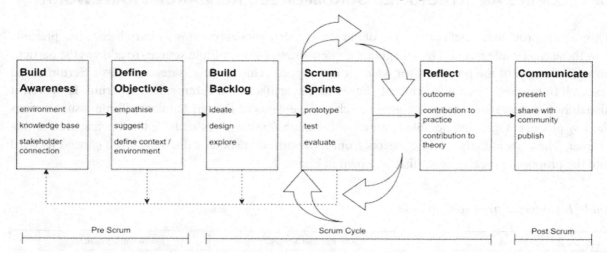

Pre-Scrum Phase

The first stage of the Pre-Scrum phase is "Build Awareness" (Figure 2) a concept taken from Vaishnavi and Kuechler's Design Science Research Cycle (2011).

Scrum projects tend to bypass the concept of building awareness because they are customer-driven. There is an assumption that the Product Owner brings awareness directly to the team. An initial research phase that focuses on the environment, the knowledge base and connecting with the stakeholders is therefore included. The environment and knowledge base concepts are taken from Design Science in Information Systems Research (Hevner et al., 2004). In an educational context, whether or not students are working for external clients, there is a need to ensure that suitable research is done into the literature as well as any technical information that might be needed. The stakeholder connection is essentially a replacement for the Scrum Product Owner, who normally channels information and requirements from customers and the host organization. In this phase, students need to identify and gain input from clients (if they are building a product), supervisors and other relevant bodies such as ethics committees and impacted communities.

This is followed by a second "Define Objectives" stage, where empathy is built with the stakeholders (a key part of Design Thinking) and suggestions are drawn from the awareness phase. The first part of a Scrum process, building the project backlog that can be used in the Sprints, requires activities driven by the Product Owner. In student research, the student (or student team) essentially becomes the Project Owner. In this role, they need to be able to define a set of objectives that suggest the core research ideas of the project, empathize with their stakeholders, and clarify the boundaries around their research context and environment. The suggestion process, taken from the Design Science Research Cycle (Vaishnavi & Kuechler, 2011) involves the abduction of research possibilities from the knowledge of the domain gained in the previous awareness building stage.

Figure 2. The "Pre Scrum" phase of the framework

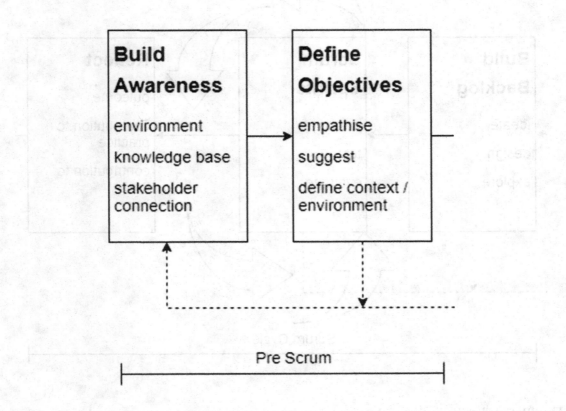

The Scrum Cycle

At the heart of the proposed research project framework is a "Scrum Cycle" (Figure 3) that embodies the key concepts of creating a project backlog, working through that backlog in a series of timeboxed sprint cycles, and ending with reflection phase (similar to the Scrum review / retrospective).

The first part of the Scrum Cycle, the "Build Backlog" stage, involves the ideation of multiple ideas, which draws concepts from both Design Thinking and Collins' (1992) Design Science of Education, whereby students need to consider multiple aspects of an innovation (multiple technologies, multiple expertise, systematic variation etc.) when scoping their backlog.

"Scrum Sprints" are focused on prototyping, testing and evaluation, in a series of timeboxes that should each contribute a specific increment towards the final project outcome, with the evaluation comprising the usual Scrum ceremonies of Sprint Review (assessing what has been achieved) and Sprint Retrospective (assessing where the Sprint process and practices could be improved). The length of a Sprint depends on the length of the student's program of research, but common Scrum timeboxes of two to four weeks would probably be appropriate for most students.

Figure 3. The "Scrum Cycle" phase of the framework

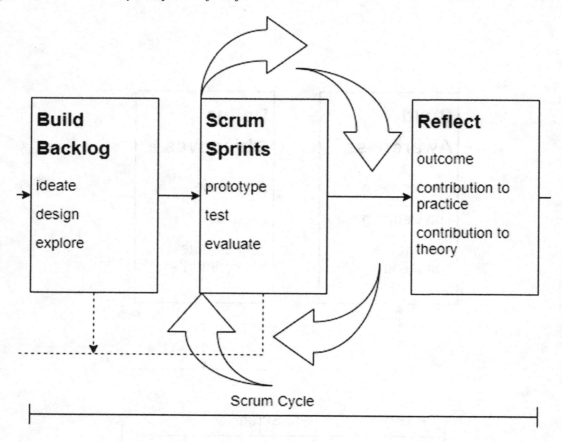

The "Reflect" stage is part of the usual Scrum project review and retrospective but has a focus on implications for theory and practice. From an academic perspective, a review is the achieved contribution of the project and the retrospective is identified as future work.

The Post-Scrum Phase

Following other academic models, the final "Post Scrum" phase deals with how the outcomes of the work are communicated (Figure 4). This phase acknowledges that a Scrum process in software development ends with the delivery of the product to the customer, but that in an academic context this is only one deliverable of the research process. The value of the communication stage is therefore not the artifact itself but the design principles of the product and the contribution to practice and theory that are embedded in the reflection stage at the end of the Scrum Cycle.

The nature of this communication will vary by there is an assumption that the work will be presented in some way for assessment, but that it should also be appropriately communicated to the community of stakeholders, and potentially also be published in a more widely accessible forum.

Framework Iterations

The main iterations within the framework presented here take place in the Scrum Sprints, but students may need to pivot back to any of the precursor stages if major adaptation is required. Although there is a single entry point to the model, the level of work in the first two stages may be minimal in well-defined projects (but it is recommended that they are still addressed).

In the other models explored in this chapter, the concept of iteration is common but the ways in which iteration takes place vary widely. Some models, such as Design Science in Information Systems Research (Hevner et al,, 2004) choose not to discuss how, when or why iteration will take place, but simply assume that some kind of "assess and refine" cycle will be involved. Other models specify explicit exit and entry points for iteration. The Design Science Research Methodology for Information Systems Research (Peffers et al., 2007) identifies iteration points from Evaluation or Communication back to Defining the Objectives or Design and Development. Still others seem to allow for iteration from any one step back through any other, such as the Generic Model for Educational Design Research (McKenney & Reeves, 2013). Such design decisions are dependent on the focus of the framework, the number and breadth of steps in the framework, the nature of the steps within which or between which iteration may take place, and the logic of iterating between specific steps, depending on their related activities. In the model presented here, there are two layers of possible iteration. One is the standard Scrum iteration of timeboxed Sprints, which takes place in the main Scrum Cycle phase. There is another set of possible integration points prior to this to enable students to redefine and re-populate the backlog in the light of changing requirements or discoveries made during implementation Sprints. In this sense, a Sprint may involve a timeboxed cycle back through the "Build Awareness", "Define Objectives" and "Build Back-log" stages. In addition, the "Build Backlog" stage may iterate back to further building of awareness and objectives definition, and there may also be an iteration back from defining objectives to building awareness. The reason for explicitly including these types of iterations in the model is to give students guidance about when they might need to revisit prior stages in order to ensure that their project remains on track, particularly given the nature of agile methods to be able to embrace change.

USAGE SCENARIOS

In order to illustrate how this model could be conceptualized within a real-world educational situation, two scenarios are outlined. These scenarios illustrate two different ways in which we believe the framework will better guide research students at the two institutions focused on in this article. As discussed at the beginning of this chapters the two contexts are a Master's program in technological futures and an undergraduate degree in computing.

Scenario 1: Master's Program in Technological Futures

The first scenario describes the way in which the adoption of this model may assist with the development of innovative technological solutions to address challenges associated with the future of work and changing, complex work environments. Many postgraduate Master's projects have begun with the aim of using emerging and disruptive technology (EDT) in this context, and a range of different outputs have been proposed. These outputs range from a digital technology solution for understanding workplace

Figure 4. The "Post Scrum" phase of the framework

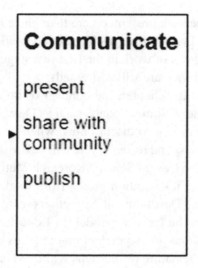

organizational charts, through to new frameworks for businesses to provide more flexible working arrangements and technological solutions to improving professional development. These students spend a significant amount of time developing a project proposal, however, guiding students through the use of robust and systematic research processes to validate the opportunity they are pursuing, and test assumptions that underlie the project can be challenging. For example, encouraging students to test the assumption that current organizational charts are not effective, and that EDT can be used in this space requires reading a lot of research from a range of different disciplines. This challenge is particularly apparent with students beginning the program with a set idea of the artifact they want to produce and are then afraid to test their assumption and find out that there is already a product in the market similar to what they were planning to develop. The need to build a bank of evidence and research (from both academic and grey literature) to help them validate the idea, and assess its feasibility, to essentially become experts on their idea can be difficult, especially if the problem is not well defined, and when research of this nature is not something they have experience doing. It is often commented by students who come from professional backgrounds that they are used to being told what the problem is that they need to address and are provided with research that confirms the problem or opportunity exists. These students work independently on their projects, but do not have all the knowledge, skills and capability to complete the project and therefore have to engage with a range of stakeholders which also proves a challenge for some students. Additionally, given the contemporary nature the future of work, and fast pace of change that is not always captured in academic research or published reports, there is often a need for students to speak with subject matter experts early in the development of their project proposals, as well as during the development of their solution. Students will benefit from a framework that helps them to manage these multiple tasks and workflows, as well as thinking critically about what they are reading, hearing, and writing. The fast-paced nature of technological development, and a wide range of EDTs that can often be used during the development of product prototypes also poses challenges. The iterative nature of the Scrum Cycle provides a framework for students to manage the development and testing of their product with the diverse range of stakeholders involved in projects.

Scenario 2: Undergraduate Degree in Computing

The second scenario focuses on the adoption of this model within an undergraduate course focusing on applying User Experience (UX) design concepts within the development of an artifact for a real company.

Formal research is not typically undertaken within an undergraduate program, however, many formal research concepts are used to ensure the output is appropriate and meets the users' requirement. Therefore, many research concepts are adopted within this course, including for user requirement elicitation, contextual inquiry and user testing. Since students are not typically exposed to formal research concepts within an undergraduate program our proposed model provides a more structured approach for scaffolding students. Scaffolding is also supported by undertaking most of the activities in a team. This team approach more fully aligns to the original concept of agile development as well as to Amiel and Reeves' (2008) analysis of design-based research and educational technology. Backlogs are, therefore, a vital part of the project, where they are used to manage teams and provide students' with accountability for tasks within the project.

This model also provides a more formalized approach for integrating many of the UX approaches. Since UX has no one model, it can often be confusing to navigate. However, the application of the integrated model provides a way for students to step through the different techniques and processes adopted within the UX discipline. For example, students build awareness and understanding of environmental needs, drawing from both user-centered and Design Thinking approaches, by adopting techniques such as contextual inquiry and competitor analysis. These approaches provide students with a clear understanding of their client/users' needs and situate their project within the wider environment. From this, students can design objectives for their product. The role of the framework is to keep students aware of the need to integrate their design tasks with both empathetic customer interactions and a focus on the contribution to learning above and beyond the digital artifact. The integration of the Scrum cycle provides a clear way for users to test assumptions and designs with users. The iteration of design provides both the opportunity for the evolution of the designs (from paper sketch to a high-fidelity prototype) but also the refinement and testing of designs drawing on both user and expert testing. Overall, the formalized nature of the proposed integrated model provides a structured approach to draw in concepts fundamental to UX, but also those of formal research and artifact development.

CONCLUSION

The work presented in this chapter is a Scrum-based research framework for innovation-based student projects that has been developed within two specific contexts, based on observations of the difficulties that students face in completing innovative technology-based projects. The framework has been developed from a synthesis of various related models from the literature, along with reflections on how a Scrum-based approach has operated thus far in the programs discussed. It has been designed to support students in their research who have been given a grounding in several process models including Scrum and design thinking. So far, development of the framework has been driven by staff observations of how effectively students have been able to adopt a Scrum-based approach to their projects, and student activities within Scrum workshops, as the team has experimented with different ideas about how to give students suitable structural guidance in the management and completion of their projects. The intent is to integrate this into a student research guide. No empirical data collection has yet taken place and future research is needed to explore how this approach can improve project outcomes for students. The next stage of this work will be to gather some formal research data to refine the framework as students use it for their innovation-based projects.

REFERENCES

Amiel, T., & Reeves, T. C. (2008). Design-based research and educational technology: Rethinking technology and the research agenda. *Journal of Educational Technology & Society*, *11*(4), 29–40.

Bai, X., Li, M., Pei, D., Li, S., & Ye, D. (2018, May). Continuous delivery of personalized assessment and feedback in agile software engineering projects. In *Proceedings of the 40th International Conference on Software Engineering: Software Engineering Education and Training* (pp. 58-67). 10.1145/3183377.3183387

Beck, K. (2001). *Manifesto for Agile Software Development*. https://agilemanifesto.org/

Brown, A. L. (1992). Design experiments: Theoretical and methodological challenges in creating complex interventions in classroom settings. *Journal of the Learning Sciences*, *2*(2), 141–178. doi:10.120715327809jls0202_2

Cobb, P., Confrey, J., diSess, A., Lehrer, R., & Schauble, L. (2003). Design Experiments in Educational Research. *Educational Researcher*, *32*(1), 9–13. doi:10.3102/0013189X032001009

Cockburn, A. (2008). *Crystal Methodologies*. http://alistair.cockburn.us/

Collins, A. (1992). Towards a design science of education. In E. Scanlon & T. O'Shea (Eds.), New Directions in Educational Technology. Springer Science & Business Media. doi:10.1007/978-3-642-77750-9_2

Conboy, K., Gleasure, R., & Cullina, E. (2015). Agile Design Science Research. In B. Donnellan, M. Helfert, J. Kenneally, D. VanderMeer, M. Rothenberger, & R. Winter (Eds.), *New Horizons in Design Science: Broadening the Research Agenda. LNCS. 9073* (pp. 168–180). Springer.

Gurusamy, K., Srinivasaraghavan, N., & Adikari, S. (2016). An Integrated Framework for Design Thinking and Agile Methods for Digital Transformation. In A. Marcus (Ed.), *Design, User Experience, and Usability: Design Thinking and Methods. LNCS 9746* (pp. 34–42). Springer., doi:10.1007/978-3-319-40409-7_4

Hevner, A. R., March, S. T., Park, J., & Ram, S. (2004). Design Science in Information Systems Research. *Management Information Systems Quarterly*, *28*(1), 75–105. doi:10.2307/25148625

IBM. (2018). *Agile, meet design thinking.* https://www.ibm.com/downloads/cas/7KL6JLMJ

Keijzer-Broers, W., & de Reuver, M. (2016). *Applying Agile Design Sprint Methods in Action Design Research: Prototyping a Health and Wellbeing Platform* (Vol. 9661). Springer.

Kelly, A. (2004). Design Research in Education: Yes, but is it Methodological? *Journal of the Learning Sciences*, *13*(1), 115–128. doi:10.120715327809jls1301_6

Kimbell, L. (2011). Rethinking design thinking: Part I. *Design and Culture*, *3*(3), 285–306. doi:10.2752/175470811X13071166525216

Koh, J. H. L., Chai, C. S., Wong, B., & Hong, H. Y. (2015). *Design Thinking for Education: Conceptions and applications in teaching and learning.* Springer.

March, S. T., & Storey, V. C. (2008). Design science in the information systems discipline: An introduction to the special issue on design science research. *Management Information Systems Quarterly*, *32*(4), 725–730. doi:10.2307/25148869

McKenney, S., & Reeves, T. C. (2014). Educational design research. In *Handbook of research on educational communications and technology* (pp. 131–140). Springer. doi:10.1007/978-1-4614-3185-5_11

Melles, G., Anderson, N., Barrett, T., & Thompson-Whiteside, S. (2015). Problem Finding through Design Thinking in Education. In P. Blessinger & J.M. Carfora (Eds.), Inquiry-Based Learning for Multidisciplinary Programs: A Conceptual and Practical Resource for Educators (Innovations in Higher Education Teaching and Learning, Volume 3) (pp.191-209). Bingley, UK: Emerald. doi:10.1108/S2055-364120150000003027

Norman, J. (2001). Design as a Framework for Innovative Thinking and Learning: How Can Design Thinking Reform Education? In E. Norman & P. Roberts (Eds.), Design and technology educational research and curriculum development: The emerging international research agenda (pp. 90-100). Loughborough University.

Peffers, K., Tuunanen, T., Rothenberger, M. A., & Chatterjee, S. (2007). A Design Science Research Methodology for Information Systems Research. *Journal of Management Information Systems*, *24*(3), 45–77. doi:10.2753/MIS0742-1222240302

Peters, M. J., Howard, K., & Sharp, M. J. A. (2012). *The management of a student research project.* Gower Publishing, Ltd.

Razzouk, R., & Shute, V. (2012). What Is Design Thinking and Why Is It Important? *Review of Educational Research*, *82*(3), 330–348. doi:10.3102/0034654312457429

Romme, A. G. L. (2004). Action research, emancipation and design thinking. *Journal of Community & Applied Social Psychology, 14*(6), 495–499. doi:10.1002/casp.794

Royce, W. (1970, August). *Managing the Development of Large Software Systems*. Paper presented at Technical Papers of Western Electronic Show and Convention (WesCon), Los Angeles, CA.

Schwaber, K., & Sutherland, J. (2017). *The Scrum Guide*. https://Scrumguides.org/docs/Scrumguide/v2017/2017-Scrum-Guide-US.pdf

Stanford. (2019). *Stanford d.school*. https://dschool.stanford.edu/

Takeda, H., Veerkamp, P., Tomiyama, T., & Yoshikawa, H. (1997). Modeling Design Processes. *AI Magazine, 11*(4), 37–48.

Takeuchi, H., & Nonaka, I. (1986, Jan.). The New New Product Development Game. *Harvard Business Review*, 137–146.

Vaishnavi, V., & Kuechler, W. (2011). Promoting Relevance in IS Research: An Informing System for Design Science Research. *Informing Science: The International Journal of an Emerging Transdiscipline, 14*, 125–138. doi:10.28945/1498

Van Den Akker, J., Gravemeijer, K., McKenney, S., & Nieveen, N. (Eds.). (2006). *Educational Design Research*. Routledge. doi:10.4324/9780203088364

Chapter 13
An Agile Method to Support Students With Special Educational Needs in Regular Education After COVID-19 Contingency

Alfredo Mendoza González
 https://orcid.org/0000-0001-6608-046X
Universidad Autonoma de Zacatecas, Mexico

Jaime Muñoz-Arteaga
 https://orcid.org/0000-0002-3635-7592
Autonomous University of Aguascalientes, Mexico

ABSTRACT

In Mexico there are units of consultants that help schools to make students with special needs be included in regular education they provide the necessary help to enhance the learning process. Their work implies adapting the learning methodology, complementing the planned academic activities, adapting learning goals to the students' needs, providing specific technological tools, analyze the knowledge acquisition, etc. Additionally, there are many factors that can affect these goals and complicate the whole intervention process. The COVID-19 pandemic is making attitudinal changes of students, together with the long academic brake, and the forced on-line learning. Together, consultants, teachers, parents, and scientists have analyzed gaps in the intervention process of the supporting units, related with collaboration, teamwork, adaptations in activities and knowledge acquisition, and proposed a solution to it. In this chapter, the authors present Scrum process as a feasible solution, making easy and stronger the collaboration, role definition, and goals prioritization.

DOI: 10.4018/978-1-7998-4885-1.ch013

Copyright © 2021, IGI Global. Copying or distributing in print or electronic forms without written permission of IGI Global is prohibited.

INTRODUCTION

In Mexico, the Support Units for Regular Education (USAER, by its name in Spanish Unidades de Servicio y Apoyo a la Educación Regular) are the entities to which the regular schools turn students with special educational needs to ensure their inclusion. The USAER team includes specialists in psychology, pedagogy, social work, and communication. The Secretary of Education in Mexico has developed a route of intervention that involves four stages: Diagnose, Intervention, Implementation and Assessment, this is called the Educational Rehabilitation Process Model (ERPM).

Despite its great definition of activities and its applicability, the ERPM does not include the implementation of Information and Communication Technologies (ICT) as a coordinated process. The inclusion of a team ICT experts, such as educational technology experts, software engineers, systems engineers, interface designers and developers, as part of the USAER team can enhance the ERPM incorporate Digital Content (in the form of learning objects, educational software, mobile applications, or a combination of them) to complement the support strategy and the whole intervention of the USAER team, with the possibility of include the school community, and the student family.

Nevertheless, the coordination and collaboration between this ICT specialists and the USAER team might be guided by a methodology that helps achieve objectives quickly according with the evolution of the students; might include the most important current learning objectives; should promote communication between different areas of expertise; and might be managed as an iterative process.

The agile methodology of SCRUM has all desired characteristics to be implemented into the ERPM. This is the main topic of the chapter: To know how the roles, tools, artefacts, teams, and work management are implemented producing a solution to enhance education of students with SEN.

One important thing to consider is the long academic break due to the COVID-19 pandemic and the loos of consciousness produced by consequence. The loss of consciousness of students after a prolonged school break is not a new research topic. Various authors have addressed this problem (Cooper, 2020), (Von Hippel, 2019), (McEachin & Atteberry, 2017), (Quinn & Polikoff, 2017); However, nowadays we are in a situation with peculiar characteristics. The period of the health contingency by COVID-19, required the suspension of classroom activities from the end of March, taking approximately three months of work at home, to close the school year. The Mexican Ministry of Education has included a reinforcement plan beginning with the Summer Fun programs and the Remedial Course for the resumption of activities. The Summer Fun, comprises a set of recreational, recreational and recreational activities for Basic Education students during the summer school break, while the remedial course involves the staggered return of students to the classrooms and will serve to answer questions and lags (SEP, 2020b). Now the question is: How should USEAR teams must adequate all this content?

New technologies such as mobile technology, augmented reality, and cloud computing provide tools with great potential to assist in the teaching-learning process for students with special educational needs associated with a disability, but that's only one point in favor. It is necessary to create adjustment schemes according to the students' needs, create agile implementation models within the current teaching-learning process, as well as evaluation methods to verify the success of the application of tools and the effective learning of students. Our proposal: implement SCRUM, understanding that educational technology tools are not everything.

Currently, USAER support services are based on the process presented in Figure 1 (SEP, 2011). As it can be seen, throughout the four moments, the activities are accompanied by monitoring instruments

Figure 1. USAER's support process. Inspired from (SEP, 2011)

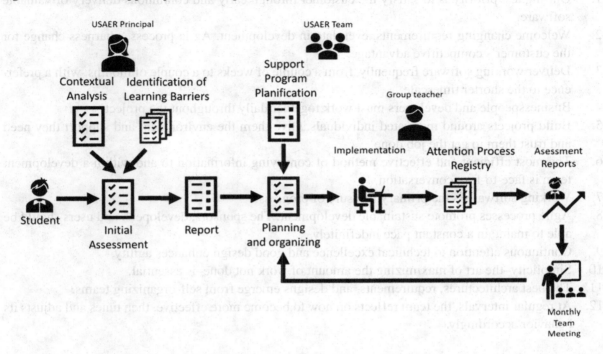

(school and classroom folders) which are used to monitor the progress of the students, and the effectiveness of the support program.

BACKGROUND

Agile software development refers to a group of software development methodologies based on iterative development, where requirements and solutions evolve through collaboration between self-organizing cross-functional teams (Musser, 2019). Agile methods or Agile processes generally promote a disciplined project management process that encourages frequent inspection and adaptation, a leadership philosophy that encourages teamwork, self-organization and accountability, a set of engineering best practices intended to allow for rapid delivery of high-quality software, and a business approach that aligns development with customer needs and company goals (May, et al 2016; Soto et al, 2018).

The values of the Agile Manifesto are (Musser, 2019):

- Individuals and interactions over processes and tools.
- Working software over comprehensive documentation.
- Customer collaboration over contract negotiation.
- Responding to change over following a plan.

Here, there are twelve principles in the Agile Philosophy (May, et al 2016):

1. Our highest priority is to satisfy the customer through early and continuous delivery of valuable software.
2. Welcome changing requirements, even late in development. Agile processes harness change for the customer's competitive advantage.
3. Deliver working software frequently, from a couple of weeks to a couple of months, with a preference to the shorter timescale.
4. Businesspeople and developers must work together daily throughout the project.
5. Build projects around motivated individuals. Give them the environment and support they need and trust them to get the job done.
6. The most efficient and effective method of conveying information to and within a development team is face-to-face conversation.
7. Working software is the primary measure of progress.
8. Agile processes promote sustainable development. The sponsors, developers, and users should be able to maintain a constant pace indefinitely.
9. Continuous attention to technical excellence and good design enhances agility.
10. Simplicity–the art of maximizing the amount of work not done–is essential.
11. The best architectures, requirements, and designs emerge from self-organizing teams.
12. At regular intervals, the team reflects on how to become more effective, then tunes and adjusts its behavior accordingly.

Scrum is one of many methodologies and frameworks that fall under the agile philosophy and is defined as a framework within which people can address complex, adaptive problems while productively and creatively delivering products of the highest possible value (Schwaber & Sutherland, 2017; Soto et al, 2018).

Scrum contains roles, activities, and artifacts (Figure 2). The three roles are the Product Owner, Scrum Master, and the Scrum Team. The activities include Sprint Planning, Sprint Execution, Daily Scrum, Sprint Review, and a Sprint Retrospective. Finally, the artifacts include a Product Backlog, Sprint Backlog, and a work increment (also known as Potentially Shippable Product Increment). For detailed description of the Scrum process, and useful documentation, reader can refer to www.scrum.org.

Next there are some useful definitions (May, et al 2016; Schwaber & Sutherland, 2017):

- **Release:** A product goal to be achieved collaboratively.
- **Sprint:** A segment of time, usually between 2-4 weeks, during which teams work to achieve specified goals toward the eventual Release.
- **Teams:** Cross-functional groups that work iteratively toward Sprint and Release goals.
- **Daily Scrum:** A short daily meeting during which each team member reports to the ScrumMaster and Team on the three Scrum questions: what have I accomplished since the last Daily Scrum, what do I plan to accomplish before the next Scrum, and what challenges might I face before the next Scrum?

Schools all over the world has begun to apply new strategies to work with students (Onieva,2018). One of the most popular on these days is the project-based learning. As indicated by its name, Project Based Learning (PBL) involves students skills enhancing and knowledge acquiring through the generation of projects; making students certainly put their ideas into action, solving real problems inside and outside

Figure 2. Scrum process

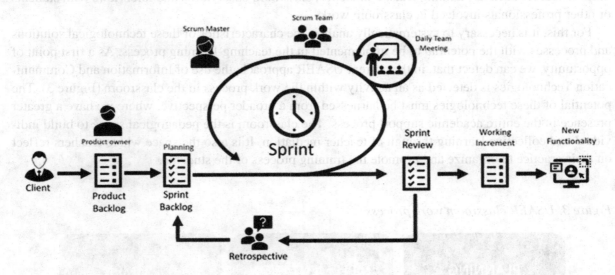

the classroom (Gannod,2015). PBL is defined as an extended task which enhances skills through a set of activities which include activity planning, information gathering, reading, listening, interviewing, etc.

Nowadays Scrum framework application in the classroom is used more frequently to enhance PBL and to stimulate rich collaborative environments (Gannod, 2015). For example, Pope-Ruark et al., (2016) applied Scrum for various English class projects and stated that Scrum could be used in any college course requiring collaboration, group projects, or problem solving. Baird and Riggins (2012) used the Scrum framework for their capstone course project. Authors found Scrum useful for maintaining student motivation due to more client interaction that forces accountability. Also, some universities around the world are modeling entire courses with the eduScrum approach, a framework that provides the foundation for teamwork throughout an entire course (Delhij et al, 2015).

Mainly, what makes Scrum promising for academic settings is that it relies on an empowered, self-organizing team to discover, implement, and evolve the best process that works for them to accomplish a shared goal (Gannod,2015). In essence, a successful Scrum team acts as a complex, adaptive system changing from state to state (Blum and Li, 2008). Successful practice of the Scrum framework often times lead to holistic solutions but can only result from rich collaborative efforts that accept change as the norm rather than a hindrance. Thus, the highly valued skills of adaptation, problem-solving, and collaboration can all be enriched if students successfully implement Scrum (Highsmith, 2013) (Onieva,2018).

SUPPORTING USAER'S PROCESS WITH SCRUM

New technologies focused on education allow highly motivating content and activities to be created for students, adaptable for enrichment with the teacher's experience and flexible to be carried out in the classroom or at home. Therefore, it is the space to identify practices, policies and cultures that favor the participation of all students, that is, inclusive. The information that USAER retrieves is obtained from various sources such as planning teacher didactics, classroom observation and interviews with students or other professionals involved in classroom work.

For this, it is necessary to systematically analyze the characteristics of these technological solutions and processes with the potential to be implemented in the teaching-learning process. As a first point of opportunity, we can detect that, in the current USAER approach, the use of Information and Communication Technologies is detected as an activity within the work process in the classroom (Figure 3). The potential of these technologies must be harnessed from a broader perspective, where we have a greater presence in the entire academic support process. The classroom is the pedagogical space to build individual and collective learning through of teacher mediation. It is also the space where teachers reflect on their practice to organize and promote the training process of the students.

Figure 3. USAER classroom work process

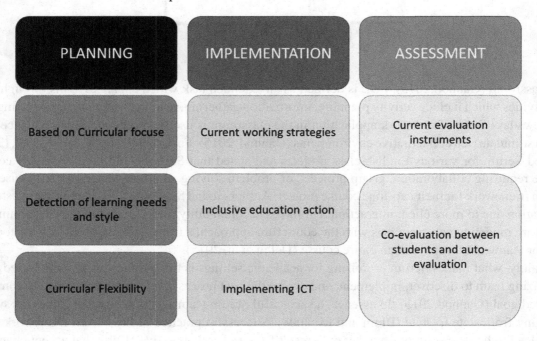

This will be carried out through an evaluation process that includes the objective analysis of the level of compliance with certain characteristics, the subjective appreciation and the opinion of techno-educational experts, allowing a comprehensive profile of these strategies, processes and tools. In the collaborative aspect, there are also points of opportunity in the process. Scientific, pedagogical and social collaboration networks allow sharing the lessons learned, the processes successfully implemented, and the measures taken to overcome the different challenges presented, which are created, implemented or refuted and enriched by all those involved in the process. Both the teaching-learning process and the digital educational tools that are implemented in it must allow this collaboration between actors, so that the monitoring of the students, as well as the adaptation according to their progress, is optima.

Regarding the attention to internal and external factors, the process of Figure 2 does not contemplate the way in which it can adapt or become more flexible. Obviously, factors such as the new normality, the new Mexican school, the remedial course, and other factors (such as the loss of consciousness due to school breaks, the change in the context of activities, as well as others resulting from the pandemic) were not considered. Therefore, it is necessary to implement measures to face them. Possibly the most interesting challenge is that you only have three weeks to adapt the contents according to the level of the students, in a staggered presence of the students.

This will be carried out through an evaluation process that includes the objective analysis of the level of compliance with certain characteristics, the subjective appreciation and the opinion of techno-educational experts, allowing a comprehensive profile of these strategies, processes and tools.

In the collaborative aspect, there are also points of opportunity in the process. Scientific, pedagogical and social collaboration networks allow sharing the lessons learned, the processes successfully implemented, and the measures taken to overcome the different challenges presented, which are created, implemented or refuted and enriched by all those involved in the process. Both the teaching-learning process and the digital educational tools that are implemented in it must allow this collaboration between actors, so that the monitoring of the students, as well as the adaptation according to their progress, is optimal.

Regarding the attention to internal and external factors, the process of Figure 2 does not contemplate the way in which it can adapt or become more flexible. Obviously, factors such as the new normality, the new Mexican school, the remedial course, and other factors (such as the loss of consciousness due to school breaks, the change in the context of activities, as well as others resulting from the pandemic) were not considered. Therefore, it is necessary to implement measures to face them. Possibly the most interesting challenge is that you only have three weeks to adapt the contents according to the level of the students, in a staggered presence of the students.

In this way, the digital strategy will combine and harmonize the operation of human and technological resources in the teaching-learning process of students with special educational needs. Serving as a guide for the continuity of face-to-face education, helping to make the best decisions according to the learning objectives, characteristics of the students and the social context.

The following Figure 4 shows the conceptual model of the Digital Strategy, immersed in the USAER service process:

Figure 4. USAER classroom work process

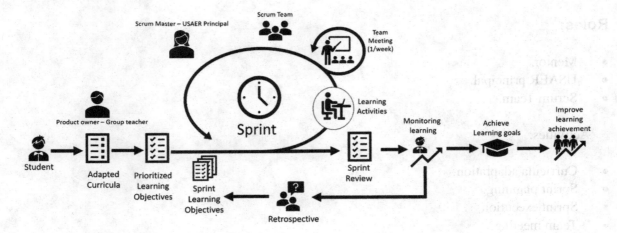

215

Our approach includes the already known roles, values, ceremonies and instruments from SCRUM process. These are the twelve Principles of Agile on the USAER goals:

1. Our highest priority is to satisfy the student learning needs, through early and continuous delivery of learning content.
2. Welcome changing in academic content, even late in the school cycle.
3. Deliver adapted academic content frequently, according with the agenda of the current school cycle, with a preference to the shorter timescale.
4. Family, group teacher, and USAER team must work together daily throughout the students.
5. Attend students' learning needs around motivated individuals. Give them the environment and support they need and trust them to get the job done.
6. The most efficient and effective method of conveying information to and within a attending team is face-to-face conversation.
7. Student's learning achievement is the primary measure of progress.
8. Agile processes promote sustainable adapted academic content. Family, teachers, USAER experts and students should be able to maintain a constant pace indefinitely.
9. Continuous attention to accessible content and good need attending enhances agility.
10. Simplicity—the art of maximizing the amount of work not being done—is essential.
11. The best intervention processes, need attending strategies, and adapted academic content emerge from self-organizing teams.
12. At regular intervals, the team reflects on how to become more effective, then tunes and adjusts its behavior accordingly.
13. Basic problem: Many students, many differences between students, many learning objectives, continuous attitudinal changes, social uncertainty.

Basic problem: Many students, many differences between students, many learning objectives, continuous attitudinal changes, social uncertainty.

Basis of solution: Each student is a project, with the objective of having significative learning according with each one's capabilities

All actions are focused in providing the best tools to achieve the prioritized learning goals.

Our proposal also involved roles, activities, and artifacts:

Roles:

- Mentor.
- USAER principal.
- Scrum Team.

Activities:

- Curricula adaptation.
- Sprint planning.
- Sprint execution.
- Team meeting.

- Learning activities execution.
- Monitoring learning.
- Retrospective.
- Learning objective adequation.

Artifacts:

- Adapted curricula.
- Learning objectives backlog.
- Sprint backlog.
- Learning activities.
- Learning increment.

CASE OF STUDY

It is very important to mention that, since March to august 2020, schools are closed to presential classes; in Mexico, the government has announced that the academic cycle 2020-2021 is going to be all in virtual mode, beginning in September (SEP, 2020a). The case of study presented here is the assignation of activities for roles, the scrum activities specification, the artifacts definitions and some scrum tools, proposed to be implemented in the next academic cycle to one kid with special educational needs, evaluated and diagnosed in the last presential cycle (August 2019).

After the detection of the student by one of his teachers, and the confirmation of others, the USAER psychologist made two evaluations, the cognitive evaluation and the evaluation of maturation in development; applying a specific battery of tests that included the WISC-2 and. The social work area carried out a socio-family assessment to detect possible external agents that could be affecting the student's development. Finally, the USAER team conducted a Case Review.

Once the USAER team carries out the Generation of the student's diagnosis, it begins with the articulation of the work team, which will integrate the directors of the institution, the teachers, the USAER team and the student's family. Together they will carry out the corresponding curricular adaptation with the abilities, capacities and limitations of the student.

STUDENT PROFILE

"Hector", presents hypoacusis, with a minimum rescue of sound. Until that moment, he has not accessed the reading-writing, nor achieved the count from 1 to 9 with concrete material; does not present autonomous displacement; in his communication skills, he does not have a signed sign language or lip reading, and he is currently not oralized. Hector, finally, has a limited memory capacity. The teachers report that they do not have the support and commitment of the mother of the family, due to the fact that she does not attend meetings or school appointments and never achieved a real relationship with the USAER support team. The evaluation of the skills (Table 1) of the Hector development was in charge of the specialists of the USAER, who by means of the application of the tests Wisc-RM and ABS S: 2 corroborated that the student has a mild intellectual disability, with an IQ of 68.

Table 1. Student assessment

Ambit	Description	Level
Language and communication	Communicates feelings, events, and ideas both orally and in writing in their native language. Describe in English aspects of your past and environment, as well as immediate needs.	Not acquired
Mathematical thinking	Understands concepts and procedures to solve various mathematical problems and to apply them in other contexts. Has a favorable attitude towards mathematics?	Not acquired
Exploring and understanding the natural and social world	You recognize some natural and social phenomena that make you curious and need to answer questions. She explores them through inquiry, analysis, and experimentation. You become familiar with some representations and models (for example, maps, diagrams, and timelines).	Not acquired
Critical thinking and problem solving	Solve problems by applying different strategies: observe, analyze, reflect and plan in order. Obtains evidence to support the solution she proposes. Explain their thought processes.	Partial
Socio-emotional skills and life project	Has attention span. Identify and put into practice their personal strengths to self-regulate their emotions and be calm to play, learn, develop empathy and live with others. Designs and undertakes short and medium-term projects (for example, improve your grades or practice a hobby.	Partial
Collaboration and teamwork	Work collaboratively. Identify their capabilities and recognize and appreciate others.	Acquired
Coexistence and citizenship	Develop your identity as a person. Know, respect and exercise your rights and obligations. It favors dialogue, contributes to peaceful coexistence and rejects all kinds of discrimination and violence.	Partial
Artistic appreciation and expression	Explore and experience different artistic manifestations. Express herself creatively through elements of music, dance, theater, and the visual arts.	Partial
Attention to the body and health	Recognize your body. Solve challenges and challenges through the creative use of your body skills. Make informed decisions about your hygiene and diet. Participate in play situations and physical activity, seeking healthy and peaceful coexistence.	Partial
Environmental care	Recognize the importance of caring for the environment. Identify local and global problems and solutions you can put into practice.	Not acquired
Digital skills	Identify a variety of tools and technologies that you use to obtain information, create, practice, learn, communicate, and play.	Partial

Context of the Problem

In order for the reader to measure the size and complexity of the problem that USAER teams have to adapt the academic curriculum, we believe that it is pertinent to describe the context of the problem.

In Mexico, basic education includes primary and secondary levels. Secondary basic education is equivalent to the first cycle of Secondary Obligatory Education in Spain and Junior High school in United States.

There are three training fields in secondary basic education, these are:

1.   Language and communication.
2.   Mathematical Thinking.
3.   Exploring and understanding the natural and social world.

Table 2 shows areas and topics for each training fields:

Table 2. Areas and topics for training fields of secondary basic education

Field	Area	Topic
Language and communication	Study	• Research, analysis. • Evaluation and recording of information. • Oral communication of information. • Production and correction of texts.
	Literature	• Read, share, produce and interpret narratives. • Read, share, produce and perform songs and poems.
	Social participation	• Use of administrative and legal documents. • Analysis of various media: print (such as magazines and newspapers) and digital (such as blogs and social networks). • Production of a variety of texts for personal purposes. • Reflection on language and texts.
	Education	• It is a transversal axis that crosses all areas and levels of Basic Education. • Must provide conceptual tools for language analysis and understanding.
Mathematical thinking	Number sense	• Numbers. • Additive problems. • Multiplicative problems.
	Form, space, and measure	• Geometric figures. • Magnitude and measurements.
	Data handling	• Probability.
	Process of change and algebraic thinking	• Proportionality. • Equivalent patterns and expressions. • Features. • Equations.
Exploring and understanding the natural and social world	The human body and health	• Structure and vital functions. • Health promotion.
	Living beings and the environment	• Interdependence and interactions between living beings and the environment. • Diversity, continuity and change.
	Science and technology	• Interactions between biology and technology.

For each topic, has been defined a set of Learning objectives for second year of secondary basic education. Next we list the learning objectives for the topic of Numbers:

- Use divisibility criteria and identify prime numbers.
- Convert decimal fractions to decimal notation and vice versa.
- Approximate some non-decimal fractions using decimal notation.
- Order fractions and decimal numbers.
- Explicit density property.
- Solving powers with integer exponent and square root approximation.

USAER Team in Action

Now, once the students that will receive academic support from USAER, the team, together with the group teacher, made the first proposal for the *adapted curricula*. Where each learning objective is modified to be reached by the student, according with his/her capabilities. Right in this point is where our proposal begins operations.

Table 3 shows the objectives for mathematical thinking, in the number sense area, with the adequations made by the Mentor and the USAER team, for the profile of Hector.

Table 3. Curricula adequations for Hector

Topic	Learning objective	USAER Adequation
Numbers	Use divisibility criteria and identify prime numbers.	Identify natural numbers.
	Convert decimal fractions to decimal notation and vice versa.	Identify fractions and how different parts form integers.
	Approximate some non-decimal fractions using decimal notation.	
	Order fractions and decimal numbers.	
	Explicit density property.	
	Solving powers with integer exponent and square root approximation.	Not considered for this student.
Additive problems	Solve addition and subtraction problems with positive and negative whole numbers, fractions, and decimals.	Know the concept of addition.
Multiplicative problems	Solve multiplication and fraction problems with decimals and division with decimals.	Know the concept of multiplication and division.
	Rank the operations to find equivalent expressions. Use of parentheses with natural, integer, decimal and fractional numbers.	Not considered for this student.

The proposal of adapted curricula together with the original learning objectives will be considered as the requirements of the project. The mentor together will define the prioritized backlog product, i. e. prioritize the learning objectives and validate that adequations in the curricula effectively match with student capabilities. Table 4 shows how the learning objectives of listed before are prioritized and form the prioritized backlog:

After this, the first sprint begins. USAER team can follow up the evolution of learning objectives for each student with a very common tool used in Scrum, the blackboard. In Figure 5 we show a possible evolution of the learning objectives of last table.

ASSESSMENT

The process here proposed has been evaluated according with 14 criteria (defined by our research team of educative technology), that involves team collaboration, workload for the student, learning goals administration, and the following up process. 10 specialists from USAER, answered the Evaluation Sheet (Annex A), all questions have answers according with a Likert scale of five values: Strongly Agree (1pt),

Table 4. Prioritized learning objectives

Learning objective	USAER Adequation	Priority
Use divisibility criteria and identify prime numbers.	Identify natural numbers.	1
Convert decimal fractions to decimal notation and vice versa.	Identify fractions and how different parts form integers.	4
Approximate some non-decimal fractions using decimal notation.		
Order fractions and decimal numbers.		
Explicit density property.		
Solving powers with integer exponent and square root approximation.	Not considered for this student.	-
Solve addition and subtraction problems with positive and negative whole numbers, fractions, and decimals.	Know the concept of addition.	2
Solve multiplication and fraction problems with decimals and division with decimals.	Know the concept of multiplication and division.	3
Rank the operations to find equivalent expressions. Use of parentheses with natural, integer, decimal and fractional numbers.	Not considered for this student.	-

Agree (2pts), Neither agree nor disagree (3pts), Disagree (4pts), and Strong Disagree (5pts). Next, we present the comparison with the current USAER attention process in Table 5:

Figure 5. Blackboard for Hector

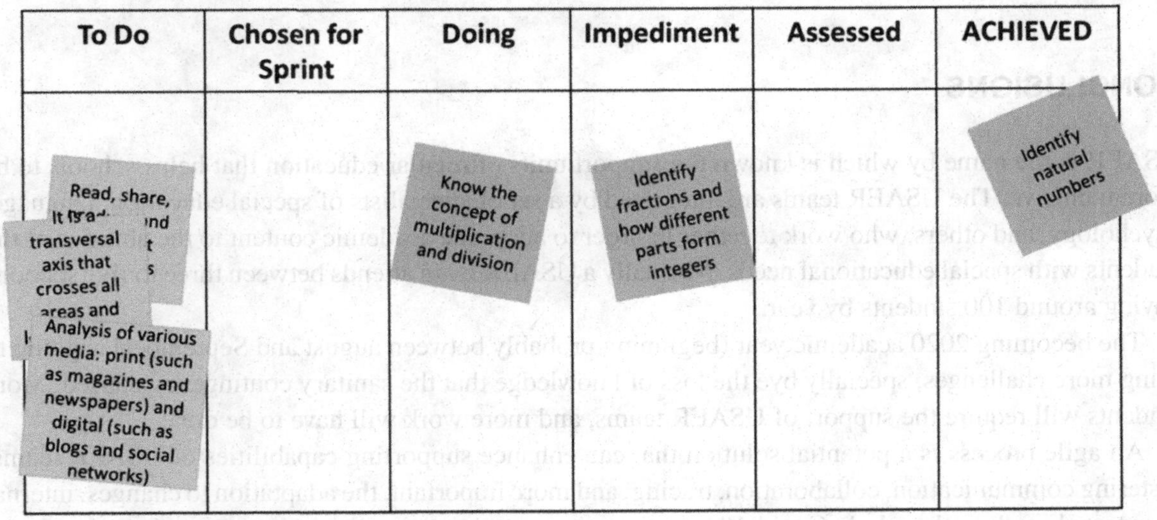

FUTURE RESEARCH DIRECTIONS

As shown in the assessment of the process, the perception of usefulness was well evaluated by USAER experts, nevertheless, the learnability seems to be a good point to enhance. This is why, the development of documentation and a training program is one of our priorities for future work.

Table 5. USAER SCRUM assessment results

Criterion	Current USAER Process	USAER-SCRUM
Team collaboration	3.2	4.7
Paring student's needs and learning objectives	3.3	3.8
Adapting academic content to changes	3.2	4.2
Learning methodology adjustment	2.47	4.7
Activities Re-assignment	2.9	4.75
Monitoring learning	2.85	4.75
Workload	3	3.6
Including expert knowledge	2.55	3.3
Involving family	2.47	4.37
ICT implementation	2.53	4.73
Easiness of use	3.75	3.2
Learnability	3.6	3.05
Reuse	3.1	3.9
Involving home and school activities	3.5	4

As experts in educative technology, our research team is also finding new ways to specify users tasks as part of the educational software design, in order to make agile also the production of those required technological solutions for each sprint, in the SCRUM-USAER process.

CONCLUSIONS

USAER is the name by which is known the support units of regular education that helps schools to be more inclusive. The USAER teams are integrated by a set of specialists of special education, language, psychology, and others, who work together in order to adapt the academic content to the abilities of the students with special educational needs. Normally a USAER team attends between three to five schools, having around 100 students by year.

The becoming 2020 academic year (beginning probably between august and September) is going to bring more challenges, specially bye the loss of knowledge that the sanitary contingency caused. More students will require the support of USAER teams, and more work will have to be done.

An agile process is a potential solution that can enhance supporting capabilities of USAER teams, fostering communication, collaboration, tracing, and more important, the adaptation to changes, internal or external, such as the whole Covid-19 situation.

REFERENCES

Baird, A., & Riggins, F. J. (2012). Planning and sprinting: Use of a hybrid project management methodology within a CIS Capstone course. *Journal of Information Systems Education*, *23*(3), 243.

Blum, C., & Li, X. (2008). Swarm intelligence in optimization. In C. Blum & D. Merkle (Eds.), *Swarm intelligence* (pp. 43–85). Springer Berlin Heidelberg. doi:10.1007/978-3-540-74089-6_2

Cooper, H. (2020). *Summer learning loss: The problem and some solutions*. Retrieved July 04, 2020, from http://www.ldonline.org/article/8057/

Delhij, A., Van Solingen, R., & Wijnands, W. (2015). *The eduScrum guide, the rules of the game*. Version 1.2 - September 2015, Reviewed by: Jeff Sutherland.

Gannod, G., Troy, D., Luczaj, J., & Rover, D. (2015). Agile way of educating. In *Proceedings of the 2015 IEEE Frontiers in Education Conference (FIE)*. 10.1109/FIE.2015.7344019

Highsmith, J. (2013). *Adaptive software development: A collaborative approach to managing complex systems*. Addison-Wesley.

May, J., York, J., & Lending, D. (2016). Teaching tip: Play ball: Bringing Scrum into the classroom. *Journal of Information Systems Education*, 27(2), 87–92.

Musser, H. (2019). *Embracing the agile mindset & Agile's core principles, the agile alliance*. Retrieved July 14. 2020, from https://www.agilealliance.org/embracing-the-agile-mindset-agiles-core-principles/

Onieva, J. (2018). *Scrum como estrategia para el aprendizaje colaborativo a través de proyectos. Propuesta didáctica para su implementación en el Aula Universitaria*. Revista de Currículum y Formación del Profesorado. doi:10.30827/profesorado.v22i2.7735

Piñero, M. L., Rondón, L. M., & Piña, V. E. (2007). *La formación de competencias transversales en y para la investigación: Una propuesta metodológica para el currículo de la UPEL-IPB. Review LAURUS. Año 13*. Viecerrectorado de Docencia. UPEL.

Pope-Ruark, R. (2015). In-troducing agile project management strategies in technical and professional communication courses. *Journal of Business and Technical Communication*, 29(1), 112–133. doi:10.1177/1050651914548456

Quinn, D., & Polikoff, M. (2017). *Summer learning loss: What is it, and what can we do about it?* Retrieved July 04, 2020, from https://www.brookings.edu/research/summer-learning-loss-what-is-it-and-what-can-we-do-about-it/

Schwaber, K., & Sutherland, J. (2017). *The Scrum guide 2017*. Retrieved July 04, 2020, from https://www.scrumguides.org/docs/scrumguide/v2017/2017-Scrum-Guide-US.pdf

SEP. (2002), *Programa nacional de fortalecimiento de la educación especial y de la integración educativa*. Cd. de México: Secretaría de Educación Pública.

SEP. (2009). *La integración educativa en el aula regular: Principios, finalidades y estrategias*. Cd. de Méxco: Secretaría de Educación Pública.

SEP. (2010). *Guía para facilitar la inclusión de alumnos y alumnas con discapacidad en escuelas que participan en el Programa Escuelas de Calidad*. Cd. de México: Secretaría de Educación Pública.

SEP. (2011). *Orientaciones para la intervención de la unidad de servicios de apoyo a la educación regular (USAER) en las escuelas de educación básica.* Secretaría de Educación Pública, Dirección de Educación Especial, Ciudad de México.

SEP (2018). *Estrategia de equidad e inclusión en la educación básica: para alumnos con discapacidad.* Aptitudes sobresalientes y dificultades severas de aprendizaje, conducta o comunicación, Cd. de México: Secretaría de Educación Pública.

SEP. (2019). *Educación especial.* Gobierno de México. Retrieved July 04, 2020, from https://aprende-encasa.sep.gob.mx/site/ed-inclusiva

SEP. (2020a). *Boletín No. 133 Regreso a clases cuando el semáforo de control de la pandemia esté en verde: SEP.* Secretaría de Educación Pública. Retrieved July 14, 2020, from https://www.gob.mx/sep

SEP. (2020b). *Regreso a clases en la nueva normalidad.* Secretaría de Educación Pública. Retrieved July 14, 2020, from https://www.gob.mx/cms/uploads/attachment/file/554867/CPM_SEP_NN-RC__29may20.pdf

Soto, F., Sucunuta, M., Rodriguez, G., Cueva, S., Jaramillo, D., & Abad, P. (2018). Agile methodologies applied in teaching-learning process in engineering: A case of study. *Proceedings of the 2018 IEEE Global Engineering Education Conference.*

Von Hippel, P. (2019). Is summer learning los real? How I lost faith in one of education research's classic results. *Education Next, 19*(4).

Appendix 1

Table 5. Evaluation sheet

Evaluation sheet				
Instructions: Select a value to each question.				
Team collaboration				
The process provides an environment that makes easy the collaboration between all team members.				
Strongly Agree	Agree	Neither agree nor disagree	Disagree	Strong Disagree
The activities assignation and the roles of each team member are perfectly balanced				
Strongly Agree	Agree	Neither agree nor disagree	Disagree	Strong Disagree
Paring student's needs and learning objectives				
All activities in the curricula can be easily pared with the student's needs				
Strongly Agree	Agree	Neither agree nor disagree	Disagree	Strong Disagree
It is easy to assign a level of difficulty of the activity according with the student capacities				
Strongly Agree	Agree	Neither agree nor disagree	Disagree	Strong Disagree
Adapting academic content to changes				
The process makes easy to change academic activities due to external changes.				
Strongly Agree	Agree	Neither agree nor disagree	Disagree	Strong Disagree
The process makes easy to change academic activities due to attitudinal changes of the student				
Strongly Agree	Agree	Neither agree nor disagree	Disagree	Strong Disagree
The process makes easy to change academic activities due to student's performance changes.				
Strongly Agree	Agree	Neither agree nor disagree	Disagree	Strong Disagree
Learning methodology adjustment				
The process makes easy to change the learning methodology due to external changes.				
Strongly Agree	Agree	Neither agree nor disagree	Disagree	Strong Disagree
The process makes easy to change the learning methodology due to student's performance changes.				
Strongly Agree	Agree	Neither agree nor disagree	Disagree	Strong Disagree
The process makes easy to change the learning methodology due to student's performance changes.				
Strongly Agree	Agree	Neither agree nor disagree	Disagree	Strong Disagree
Activities Re-assignment				
The process makes easy to re-design activities where the student does not success in achieveing learning goals.				
Strongly Agree	Agree	Neither agree nor disagree	Disagree	Strong Disagree
The process makes easy to re-assign unsuccessful learning activities				
Strongly Agree	Agree	Neither agree nor disagree	Disagree	Strong Disagree
Monitoring learning				
The process makes easy to follow student progress				
Strongly Agree	Agree	Neither agree nor disagree	Disagree	Strong Disagree
The progress of the student can be seen by any member of the team				
Strongly Agree	Agree	Neither agree nor disagree	Disagree	Strong Disagree
Workload				
The process makes easy to increment/decrement the workload according with the student's progress				
Strongly Agree	Agree	Neither agree nor disagree	Disagree	Strong Disagree
The amount of workload is defined according to the student's abilities and progress				
Strongly Agree	Agree	Neither agree nor disagree	Disagree	Strong Disagree
Including expert knowledge				
It is easy to include expert's knowledge into the learning process and activities.				
Strongly Agree	Agree	Neither agree nor disagree	Disagree	Strong Disagree
It is easy for experts to find out where their expertise can be applied				
Strongly Agree	Agree	Neither agree nor disagree	Disagree	Strong Disagree
Involving family				
The process effectively incorporates family members into the learning process				
Strongly Agree	Agree	Neither agree nor disagree	Disagree	Strong Disagree
It is easy to assign roles and activities to any family member.				
Strongly Agree	Agree	Neither agree nor disagree	Disagree	Strong Disagree
The process makes easy the communication with the student's family				
Strongly Agree	Agree	Neither agree nor disagree	Disagree	Strong Disagree
ICT implementation				
The process makes easy to incorporate ICT into the learning activities.				
Strongly Agree	Agree	Neither agree nor disagree	Disagree	Strong Disagree
The process makes easy to select the type of technology that better fits for certain activity				
Strongly Agree	Agree	Neither agree nor disagree	Disagree	Strong Disagree

continued on following page

Table 5. Continued

Evaluation sheet				
It is easy to know the best characteristics of the required technology				
Strongly Agree	Agree	Neither agree nor disagree	Disagree	Strong Disagree
Easiness of use				
It is easy to implement the process into the school program				
Strongly Agree	Agree	Neither agree nor disagree	Disagree	Strong Disagree
Artifacts and tools are easy to be applied				
Strongly Agree	Agree	Neither agree nor disagree	Disagree	Strong Disagree
Learnability				
It is easy to learn how the whole process works				
Strongly Agree	Agree	Neither agree nor disagree	Disagree	Strong Disagree
It is easy to learn how the phases of the process works alone				
Strongly Agree	Agree	Neither agree nor disagree	Disagree	Strong Disagree
It is easy to learn how all the phases work together				
Strongly Agree	Agree	Neither agree nor disagree	Disagree	Strong Disagree
The artifacts and tools are easy to learn				
Strongly Agree	Agree	Neither agree nor disagree	Disagree	Strong Disagree
Reuse				
Pre-defined activities can be easily applied over other objectives or student's process				
Strongly Agree	Agree	Neither agree nor disagree	Disagree	Strong Disagree
Lessons learned, and good practices can be easily documented and implemented				
Strongly Agree	Agree	Neither agree nor disagree	Disagree	Strong Disagree
Involving home and school activities				
Activities can be easily defined for school or home				
Strongly Agree	Agree	Neither agree nor disagree	Disagree	Strong Disagree

Section 5
Organization Assessment

Chapter 14
The Market Value of Scrum:
A Note on References to Scrum in U.S. Corporate Financial Reports

Sathiadev Mahesh
University of New Orleans, USA

Kenneth R. Walsh
University of New Orleans, USA

Cherie C. Trumbach
University of New Orleans, USA

ABSTRACT

Scrum technologies have been applied in business software for two decades and are an important part of organizations' innovation processes. This exploratory study examines whether the use of Scrum within an organization can be detected from its financial statements by reviewing references to scrum in corporate financial reports filed with the US Securities and Exchange Commission (SEC). While scrum use is widespread in software development, there are very few references to scrum in corporate financial reports. Fewer than one-half percent of businesses filing reports with the Securities and Exchange Commission include scrum capabilities in their business strategy or business competency sections. It appears that senior management has not yet recognized the value of the technology and evaluated its impact on investor evaluation of business prospects. Investors need to seek other media to evaluate scrum implementation at the business.

DOI: 10.4018/978-1-7998-4885-1.ch014

Copyright © 2021, IGI Global. Copying or distributing in print or electronic forms without written permission of IGI Global is prohibited.

INTRODUCTION

Useful information can be gleaned from a careful analysis of corporate reports, especially corporate annual financial reports, prepared to meet regulatory guidelines. Text analysis of reports can yield useful insights into how technology is viewed by management and into how management views technology impacts investors' evaluation of the business operations. Our study focuses on the release of information regarding the adoption of a new software methodology. This research is limited to US financial reports to limit the need for language translation and due to the sample available for study. Our goal is to determine the number of references to scrum and related agile technologies in these reports and analyze trends in introducing and using these terms. We find relatively few refences to scrum in the thousands of reports. However, all the references to scrum found in this study are positive with no business stating a cessation of using scrum or finding an alternative means of development to be superior.

BACKGROUND

Corporate Financial reports are prepared for two audiences; the regulatory agency which requires a report meeting statutory guidelines with severe penalties for non-compliance, and the market which increasingly uses the electronically filed data for evaluating business operations and profitability. Even in 2000, an analysis of disclosures in electronically (EDGAR) filed reports shows that incremental information useful for investors is found in these reports while the delay in paper filing eliminates any benefits to investors (Qi, Wu, & Haw, 2000). Palmieri, Perrin & Whitehouse (2018) discuss the use of language in financial communication and the AILA network in financial communication research.

Research using financial reporting often uses financial data and accounting ratios as determinants of profitability. For example, Sultan (2014) found that return on equity (ROE) was the best measure of the health of the Bagdad soft-drink industry in the years 2004 to 2013. However, such accounting ratio analysis gives little insight into the innovation processes at work within the organization that have potential for future profitability. Muneer et al. (2017) showed how an organization's financial reporting method can lead to profitability. Such analysis gives some insight into the relationship between the practices of the firm and profitability, however the financial reporting practices of the firm may or may not relate to its use of innovative processes.

During the past two decades the increasing use of automated tools to analyze data, including text data, has resulted in the printed corporate report becoming a quaint anachronism, and rarely read seriously. Investors analyze the data in electronically filed reports. Jarvenpaa & Ives (1990) analyzed 600 letters to shareholders included in corporate reports and used a count of the number of IT phrases as a proxy of the perceived importance of information technology to the business. This type of content analysis has its roots in WWII efforts of military intelligence and is a useful tool for analyzing the prevalence and perceived importance of a new technology (Lacity & Janson, 1994). Abbasi & Chen (2008) document different linguistic features used for text analysis including language and processing features. It has been shown that executives used specific terms to consistently demonstrate a sustained focus on trustworthiness and moving in a specified strategic direction (Crawford, 2011).

The tone employed in earnings press releases is found to influence stock market pricing (Huang, Krishnan, & Lin, 2018). They use word-lists created for 10-K analysis and use a frequency count of net positive words to total words. Note that their study uses press releases rather than 10-K reports filed by the business with the SEC. While press releases are highly relevant for market evaluation of special events, including crises or opportunities, the 10-K reports are more relevant for how the business values the use of specific technologies. Another study by Erickson, Weber and Segovia (2011) uses a critical analysis of the language used by the business to explain weaknesses in its operations with specific reference to Section 404 of Sarbanes-Oxley Act requirements for the reporting of internal control failures. In this study the emphasis is on the language used to report failures.

Weitz, Henry & Rosenthal (2014) examine the use of non-financial metrics about website visits used by social media companies to communicate the value of business operations in corporate annual 10-K and quarterly 10-Q filings. They point out the lack of value from this data due to the lack of standards for reporting the data. While financial data is reported according to well-established standards, website data reporting standards are still fluid, and with rapid changes in the technology, not amenable to strict guidelines. The 10-K and 10Q reports are found to miss many useful metrics and include metrics that are not comparable due to differences in how they are calculated by different companies.

Text mining of sustainability reports made by five Brazilian companies from 2009 to 2016 shows a high level of similarity in these reports even though they functioned in very different sectors (Clemente, Ribiero, de Paula & Mendonca, 2019). One conclusion drawn from the study is that businesses tend to make socially appropriate statements on the topic of sustainability. Another, more detailed study of 10-K and related reports filed by 180 firms in the tech sector focused on global mind-set included in the reports (Beldebos et.al, 2017). A global mind-set indicator was developed in the study and shown to correlate with financial performance. A text analysis of 240 advertising slogans by Dowling and Kabanoff (1996) using content analysis showed five clear clusters.

This shows that analysis of corporate financial reports will yield useful information about the perceived importance of a new technology to business management and stockholders. While our study is limited to U.S. SEC filing and this limits the global application of this report, it does provide information on the perceived impact of scrum technologies on evaluating the value of U.S. listed companies. It must also be noted that many global companies have a major presence in the U.S. market and are required to file financial reports when their stock is listed on U.S. exchanges.

DATA AND ANALYSIS

Public listed companies in the US are required to file annual financial reports following strict guidelines laid out by the Securities and Exchange Commission (SEC). These include annual 10-K reports filed by US Companies and 20-F reports filed by non-US companies with US listed shares. 10-K reports filed annually should provide a "comprehensive overview of the business and financial condition" according to SEC guidelines. While the primary focus of the report is to provide audited financial statements, there is also a business condition requirement which covers the operations of the business and requires that management publicly announce any business actions that impact the operations of the enterprise. This includes the adoption of new technology that can make the business more profitable or expose the business to implementation risks that could negatively impact the business. Much research in the financial arena has focused on the numbers released in the statement and the calculation of appropriate financial ratios. However, this refers to the past year or quarter in the case of 10-Q quarterly reports. The descriptive statements made in the sections on business operations on the other hand focus on potential future impact of business practices. References to scrum and scrum related terms in these reports are analyzed in this study.

Searches were made from multiple data sources including the SEC Edgar site which provides a full-text search of the past four years of filed documents and Nexis document search of the SEC filings which goes back over two decades covering the entire period when scrum has been used in business. Economic data from the St. Louis Fed (https://alfred.stlouisfed.org) estimates about 4500 listed companies in the US (13.3355 per million * 335 million) while an analysis of companies filing 10-K reports showed 8677 10-K's filed in 2019. However, many of these reports were filed by investment trusts and not businesses with operations in the US or elsewhere. A detailed analysis of 1000 randomly selected 10- K filings from 2019 showed less than 80% referred to businesses with operations, providing an estimate of 6942 companies. Using a sample of 250 20-F filings in 2019 it is estimated that 1371 businesses with operations filed 20-F reports.

What is interesting is that of these 8315 companies only 39 reports referred to scrum. The study includes not just 2019 filings but all references to scrum in financial reports filed during the past two decades. Hence, these *thirty-nine* companies include some that ceased to exist during the period, which means that much less than $39/8315 = 0.44\%$ of publicly listed companies believed it was relevant for their investors to be informed about the business use of scrum technologies. Of these thirty-nine companies, nine refer to scrum merely as one of the skills of their executives, and that with only reference to one executive on their board. Two other companies refer to scrum in a tangential manner. One uses the term "scrum" in a completely unrelated manner with no reference to software development. Another merely refers to meeting a customer about scrum. In these two cases it is not highlighted as a unique competence that benefits the company in any special manner. This yields a total of *twenty-eight* companies that refer to scrum as a significant part of their operations and a source of value to investors.

While there are many references to scrum replacing traditional waterfall development, there are absolutely no references to scrum being replaced with a superior or more innovative technology. While market assessments of business value have viewed e-commerce implementations as valuable and top management has consistently communicated their e-commerce strategy in reports. However, this has not happened in the case of scrum.

Analysis of the data in Table 2 shows that two of the companies made multiple references to scrum as part a report that referred to multiple service contracts that required scrum methodology. Overall, the companies referred to scrum once or twice in their report. The reference was part of the business Research and Development or Business Plan and referred to using agile scrum development methodology.

The text in the reports were typically repeated multiple years by companies with few changes from year to year. The earliest reference to scrum is in 2007 and it continues to be used in reports filed in 2020. However, as we saw earlier, very few companies communicate their use of scrum to their shareholders. Almost all the companies listed in the table are involved in software development as their primary business. Only three companies can be classified as involved in other fields of business.

Software development companies typically announce the number of scrum certifications or their association with professional organizations for agile-scrum development. They communicate the number of employees trained in scrum and certified in agile technologies and their commitment to professional organizations for agile development of software. Infosys in particular highlights its shift away from waterfall development.

Table 1. Forms filed with SEC including the term "scrum" and with reference to Software development

Form	Year	Company Name	Scrum References	Sub-heading
6-K	2018	Banco Santander	1	Cultural Change
10-K	2012-2013	CA Technologies	4	R & D
20-F	2012-2015	Click Software	2	Agile Methodology
S 1-A	2019	Data Vision Inc	1	
20-F	2018-2019	Endava plc	7	Frameworks
20-F	2017-2019	Exfo Inc	1	R & D
20-F	2013-2016	Globant, S.A.	2	Delivery Model
10K	2011-2012	Immersion, Corp	1	R & D
20-F	2014-2020	Infosys Ltd	1 to 3 increase	Solutions & Capabilities
20F	2017-2019	ING Groep	1	Innovation Culture
10-K	2014-2018	Learning Tree International	1	Curriculum
20-F	2014-2018	Luxoft Holding Inc	4 to 1 reduction	
10K	2008-2011	Lyris, Inc	1	R & D
10K	2015	Mantech, Intl	1	Solutions & Services
S1	2017	Nabufit Global	2	R & D
10-K	2015	NCI, Inc	1	Software Development
10-K	2018	Nielsen Holdings plc	15[1]	Service Agreement
20-F	2020	PagSeguro Digital Ltd	1	Product Development
10-K	2017-2018	Plyzer Technologies Inc	1	Business Plan
10-K	2013-2015	Rally Software	1 to 2 increase	Business Plan
10-K	2013-2016	Sciquest, Inc	1	Business
10-K	2019-2020	SolarWinds Corp	1	New Ways of Working
S-1	2008-2011	Success Factors	1	Business
10-Q	2017	Synacor Inc	5[1]	Service Agreement
6-K	2020	Telefonica S A	1	New Ways of Working
10-Q	2017-2020	UPAY	1	Revenue Recognition
10-K	2011-2012	Vidaroo Corp	2	Business Strengths
20-F	2019-2020	Wipro Ltd	2	Business Strategy

[1] These two documents refer to scrum as part of contracts multiple times.

(i) Infosys a leading software developer and outsourced IT services provider incorporates the use of scrum consistently from 2014 to 2020. Examples of statements in the reports include "Infosys has taken the lead *to move away from the traditional waterfall development* approach to an Agile and Scrum based approach … solutions embody the best practices developed from more than 1000 projects"

(ii) CA technologies from 2012 to 2013 states that "Our professionals are certified across key standards, including Scrum Alliance … and are certified in CSM (Certified Scrum Master) and CSP (Certified Scrum Professional) … *implementing agile practices and methodologies*"

(iii) Immersion Corp states in 2011 and 2012 that "we *transitioned from a product design process* based on ISO 9001 guidance to the customer-focused Agile Scrum project management process."

(iv) Luxoft Holding refers to scrum from 2014 to 2018 and updates data in its reports as more employees are trained in scrum. Its statement in the 2018 report reads "As of March31, 2017 we employ *more than 600 professionals with IC Agile Certified Professional, Professional Scrum Master or Certified Scrum Master certifications* and more than 3,000 professionals who work on Agile projects and consistently evolve our Agile practice and its applicable methodologies."

(V) Vidaroo refers to its use of Scrum in reports filed in 2011-2012 and states that "… uses an iterative framework for project management called SCRUM".

Other software companies make a short reference to scrum without going into details of the number of employees trained in scrum. Often this is a *grab-bag of terms* which refer to completely different technologies.

For example, Mantech in 2015 states "Activities cross a variety of development methodologies, including waterfall, prototype model, incremental, iterative, V-Model, Spiral, Agile and Scrum." Waterfall and Agile Scrum are two completely different and contradictory approaches to software development. This appears to be an effort to cover all bases and does not communicate a specialization in any technology or a claim that one technology is better than another.

Success Factors in its reports filed between 2008 and 2011 states "Our engineering process is based on a combination of three methodologies: traditional waterfall …; a SCRUM development methodology for agility… and the Extreme Programming methodology …" Note the reference to all forms of software development.

One example of the inclusion of scrum in reports by companies in other fields, i.e. in a line of business other than software development, is a special 6-K report filed by Banco Santander in 2018. The business claims success from the innovative software development technology to support its banking operations and demonstrates its achievement by referring to an award for scrum based agile development. This is in fact the only example of a report filed by a bank with the SEC in the past twenty years that refers to use of scrum and communicates this to its current and prospective shareholders.

Banco Santander in its 6-A filed in 2018 states "The Group is promoting the adoption of Agile methodologies based on…, with multidisciplinary teams … awarded the Agile Best DevOps Finance Project prize … as part of the Strategic Insurance Plan."

Another example is ING Groep, a global insurance company that from 2017 to 2019 states "We accelerate innovation … combines Lean Start-up, Agile Scrum and Design Thinking methods … based on customer feedback."

Many of the reports referencing use of scrum include a *brief one sentence description* of scrum since most investors are not aware of the technology. Example include statements such as "SCRUM provides a vast visual picture of how far development is according to the original plan" in Nabufit Global's 2017 report and "… collaborative teams called SCRUM team, ensuring that each increment is fully tested and validated" in Exfo Inc's 2017 to 2019 reports. Globant S.A. states ""Scrum" means an iterative and incremental agile software development method for managing software projects" in its 2013 and 2014 reports but then drops the explanation is later statements.

References to features of scrum such as backlogs, sprints, scrum masters, and scrum Kanban were even rarer. For example, from the nearly 8000 businesses which filed annual reports, only two companies referred to sprints used in business operations. Synacor in its 2017 report states that "…Project Team will work in 2-weeks sprint-cycles…" and UPAY in its 2017 to 2020 reports states "…scrum methodology with 2-week development sprints…". Four companies refer to scrum kanbans used in managing backlogs for project management.

FUTURE RESEARCH DIRECTIONS

This is an exploratory study. Future research should look at references in business press releases, social media and other top management communications to analyze the impact of scrum in their outreach to investors. Another trove of data to be analyzed is stock analysis reports by investors. Does the broader investment community understand the economic value of scrum in a business and does it value successful implementation and penalize the failure in implementing scrum or even the failure to try to implement scrum.

SUMMARY AND CONCLUSION

The study is based on data scraped from reports filed with the U.S. SEC. While companies also prepare annual reports with more descriptive data, very few investors at present access printed reports or their electronic versions. Hence, electronically filed SEC reports remain the primary source of public information available to investors and this study provides an assessment of the relevance of scrum to investors in listed companies.

This study shows that top management of very few companies communicate their scrum capabilities to their stockholders. Less than *one-half percent of listed companies filing SEC reports* in the US refer to their scrum capabilities. Only a small number of software development companies, largely specializing in outsourced software development make claims about their agile scrum capabilities to investors.

There was no technology claimed to replace scrum while there were many references to scrum replacing traditional waterfall development. The complete absences of any negative comments about scrum can be concluded that scrum is perceived as a useful technology, and has not been replaced with a newer or more suitable approach. However, either top management has not perceived the economic value of scrum to corporate market valuation, or individual investors have not clamored for more information of scrum implementation at businesses.

REFERENCES

Abbasi, A., & Chen, H. (2008). Cybergate: A Design Framework and System for Text Analysis of Computer-Mediated Communication. *Management Information Systems Quarterly*, *32*(4), 811–837. doi:10.2307/25148873

Belderbos, R., Grabowska, M., Leten, B., Kelchtermans, S., & Ugur, N. (2017). On the Use of Computer-Aided Text Analysis in International Business Research. *Global Strategy Journal*, *7*(3), 312–331. doi:10.1002/gsj.1162

Clemente, A., Ribeiro, F., de Paula da Silva, O. A., & Mendonça Oliveira, N. (2019). Analysis of Contents of Annual Sustainability Reports of Industrial Companies Participating in the Sustainability Index of the Brazilian Stock Exchange. *Brazilian Journal of Management / Revista de Administração Da UFSM, 12*, 1211–1226. https://doi-org.ezproxy.uno.edu/10.5902/1983465937995

Crawford, C. B. (2011). Ethics and Ethos in Financial Reporting: Analyzing Persuasive Language in Earnings Calls. *Business Communication Quarterly, 74*(3), 298–312. doi:10.1177/1080569911413810

Dowling, G. R., & Kabanoff, B. (1996). Computer-Aided Content Analysis: What Do 240 Advertising Slogans Have in Common? *Marketing Letters, 7*(1), 63–75. doi:10.1007/BF00557312

Erickson, S. L., Weber, M., & Segovia, J. (2011). Using Communication Theory to Analyze Corporate Reporting Strategies. *Journal of Business Communication, 48*(2), 207–223. doi:10.1177/0021943611399728

Huang, X., Krishnan, S., & Lin, P. (2018). Tone Analysis and Earnings Management. *Journal of Accounting & Finance, 18*(8), 46–61. https://doi-org.ezproxy.uno.edu/10.33423/jaf.v18i8.110

Jarvenpaa, S., & Ives, B. (1990). Information technology and corporate strategy: A view from the top. *Information Systems Research, I*, 4, 351–375.

Lacity, M. C., & Janson, M. A. (1994). Understanding Qualitative Data: A Framework of Text Analysis Methods. *Journal of Management Information Systems, 11*(2), 137–155. doi:10.1080/07421222.1994.11518043

Muneer, S., Ahmad, R. A., & Ali, A. (2017). Impact of Financial Management Practices on SMEs Profitability with Moderating Role of Agency Cost. *Information Management and Business Review, 9*(1), 23–30. doi:10.22610/imbr.v9i1.1593

Palmieri, R., Perrin, D., & Whitehouse, M. (2018). The Pragmatics of Financial Communication. Part 1: From Sources to the Public Sphere. *International Journal of Business Communication, 55*(2), 127–134. doi:10.1177/2329488418758449

Qi, D., Wu, W., & Haw, I.-M. (2000). The Incremental Information Content of SEC 10-K Reports Filed under the EDGAR System. *Journal of Accounting, Auditing & Finance, 15*(1), 25–46. doi:10.1177/0148558X0001500102

Sultan, A. S. (2014). Financial Statements Analysis - Measurement of Performance and Profitability: Applied Study of Baghdad Soft-Drink Industry. *Research Journal of Finance and Accounting, 5*(4), 49–56.

Weitz, R., Henry, T., & Rosenthal, D. (2014). Limitations of Nonfinancial Metrics Reported by Social Media Companies. *Journal of International Technology & Information Management, 23*(3/4), 11–44.

Compilation of References

14. th Annual State of Agile Report. (2020). Retrieved from https://stateofagile.com/#ufh-i-615706098-14th-annual-state-of-agile-report/7027494

Abbasi, A., & Chen, H. (2008). Cybergate: A Design Framework and System for Text Analysis of Computer-Mediated Communication. *Management Information Systems Quarterly*, *32*(4), 811–837. doi:10.2307/25148873

Abrahamsson, P., Pikkarainen, M., Salo, O., Haikara, J., & Still, J. (2008). The impact of agile practices on communication in software development. *Empirical Software Engineering*.

Aghina, W., Ahlback, K., De Smet, A., Lackey, G., Lurie, M., Muraka, M., & Handscomb, C. (2018, Jan). *The Five trademarks of Agile Organisations.* https://www.mckinsey.com/business-functions/organization/our-insights/the-five-trademarks-of-agile-organizations

Aghina, W., Ahlback, K., De Smet, A., Lackey, G., Lurie, M., Murarka, M., & Handscomb, C. (2018, January). Retrieved February 10, 2020, from https://www.mckinsey.com/business-functions/organization/our-insights/the-five-trademarks-of-agile-organizations

Aghina, W., Handscomb, C., Ludolph, J., West, D., & Yip, A. (2018, Dec 20). *How to select and develop individuals for successful Agile teams: A practical guide.* https://mckinsey.com/business-functions/organization/our-insights/how-to-select-and-develop-individuals-for-successful-agile-teams-a-practical-guide

Agile Actors. (2020). *Solutions to common remote work issues during COVID.* Downloaded August 24, 2020, from https://www.scruminc.com/solutions-to-common-remote-work-issues-during-covid/

Agile Alliance. (2001). *Manifesto for Agile Software Development. Section: Principles.* www.agilemanifesto.org

Agile CxO. (2017). *The Agile leadership Check book: Leading in a Self-Organising world.* https://agilecxo.org/wp-content/uploads/2017/09/agilecxocheckbookv7.pdf

Allisy-Roberts, P., Ambrosi, P., Bartlett, D. T., Coursey, B. M., DeWerd, L. A., Fantuzzi, E., & McDonald, J. C. (2017). The 11th Annual State of Agile Report. *Journal of the ICRU*, *6*(2), 7–8. doi:10.1093/jicru_ndl025

Almadhoun, W., & Hamdan, M. (2020). Optimizing the self-organizing team size using a genetic algorithm in agile practices. *Journal of Intelligent Systems*, *29*(1), 1151–1165. doi:10.1515/jisys-2018-0085

Almeida, F. (2017). Challenges in Migration from Waterfall to Agile Environments. *World Journal of Computer Application and Technology,* 1–11. Retrieved from https://pdfs.semanticscholar.org/555d/47e2b9846f38ef66c137afbb3fc0d7bdf3b7.pdf?_ga=2.38570467.1502277820.1576607231-1259273190.1576607231

American Law Institute. (2020). *Restatement of law, second, contracts.* Retrieved February 11, 2020, from https://www.ali.org/publications/show/contracts/

Amiel, T., & Reeves, T. C. (2008). Design-based research and educational technology: Rethinking technology and the research agenda. *Journal of Educational Technology & Society*, *11*(4), 29–40.

Ananda, S., Burke, E. K., Chenc, T. Y., Clark, J., Cohene, M. B., Grieskampf, W., Harmang, M., Harrold, M., Phil, J., & McMinn, P. H. (2013). An orchestrated survey of methodologies for automated software test case generation. *Journal of Systems and Software*, *86*(8), 1978–2001. doi:10.1016/j.jss.2013.02.061

Anderson, S. D., & Wanberg, K. W. (1991). A convergent validity model of emergent leadership in groups. *Small Group Research*, *22*(3), 380–397. doi:10.1177/1046496491223006

Arbogast, T., Larman, C., & Mallik, B. (2012). Agile contracts primer. *Practices for Scaling Lean & Agile Development: Large, Multisite, & Offshore Product Development with Large-Scale Scrum*. Retrieved February 5, 2020, from https://agilecontracts.org/agile contracts primer.pdf

Argyris, C. (2002). Double-loop learning, teaching, and research. *Academy of Management Learning & Education*, *1*(2), 206–218. doi:10.5465/amle.2002.8509400

Armour, P. G. (2014). The business of software: Estimation is not evil. *Communications of the ACM*, *57*(1), 42–43. doi:10.1145/2542505

Aronson, J., Fried, C., & Good, C. (2002). Reducing the effects of stereotype threat on African American college students by shaping theories of intelligence. *Journal of Experimental Social Psychology*, *38*(2), 113–125. doi:10.1006/jesp.2001.1491

Aversano, L., & Tortorella, M. (2004). An assessment strategy for identifying legacy system evolution requirements in eBusiness context. *Journal of Software Maintenance & Evolution: Research & Practice*, *16*(4/5), 255-276.

Aytac, T., Dagli, G., Altinay, Z., & Altinay, F. (2019). The role of learning management in agile management for consensus culture. *The International Journal of Information and Learning Technology*, *36*(4), 364–372. doi:10.1108/IJILT-02-2019-0017

Baham, C. (2019). Implementing Scrum Wholesale in the Classroom. *Journal of Information Systems Education*, *30*(3), 1.

Baham, C. (2019). Teaching tip: Implementing Scrum wholesales in the classroom. *Journal of Information Systems Education*, *30*(3), 141–159.

Baig, A., Hall, B., Jenkins, P., Lamarre, E., & McCarthy, B. (2020). *The covid-19 recovery will be digital: A plan for the first 90 days*. Retrieved August 24, 2020, from https://www.mckinsey.com/business-functions/mckinsey-digital/our-insights/the-covid-19-recovery-will-be-digital-a-plan-for-the-first-90-days

Baird, A., & Riggins, F. J. (2012). Planning and sprinting: Use of a hybrid project management methodology within a CIS Capstone course. *Journal of Information Systems Education*, *23*(3), 243.

Bai, X., Li, M., Pei, D., Li, S., & Ye, D. (2018, May). Continuous delivery of personalized assessment and feedback in agile software engineering projects. In *Proceedings of the 40th International Conference on Software Engineering: Software Engineering Education and Training* (pp. 58-67). 10.1145/3183377.3183387

Balaji, S., & Murugaiyan, M. S. (2012). Waterfall vs. V-model vs. Agile: A comparative study on SDLC. *International Journal of Information Technology and Business Management*, *2*(1), 26–30.

Banker, R. D., Davis, G. B., & Slaughter, S. A. (1998). Software development practices, software complexity, and software maintenance performance: A field study. *Management Science*, *44*(4), 433–450. doi:10.1287/mnsc.44.4.433

Bannerman, P. L., Hossain, E., & Jeffery, R. (2012). Scrum practice mitigation of global software development coordination challenges: A distinctive advantage? *2012 45th Hawaii International Conference on System Sciences*, 5309–5318.

Barki, H., & Hartwick, J. (2001). Interpersonal conflict and its management in information system development. *Management Information Systems Quarterly*, *25*(2), 195–228. doi:10.2307/3250929

Barlow, J. B. (2011). Overview and Guidance on Agile Development in Large Organizations. Comm. of the Ass. for Inform. *Systems*, *29*(1), 25–44.

Barlow, J. B., Keith, M. J., Wilson, D. W., Schuetzler, R. M., Lowry, P. B., Vance, A., & Giboney, J. S. (2011). Overview and guidance on Agile development in large organizations. *Communications of the Association for Information Systems*, *29*, 25–44. doi:10.17705/1CAIS.02902

Barrick, M. R., & Mount, M. K. (1991). The big five personality dimensions and job performance: A meta-analysis. *Personnel Psychology*, *44*(1), 1–26. doi:10.1111/j.1744-6570.1991.tb00688.x

Barton, D., Carey, D., & Charan, R. A. M. (2018). One Bank's Agile Team Experiment "How ING Revamped its Retail Operation. *Harvard Business Review*, *96*(2), 59–61.

Bass, J. M., Beecham, S., Razzak, M. A., Canna, C. N., & Noll, J. (2018). An empirical study of the Product Owner role in Scrum. *Proceedings of the 40th International Conference on Software Engineering: Companion Proceeedings*, 123–124. 10.1145/3183440.3195066

Bastone, N. (2018). *The 29 tech companies with the best company culture in 2018*. Retrieved from https://www.businessinsider.com/best-tech-companies-to-work-at-glassdoor-2018-11

Beck, K. (2001). *Manifesto for Agile Software Development*. https://agilemanifesto.org/

Beck, K., Beedle, M., Van Bennekum, A., Cockburn, A., Cunningham, W., Fowler, M., ... & Kern, J. (2001). *The agile manifesto*. Academic Press.

Beck, K., Beedle, M., Van Bennekum, A., Cockburn, A., Cunningham, W., Fowler, M., ... Kern, J., R. (2001). *Manifesto for agile software development*. Academic Press.

Beck, K., Beedle, M., van Bennekum, A., Cockburn, A., Cunningham, W., Fowler, M., Grenning, J., Highsmith, J., Hunt, A., Jeffries, R., Kern, J., Marick, B., Martin, R. C., Mellor, S., Schwaber, K., Sutherland, J., & Thomas, D. (2001). *Manifesto for Agile Software Development*. Retrieved March 9, 2018, from https://agilemanifesto.org/

Beck, K., Cockburn, A., Jeffries, R., & Highsmith, J. (2001). *Agile manifesto*. http://www.agilemanifesto.org

Beck, K. (1999). Embracing change with extreme programming. *Computer*, *32*(10), 70–77. doi:10.1109/2.796139

Beck, K. (2003). *Test-Driven Development: By Example*. Pearson Education.

Belderbos, R., Grabowska, M., Leten, B., Kelchtermans, S., & Ugur, N. (2017). On the Use of Computer-Aided Text Analysis in International Business Research. *Global Strategy Journal*, *7*(3), 312–331. doi:10.1002/gsj.1162

Bell, B. S., Kanar, A. M., & Kozlowski, S. W. (2008). Current issues and future directions in simulation-based training in North America. *International Journal of Human Resource Management*, *19*(8), 1416–1434. doi:10.1080/09585190802200173

Bernstein, A. (2015, Aug. 25). How to write supplier contracts for agile software development. *Computer Weekly*, 21-24.

Bhoola, V., & Mallik, D. (2014). Determinants of agile practices: A Gini index approach. *Vilakshan, XIMB. Journal of Management*, *11*(2), 95–114.

Bick, S., Spohrer, K., Hoda, R., Scheerer, A., & Heinzl, A. (2018). Coordination challenges in large-scale software development: A case study of planning misalignment in hybrid settings. *IEEE Transactions on Software Engineering*, *44*(10), 932–950. doi:10.1109/TSE.2017.2730870

Binder, R. V. (2000). *Testing Object-Oriented Systems: Models, Patterns, and Tolls*. Addison-Wesley.

Birkinshaw, J. (2017). What to Expect From Agile. *MIT Sloan Management Review*. Retrieved from https://sloanreview.mit.edu/article/what-to-expect-from-agile/

Birkinshaw, J. (2018). What to expect from agile. *MIT Sloan Management Review*, *59*(2), 39–42.

Blum, C., & Li, X. (2008). Swarm intelligence in optimization. In C. Blum & D. Merkle (Eds.), *Swarm intelligence* (pp. 43–85). Springer Berlin Heidelberg. doi:10.1007/978-3-540-74089-6_2

Boehm, B. (1988). A spiral model of software development and enhancement. *IEEE Computer*, *21*(5), 61–72. doi:10.1109/2.59

Boehm, B. (2002). Get Ready for Agile Methods, with Care. *IEEE Computer*, *35*(1), 64–69. doi:10.1109/2.976920

Boehm, B. W. (1983). Seven basic principles of software engineering. *Journal of Systems and Software*, *3*(1), 3–24. doi:10.1016/0164-1212(83)90003-1

Boehm, B., & Papaccio, P. (1988). Understanding and controlling software costs. *IEEE Transactions on Software Engineering*, *14*(10), 1462–1477. doi:10.1109/32.6191

Boehm, B., & Turner, B. (2003). *Balancing Agility and Discipline: A Guide for the Perplexed*. Addison Wesley Pearson Education.

Boehm, R., & Turner, B. (2003b). Using risk to balance agile and plan-driven methods. *Computer*, *36*(6), 57–66. doi:10.1109/MC.2003.1204376

Bouray, R. P., & Richards, G. E. (2018). Accounting for external-use software development costs in an agile environment. *Journal of Accountancy*. Retrieved August 12, 2020, from https://www.journalofaccountancy.com/news/2018/mar/accounting-for-external-use-software-development-costs-201818259.html

Brightwell, I. (2017). *Is a 'fixed price' agile contract possible?* Retrieved February 5, 2020, from http://web.b.ebscohost.com/ehost/detail/detail?vid=7&sid+afafbb04-744b-4f89-a249-1523bfdd2f41%sessionmgr102&bdata=JnNpdGU9ZWhvc3QtbG12ZSZzY29wZT1zaXR1#AN=124565087&db=bth

Brown, A. L. (1992). Design experiments: Theoretical and methodological challenges in creating complex interventions in classroom settings. *Journal of the Learning Sciences*, *2*(2), 141–178. doi:10.120715327809jls0202_2

Brown, S., & Vaughan, C. (2010). *Play: How it shapes the brain, opens the imagination, and invigorates the soul*. Penguin.

Budner, S. (1962). Intolerance of ambiguity as a personality variable. *Journal of Personality*, *30*(1), 29–50. doi:10.1111/j.1467-6494.1962.tb02303.x PMID:13874381

Burden, A., Ouderaa, E. V., Venkataraman, R., Nystrom, T., & Shukla, P. P. (2018, June 19). *Technical Debt Might Be Hindering Your Digital Transformation*. Retrieved August 12, 2020, from https://sloanreview.mit.edu/article/technical-debt-might-be-hindering-your-digital-transformation/

Burrell, L., & Gherson, D. (2018). Co-creating the Employee Experience: A Conversation with Diane Gherson, IBM's Head of HR. *Harvard Business Review*, *96*(2), 54–58.

Cantoni, L., Botturi, L., Faré, M., & Bolchini, D. (2009). Playful holistic support to HCI requirements using LEGO bricks. In *International Conference on Human Centered Design* (pp. 844-853): (pp. 844-853). Springer. 10.1007/978-3-642-02806-9_97

Cappelli, P. (2015). Why we love to hate HR... and what HR can do about it. *Harvard Business Review, 93*(7/8), 54–61.

Cappelli, P., & Tavis, A. (2018). HR goes agile. *Harvard Business Review, 96*(2), 46–52.

Carr, N. G. (2003). IT doesn't matter. *Harvard Business Review, 81*(5), 41–49. PMID:12747161

Castillo, F. (2016). Agile-Scrum Project Management. In *Managing Information Technology* (pp. 199–210). Springer.

Chamorro-Premuzic, T. (2015). Ace the assessment. *Harvard Business Review, 93*(7/8), 118–121.

Chand, K. (2016). *What is Agile contracting methodology?* Retrieved February 5, 2020, from https://www.lexology.com/library/detail.aspx?g=b96675c0-6e23-47cb-be8b-e3cc0966250e

ChandrasekharanA. (2018). *Transformation Fatigue.* Retrieved from https://www.agilealliance.org/resources/sessions/the-inevitability-of-enterprise-agile-transformation-fatigue-how-do-you-reset-2/

Chan, Y., & Reich, B. (2007). IT alignment: What have we learned. *Journal of Information Technology, 22*(4), 297–315. doi:10.1057/palgrave.jit.2000109

City, S. L. (2009). *Scrum Lego City.* Retrieved from https://www.agile42.com/en/training/scrum-lego-city/

Clemente, A., Ribeiro, F., de Paula da Silva, O. A., & Mendonça Oliveira, N. (2019). Analysis of Contents of Annual Sustainability Reports of Industrial Companies Participating in the Sustainability Index of the Brazilian Stock Exchange. *Brazilian Journal of Management / Revista de Administração Da UFSM, 12*, 1211–1226. https://doi-org.ezproxy.uno.edu/10.5902/1983465937995

Clem, J. M., Mennicke, A. M., & Beasley, C. (2014). Development and validation of the experiential learning survey. *Journal of Social Work Education, 50*(3), 490–506. doi:10.1080/10437797.2014.917900

Cobb, P., Confrey, J., diSess, A., Lehrer, R., & Schauble, L. (2003). Design Experiments in Educational Research. *Educational Researcher, 32*(1), 9–13. doi:10.3102/0013189X032001009

Cockburn, A. & Williams, L. (2003). Agile software development: it's about feedback and change. *IEEE Computer, 36*(6), 39–43.

Cockburn, A. (2008). *Crystal Methodologies.* http://alistair.cockburn.us/

Cockburn, A., & Highsmith, J. (2001). Agile software development: The people factor. *IEEE Computer, 34*(11), 131–133. doi:10.1109/2.963450

Codington-Lacerte, C. (2018). *Agile software development.* Salem Press Encyclopedia.

Cohn, M. (2009). *Succeeding with Agile.* Addison-Wesley Professional. https://learning.oreilly.com/library/view/succeeding-with-agile/9780321660534/?ar=#toc

Collins, A. (1992). Towards a design science of education. In E. Scanlon & T. O'Shea (Eds.), New Directions in Educational Technology. Springer Science & Business Media. doi:10.1007/978-3-642-77750-9_2

Comella-Dorda, S., Garg, L., Thareja, S., & Vasquez-McCall, B. (2019). *Revisiting agile teams after an abrupt shift to remote.* Retrieved August 23, 2020 from https://wwww.mckinsey.com/business-functions/organization/our-insights/revisiting-agile-teams-after-an-abrupt-shift-to-remote#

Conboy, K. (2009). Agility from first principles: Reconstructing the concept of agility in information systems development. *Information Systems Research*, *20*(3), 329–354. doi:10.1287/isre.1090.0236

Conboy, K., Coyle, S., Wang, X., & Pikkarainen, M. (2011). People over Process: Key Challenges in Agile Development. *IEEE Software*, *28*(4), 48–57. doi:10.1109/MS.2010.132

Conboy, K., Gleasure, R., & Cullina, E. (2015). Agile Design Science Research. In B. Donnellan, M. Helfert, J. Kenneally, D. VanderMeer, M. Rothenberger, & R. Winter (Eds.), *New Horizons in Design Science: Broadening the Research Agenda. LNCS. 9073* (pp. 168–180). Springer.

Conboy, K., & Morgan, L. (2011). Beyond the customer: Opening the agile systems development process. *Information and Software Technology*, *53*(5), 535–542. doi:10.1016/j.infsof.2010.10.007

Cooper, H. (2020). *Summer learning loss: The problem and some solutions*. Retrieved July 04, 2020, from http://www.ldonline.org/article/8057/

Cooper, R. G., & Sommer, A. F. (2016). From experience: The agile-stage-gate hybrid model: A promising new approach and a new research opportunity. *Journal of Product Innovation Management*, *33*(5).

Costa, C. (2020). *Software development agreements: Polar Pro Filters Inc. v. Frogslayer LLC*. Retrieved August 17, 2020, from http://ccosta.com/index.php/2020/05/03/software-development-agreements-polar-pro-filters-inc-v-frogslayer-llc-2/

Crawford, C. B. (2011). Ethics and Ethos in Financial Reporting: Analyzing Persuasive Language in Earnings Calls. *Business Communication Quarterly*, *74*(3), 298–312. doi:10.1177/1080569911413810

Crispin, L., & Gregory, J. (2009). *Agile Testing: a Practical Guide for Testers and Agile Teams*. Addison-Wesley Professional.

Crosby, P. (2019). *How to recognize and prevent Transformation Fatigue*. Retrieved from https://theuncommonleague.com/blog/transformation-fatigue

Crotty, J., & Horrocks, I. (2017). Managing legacy system costs: A case study of a meta-assessment model to identify solutions in a large financial services company. *Applied Computung and Informatics*, *13*(2), 175–183. doi:10.1016/j.aci.2016.12.001

Csikszentmihalyi, M. (1990). *Flow: The Psychology Of Optimal Experience*. Perennial Modern Classics.

Cubric, M. (2013). An agile method for teaching agile in business schools. *International Journal of Management Education*, *11*(3), 119–131. doi:10.1016/j.ijme.2013.10.001

Cunningham, W. (2001). *Agile Manifesto, 2001*. http://www.agilemanifesto.org

Curtis, B., Krasner, H., & Iscoe, N. (1988). A field study of the software design process for large systems. *Communications of the ACM*, *31*(11), 1268–1287. doi:10.1145/50087.50089

Darrin, M. A. G., & Devereux, W. S. (2017). The Agile Manifesto, design thinking and systems engineering. *2017 Annual IEEE International Systems Conference (SysCon)*, 1-5. 10.1109/SYSCON.2017.7934765

Dataitlaw. (2019). *5 basic legal issues of agile software development*. Retrieved February 4, 2020, from https://www.dataitlaw.com/5-basic-legal-issues-of-agile-software-development/

De Smet, A., Lurie, M., & St George, A. (2018). *Leading Agile Transformation: The new capabilities leaders need to build 21ˢᵗ Century Organisations*. McKinsey & Company.

Deemer, P., Benefield, G., Larman, C., & Vodde, B. (2012). A lightweight guide to the theory and practice of Scrum-Scrum. *Ver, 2,* 2012.

Definition of Agile. (n.d.). Retrieved February 11, 2020, from https://www.dictionary.com/browse/agile?s=t

Dekkers, J., & Donatti, S. (1981). The integration of research studies on the use of simulation as an instructional strategy. *The Journal of Educational Research, 74*(6), 424–427. doi:10.1080/00220671.1981.10885343

Delhij, A., Van Solingen, R., & Wijnands, W. (2015). *The eduScrum guide, the rules of the game.* Version 1.2 - September 2015, Reviewed by: Jeff Sutherland.

DemingE. (1982). Retrieved from https://deming.org/quotes

Denning, S. (2019). *The five biggest challenges facing Agile.* www.forbes.com

Dennis, A., Wixom, B. H., & Roth, R. M. (2018). *Systems Analysis and Design* (7th ed.). John Wiley.

Devedzic, V., & Milenković, S. R. (2011). Teaching agile software development: A case study. *IEEE Transactions on Education, 54*(2), 273–278. doi:10.1109/TE.2010.2052104

Donovan, J., & Benko, C. (2016). AT&T's talent overhaul. *Harvard Business Review,* 68–73.

Dowling, G. R., & Kabanoff, B. (1996). Computer-Aided Content Analysis: What Do 240 Advertising Slogans Have in Common? *Marketing Letters, 7*(1), 63–75. doi:10.1007/BF00557312

Druskat, V., & Wheeler, J. (2001). Managing from the boundary: The effective leadership of self-managing work teams. *Academy of Management Annual Meeting Proceedings.* 10.5465/apbpp.2001.6133637

Dubey, A., Jain, A., & Mantri, A. (2015, March). Comparative study: Waterfall v/s agile model. *International Journal of Engineering Sciences & Research Technology, 4*(3). http://www.ijesrt.com

Dutton, G. (2018). Choosing the right agile strategy. *Training (New York, N.Y.),* 34–36. Retrieved February 10, 2020, from http://pubs.royle.com/publication/?i=482831&p=36#{%22page%22:%2236%22,%22issue_id%22:482831,%22publication_id%22:%2220617%22}

Dweck, C. S., & Leggett, E. L. (1988). A social-cognitive approach to motivation and personality. *Psychological Review, 95*(2), 256–273. doi:10.1037/0033-295X.95.2.256

Dybå, T., Dingsøyr, T., & Moe, N. B. (2014). Agile project management. In Software Project Management in a Changing World. Springer-Verlag. doi:10.1007/978-3-642-55035-5_11

Dybå, T., & Dingsøyr, T. (2015). Agile project management: from self-managing teams to large-scale development. *Proceedings of 2015 IEEE/ACM 37th IEEE International Conference on Software Engineering (ICSE),* 945-946. 10.1109/ICSE.2015.299

Edwards, I., Bickerstaff, R., & Bartsch, C. (n.d.). *Bird & Bird & contracting for agile software development projects.* Retrieved February 6, 2020, from https://www.twobirds.com/~/media/pdfs/brochures/contracting-for-agile-software-development-projects.pdf?la=en

Eisenberg, M. A. (2009). The role of fault in contract law: Unconscionability, unexpected circumstances, interpretation, mistake, and performance. *Michigan Law Review, 107,* 1413–1430.

Erickson, S. L., Weber, M., & Segovia, J. (2011). Using Communication Theory to Analyze Corporate Reporting Strategies. *Journal of Business Communication, 48*(2), 207–223. doi:10.1177/0021943611399728

Faraj, S., & Azad, B. (2012). The materiality of technology: An affordance perspective. *Materiality and organizing: Social interaction in a technological world*, 237-258.

Fe, S. A. (2019). *Principle #6 – Visualize and limit WIP, reduce batch sizes, and manage queue lengths*. Retrieved from https://www.scaledagileframework.com/visualize-and-limit-wip-reduce-batch-sizes-and-manage-queue-lengths/

Fernandes, J. M., & Sousa, S. M. (2010, March). Playscrum-a card game to learn the scrum agile method. In *2010 Second International Conference on Games and Virtual Worlds for Serious Applications* (pp. 52-59). IEEE. 10.1109/VS-GAMES.2010.24

Fernández-Aráoz, C. (2014). 21st Century Talent Spotting. *Harvard Business Review*, *92*(6), 46–56. PMID:25051855

Fernandez, D., & Fernandez, J. (2008). Agile project management – Agilism versus traditional approaches. *Journal of Computer Information Systems*, *49*(2), 10–16.

Flo-Products Co. v. Valley Farms Dairy Co. 718 S.W. 2d 207 (Ct. Appl. MO.).

Fowler, M., & Highsmith, J. (2001). Agile methodologists agree on something. *Software Development*, *9*, 28–32.

Freeman, L. A. (2003). Simulation and role playing with LEGO® blocks. *Journal of Information Systems Education*, *14*(2), 3.

Frenkel-Brunswik, E. (1948). Intolerance of ambiguity as an emotional perceptual personality variable. *Journal of Personality*, *18*(1), 108–143. doi:10.1111/j.1467-6494.1949.tb01236.x

Freud, S (1917). *A difficulty in the path of psycho-analysis*. Academic Press.

Friedman, T. L. (2014). How to get a job at Google. *The New York Times*, 22.

Friess, E. (2019). Scrum language use in a software engineering firm: An exploratory study. *IEEE Transactions on Professional Communication*, *62*(2), 130–147. doi:10.1109/TPC.2019.2911461

Gangadharan, G., Kuiper, E., Janssen, M., & Luttighuis, P. (2013). IT innovation squeeze: propositions and a methodology for deciding to continue or decommission legacy systems. In Y. K. Dwivedi, H. Z. Henriksen, D. Wastell, & R. De' (Eds.), *Grand Successes and Failures in IT. Public and Private Sectors. TDIT 2013. IFIP Advances in Information and Communication Technology, 402, 481-494*. Springer. doi:10.1007/978-3-642-38862-0_30

Gannod, G., Troy, D., Luczaj, J., & Rover, D. (2015). Agile way of educating. In *Proceedings of the 2015 IEEE Frontiers in Education Conference (FIE)*. 10.1109/FIE.2015.7344019

Garel, G. (2013). A history of project management models: From pre-models to the standard models. *International Journal of Project Management*, *31*(5), 663–669. doi:10.1016/j.ijproman.2012.12.011

Garud, R. (1997). On the distinction between know-how, know-what, and know-why. *Advances in Strategic Management*, *14*, 81–102.

Gauntlett, D. (2007). *Creative exploration—New approaches to identities and audiences*. Routledge. doi:10.4324/9780203961407

Gieles, H., & van der Meer, W. (2017). *Talent management as the beating heart of an Agile Organization*. Academic Press.

Gill, A. Q. (2014). Hybrid adaptive software development capability: An empirical study. *Journal of Software*, *9*(10), 2614–2621. doi:10.4304/jsw.9.10.2614-2621

Gkritsi, A. (2011). *Scrum Game: an agile software management game* (Doctoral dissertation). University of Southampton.

Goleman, D. (1995). *Emotional Intelligence: Why it can matter more than IQ*. Bantom Books.

Gonçalves, E. F., Drumond, G. M., & Méxas, M. P. (2017). Evaluation of PMBOK and Scrum practices for software development in the vision of specialists. *Independent Journal of Management & Production, 8*(5), 569–580. doi:10.14807/ijmp.v8i5.598

Gren, L., Torkar, R., & Feldt, R. (2017). Group development and Group Maturity when building Agile teams: A qualitative and quantitative investigation at Eight large companies. *Journal of Systems and Software, 124*(Feb), 104–119. doi:10.1016/j.jss.2016.11.024

Guo, S., Tong, W., Zhang, J., & Liu, Z. (2011). An Application of Ontology to Test Case Reuse. *International Conference on Mechatronic Science, Electrical Engineering and Computer*.

Gupta, M., George, J. F., & Xia, W. (2019). Relationships between IT department culture and agile software development practices: An empirical investigation. *International Journal of Information Management, 44*, 13–24. doi:10.1016/j.ijinfomgt.2018.09.006

Gurusamy, K., Srinivasaraghavan, N., & Adikari, S. (2016). An Integrated Framework for Design Thinking and Agile Methods for Digital Transformation. In A. Marcus (Ed.), *Design, User Experience, and Usability: Design Thinking and Methods. LNCS 9746* (pp. 34–42). Springer., doi:10.1007/978-3-319-40409-7_4

Hamer v. Sidway 124 N.Y. 538, 27 N.E. 256 (Ct. App. N. Y.).

Handscombe, C., Allan, J., Khushpreet, K., Belkis, V., & Ahmad, Z. (2018). *How to mess up your Agile Transformation in 7 easy (mis) steps*. Retrieved from https://www.mckinsey.com/business-functions/organization/our-insights/how-to-mess-up-your-agile-transformation-in-seven-easy-missteps

Hassett, J., & Burke, E. (2017). Why the agile approach is so important to law firms. *Of Council, 36*(10), 6-9.

Hastie, S., & Engineer, C. K. (2004). The Agile Mindset: what does it take to make this stuff work? Software Education Associates Ltd.

Hayat, F., Rehman, A. U., Arif, K. S., Wahab, K., & Abbas, M. (2019). *The influence of agile methodology (Scrum) on software project management*. IEEE Computer Society.

Hayat, F., Rehman, A. U., Arif, K. S., Wahab, K., & Abbas, M. (2019). The Influence of Agile Methodology (Scrum) on Software Project Management. In *2019 20th IEEE/ACIS International Conference on Software Engineering, Artificial Intelligence, Networking and Parallel/Distributed Computing (SNPD)* (pp. 145-149). IEEE.

Hayat, F., Rehman, A. U., Arif, K. S., Wahab, K., & Abbas, M. (2019, July). The Influence of Agile Methodology (Scrum) on Software Project Management. In *2019 20th IEEE/ACIS International Conference on Software Engineering, Artificial Intelligence, Networking and Parallel/Distributed Computing (SNPD)* (pp. 145-149). IEEE.

Herold, D. M., & Parsons, C. K. (1985). Assessing the feedback environment in work organizations: Development of the job feedback survey. *The Journal of Applied Psychology, 70*(2), 290–305. doi:10.1037/0021-9010.70.2.290

Heslin, P. A., & VandeWalle, D. (2010). Performance appraisal procedural justice: The role of a manager's implicit person theory. *Journal of Management, 12*, 1201–1214.

Heslin, P., Latham, G., & VandeWalle, D. (2005). The effect of implicit person theory on performance appraisals. *The Journal of Applied Psychology, 90*(5), 842–856. doi:10.1037/0021-9010.90.5.842 PMID:16162058

Heslin, P., Vandewalle, D., & Latham, G. (2006). Keen to help? Managers' implicit person theories and their subsequent employee coaching. *Personnel Psychology, 59*(4), 871–902. doi:10.1111/j.1744-6570.2006.00057.x

Hevner, A. R., March, S. T., Park, J., & Ram, S. (2004). Design Science in Information Systems Research. *Management Information Systems Quarterly*, *28*(1), 75–105. doi:10.2307/25148625

Highsmith, J. (2002). What Is agile software development? *Crosstalk*, *15*(10), 4–9.

Highsmith, J. (2013). *Adaptive software development: A collaborative approach to managing complex systems*. Addison-Wesley.

Hobbs, B., & Petit, Y. (2017). Agile methods on large projects in large organizations. *Project Management Journal*, *48*(3), 3–19. doi:10.1177/875697281704800301

Holiday, R. (2016). *5 Deadly Kinds of Ego That Prey Upon Your Success*. Retrieved from https://www.entrepreneur.com/article/276972

Hron, M., & Obwegeser, N. (2018). Scrum in practice: an overview of Scrum adaptations. *Proceedings of the 51st Hawaii International Conference on System Sciences*. 10.24251/HICSS.2018.679

Hsia, H. C. (2018). *Common Misinterpretations of Scrum*. Retrieved from https://www.scrum.org/resources/blog/common-misinterpretations-scrum

Huang, X., Krishnan, S., & Lin, P. (2018). Tone Analysis and Earnings Management. *Journal of Accounting & Finance*, *18*(8), 46–61. https://doi-org.ezproxy.uno.edu/10.33423/jaf.v18i8.110

IBM. (2018). *Agile, meet design thinking*. https://www.ibm.com/downloads/cas/7KL6JLMJ

Ihme, T. (2012). *Scrum adoption and architectural extensions in developing new service applications of large financial IT systems*. The Brazilian Computer Society. doi:10.100713173-012-0096-0

Ionel, N. (2009). Agile software development methodologies: An overview of the current state of research. *Annals of Faculty of Economics*, *4*(1).

Ipate, F., & Holcombe, M. (1997). An integration testing method that is proved to find all faults. *International Journal of Computer Mathematics*, *63*(3-4), 159–178. doi:10.1080/00207169708804559

Jalote, P., & Jain, G. (2006). Assigning tasks in a 24-hours software development model. *Journal of Systems and Software*, *79*(7), 904–911. doi:10.1016/j.jss.2005.06.040

James, A. (2013). Lego Serious Play: a three-dimensional approach to learning development. *Journal of Learning Development in Higher Education*, (6).

James, A., & Nerantzi, C. (Eds.). (2019). *The Power of Play in Higher Education: Creativity in tertiary learning*. Springer. doi:10.1007/978-3-319-95780-7

Jarvenpaa, S., & Ives, B. (1990). Information technology and corporate strategy: A view from the top. *Information Systems Research*, *I*, 4, 351–375.

Jeong, K.-Y., & Bozkurt, I. (2014). Evaluating a project management simulation training exercise. *Simulation & Gaming*, *45*(2), 183–203. doi:10.1177/1046878113518481

Jiang, L., & Eberlein, A. (2009). An analysis of the history of classical software development and agile development. *IEEE International Conference on Systems, Man, and Cybernetics*. 10.1109/ICSMC.2009.5346888

Jilin, C., Hneif, M., & Ow, S. H. (2009). Review of Agile Methodologies in Software Development 1. *International Journal of Research and Reviews in Applied Sciences*, *1*(1), 2076–73. doi:10.1109/MEC.2011.6025579

Job, J. (2019). *7 Vital Differences between Agile Adoption and Agile Transformation.* Retrieved from https://responsiveadvisors.com/blog

Johnson, J., & Mulder, H. (2017). *Big, Bang, Boom Revisited: Why large projects fail, A case study research of NPAC.* www.standishgroup.com/sample-research-files/BBB2017-Final-2.pdf

Joiner, B., & Josephs, S. (2007). *Developing Agile leaders.* www.researchgate.net/publication/242157752

Jovanovic, P., & Beric, I. (2018). Analysis of the available project management methodologies," management. *Journal of Sustainable Business and Management Solutions in Emerging Economies, 23*(3), 1. doi:10.7595/management.fon.2018.0027

Jrad, R. B. N., & Sundaram, D. (2015). Challenges of inter-organizational information and middleware system projects: Agility, complexity, success, and failure. *6th International Conference on Information, Intelligence, Systems and Applications (IISA).* 10.1109/IISA.2015.7387960

Kaczor, K. (2019). *Agile leadership in and beyond the Scrum team(s).* Scrum.org white paper.

Kaleshovska, N., Josimovski, S., Pulevska-Ivanovska, L., Postolov, K., & Janecski, Z. (2015). The contribution of SCRUM in managing successful software development projects. *Economic Development / Ekonomiski Razvoj, 17*(1/2), 175-194.

Kanth, S. K. (2009). Agile methodology in product testing. *Journal of the Quality Assurance Institute, 23*(1), 18–23.

Keijzer-Broers, W., & de Reuver, M. (2016). *Applying Agile Design Sprint Methods in Action Design Research: Prototyping a Health and Wellbeing Platform* (Vol. 9661). Springer.

Kelly, A. (2004). Design Research in Education: Yes, but is it Methodological? *Journal of the Learning Sciences, 13*(1), 115–128. doi:10.120715327809jls1301_6

Kenton, W. (2020). *Hersey – Blanchard Model.* www.investopedia.com

Khan, P. M., & Beg, M. M. S. (2012). Measuring cost of quality (CoQ) on SDLC Projects is indispensable for effective software quality assurance. *International Journal of Soft computing and Software Engineering, 2*(9). doi:10.7321/jscse.v2.n9.1

Khmelevsky, Y., Li, X., & Madnick, S. (2017). Software development using agile and Scrum in distributed teams. *2017 Annual IEEE International Systems Conference (SysCon)*, 1–4. 10.1109/SYSCON.2017.7934766

Kimbell, L. (2011). Rethinking design thinking: Part I. *Design and Culture, 3*(3), 285–306. doi:10.2752/175470811X13071166525216

Kluger, A. N., & DeNisi, A. (1996). The effects of feedback interventions on performance: A historical review, a meta-analysis, and a preliminary feedback intervention theory. *Psychological Bulletin, 119*(2), 254–284. doi:10.1037/0033-2909.119.2.254

Kneuper, R. (2017). *Sixty years of software development life cycle models. IEEE Annals of the History of Computing.*

Ko, D.-G., & Kirsch, L. J. (2017). The hybrid IT project manager: One foot each in the IT and business domains. *International Journal of Project Management, 35*(3), 307–319. doi:10.1016/j.ijproman.2017.01.013

Koh, J. H. L., Chai, C. S., Wong, B., & Hong, H. Y. (2015). *Design Thinking for Education: Conceptions and applications in teaching and learning.* Springer.

Kolb, A. Y., & Kolb, D. A. (2005). Learning styles and learning spaces: Enhancing experiential learning in higher education. *Academy of Management Learning & Education, 4*(2), 193–212. doi:10.5465/amle.2005.17268566

Kolb, A. Y., & Kolb, D. A. (2010). Learning to play, playing to learn: A case study of a ludic learning space. *Journal of Organizational Change Management, 23*(1), 26–50. doi:10.1108/09534811011017199

Kolb, D. A. (2014). *Experiential Learning: Experience as the Source of Learning and Development*. FT Press.

Kortum, F., Klunder, J., & Schneider, K. (2019). Behaviour driven dynamics in Agile Development: The effect of fast feedback on teams. *International Conference on Software and Systems Process*, Montreal, Canada.

Kristiansen, P., & Rasmussen, R. (2014). *Building a better business using the lego serious play method*. John Wiley & Sons.

Kristof-Brown, A. L., Zimmerman, R. D., & Johnson, E. C. (2005). Consequences of Individuals'' Fit at Work: A Meta-Analysis of Person–Job, Person–Organization, Person–Group, and Person–Supervisor Fit. *Personnel Psychology, 58*(2), 281–342. doi:10.1111/j.1744-6570.2005.00672.x

Krivitsky, A. (2017). *lego4scrum 3.0 - A Complete Guide to lego4scrum - A great way to teach the Scrum framework and Agile thinking*. https://leanpub.com/

Laakkonen, K. (2014). *Contracts in agile software development*. Aalto University School of Science.

Labs, P. (2015). *State of DevOps 2015 Report*. IT Revolution Press. https://puppet.com/resources/white-paper/2015-state-of-devops-report

Lacity, M. C., & Janson, M. A. (1994). Understanding Qualitative Data: A Framework of Text Analysis Methods. *Journal of Management Information Systems, 11*(2), 137–155. doi:10.1080/07421222.1994.11518043

Laplante, P. A., & Neill, C. J. (2004). "The demise of the Waterfall model is Imminent" and other urban myths. *ACM Queue; Tomorrow's Computing Today, 1*(10), 10–15. doi:10.1145/971564.971573

Larman, C. (2003). *Agile and Iterative Development: A Manager's Guide*. Addison-Wesley.

Larusdottir, M., Cajander, A., & Gulliksen, J. (2014). Informal feedback rather than performance measurements – User-centred evaluation. *Behaviour & Information Technology, 33*(11), 1118–1135. doi:10.1080/0144929X.2013.857430

Law, E., & Larusdottir, M. (2015). Whose Experience Do We Care About? Analysis of the Fitness of ScrumScrum and Kanban to User Experience. *International Journal of Human-Computer Interaction, 31*(9), 584–602. doi:10.1080/10447318.2015.1065693

Lean, C. X. (2019). *What is Servant Leadership in Agile Project Management?* www.leancxscore.com

Leau, Y. B., Loo, W. K., Tham, W. Y., & Tan, S. F. (2012). Software development life cycle agile vs. traditional approaches. *2012 International Conference on Information and Network Technology (ICINT 2012), 37*, 162-167.

Lee, G., & Xia, W. (2010). Toward Agile: An integrated analysis of quantitative and qualitative field data on software development agility. *Management Information Systems Quarterly, 34*(1), 87–114. doi:10.2307/20721416

Lee, S., & Young, H. (2013). Agile Software Development Framework in a Small Project Environment. *Journal of Information Systems, 9*(1).

Leffingwell, D. (2012). *Agile Software Requirements: Lean Requirements Practices for Teams, Programs, and the Enterprise*. Pearson Education.

Legal Executive Institute, & Reuters, T. (2017). *US companies vastly outspend rest of the world on legal services, Acritas study shows*. Retrieved August 11, 2020, from https://www.legalexecutiveinstitute.com/acritas-legal-services-spending-study/#:~:text=US%20companies%20spend%20a%20whopping,new%20study%20by%20Acritas%20Research

Legal Information Institute. (2002). *UCC article 2 – Sales*. Retrieved February 11, 2020, from https://www.law.cornell.edu/ucc/index.html

Léger, P.-M. (2006). *Using a Simulation Game Approach to Teach Enterprise Resource Planning Concepts*. HEC Montréal, Groupe de recherche en systèmes d'information. Retrieved from http://proxy2.hec.ca/login?url=http:// proquest.umi.com/pqdweb?did=1211107151&Fmt=7&clientId=10342&RQT=309&VName=PQD

Lei, H., Ganjeizadeh, F., Jayachandran, P. K., & Ozcan, P. (2017). A statistical analysis of the effects of Scrum and Kanban on software development projects. *Robotics and Computer-integrated Manufacturing*, *43*, 59–67. doi:10.1016/j.rcim.2015.12.001

Li, P. (2015). JIRA Essentials: Use the features of JIRA to manage projects and effectively handle bugs and software issues (3rd ed.). Packt Publishing.

Li, E. Y. (1990). Software testing in aa system development process: A life cycle perspective. *Journal of Systems Management*, *41*(8), 23–31.

Lin, C. P., Joe, S. W., Chen, S. C., & Wang, H. J. (2015). Better to be flexible than to have flunked. *Journal of Service Management*, *26*(5), 823–843. doi:10.1108/JOSM-08-2014-0201

Lindvall, M., Muthig, D., Dagnino, A., Wallin, C., Stupperich, M., Kiefer, D., May, J., & Kahkonen, T. (2004). Agile Software Development in Large Organizations. *IEEE Computer Society*, *4*(12), 26–34. doi:10.1109/MC.2004.231

Livni, E. (2018). *I was a contract worker in Google's caste system—and it wasn't pretty*. Retrieved from https://finance.yahoo.com/news/contract-worker-google-caste-system-144104055.html

Lock, D. (2019). *14 symptoms of change fatigue*. Retrieved from https://daniellock.com/14-symptoms-of-change-fatigue/

Louisiana Civil Code. (n.d.). *Title iv – Conventional obligations or contracts*. Retrieved February 11, 2020, from https://lcco.law.lsu.edu/?uid=73&ver=en

Lukasiewicz, K., & Miler, J. (2012). Improving agility and discipline of software development with the Scrum and CMMI. *Institute of Engineering and Technology*, *6*(5), 416–422.

Luthans, F., & Stajkovic, A. D. (1999). Reinforce for performance: The need to go beyond pay and even rewards. *The Academy of Management Perspectives*, *13*(2), 49–57. doi:10.5465/ame.1999.1899548

Lynch, W. (2019). *The brief history of Scrum*. Retrieved August 21, 2020, from https://medium.com/@warren2lynch/the-brief-of-history-of-scrum-15efb73b4701#:~:text=Jeff%20Sutherland%20originated%20the%20first,a%20formal%20process%20in%201995

Maassen, M. A. (2018). Opportunities and risks of the agile software development management in the IT field. Case study: IT companies between 2009-2018. *Review of International Comparative Management*, *19*(3), 234–243. doi:10.24818/RMCI.2018.3.234

Mackay, J. (2019). *Context switching can kill up to 80% of your productive time (here's what to do about it)*. Retrieved from https://blog.rescuetime.com/context-switching/

Mahadevan, L., Kettinger, W., & Meservy, T. (2015). Running on hybrid: Control changes when introducing an Agile methodology in a traditional "Waterfall" system development environment. *Communications of the Association for Information Systems*, *36*(5). Advance online publication. doi:10.17705/1CAIS.03605

Mahajan, A. (2013). *The importance of HR in agile adoption*. Scrum Alliance. https://www.scrumalliance.org/community/articles/2013/january/the-importance-ofhr-in-agile-adoption

Mahanti, A. (2006). Challenges in Enterprise adoption of agile methods – a survey. *Journal of Computing and Information Technology – CIT*, 197-206.

Mall, R. (2006). *Fundamental of Software Engineering* (2nd ed.). Prentice Hall.

Mann, R. A., & Roberts, B. S. (2014). *Business law and the regulation of business* (11th ed.). Southwestern, Cengage Learning.

March, S. T., & Storey, V. C. (2008). Design science in the information systems discipline: An introduction to the special issue on design science research. *Management Information Systems Quarterly*, *32*(4), 725–730. doi:10.2307/25148869

Marriott, E. (2016). *The history of the world in bite-sized chunks*. London, UK: Michael O'Hara Books Limited.

Martin, A. (2000). A simulation engine for custom project management education. *International Journal of Project Management*, *18*(3), 201–213. doi:10.1016/S0263-7863(99)00014-9

Maruping, L. M., Venkatesh, V., & Agarwal, R. (2009). A control theory perspective on Agile methodology use and changing user requirements. *Information Systems Research*, *20*(3), 377-399.

Maruping, L. M., Venkatesh, V., & Agarwal, R. (2009). A control theory perspective on agile methodology use and changing user requirements. *Information Systems Research*, *20*(3), 377–399. doi:10.1287/isre.1090.0238

Maruping, L., & Matook, S. (forthcoming). The Multiplex Nature of the Customer Representative Role in Agile Information Systems Development. *Management Information Systems Quarterly*.

Masa'deh, R., Tarhini, A., Al-Dmour, R. H., & Obeidat, B. Y. (2015). Strategic IT-business alignment as managers' explorative and exploitative strategies. *European Scientific Journal*, *11*(7), 438–457.

Masood, Z., Hoda, R., & Blincoe, K. (2018). Adapting Agile Practices in University Contexts. *Journal of Systems and Software*, *144*, 501–510. doi:10.1016/j.jss.2018.07.011

Mathur, G., Jugdev, K., & Fung, T. S. (2013). Project management assets and project management performance outcomes. *Management Research Review*, *36*(2), 112–135. doi:10.1108/01409171311292234

Matook, S., & Maruping, L. (2014). A Competency Model for Customer Representatives in Agile Software Development Projects. *MIS Quarterly Executive*, *13*(2). https://aisel.aisnet.org/misqe/vol13/iss2/3

Matturro, G., Cordovés, F., & Solari, M. (2018). role of Product Owner from the practitioner's perspective. An exploratory study. *Proceedings of the International Conference on Software Engineering Research and Practice (SERP)*, 113–118.

Mautz, S. (2019). *These 5 Toxic Factors Cause People to Quit Even Before They Have Another Job, According to a Recent Study*. Retrieved from https://www.inc.com

May, J., York, J., & Lending, D. (2016). Play ball: Bringing scrum into the classroom. *Journal of Information Systems Education*, *27*(2), 1.

May, J., York, J., & Lending, D. (2016). Teaching tip: Play ball: Bringing Scrum into the classroom. *Journal of Information Systems Education*, *27*(2), 87–92.

Mayrhauser, A., France, R., Scheetz, M., & Dahlman, E. (2000). Generating test-cases from an object-oriented model with an artificial-intelligence planning system. Reliability. *IEEE Transactions on.*, *49*, 26–36. doi:10.1109/24.855534

McAvoy, J., & Sammon, D. (2005). Agile methodology adoption decisions: An innovative approach to teaching and learning. *Journal of Information Systems Education*, *16*(4), 409.

McCord, P. (2014). How Netflix Reinvented HR: Trust People, Not Policies. Reward Candor and Throwaway the Standard Playbook. *Harvard Business Review, 90*(3), 71–76.

McCreery, J. K. (2003). Assessing the value of a project management simulation training exercise. *International Journal of Project Management, 21*(4), 233–242. doi:10.1016/S0263-7863(02)00026-1

McGregor, L., & Doshi, N. (2018). Why Agile goes awry – and how to fix it. *Harvard Business Review*. Retrieved February 10, 2020, from https://hbr.org/2018/10/why-agile-goes-awry-and-how-to-fix-it

McKenney, S., & Reeves, T. C. (2014). Educational design research. In *Handbook of research on educational communications and technology* (pp. 131–140). Springer. doi:10.1007/978-1-4614-3185-5_11

Medeiros, D. B., Neto, P. D. A. D. S., Passos, E. B., & De Souza Araújo, W. (2015). Working and playing with Scrum. *International Journal of Software Engineering and Knowledge Engineering, 25*(06), 993–1015. doi:10.1142/S021819401550014X

Melles, G., Anderson, N., Barrett, T., & Thompson-Whiteside, S. (2015). Problem Finding through Design Thinking in Education. In P. Blessinger & J.M. Carfora (Eds.), Inquiry-Based Learning for Multidisciplinary Programs: A Conceptual and Practical Resource for Educators (Innovations in Higher Education Teaching and Learning, Volume 3) (pp.191-209). Bingley, UK: Emerald. doi:10.1108/S2055-364120150000003027

Mendoza, I., Kalinowski, M., Souza, U., & Felderer, M. (2019, January). Relating verification and validation methods to software product quality characteristics: results of an expert survey. In *International Conference on Software Quality* (pp. 33-44). Springer. 10.1007/978-3-030-05767-1_3

Meredith, J. R., Shafer, S. M., & Mantel, S. J. Jr. (2018). *Project management: a strategic managerial approach* (10th ed.). John Wiley & Sons, Inc.

Merriam-Webster.com Dictionary. (n.d.a). *Culture* Retrieved from https://www.merriam-webster.com/dictionary/culture

Merriam-Webster.com Dictionary. (n.d.b). *Fatigue.* Retrieved from https://www.merriam-webster.com/dictionary/fatigue

Mersino, A. (2018). *Agile leaders' role during an Agile transformation.* www.vitalitychicago.com/blog/what-leaders-role-agile-transformation

Mersino, A. (2019). *Most Agile Transformations Will Fail.* Retrieved from https://vitalitychicago.com/blog/most-agile-transformations-will-fail/

Meyer, B. (2018). Making sense of agile methods. *IEEE Software, 35*(2), 91–94. doi:10.1109/MS.2018.1661325

Michael, J. (2006). Where's the evidence that active learning works? *Advances in Physiology Education, 30*(4), 159–167. doi:10.1152/advan.00053.2006 PMID:17108243

Miller, S. (2015). *Ten things you need to know as in-house counsel.* Retrieved August 11, 2020, from https://sterling-miller2014.wordpress.com/2015/07/07/ten-things-explaining-litigation-to-the-board-and-the-ceo/

Mitchell, I. (2018). *Twenty Top Fails in Executive Agile Leadership.* Retrieved from https://www.scrum.org/resources/

Moe, N. B., Dingsøyr, T., & Dybå, T. (2010). A teamwork model for understanding an agile team: A case study of a Scrum project. *Information and Software Technology, 52*(5), 480–491. doi:10.1016/j.infsof.2009.11.004

Moe, N., Dingsoyr, T., & Kvangardsnes, O. (2009). Understanding Shared Leadership in Agile development: A case study. *Proceedings of 42nd Hawaii International conference on System Sciences.*

Moore, G. (1991). *Crossing the chasm.* HarperCollins Publishers.

Morgan, G. (2006). *Images of Organizations*. Sage Publications.

Mulder, H. (1994). *The Chaos Report*. Academic Press.

Muneer, S., Ahmad, R. A., & Ali, A. (2017). Impact of Financial Management Practices on SMEs Profitability with Moderating Role of Agency Cost. *Information Management and Business Review*, *9*(1), 23–30. doi:10.22610/imbr.v9i1.1593

Murphy, M. C., & Dweck, C. S. (2010). A culture of genius: How an organization's lay theory shapes people's cognition, affect, and behavior. *Personality and Social Psychology Bulletin*, *36*(3), 283–296. doi:10.1177/0146167209347380 PMID:19826076

Musser, H. (2019). *Embracing the agile mindset & Agile's core principles, the agile alliance*. Retrieved July 14. 2020, from https://www.agilealliance.org/embracing-the-agile-mindset-agiles-core-principles/

Myers, G. J. (2004). *The Art of Software Testing* (2nd ed.). John Wiley & Sons.

Nederhof, A. J. (1985). Methods of coping with social desirability bias: A review. *European Journal of Social Psychology*, *15*(3), 263–280. doi:10.1002/ejsp.2420150303

Nelson, R. R. (2007). IT project management: Infamous failures, classic mistakes, and best practices. *MIS Quarterly Executive*, *6*(2), 67–78.

Nidumolu, S. (1995). The effect of coordination and uncertainty on software project performance: Residual performance risk as an intervening variable. *Information Systems Research*, *6*(3), 191–219. doi:10.1287/isre.6.3.191

Norman, J. (2001). Design as a Framework for Innovative Thinking and Learning: How Can Design Thinking Reform Education? In E. Norman & P. Roberts (Eds.), Design and technology educational research and curriculum development: The emerging international research agenda (pp. 90-100). Loughborough University.

Onieva, J. (2018). *Scrum como estrategia para el aprendizaje colaborativo a través de proyectos. Propuesta didáctica para su implementación en el Aula Universitaria*. Revista de Currículum y Formación del Profesorado. doi:10.30827/profesorado.v22i2.7735

Oomen, S., De Waal, B., Albertin, A., & Ravesteyn, P. (2017). How can Scrum be succesful? Competences of the ScrumScrum Product Owner. *Proceedings of the European Conference on Information Systems*.

Oprins, R. J., Frijns, H. A., & Stettina, C. J. (2019, May). Evolution of Scrum Transcending Business Domains and the Future of Agile Project Management. In *International Conference on Agile Software Development* (pp. 244-259). Springer. 10.1007/978-3-030-19034-7_15

Overhage, S., & Schlauderer, S. (2012). Investigating the long-term acceptance of Agile methodologies: An empirical study of developer perceptions in SCRUM projects. *45th Hawaii International Conference on System Sciences*. 10.1109/HICSS.2012.387

Ozierańska, A., Skomra, A., Kuchta, D., & Rola, P. (2016). The critical factors of Scrum implementation in IT project – the case study. *Journal of Economics and Management*, *25*(3), 79–96. doi:10.22367/jem.2016.25.06

Ozkan, N., & Kucuk, C. (2016). A systematic approach to project-related concepts of Scrum. *Review of International Comparative Management*, *17*(4), 320–333.

Paasivaara, M., Heikkilä, V., Lassenius, C., & Toivola, T. (2014). Teaching students scrum using LEGO blocks. *Companion Proceedings of the 36th International Conference on Software Engineering*. 10.1145/2591062.2591169

Paasivaara, M., Lassenius, C., & Heikkilä, V. T. (2012). Inter-team coordination in large-scale globally distributed Scrum: Do Scrum-of-Scrums really work? *Proceedings of the ACM-IEEE International Symposium on Empirical Software Engineering and Measurement*, 235–238. 10.1145/2372251.2372294

Pal, K. (2019). Markov Decision Theory Based Crowdsourcing Software Process Model. In Crowdsourcing and Probabilistic Decision-Making in Software Engineering: Emerging Research and Opportunities. IGI Publication.

Pal, K. (2020). Framework for Reusable Test Case Generation in Software Systems Testing. In Software Engineering for Agile Application Development. IGI Global Publication.

Palmieri, R., Perrin, D., & Whitehouse, M. (2018). The Pragmatics of Financial Communication. Part 1: From Sources to the Public Sphere. *International Journal of Business Communication*, 55(2), 127–134. doi:10.1177/2329488418758449

Papert, S. A. (1990). *Mindstorms: Children, computers, and powerful ideas*. Basic Books.

Parker, D., Holesgrove, M., & Pathak, R. (2015). Improving Productivity with self-organised teams and Agile leadership. *International Journal of Productivity and Performance Management*, 64(1), 112–128. doi:10.1108/IJPPM-10-2013-0178

Parris, D., & Peachey, D. (2013). A systematic Literature review of Servant Leadership theory in Organisational Context. *Journal of Business Ethics*, 113(3), 377–393. doi:10.100710551-012-1322-6

Peabody, M. A., & Noyes, S. (2017). Reflective boot camp: Adapting LEGO® SERIOUS PLAY® in higher education. *Reflective Practice*, 18(2), 232–243. doi:10.1080/14623943.2016.1268117

Pearce, C., & Sims, H. (2002). Vertical versus Shared Leadership as Predictors of the effectiveness of change management teams: An examination of Aversive, Directive, Transactional, Transformational and Empowering leader behaviours. *Group Dynamics*, 6(2), 172–197. doi:10.1037/1089-2699.6.2.172

Peffers, K., Tuunanen, T., Rothenberger, M. A., & Chatterjee, S. (2007). A Design Science Research Methodology for Information Systems Research. *Journal of Management Information Systems*, 24(3), 45–77. doi:10.2753/MIS0742-1222240302

Peters, M. J., Howard, K., & Sharp, M. J. A. (2012). *The management of a student research project*. Gower Publishing, Ltd.

Peterson, O. (2019). *What is Fake Agile? Understanding the Dark Side of Agile and How to Avoid It*. Retrieved from https://www.process.st/fake-agile/?utm_campaign=Submission&utm_medium=Community&utm_source=GrowthHackers.com

Pike, C. (2002). Exploring the conceptual space of LEGO: Teaching and learning the psychology of creativity. *Psychology Learning & Teaching*, 2(2), 87–94. doi:10.2304/plat.2002.2.2.87

Piñero, M. L., Rondón, L. M., & Piña, V. E. (2007). *La formación de competencias transversales en y para la investigación: Una propuesta metodológica para el currículo de la UPEL-IPB. Review LAURUS. Año 13*. Viecerrectorado de Docencia. UPEL.

Poindexter, W., & Berez, S. (2017). Agile Is Not Enough. *MIT Sloan Management Review*. Retrieved from https://sloanreview.mit.edu/article/agile-is-not-enough/

Polar Pro Filters Inc. v. Frogslayer, LLC No. H-19-1706, slip op. (S. D. Tex. Oct. 22, 2019).

Pope-Ruark, R. (2015). In-troducing agile project management strategies in technical and professional communication courses. *Journal of Business and Technical Communication*, 29(1), 112–133. doi:10.1177/1050651914548456

Preimesberger, C. (2020). *Startup vantiq comes to rescue in covid-19 use cases*. Retrieved August 21, 2020, from https://www.eweek.com/innovation/startup-vantiq-comes-to-rescue-in-covid-19-use-cases

Preston, G., Moon, J., Simon, R., Allen, S., & Kossi, E. (2015). The relevance of emotional intelligence in project leadership. *Journal of Information Technology and Economic Development*, *6*(1), 16.

Prince, M. (2004). Does active learning work? A review of the research. *Journal of Engineering Education*, *93*(3), 223–231. doi:10.1002/j.2168-9830.2004.tb00809.x

Prokopets, M. (n.d.). *The 5 Scrum Values and Why They Matter*. Retrieved from https://usefyi.com

Przybilla, L., Wiesche, M., & Krcmar, H. (2019). Emergent Leadership in Agile Teams--an Initial Exploration. *SIGMIS-CPR '19*.

Qi, D., Wu, W., & Haw, I.-M. (2000). The Incremental Information Content of SEC 10-K Reports Filed under the EDGAR System. *Journal of Accounting, Auditing & Finance*, *15*(1), 25–46. doi:10.1177/0148558X0001500102

Quinn, D., & Polikoff, M. (2017). *Summer learning loss: What is it, and what can we do about it?* Retrieved July 04, 2020, from https://www.brookings.edu/research/summer-learning-loss-what-is-it-and-what-can-we-do-about-it/

Rahman, H., Shafique, M. N., & Rashid, A. (2018). Project success in the eyes of project management information system and project team members. *Abasyn Journal of Social Sciences*, *AICTBM-18*, 1–6.

Raysman, R., & Brown, P. (2019). Software development agreement dispute produces a split decision. *New York Law Journal Online*. Retrieved November 8, 2019, from https://www.law.com/newyorklawjournal/2019/11/08/software-development-agreement-dispute-produces-a-split-decision/

Razzouk, R., & Shute, V. (2012). What Is Design Thinking and Why Is It Important? *Review of Educational Research*, *82*(3), 330–348. doi:10.3102/0034654312457429

Read, A., & Briggs, R. O. (2012). The Many Lives of an Agile Story: Design Processes, Design Products, and Understandings in a Large-Scale Agile Development Project. *2012 45th Hawaii International Conference on System Sciences, Maui, HI*, 5319-5328.

Rehburg, B., Danoesastro, M., Kaul, S., & Stutts, L. (2019). *How to remain remotely agile through covid-19*. Retrieved August 22, 2020, from https://www.bcg.com/en-us/publications/2020/remaining-agile-and-remote-through-covid.aspx

Repenning, N. P., Kieffer, D., & Repenning, J. (2018). A new approach to designing work. *MIT Sloan Management Review*, *59*(2), 29–38.

Resnick, M., & Silverman, B. (2005, June). Some reflections on designing construction kits for kids. In *Proceedings of the 2005 conference on Interaction design and children* (pp. 117-122). 10.1145/1109540.1109556

Rigby, D. K., Sutherland, J., & Takeuchi, H. (2016). The secret history of Agile innovation. *Harvard Business Review Digital Articles*, 2-5. https://hbr.org/2016/04/the-secret-history-of-agile-innovation

Rigby, D. K., Sutherland, J., & Noble, A. (2018). Agile at scale. *Harvard Business Review*, *96*(3), 88–96.

Rigby, D. K., Sutherland, J., & Takeuchi, H. (2016). Embracing Agile. *Harvard Business Review*, *94*(5), 40–50.

Riggins, J. (2019). *Three challenges to the new Agile leader*. Aginext Community.

Rising, L., & Janoff, N. (2000). The Scrum software development process for small teams. *IEEE Software*, *17*(4), 26–32. doi:10.1109/52.854065

Rodrigues, A., & Bowers, J. (1996). Systems dynamics in project management: A comparative analysis with traditional methods. *System Dynamics Review*, *12*(2), 121–139. doi:10.1002/(SICI)1099-1727(199622)12:2<121::AID-SDR99>3.0.CO;2-X

Rodriguez, G., Soria, Á., & Campo, M. (2015). Virtual Scrum: A teaching aid to introduce undergraduate software engineering students to scrum. *Computer Applications in Engineering Education*, *23*(1), 147–156. doi:10.1002/cae.21588

Rodríguez, G., Soria, Á., & Campo, M. (2016). Measuring the impact of agile coaching on students' performance. *IEEE Transactions on Education*, *59*(3), 202–209. doi:10.1109/TE.2015.2506624

Rodriguez, P., Markkula, J., Oivo, M., & Turula, K. (2012). Survey on agile and lean usage in finnish software industry. *Proceeding of ACM-IEEE international symposium on Empirical software engineering and measurement*, 139-148. 10.1145/2372251.2372275

Roebuck, K. (2012). *System Development Life Cycle (SDLC): High-impact Strategies – What You Need to Know: Definition, Adoption, Impact, Benefits, Maturity, Vendors*. Emereo Publishing.

Rola, P., Kuchta, D., & Kopczyk, D. (2016). Conceptual model of working space for Agile (Scrum) project team. *Journal of Systems and Software*, *118*, 49–63. doi:10.1016/j.jss.2016.04.071

Romme, A. G. L. (2004). Action research, emancipation and design thinking. *Journal of Community & Applied Social Psychology*, *14*(6), 495–499. doi:10.1002/casp.794

Roning, P. (2019). *Agile Leadership Took kit*. Addison – Wesley.

Roos, J., Victor, B., & Statler, M. (2004). Playing seriously with strategy. *Long Range Planning*, *37*(6), 549–568. doi:10.1016/j.lrp.2004.09.005

Rosenkranz, C., Vranešić, H., & Holten, R. (2014). Boundary interactions and motors of change in requirements elicitation: A dynamic perspective on knowledge sharing. *Journal of the Association for Information Systems*, *15*(6), 2.

Royce, W. (1970, August). *Managing the Development of Large Software Systems*. Paper presented at Technical Papers of Western Electronic Show and Convention (WesCon), Los Angeles, CA.

Royce, W. (1970). Managing the Development of Large Software Systems. *Proceedings of IEEE WESCON*, 26.

Royce, W. W. (1970). Managing the development of large software systems. *Proceedings of IEEE WESCON*, 1-9.

Rubin, K. S. (2012). *Essential Scrum: A practical guide to the most popular agile process*. Addison-Wesley.

Rubin, K. S. (2013). *Essential Scrum: A Practical Guide to the Most Popular Agile Process*. Addison-Wesley.

Salas, E., Rosen, M. A., Held, J. D., & Weissmuller, J. J. (2009). Performance measurement in simulation-based training: A review and best practices. *Simulation & Gaming*, *40*(3), 328–376. doi:10.1177/1046878108326734

Salas, E., Wildman, J. L., & Piccolo, R. F. (2009). Using simulation-based training to enhance management education. *Academy of Management Learning & Education*, *8*(4), 559–573.

Schlauderer, S., & Overhage, S. (2013). *Exploring the customer perspective of agile development: Acceptance factors and on-site customer perceptions in Scrum projects*. Academic Press.

Schmidt, C., Kude, T., Heinzl, A., & Mithas, S. (2014). How Agile practices influence the performance of software development teams: The role of shared mental models and backup. *Proceedings of the International Conference on Information Systems*.

Schmitz, K. (2018). A three cohort study of role-play instruction for agile project management. *Journal of Information Systems Education*, *29*(2), 93–103.

Schwaber, K. & Sutherland, J. (2009). Scrum guide. Scrum Alliance, Seattle. *Journal of Mini-Micro Systems, 27*, 2150-2155.

Schwaber, K. (1995). *ScrumScrum Development Process*. OOPSLA'95 Workshop on Business Object Design and Implementation, Austin, TX.

Schwaber, K., & Sutherland, J. (2017). *The Scrum guide 2017*. Retrieved July 04, 2020, from https://www.scrumguides. org/docs/scrumguide/v2017/2017-Scrum-Guide-US.pdf

Schwaber, K., & Sutherland, J. (2017). *The Scrum Guide*. https://Scrumguides.org/docs/Scrumguide/v2017/2017-Scrum-Guide-US.pdf

Schwaber, K., & Sutherland, J. (2017). *The Scrum Guide*. Retrieved from https://www.scrumguides.org/docs/scrumguide/ v2017/2017-Scrum-Guide-US.pdf

Schwaber, K., & Sutherland, J. (2017). *The Scrum Guide: the definitive guide to scrum: The rules of the game*. Retrieved from www.scrum.org

Schwaber, K. (2004). *Agile project management with Scrum*. Microsoft.

Schwaber, K. (2009). *Agile Project Management with ScrumScrum*. Microsoft Press.

Schwaber, K., & Beedle, M. (2002). *Agile Software Development with SCRUM*. Prentice-Hall.

Schwaber, K., & Sutherland, J. (2012). *Software in 30 Days: How agile managers beat the odds, delight their customers, and leave competitors in the dust*. John Wiley & Sons. doi:10.1002/9781119203278

Scrum Alliance. (2020). *Overview: What is Scrum?* Retrieved July 27, 2020, from https://www.Scrumalliance.org/ about-Scrum/overview

Scrum.Org. (n.d.a). *Scrum Values*. Retrieved from https://www.scrum.org/resources/what-is-scrum

Scrum.Org. (n.d.b). *What is Scrum*. Retrieved from https://www.scrum.org/resources/what-is-scrum

ScrumAlliance.Org. (2017-2018). *State of Scrum Report, Scaling and Agile Transformation*. Retrieved from https://www. scrumalliance.org/learn-about-scrum/state-of-scrum

Scully, J. (2014, Jan.). Agile HR delivery. *Workforce Solutions*, 8-11.

Senapathi, M., & Srinivasan, A. (2014). An empirical investigation of the factors affecting agile usage. *Proceedings of the 18th International Conference on Evaluation and Assessment in Software Engineering*, *10*. 10.1145/2601248.2601253

SEP (2018). *Estrategia de equidad e inclusión en la educación básica: para alumnos con discapacidad*. Aptitudes sobre-salientes y dificultades severas de aprendizaje, conducta o comunicación, Cd. de México: Secretaría de Educación Pública.

SEP. (2002), *Programa nacional de fortalecimiento de la educación especial y de la integración educativa*. Cd. de México: Secretaría de Educación Pública.

SEP. (2009). *La integración educativa en el aula regular: Principios, finalidades y estrategias*. Cd. de Méxco: Secretaría de Educación Pública.

SEP. (2010). *Guía para facilitar la inclusión de alumnos y alumnas con discapacidad en escuelas que participan en el Programa Escuelas de Calidad*. Cd. de México: Secretaría de Educación Pública.

SEP. (2011). *Orientaciones para la intervención de la unidad de servicios de apoyo a la educación regular (USAER) en las escuelas de educación básica*. Secretaría de Educación Pública, Dirección de Educación Especial, Ciudad de México.

SEP. (2019). *Educación especial*. Gobierno de México. Retrieved July 04, 2020, from https://aprendeencasa.sep.gob. mx/site/ed-inclusiva

SEP. (2020a). *Boletín No. 133 Regreso a clases cuando el semáforo de control de la pandemia esté en verde: SEP.* Secretaría de Educación Pública. Retrieved July 14, 2020, from https://www.gob.mx/sep

SEP. (2020b). *Regreso a clases en la nueva normalidad.* Secretaría de Educación Pública. Retrieved July 14, 2020, from https://www.gob.mx/cms/uploads/attachment/file/554867/CPM_SEP_NN-RC__29may20.pdf

Sharma, M. K. (2017). A study of SDLC to develop well engineered software. *International Journal of Advanced Research in Computer Science, 8*(3).

Sharp, J. H., & Lang, G. (2019). Agile in teaching and learning: Conceptual framework and research agenda. *Journal of Information Systems Education, 29*(2), 1.

Shenoy, A. (2019). Common misconceptions about Agile. *PM World Journal, 8*(10), 1–4.

Sherman, M., Edison, S., Rehberg, B. & Danoesastro. (2017). *Taking agile way beyond software.* Boston Consulting Group. https://www.bcg.com/enau/publications/2017/technology-digital-organization-taking-agile-way-beyondsoftware.aspx

Shipilov, A., & Godart, F. (2015). Luxury's talent factories. *Harvard Business Review, 93*(6), 98–104.

Sibona, C., Pourreza, S., & Hill, S. (2018). Origami: An active learning exercise for Scrum project management. *Journal of Information Systems Education, 29*(2), 105–116.

Siddique, L., & Hussein, B. A. (2016). Grounded theory study of the contracting process in agile projects in Norway's software industry. *The Journal of Modern Project Management*, 53-63. Retrieved February 10, 2020, from https://www.researchgate.net/publication/303336244_Grounded_Theory_Study_of_the_Contracting_Process_in_Agile_Projects_in_Norway's_Software_Industry

Sinclair, C. (2012). How to guide your lawyers in brokering agile software contracts. *Computer Weekly*, 23-29. Retrieved February 5, 2020, from http://web.b.ebscohost.com/ehost/pdfviewer?vid=8&sid=afafbb04-744b-4f89-a249-1523bfdd241%40sessionmgr102

Singh, R., Kumar, D., & Sagar, B. B. (2019). Analytical study of agile methodology in information technology sector. *4th International Conference on Information Systems and Computer Networks (ISCON)*. 10.1109/ISCON47742.2019.9036280

Skinner, B. F. (1953). *Science and Human Behavior*. Macmillan.

Slaughter, S. (1993). Innovation and learning during implementation: A comparison of user and manufacturer innovations. *Research Policy, 22*(1), 81–95. doi:10.1016/0048-7333(93)90034-F

Smith-Daniels, D. E., & Smith-Daniels, V. L. (2008). Trade-offs, biases, and uncertainty in project planning and execution: A problem-based simulation exercise. *Decision Sciences Journal of Innovative Education, 6*(2), 313–341. doi:10.1111/j.1540-4609.2008.00177.x

Smits, H., & Pshigoda, G. (2007). *Implementing Scrum in a distributed software development organization. Agile 2007 (AGILE 2007), 371–375.*

Sommer, A. F., Slavensky, A., Nguyen, V. T., Steger-Jenson, K., & Dukovska-Popovska, I. (2013). Scrum integration in stage-gate models for collaborative product development – A case study of three industrial manufacturers. *IEEE International Conference on Industrial Engineering and Engineering Management (IEEM)*. 10.1109/IEEM.2013.6962616

Sommerville, I. (2019). *Software Engineering*. Addison Wesley.

Soto, F., Sucunuta, M., Rodriguez, G., Cueva, S., Jaramillo, D., & Abad, P. (2018). Agile methodologies applied in teaching-learning process in engineering: A case of study. *Proceedings of the 2018 IEEE Global Engineering Education Conference.*

Srinivasan, R., Quan, T., & Reed, P. (2014). *Accounting for agile projects*. Project Management Institute. Retrieved from https://www.pmi.org/learning/library/accounting-agile-projects-9303

Srivastava, P., & Jain, S. (2017). A leadership framework for distributed self-organised scrum teams. *Team Performance Management, 23*(7).

Srivastava, P., & Jain, S. (2017). A leadership framework for distributed self-organized scrum teams. *Team Performance Management, 23*(5/6), 293–314. doi:10.1108/TPM-06-2016-0033

Stainton, A. J., Johnson, J. E., & Borodzicz, E. P. (2010). Educational validity of business gaming simulation: A research methodology framework. *Simulation & Gaming, 41*(5), 705–723. doi:10.1177/1046878109353467

Stanford. (2019). *Stanford d.school*. https://dschool.stanford.edu/

Statler, M., Heracleous, L., & Jacobs, C. D. (2011). Serious play as a practice of paradox. *The Journal of Applied Behavioral Science, 47*(2), 236–256. doi:10.1177/0021886311398453

Steelman, L. A., Levy, P. E., & Snell, A. F. (2004). The feedback environment scale: Construct definition, measurement, and validation. *Educational and Psychological Measurement, 64*(1), 165–184. doi:10.1177/0013164403258440

Steghöfer, J.-P., Burden, H., Alahyari, H., & Haneberg, D. (2017). No silver brick: Opportunities and limitations of teaching scrum with lego workshops. *Journal of Systems and Software, 131*, 230–247. doi:10.1016/j.jss.2017.06.019

Stoica, M., Ghilic-Micu, B., Mircea, M., & Uscatu, C. (2016). Analyzing agile development - from waterfall style to Scrumban. *Informações Econômicas, 20*(4), 5–14. doi:10.12948/issn14531305/20.4.2016.01

Stoica, M., Mircea, M., & Ghilic-Micu, B. (2013). Software development: Agile vs. traditional. *Informações Econômicas, 17*(4), 64–76. doi:10.12948/issn14531305/17.4.2013.06

Stray, V., Hoda, R., Passivara, M., & Krutchen, P. (2020). *What an Agile leader does: The Group dynamics perspective*. https://www.ncbi.nlm.nih.gov/pmc/articles /PMC7251611/

Sultan, A. S. (2014). Financial Statements Analysis - Measurement of Performance and Profitability: Applied Study of Baghdad Soft-Drink Industry. *Research Journal of Finance and Accounting, 5*(4), 49–56.

Sutherland, J., & Schwaber, K. (2016). *The Scrum Guide: The Definitive Guide to Scrum: The Rules of the Game*. Academic Press.

Sutherland, J., Viktorov, A., Blount, J., & Puntikov, N. (2007). Distributed Scrum: Agile project management with outsourced development teams. *2007 40th Annual Hawaii International Conference on System Sciences (HICSS'07)*, 274a-274a.

Sutherland, J. (2014). *ScrumScrum: The Art of Doing Twice the Work in Half the Time*. Crown Publishing.

Sverrisdottir, H. S., Ingason, H. T., & Jonasson, H. I. (2013). The role of the Product Owner in ScrumScrum comparison between theory and practices. *Proceedings of the 27th IPMA World Congress*.

Taipalus, T., Seppänen, V., & Pirhonen, M. (2018). Coping with uncertainty in an agile systems development course. *Journal of Information Systems Education, 29*(2).

Takeda, H., Veerkamp, P., Tomiyama, T., & Yoshikawa, H. (1997). Modeling Design Processes. *AI Magazine, 11*(4), 37–48.

Takeuchi, H., & Nonaka, I. (1986). The new new product development game. *Harvard Business Review, 64*(1), 137–146.

Takeuchi, H., & Nonaka, I. (1986, Jan.). The New New Product Development Game. *Harvard Business Review*, 137–146.

Talby, D., Keren, A., Hazzan, O., & Dubinsky, Y. (2006). Agile Software Testing in a Large-scale Project. *Software*, *23*(4), 30–37. doi:10.1109/MS.2006.93

Tanner, M., & Mackinnon, A. (2015). Sources of interruptions experienced during a Scrum sprint. *The Electronic Journal of Information Systems Evaluation*, *18*(1), 3–18.

Taylor, K. J. (2016). Adopting agile software development: The project manager experience. *Information Technology & People*, *29*(4), 670–687. doi:10.1108/ITP-02-2014-0031

Taylor, S. S., & Statler, M. (2014). Material matters: Increasing emotional engagement in learning. *Journal of Management Education*, *38*(4), 586–607. doi:10.1177/1052562913489976

Tiwari, S. R., Nafees, L., & Krishnan, O. (2014). Simulation as a pedagogical tool: Measurement of impact on perceived effective learning. *International Journal of Management Education*, *12*(3), 260–270. doi:10.1016/j.ijme.2014.06.006

Tripp, J., Saltz, J., & Turk, D. (2018, January). Thoughts on current and future research on agile and lean: ensuring relevance and rigor. *Proceedings of the 51st Hawaii International Conference on System Sciences*. 10.24251/HICSS.2018.681

Unger-Windeler, C., & Schneider, K. (2019). Expectations on the Product Owner Role in Systems Engineering-A Scrum Team's Point of View. *2019 45th Euromicro Conference on Software Engineering and Advanced Applications (SEAA)*, 276–283.

Ungvarsky, J. (2019). *Systems development life cycle (SDLC)*. Salem Press Encyclopedia of Science.

UnknownA. (n.d.). Retrieved from https://www.reddit.com/r/quotes/comments/

Vaishnavi, V., & Kuechler, W. (2011). Promoting Relevance in IS Research: An Informing System for Design Science Research. *Informing Science: The International Journal of an Emerging Transdiscipline*, *14*, 125–138. doi:10.28945/1498

Van Den Akker, J., Gravemeijer, K., McKenney, S., & Nieveen, N. (Eds.). (2006). *Educational Design Research*. Routledge. doi:10.4324/9780203088364

Van Der Star, A. (2017). *Team Morale and team happiness indicators*. Retrieved from https://www.productowneroftheyear.com/team-morale-and-team-happiness-indicators/

van Ruler, B. (2019). Agile communication evaluation and measurement. *Journal of Communication Management*, *23*(3), 265–280.

van Veenendaal, E. (2009). Scrum & Testing: Back to the Future. *Testing Experience, 3*.

van Veenendaal, E. (2010). Scrum & Testing: Assessing the risks. *Agile Record, 3*.

Verheyen, G. (2019). *Scrum: A Pocket Guide* (2nd ed.). Van Haren Publishing.

Verma, S. (2014). Analysis of strengths and weaknesses od SDLC models. *International Journal of Advance Research in Computer Science and Management Studies*, *2*(3). http://www.ijarcsms.com/docs/paper/volume2/issue3/V2I3-0094.pdf

Version One. (2018). *12th Annual State of Agile Report*. Retrieved June 15, 2018, from https://www.stateofagile.com/#ufh-i-423641583-12th-annual-state-of-agile-report/473508

VersionOne. (2011). State of Agile Survey 2011 - The State of Agile Development. *Journal of Computational Science*, *33*, 290–291.

Vijayasarathy, L. R., & Butler, C. W. (2016). Choice of software development methodologies: Do organizational, project, and team characteristics matter? *IEEE Software*, *33*(5), 86–94. doi:10.1109/MS.2015.26

Vilmate. (2019). *Why communication is a driver of Agile project success?* https://vilmate.com/blog/communication-challenges-in-agile/

Vinaja, R. (2019). The Scrum Culture: Introducing Agile Methods in Organizations. Springer Nature.

Vinje, N. (2018). *Do Team Building Exercises Really Work?* Retrieved from https://glideconsultingllc.com/team-building-exercises-really-work/

Vitharana, P., Zahedi, F., & Jain, H. K. (2016). Enhancing analysts' mental models for improving requirements elicitation: A two-stage theoretical framework and empirical results. *Journal of the Association for Information Systems*, *17*(12), 1. doi:10.17705/1jais.00444

Von Hippel, P. (2019). Is summer learning los real? How I lost faith in one of education research's classic results. *Education Next*, *19*(4).

Von Wangenheim, C. G., Savi, R., & Borgatto, A. F. (2013). SCRUMIA—An educational game for teaching SCRUM in computing courses. *Journal of Systems and Software*, *86*(10), 2675–2687. doi:10.1016/j.jss.2013.05.030

Waguespack, L. J., & Schiano, W. T. (2012). SCRUM project architecture and thriving systems theory. *2012 45th Hawaii International Conference on System Sciences*, 4943-4951. 10.1109/HICSS.2012.513

Ward, D. B. (2019). *8 do's and dont's of agile contract*s. Retrieved February 3, 2020, from https://telegraphhillsoftware.come/8-dos-donts-agile-contracts-v2/

Waterman, M. (2018). Agility, risk, and uncertainty, part 1: Designing an agile architecture. *IEEE Software*, *35*(2), 99–101. doi:10.1109/MS.2018.1661335

Webster, J., & Martocchio, J. J. (1993). Turning work into play: Implications for microcomputer software training. *Journal of Management*, *19*(1), 127–146. doi:10.1177/014920639301900109

Weitz, R., Henry, T., & Rosenthal, D. (2014). Limitations of Nonfinancial Metrics Reported by Social Media Companies. *Journal of International Technology & Information Management*, *23*(3/4), 11–44.

Werder, K., & Maedche, A. (2018). Explaining the emergence of team agility: A complex adaptive systems perspective. *Information Technology & People*, *31*(3), 819–844. doi:10.1108/ITP-04-2017-0125

West, D., Grant, T., & Gerush, M., & D'silva, D. (2010). Agile Development: Mainstream Adoption has Changed Agility. *Forrester Research*, *2*(1), 41.

What Is Velocity in Agile? (2019, September 26). Retrieved July 23, 2020, from https://www.agilealliance.org/glossary/velocity/

Whetten, D. A. (2007). Principles of effective course design: What I wish I had known about learning-centered teaching 30 years ago. *Journal of Management Education*, *31*(3), 339–357. doi:10.1177/1052562906298445

Whitworth, E., & Biddle, R. (2007). Motivation and cohesion in agile teams. In G. Concas, E. Damiana, & M. Scotto (Eds.), Lecture Notes in Computer Science: Vol. 4536. *Agile Processes in Software Engineering and Extreme Programming. XP 2007*. Springer. doi:10.1007/978-3-540-73101-6_9

Wikipedia. (2020). Retrieved from https://en.wikipedia.org/wiki/Value_(ethics)

Wilding, R. (1999). The Role of Time Compression and Emotional Intelligence in Agile Supply Chains. *Supply Chain Practice*, *1*(4).

Williams, M., Ariyachandra, T., & Frolick, M. (2017). Business intelligence – success through agile implementation. *The Journal of Management and Engineering Integration*, *10*(1), 14–20.

Xu, R., Chen, B., Chen, B., Wu, M., & Xiong, Z. (2003). Investigation on the pattern for Construction of Reusable Test Cases in Object-oriented Software. *Journal of Wuhan University*, *49*(005), 592–596.

Youssef, M. A. (1992). Agile manufacturing: A necessary condition for competing in global markets. *Industrial Engineering, 18*(20).

Zenasni, F., Besancon, M., & Lubart, T. (2008). Creativity and tolerance of ambiguity: An empirical study. *The Journal of Creative Behavior*, *42*(1), 61–73. doi:10.1002/j.2162-6057.2008.tb01080.x

About the Contributors

Kenneth R. Walsh is an Associate Professor in the Information Systems Group of the Management and Marketing Department, College of Business, at the University of New Orleans. He is published widely in the scientific community with articles in the Communications of the ACM, Information and Management, Journal of Computer Information Systems, and many others. Dr. Walsh has conducted consulting or research engagements with many organizations including the National Science Foundation, US Navy, City of New Orleans, New Orleans RTA ,and the Louisiana Partnership for Innovation, among others. Dr. Walsh received hi Ph.D. from the University of Arizona. Before devoting is life to research, he was a Senior Systems Analyst for Exxon leading project to develop database systems for oil and gas production. When not conducting research, Dr. Walsh enjoys sailing.

Sathiadev Mahesh, Professor of Management, has been on faculty of the University of New Orleans since 1984. Dr. Mahesh received his Ph.D. from Purdue University in 1984. He has an M.B.A. from Oklahoma State University and degrees in Engineering from the I.I.T. Madras and the University of Madras, India. His research has been published in many journals including Decision Sciences, Omega, Information Resources Management Journal, the Journal of Organizational Change Management, The Health Care Manager, and the Journal of Health & Human Services Administration. He has worked on many systems development projects and has experience with a wide range of business applications. In addition, Dr. Mahesh has worked in business process improvement, including process quality improvement. He is a past vice president of education for the local APICS chapter and has taught many certification modules. Dr. Mahesh teaches courses in MIS and operations management.

* * *

Corey Baham is an Assistant Professor of Management Science and Information Systems at the Spears School of Business at Oklahoma State University. His current research focuses on agility in IS development, systems recovery, and firm dexterity. His work has been published in the Journal of Management Information Systems, Communications of the Association of Information Systems and major IS conference proceedings. In addition to research, he teaches courses in Systems Analysis and Design, Advanced Web Applications, and Qualitative and Mixed Methods research. He currently serves as a faculty advisor for the PhD Project's Information Systems Doctoral Student Association.

S. M. Balasubramaniyan is a professional with more than 40 years of Industry experience in Telecom, IT and Quality domains. Held leadership roles in Product and Services organisation with Indian and International experiences besides Board member's role in Indian and International Societies and professional bodies, Guest lectures in Academia, Executive speaker in National and International conferences. Currently an entrepreneur and leading a Hi-Tech Embedded systems design services organisation.

Simon Bourdeau, PMP, is an Assistant Professor of MIS at ESG-UQAM, Montréal, since 2012. He is also a member/researcher in various research groups and centres, including the CEFRIO, the CI-RANO and the GReSI (HEC Montréal). He holds a Ph.D. in information systems from HEC Montréal. His research interests are IS project management, project teams' dynamic (i.e. collaboration, creativity, diversity, resistance, conflicts), digital transformation, operational risks, and innovation. His studies have been published in various journals such as IEEE Software, European Journal of Information Systems, Management Research Review and Educational Technology Research and Development. Since 2013, he is also a Lego Facilitator© Serious Play ™ certified and uses this methodology in teaching, research as well as in private and public organizations.

Aruna Chandrasekharan has her roots in IT. She started as a software developer in 1992 and then had her "Aha" moment in Agile in 2007. For the past 12 years, Aruna Chandrasekharan has been an Enterprise Change Agent and has had the privilege of being a part of 5 large transformation efforts since then. Aruna is particularly interested in a holistic approach to transformation across all levels and divisions of organizations with special emphasis on leadership. Leaders who educate themselves, understand their purpose in an enterprise transformation and have the humility and accountability to "walk the walk", are the ones who can truly sustain an ever evolving transformation.

Edward T. Chen is a professor of Management Information Systems in the Operations and Information Systems Department at the University of Massachusetts Lowell. Dr. Chen has published numerous research articles in scholarly journals such as Information & Management, Journal of Computer Information Systems, Project Management, Comparative Technology Transfer and Society, Journal of International Technology and Information Management, and International Journal of Innovation and Learning. Dr. Chen has been served as vice-president, journal editor, board director, editorial reviewer, track chair, and session chair of many professional associations and conferences. Professor Chen has received the Irwin Distinguished Paper Award at the Southwestern Federation of Administrative Disciplines conference, the Best Paper Award at the International Conference on Accounting and Information Technology, and the Best Paper Award at the Annual Meeting of Northeast Decision Science Institute. His main research interests are in the areas of Project Management, Machine Learning, and Healthcare IT.

James Davis is faculty at Louisiana State University in the Stephenson Department of Entrepreneurship & Information Systems where he teaches data science, project management, and tech entrepreneurship classes. He has written a series of online books on software development and the Python programming language. He holds the project management professional (PMP), scaled agile program consultant (SPC), scrum professional (CSP), scrum master (CSM, SSM) certifications and has made numerous presentations for the Project Management Institute and Scrum Alliance. He is also a retired lieutenant colonel with his military service split between the active army and army reserve to include combat tours in Iraq and Afghanistan. He is an accomplished entrepreneur and has been the technology lead (CTO) in a successful startup company.

Van Goodwin founded Van Allen Strategies in 2014, a consulting firm supporting corporate clients in software development and major technical infrastructure projects. His work focuses on helping private sector companies manage change around implementations of new technologies. Prior to founding his company, he was a 12-year technology consulting veteran, primarily for government agencies and higher education. Before his private sector career, he also supported academic research around the efficacy of virtual, geographically disperse teams.

Jacqueline Jewkes has 53 years of experience as a programmer and systems analyst working on large mainframe projects for banking and financial institutions. Her experience covers developing new projects as well as enhancements to and maintenance of large legacy systems. Her varied background included working with end-users to meet the needs of multi-national clients, mainly in Boston and London. In addition she was involved in training off-shore technical teams in India. Her experience covered defining projects, working with both technical and business people through development and testing to bring projects to a successful conclusion.

Bill Karakostas is an independent researcher. He has a 30 year career in the software industry, and in Academia, as an Associate Professor at City University London and as an Assistant Professor at the University of Manchester-UMIST in the UK. Bill received the MSc and PhD in Software Engineering from the University of Manchester, United Kingdom. Bill has published over 200 research papers and three books on systems requirement engineering, model-driven service engineering, and service customization. His research interest includes Cloud and Service Computing and IoT. He is a member of the IEEE Computer Society.

James W. Logan is a Professor of Strategic Management in the Department of Management and Marketing at the University of New Orleans. He earned B.S. and Ph.D. degrees from Louisiana State University, and an M.P.A. from Texas Christian University. Professor Logan has been a faculty member in the University of New Orleans College of Business Administration since 1988. A former Dean of the College of Business Administration at the University of New Orleans, he has also worked with a large variety of technology related companies and organizations, primarily in the areas of technology management, the effect of new technology on corporate strategy, and increasing the innovation capacity of existing organizations. Dr. Logan has consulted with a variety of organizations in the health care, strategic planning, and technology management areas. He has published numerous articles, proceedings, and book chapters primarily dealing with the areas of technology management and decision making in turbulent and challenging environments.

Kathryn MacCallum is an Associate Professor of Digital Education Futures within the School of Educational Studies and Leadership at the University of Canterbury, New Zealand. Prior to this, Kathryn was an Associate Professor of Computing at Eastern Institute of Technology, Napier, New Zealand. Kathryn's research has centred around exploring how technology can be effectively used to support teaching and learning. She has been involved in a number of research projects, both in New Zealand and internationally, developing innovative approaches to the integration of technology within all sectors of education. She has authored over 40 articles on this topic, and also serves as Editor in Chief for a number of international journals focusing on education technology.

Alfredo Mendoza-González is member of the National System of Researchers. He is an expert in accessibility in new technologies for users with intellectual disabilities. He develops research in Educational Technology, Artificial Intelligence and Human-Computer Interaction. He has presented his work in indexed and audited reviews of international impact, as well as specialized national and international forums. He completed a post-doctorate internship at the Automotive Industry Research Center in Mexico of the Autonomous University of Zacatecas through the Program for Professional Teaching Development in 2018. He is associated professor of the Polytechnic University of Aguascalientes in the Master of Science of the Engineering and has attended as a visiting professor in the Master of Engineering Sciences at the Autonomous University of Zacatecas and as an associate professor in Computer Systems Engineering and Intelligent Computing Engineering at the Autonomous University of Aguascalientes. He is a former student of the Autonomous University of Aguascalientes of Computer Systems Engineering (2009) and of the Master of Science with Option to Computation and Applied Mathematics (2013). He was the highest score of the 2014-2017 generation of the Interinstitutional Doctorate of Computer Sciences of the Autonomous University of Tabasco.

Jaime Muñoz-Arteaga is a professor at Universidad Autónoma de Aguascalientes (UAA), Aguascalientes, México. His research topics are in the domain of human-computer interaction, e-learning and web engineering.

Kamalendu Pal is with the Department of Computer Science, School of Mathematics, Computer Science and Engineering, City, University of London. Kamalendu received his BSc (Hons) degree in Physics from Calcutta University, India, Postgraduate Diploma in Computer Science from Pune, India; MSc degree in Software Systems Technology from Sheffield University, Postgraduate Diploma in Artificial Intelligence from Kingston University, MPhil degree in Computer Science from University College London, and MBA degree from University of Hull, United Kingdom. He has published dozens of research papers in international journals and conferences. His research interests include knowledge-based systems, decision support systems, computer integrated design, software engineering, and service oriented computing. He is in the editorial board of international computer science journals and is a member of the British Computer Society, the Institution of Engineering and Technology, and the IEEE Computer Society.

David Parsons is National Postgraduate Director for The Mind Lab in Auckland, New Zealand. He holds a PhD in Information Technology and a Master's degree in Computer Science, and has wide experience in both academia and the IT industry. He is the founding editor in chief of the International Journal of Mobile and Blended Learning (IJMBL) and has published widely on technology enhanced learning, software development and agile methods. He is current President of the International Association for Mobile Learning, a certified member of the Association for Learning Technologies and a member of the Australasian Society for Computers in Learning in Tertiary Education and the Agile Alliance.

Dinah Payne, Professor of Management and the Freeport Mc-Mo-Ran Endowed Professor of Business Ethics, a licensed attorney since 1986, has been at the University of New Orleans since 1988. Her research interests include domestic and international business ethics, business law, international management and international law. She has participated in domestic and international teaching and learning experiences, including the UNO-Innsbruck Summer School, the Semester at Sea Program and seminars in Costa Rica, Mexico, New Zealand, Italy and Belgium. Most recently, she has completed an international faculty development seminar at the University of South Carolina and presented papers in Canada and the UK. She is the recipient of the Gordon "Nick" Mueller International Service Award and the CityBusiness Leaders in Law, 2018 Award. She is also the University's Student Ombudsperson, whose charge is to act as a neutral party advocating fairness in dispute resolution when students raise questions or concerns.

Marie-Claude Petit is lecturer in Project Management at ESG-UQAM since 2013. She holds a Ph.D. in Industrial Engineering from Polytechnique Montreal, and a M.Sc. in Project Management from ESG-UQAM. She is a student member of OPIEVA (Interuniversity Observatory of Innovative Practices in Learning Assessment) and pursues a postgraduate program at the Education Sciences Faculty at UQAM. Her main research interests are active-based methods and strategies for learning Project Management, asynchronous/synchronous online teaching and learning, and distributed project team dynamics and communication.

Alejandro Romero-Torres is a professor at the School of Management (ESG) from Université du Québec à Montréal (UQAM) and associate researcher for different research centres, such as research chair on project management (UQAM), research chair on management of aeronautical projects (UQTR) and inter-university research centre on organization analysis CIRANO. He is direction of the laboratory of innovative practices in project context and the observatory of Quebec project (ESG UQAM). Since 2017, he was nominated as director of the programs in project management at UQAM. He holds an Information Technology Engineering Degree (Universidad Anahuac, Mexico), M. Sc. and Ph.D. in Technology Management (Ecole Polytechnique de Montréal, Canada). Alejandro Romero has developed a research agenda on digital transformation in project management.

Andrew Schwarz is a professor in the Stephenson Entrepreneurship and Information Systems Department in the E. J. Ourso College of Business Administration at Louisiana State University. Prior to pursuing his Ph.D., Andrew completed his undergraduate degree at Florida Atlantic University in Boca Raton, Florida, where he majored in social psychology and minored in sociology. Following completion of his bachelor's degree, Andrew worked in the market research industry for Fortune 500 firms, before returning to academia. In 2003, Andrew graduated with a Ph.D. in Management Information Systems from the University of Houston. Andrew has been recognized as a top business leader in Baton Rouge and honored with multiple teaching and service awards locally and across the globe. He is currently is on the MBA faculty at LSU and is ranked in the top 1% of the globe in terms of research productivity in top tier academic journals.

Hayley Sparks has a PhD in Geography from The University of Auckland, New Zealand and is now the National Academic Manager at The Mind Lab. Her doctoral research explored how systems of privilege operate to shape the everyday lived realities of young people who attend elite private schools. Her research interests primarily sit at the intersection of geography and education to understand relationships between people and place, including the role of digital technology in education, and the value of practice-based research.

Matt Zingoni is an associate professor of Human Resources Management at the University of New Orleans. Dr. Zingoni received his PhD from Syracuse University and holds an MBA from Bentley University, a BS in Investment Management from Duquesne University and senior certification from the Society of Human Resource Management. Prior to joining the faculty at UNO in 2012, Dr. Zingoni worked in the wealth management industry and as a corporate training consultant. Dr. Zingoni conducts research in the areas of performance management and employee development, with a focus on employee's persistence and resiliency after failure. His research has been published in journals in both the fields of Business and Applied Psychology.

Index

Purchase Print, E-Book, or Print + E-Book

IGI Global's reference books are available in three unique pricing formats:
Print Only, E-Book Only, or Print + E-Book.
Shipping fees may apply.

www.igi-global.com

Recommended Reference Books

ISBN: 978-1-5225-5912-2
© 2019; 349 pp.
List Price: $215

ISBN: 978-1-5225-8176-5
© 2019; 2,218 pp.
List Price: $2,950

ISBN: 978-1-5225-7811-6
© 2019; 317 pp.
List Price: $225

ISBN: 978-1-5225-7268-8
© 2019; 316 pp.
List Price: $215

ISBN: 978-1-5225-7455-2
© 2019; 288 pp.
List Price: $205

ISBN: 978-1-5225-8973-0
© 2019; 200 pp.
List Price: $195

Do you want to stay current on the latest research trends, product announcements, news and special offers?

Join IGI Global's mailing list today and start enjoying exclusive perks sent only to IGI Global members.
Add your name to the list at **www.igi-global.com/newsletters**.

Publisher of Peer-Reviewed, Timely, and Innovative Academic Research

www.igi-global.com   Sign up at www.igi-global.com/newsletters   facebook.com/igiglobal   twitter.com/igiglobal   linkedin.com/igiglobal

Ensure Quality Research is Introduced to the Academic Community

Become an IGI Global Reviewer for Authored Book Projects

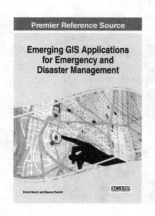

The overall success of an authored book project is dependent on quality and timely reviews.

In this competitive age of scholarly publishing, constructive and timely feedback significantly expedites the turnaround time of manuscripts from submission to acceptance, allowing the publication and discovery of forward-thinking research at a much more expeditious rate. Several IGI Global authored book projects are currently seeking highly-qualified experts in the field to fill vacancies on their respective editorial review boards:

Applications and Inquiries may be sent to:
development@igi-global.com

Applicants must have a doctorate (or an equivalent degree) as well as publishing and reviewing experience. Reviewers are asked to complete the open-ended evaluation questions with as much detail as possible in a timely, collegial, and constructive manner. All reviewers' tenures run for one-year terms on the editorial review boards and are expected to complete at least three reviews per term. Upon successful completion of this term, reviewers can be considered for an additional term.

If you have a colleague that may be interested in this opportunity, we encourage you to share this information with them.

IGI Global Proudly Partners With eContent Pro International

Receive a 25% Discount on all Editorial Services

Editorial Services

IGI Global expects all final manuscripts submitted for publication to be in their final form. This means they must be reviewed, revised, and professionally copy edited prior to their final submission. Not only does this support with accelerating the publication process, but it also ensures that the highest quality scholarly work can be disseminated.

English Language Copy Editing

Let eContent Pro International's expert copy editors perform edits on your manuscript to resolve spelling, punctuaion, grammar, syntax, flow, formatting issues and more.

Scientific and Scholarly Editing

Allow colleagues in your research area to examine the content of your manuscript and provide you with valuable feedback and suggestions before submission.

Figure, Table, Chart & Equation Conversions

Do you have poor quality figures? Do you need visual elements in your manuscript created or converted? A design expert can help!

Translation

Need your documjent translated into English? eContent Pro International's expert translators are fluent in English and more than 40 different languages.

Hear What Your Colleagues are Saying About Editorial Services Supported by IGI Global

"The service was very fast, very thorough, and very helpful in ensuring our chapter meets the criteria and requirements of the book's editors. I was quite impressed and happy with your service."

– Prof. Tom Brinthaupt,
Middle Tennessee State University, USA

"I found the work actually spectacular. The editing, formatting, and other checks were very thorough. The turnaround time was great as well. I will definitely use eContent Pro in the future."

– Nickanor Amwata, Lecturer,
University of Kurdistan Hawler, Iraq

"I was impressed that it was done timely, and wherever the content was not clear for the reader, the paper was improved with better readability for the audience."

– Prof. James Chilembwe,
Mzuzu University, Malawi

Email: customerservice@econtentpro.com   **www.igi-global.com/editorial-service-partners**

www.igi-global.com

Celebrating Over 30 Years of Scholarly
Knowledge Creation & Dissemination

InfoSci®-Books

A Database of Over 5,300+ Reference Books Containing Over 100,000+ Chapters Focusing on Emerging Research

GAIN ACCESS TO **THOUSANDS** OF REFERENCE BOOKS AT **A FRACTION** OF THEIR INDIVIDUAL LIST **PRICE**.

InfoSci®-Books Database

The **InfoSci®-Books** database is a collection of over 5,300+ IGI Global single and multi-volume reference books, handbooks of research, and encyclopedias, encompassing groundbreaking research from prominent experts worldwide that span over 350+ topics in 11 core subject areas including business, computer science, education, science and engineering, social sciences and more.

Open Access Fee Waiver (Offset Model) Initiative

For any library that invests in IGI Global's InfoSci-Journals and/ or InfoSci-Books databases, IGI Global will match the library's investment with a fund of equal value to go toward **subsidizing the OA article processing charges (APCs) for their students, faculty, and staff** at that institution when their work is submitted and accepted under OA into an IGI Global journal.*

INFOSCI® PLATFORM FEATURES

- No DRM
- No Set-Up or Maintenance Fees
- A Guarantee of No More Than a 5% Annual Increase
- Full-Text HTML and PDF Viewing Options
- Downloadable MARC Records
- Unlimited Simultaneous Access
- COUNTER 5 Compliant Reports
- Formatted Citations With Ability to Export to RefWorks and EasyBib
- No Embargo of Content (Research is Available Months in Advance of the Print Release)

*The fund will be offered on an annual basis and expire at the end of the subscription period. The fund would renew as the subscription is renewed for each year thereafter. The open access fees will be waived after the student, faculty, or staff's paper has been vetted and accepted into an IGI Global journal and the fund can only be used toward publishing OA in an IGI Global journal. Libraries in developing countries will have the match on their investment doubled.

To Learn More or To Purchase This Database:
www.igi-global.com/infosci-books

eresources@igi-global.com • Toll Free: 1-866-342-6657 ext. 100 • Phone: 717-533-8845 x100

www.igi-global.com

IGI Global
DISSEMINATOR OF KNOWLEDGE
www.igi-global.com

Publisher of Peer-Reviewed, Timely, and
Innovative Academic Research Since 1988

IGI Global's Transformative Open Access (OA) Model:
How to Turn Your University Library's Database Acquisitions Into a Source of OA Funding

In response to the OA movement and well in advance of Plan S, IGI Global, early last year, unveiled their OA Fee Waiver (Offset Model) Initiative.

Under this initiative, librarians who invest in IGI Global's InfoSci-Books (5,300+ reference books) and/or InfoSci-Journals (185+ scholarly journals) databases will be able to subsidize their patron's OA article processing charges (APC) when their work is submitted and accepted (after the peer review process) into an IGI Global journal.*

How Does it Work?

1. When a library subscribes or perpetually purchases IGI Global's InfoSci-Databases including InfoSci-Books (5,300+ e-books), InfoSci-Journals (185+ e-journals), and/or their discipline/subject-focused subsets, IGI Global will match the library's investment with a fund of equal value to go toward subsidizing the OA article processing charges (APCs) for their patrons.

   Researchers: Be sure to recommend the InfoSci-Books and InfoSci-Journals to take advantage of this initiative.

2. When a student, faculty, or staff member submits a paper and it is accepted (following the peer review) into one of IGI Global's 185+ scholarly journals, the author will have the option to have their paper published under a traditional publishing model or as OA.

3. When the author chooses to have their paper published under OA, IGI Global will notify them of the OA Fee Waiver (Offset Model) Initiative. If the author decides they would like to take advantage of this initiative, IGI Global will deduct the US\$ 1,500 APC from the created fund.

4. This fund will be offered on an annual basis and will renew as the subscription is renewed for each year thereafter. IGI Global will manage the fund and award the APC waivers unless the librarian has a preference as to how the funds should be managed.

Hear From the Experts on This Initiative:

"I'm very happy to have been able to make one of my recent research contributions, 'Visualizing the Social Media Conversations of a National Information Technology Professional Association' featured in the *International Journal of Human Capital and Information Technology Professionals*, freely available along with having access to the valuable resources found within IGI Global's InfoSci-Journals database."

– **Prof. Stuart Palmer**,
Deakin University, Australia

For More Information, Visit: www.igi-global.com/publish/contributor-resources/open-access or contact IGI Global's Database Team at eresources@igi-global.com.

Are You Ready to Publish Your Research?

IGI Global offers book authorship and editorship opportunities across 11 subject areas, including business, computer science, education, science and engineering, social sciences, and more!

Benefits of Publishing with IGI Global:

- Free one-on-one editorial and promotional support.

- Expedited publishing timelines that can take your book from start to finish in less than one (1) year.

- Choose from a variety of formats including: Edited and Authored References, Handbooks of Research, Encyclopedias, and Research Insights.

- Utilize IGI Global's eEditorial Discovery® submission system in support of conducting the submission and blind review process.

- IGI Global maintains a strict adherence to ethical practices due in part to our full membership with the Committee on Publication Ethics (COPE).

- Indexing potential in prestigious indices such as Scopus®, Web of Science™, PsycINFO®, and ERIC – Education Resources Information Center.

- Ability to connect your ORCID iD to your IGI Global publications.

- Earn royalties on your publication as well as receive complimentary copies and exclusive discounts.

Get Started Today by Contacting the Acquisitions Department at:

acquisition@igi-global.com

www.igi-global.com/infosci-ondemand

InfoSci®-OnDemand

Continuously updated with new material on a weekly basis, InfoSci®-OnDemand offers the ability to search through thousands of quality full-text research papers. Users can narrow each search by identifying key topic areas of interest, then display a complete listing of relevant papers, and purchase materials specific to their research needs.

Comprehensive Service
- Over 125,000+ journal articles, book chapters, and case studies.
- All content is downloadable in PDF and HTML format and can be stored locally for future use.

No Subscription Fees
- One time fee of $37.50 per PDF download.

Instant Access
- Receive a download link immediately after order completion!

"It really provides an excellent entry into the research literature of the field. It presents a manageable number of highly relevant sources on topics of interest to a wide range of researchers. The sources are scholarly, but also accessible to 'practitioners'."

- Lisa Stimatz, MLS, University of North Carolina at Chapel Hill, USA

"It is an excellent and well designed database which will facilitate research, publication, and teaching. It is a very useful tool to have."

- George Ditsa, PhD, University of Wollongong, Australia

"I have accessed the database and find it to be a valuable tool to the IT/IS community. I found valuable articles meeting my search criteria 95% of the time."

- Prof. Lynda Louis, Xavier University of Louisiana, USA

Recommended for use by researchers who wish to immediately download PDFs of individual chapters or articles.

www.igi-global.com/e-resources/infosci-ondemand

IGI Global
DISSEMINATOR OF KNOWLEDGE

www.igi-global.com

Printed in the United States
By Bookmasters

Printed in the United States
By Bookmasters